The Temperament Perspective

Working with Children's Behavioral Styles

by

Jan Kristal, M.A.
Dominican University of California
San Rafael, California

·P A U L·H·
BROOKES
PUBLISHING CO.®

New York • London • Sydney

Paul H. Brookes Publishing Co.
Post Office Box 10624
Baltimore, Maryland 21285-0624

www.brookespublishing.com

Typeset by Integrated Publishing Solutions, Inc.,
Grand Rapids, Michigan.
Manufactured in the United States of America
by Versa Press, East Peoria, Illinois.

The individuals described in this book are composites
or real people whose situations are masked, and are
based on the author's actual experiences. Individuals'
names have been changed and identifying details have
been altered to protect confidentiality.

Library of Congress Cataloging-in-Publication Data

Kristal, Jan
  The temperament perspective : working with children's
behavioral styles / by Jan Kristal.—1st ed.
    p. cm.
  Includes bibliographical references and index.
  ISBN 1-55766-791-8 (pbk.)
  1. Temperament in children.   I. Title
BF723.T53K75 2004
155.4'1826—dc22

                             2004022818

British Library Cataloguing in Publication data
are available from the British Library.

The Temperament
Perspective

Contents

About the Author

Jan Kristal, M.A., Temperament Counselor, private practice; Faculty Member, Department of Psychology, Dominican University of California, 50 Acacia Drive, San Rafael, California 94901

In addition to her private practice as a temperament counselor, Ms. Kristal serves as a faculty member at Dominican University, where she teaches classes in child and adolescent development and temperament and child behavior. She received a bachelor's degree in child psychology at the University of Minnesota and a master's degree in developmental psychology from San Francisco State University (SFSU). In 1986, Ms. Kristal was part of a study for parents and physicians at Kaiser Permanente Medical Group that focused on how children's temperaments affect daily issues and behavioral challenges. Subsequent training in temperament counseling led to her being hired by Kaiser Permanente as the first temperament counselor in the San Rafael department of pediatrics. She later became a consultant with Kaiser Northern California's Regional Health Education Department and trained other practitioners as temperament counselors in Kaiser facilities on the West Coast and Hawaii. In 1991 she developed temperament-based parenting classes for Kaiser Permanente, and in 1994, she co-authored the *Instructor's Manual for Temperament-Based Parenting Classes* with Helen Neville, R.N., and Rona Renner, R.N., for Kaiser Permanente. From 1995 to 2000 she taught a class called Temperament and Children's Behavior at SFSU.

Following in the footsteps of her mentors Stella Chess, M.D., Alexander Thomas, M.D., James Cameron, Ph.D., David Rosen, M.D., and others, Ms. Kristal is a leader in temperament research, practice, and theory.

Foreword

Jan Kristal's book, *The Temperament Perspective: Working with Children's Behavioral Styles,* is very timely. It comes in an era when practitioners have accepted temperament as a clinical tool, but only recently have studies of large numbers of families shown how to apply temperament theory and concepts in many arenas. Since 1989, Ms. Kristal has been the pioneering temperament counselor for the Kaiser Permanente Temperament Project. The insights gained from 25,000 pediatric patients in the project and from hundreds of children in her private practice are the backbone of this lively and well-organized guide. Researchers and practitioners who have found temperament to be compelling and important include pediatricians, nurses, educators, child psychologists, psychotherapists, child care providers, social workers, and parents. This book is addressed to them.

To place her work in context, Ms. Kristal begins with the Thomas and Chess definition of temperament and then gives a succinct history of the New York Longitudinal Study design and results. She summarizes the data of other researchers, including their modifications and the amended definitions of temperament. She then guides the reader through the ways in which temperament is expressed within various age groups. In describing each group, trait, and combination of traits, Ms. Kristal presents issues from her work with parents, child care providers, teachers, health care providers, and mental health professionals and suggests how to best address their concerns. She discusses goodness of fit, learning problems, social behavior, teacher attitudes, and discipline. The many pertinent descriptions of child–environment interactions, problems, and solutions help the reader learn how to prevent potential problems and handle existing ones.

The book focuses on learning because child development is a learning process for both parents and children. The infant and the maturing child constantly learn about the world around them: the rhythms of sleeping and waking; hunger and food; discomforts and what alleviates them; the smells, sounds, and sights of caregivers; and the pleasures of daily events. At the same time, caregivers are learning to recognize the unique style of their child's responses and to anticipate reactions. Most children and most parents share this learning minuet with more pleasure than problem. But sometimes, the fit is not good and caregivers need help. At these moments, the caregiver's awareness of the child's abilities, strengths, weaknesses, and temperament can ease the learning process. At other times, a professional working with a child may not understand the nuances of a difficult temperament and misinterpret the behavior. *The Temperament Perspective* helps practitioners and parents become aware of individual differences, understand the relationship between temperament and behavior, learn appropriate responses to increase goodness of fit, and develop strategies to work with problematic behavior and prevent misdiagnoses.

An essential element of the application of temperament theory to child rearing and problem prevention is the temperament counselor's knowledge of child development. There is always the possibility that a behavior goes beyond the extremes of temperament and into pathology. Is the child who cries every time she separates from her parents merely exhibiting unusual shyness or is she depressed or anxious? Is the family of the tantrum-prone young tyrant in need of temperament-based counseling, or should a psychiatric evaluation be considered? This book differentiates temperament from pathology and helps clinicians discriminate between them.

As one of the founders of temperament theory, I find it splendid that *The Temperament Perspective* is so accessible, substantial, and useful in summing up temperament theory and its clinical applications. It is an excellent template for teaching the skills and knowledge needed for incorporating temperament concepts into an educator's or clinician's work with children or in training temperament counselors to work directly with families or with other practitioners.

Stella Chess, M.D.
Professor of Child Psychiatry
New York University Medical Center

Preface

I first learned about temperament after I had children of my own. My undergraduate studies in child psychology in the early 1970s focused on the role of environment and early experience in children's behavior. Armed with my degree, I felt prepared for the world of motherhood. My first daughter was quiet and easy to reason with and to discipline. I assumed I was successful because of my knowledge of child psychology, our stable environment, and our parenting abilities.

Then, my second daughter was born. She was LOUD and had a mind of her own. Discipline often became a power struggle. What worked with my older daughter did not work with her. I did not understand why her responses differed from her sister's when her environment and caregiving were the same. This did not fit with my belief that the environment accounted for behavior. My daughters had come into the world with very different temperaments, a concept I did not fully understand until much later.

In 1986, while in graduate school at San Francisco State University, I became involved in a research project at Kaiser Permanente Medical Center. David Rosen, M.D., then chief of psychiatry, and James Cameron, Ph.D., a clinical child psychologist, began a study to examine the effects of providing parents of infants with anticipatory temperament guidance. This research evolved into an innovative clinical program that assessed children's temperament and then advised parents about daily issues and behavioral problems that stemmed from their particular child's temperament. The program also educated physicians about using temperament concepts in their practices with children and parents. Our program was based on the research and clinical techniques of Alexander Thomas, M.D., and Stella Chess, M.D., pioneers of temperament theory and authors of the New York Longitudinal Study. Their research was the first to show that certain combinations of temperament traits often result in behaviors that can develop into problems. The studies conducted by these pioneers and others revealed what I did not understand as a new mother—that once parents and practitioners understand temperament, they can gain insight on behavior, anticipate problems, and determine strategies to address difficulties.

The field of temperament research and clinical work has grown tremendously since the 1980s. Teachers, health care providers, psychotherapists, child care providers, and other professionals increasingly use temperament concepts in their work with children. Universities are beginning to offer classes in temperament and child behavior. I have written this book as a guide for professionals who want to incorporate temperament into their work, a text for classes on temperament, and a resource for parents who want more information than is available in a general book on parenting.

During the course of conducting research for this book, I reviewed more than 600 clinical cases to examine which temperament combinations tended to be referred the most and least for clinical evaluation and intervention, the kinds of behaviors reported challenging by parents, and the strategies that worked best in solving temperament-related problems. The book introduces other temperament research when relevant and uses vignettes to provide examples of temperament-related behavior and strategies. The children described in these vignettes are either composites or real people whose situations are masked to protect confidentiality and are loosely based on my clinical work at Kaiser Permanente, my private practice, and clients seen by my colleagues who are child therapists. The strategies discussed are based on my clinical work as well as that of Drs. Cameron, Chess, and Thomas.

Chapters are divided into three sections. Section I defines temperament, discusses different theories, describes how interactions between temperament and environment affect behavior, and presents ways to assess temperament. Section II examines individual differences in temperaments of children in three age groups: infancy, early childhood, and school-age (middle childhood). It describes typical behaviors of children with various temperaments and temperament combinations, temperament-related problems likely to occur at each age, and techniques for managing behavioral issues. Section III explains how to use temperament information to work with parents or with children in child care, school, health care, and psychotherapy settings. It concludes by discussing conditions that at first appear to be temperament-based, but may, in fact, be more serious. Appendices provide resources such as information about temperament questionnaires and assessments, books, videos, and web sites.

As we recognize temperament as an integral part of each child, we will see children as unique individuals and embrace their differences. We will welcome the special characteristics each child brings to an interaction rather than expect sameness or criticize the differences. I hope that this book provides an accessible way for professionals, clinicians, and parents to understand temperament and incorporate the concepts to enhance their work with children, and that knowledge of temperament will enable them to look at children, other adults, and even themselves with a better appreciation for individual differences.

Acknowledgments

This book began several years ago when Stella Chess and Alexander Thomas convinced me of its need, then encouraged and supported my efforts. They are foremost among the many people to whom I am grateful for their insights and wisdom. I also thank Stella for her availability to answer any question and to discuss the families with whom I worked, and for her wonderful examples of using temperament in clinical practice.

I would not have completed this book without the assistance of many other people as well, and I thank them here.

James Cameron, Ph.D., and David Rosen, M.D., taught me about temperament counseling and provided much of the research and clinical data on which the book is based; and Alice Shannon, M.F.T., my friend and colleague, helped with temperament training when the program was in its research phase at Kaiser Permanente and continues to provide insights about temperament. The Kaiser Permanente/Northern California pediatricians at San Rafael, Petaluma, and Novato with whom I worked over the years believed in the value of the temperament program and helped make it a success. Aimy Taniguchi, M.D., chief of pediatrics, in particular, supported and budgeted for the program. I would also like to thank Dr. Becky Loewy, professor at San Francisco State University, who suggested that I develop a temperament class for SFSU.

Linda Steck, Ph.D., read numerous drafts of this book, provided editorial comments and suggestions, and tried to keep me from using the "dreaded passive voice." My journalist daughter, Nicole, also provided initial editing on first drafts.

Many therapists and colleagues gave me feedback about how they used temperament in their practices. In addition, Ruth Jaeger, LCSW, and Marjorie Walters, Ph.D., provided comments on the therapy chapter and Elaine Aron, Ph.D., gave me feedback about the book and brainstormed with me about the trait of sensitivity. Several teachers shared with me how they used temperament in their classrooms. Laurette Rogers, M.S., teacher extraordinaire and environmental educational program director, and Florence Webb, Ph.D., educational consultant, provided insights and suggestions on the education chapter.

I was fortunate to have students who helped me sort through the clinical cases for the book: Mariel Garcia, Elizabeth Gardner, and Liz Gremillon.

My editors at Paul H. Brookes Publishing Co. made this publication process an enjoyable collaboration. Heather Shrestha first saw the need for this book and then made my writing clear and consistent, and Leslie Eckard made the ideas flow and the book come alive, turning it into a polished piece of work.

Thank you to all the Kaiser Temperament Counselors who shared their stories and helped make the Kaiser program a success. I am grateful to all the families I've worked with who have taught me so much about temperament and goodness of fit.

And, finally, I thank my daughters, Nicole and Vanessa, for teaching me firsthand about differences in temperament, and my husband, Alan, whose easygoing temperament has balanced my intensity so well for all of these years, especially while I was writing this book.

To the temperament pioneers and my mentors

Alexander Thomas, M.D.
(1914–2003)
and
Stella Chess, M.D.

SECTION I

Understanding Temperament

CHAPTER 1

The Concept of Temperament

What Is It? Who Uses It?

• •

A worried mother, Jenny, called a temperament specialist about her 3-year-old son, Josh, who seemed out of control. Josh often became frustrated or angry over seemingly small events and had violent tantrums in which he would bang his head on the floor, crawl under furniture, and scream. His parents tried to distract him with various activities and to hold him gently when he acted this way, but he refused to calm down. Jenny explained that he was irritable most of the time, and she never knew what would enrage him. The whole family revolved around Josh—trying not to upset him and then trying to calm him when he "flipped out." Josh's behavior also caused problems between his parents because they disagreed on how to work with his behavior challenges.

"We can't take him anywhere because of his potential meltdowns. I am afraid to get baby sitters or send him to preschool because I don't think anyone can manage him," Jenny said. "He is entirely different from his older sister, who is so easy to deal with. This affects her, too, because we focus so much on Josh's behavior. My pediatrician suggested temperament testing and I want to know more about it, but I'm worried there is something wrong. My pediatrician says it's probably 'normal,' but she doesn't see the kind of behavior that I do."

The temperament specialist explained how a temperament assessment for her son could help her understand, work with, and possibly prevent Josh's negative behavior. Jenny hesitated and said, "His behavior is so extreme that I made an appointment to see a child neurologist before calling you. Even though this sounds helpful, I think I'll keep the appointment with the neurologist and see what he has to say."

Two months later, the temperament specialist received another call from Jenny. "I don't know if you remember me, but I called before about my son's extreme behavior. We spent hundreds of dollars having Josh tested and the doctor said that he is perfectly normal developmentally, even advanced in some areas. He then told us, 'You just have a difficult child. Good luck!' and sent us on our way. I still don't know what to do. Can you help?"

Happily, the neurologist had some idea of temperament, but not enough to help this family. A temperament assessment provided valuable insight. Josh was very sensitive and became overstimulated in busy environments. Obstacles and delays frustrated him and he had difficulty with any change, transition, or intrusion. The combination of these temperament traits, combined with strong, loud reactions, often resulted in angry tantrums.

Concerns like Jenny's are not uncommon with children of certain temperaments. Strategies for working with Josh's temperament include giving him ample warning before making any transition or intrusion and developing consistent, straightforward routines so that he knows what to expect. The temperament specialist also recommended keeping stimulating experiences to a minimum and providing regular quiet times each day to decrease overstimulation. At the first signs of his escalating intensity, his parents could avoid the dreaded tantrum by redirecting him to another task or by using calming activities such as blowing bubbles or reading him a story.

After two meetings, Josh's mother began to implement her new knowledge of temperament into everyday interactions with her son and watched his behavior improve. She could see how his temperament related to his behavior and could prevent meltdowns by anticipating potential problems. This made a great difference in Josh's behavior and to his family. Jenny and her husband argued less about discipline and, instead, worked together to respond appropriately to his temperament. Josh became less volatile, and his extreme behavior became more manageable as his environment stabilized and his parents' responses became more consistent. The family still experienced some ups and downs, but Jenny was able to understand what triggered Josh's challenging behavior. She became more proactive in her approach, and worked with the negative behaviors more easily when they did occur. It was apparent that Josh was a "normal" 3-year-old, as the pediatrician had said, but his particular combination of temperament traits resulted in challenging behavior.

• •

All children are unique and approach the world with their own style of behavior or temperament. Some rush into new situations actively, whereas others stand back and watch. Some seem to go with the flow, whereas others are inflexible and demanding. Why is one infant fussy and irritable for days before a new tooth appears and yet another sprouts a tooth with no indication that she[1] was teething? Why do sensitive, responsive parents sometimes have problematic children, whereas some unstable parents have well-adjusted children?

Temperament is a child's innate way of approaching and experiencing the world. Most children seem to approach the world with ease; however, others find challenges at every turn. Different temperaments engender different reactions. Children react to their environments and those around them because of their temperaments. Likewise, adults and peers (or others) respond to children's temperaments.

Although a wide variety of temperament styles is possible, several stand out. Children who are sensitive and timid react with caution and hesitancy. Children who have energetic and flexible temperaments

---

[1] To be fair to both genders in describing children in this book, pronouns will be alternated.

eagerly dive into situations, whereas children who are energetic and inflexible are often forcefully defiant and present real challenges to caregivers. Children who have low energy and are inflexible express their obstinacy in quiet ways. Even the most challenging temperaments have positive qualities, however. There are no "good" or "bad" temperaments.

Parents, teachers, or others who work with children may blame themselves for a child's difficult behavior. Or they may believe that there is something wrong with the child, especially if the behavior seems different from the behavior of most children. If they do not understand the child's unique temperament, they may reach unrealistic conclusions or seek unnecessary professional help. Intense tantrums, aggression, high activity, withdrawal, and noncompliance are normal behaviors of children with specific temperaments. When parents or others who work with children learn that temperament can help explain difficult behavior, their feeling of relief is palpable.

What advice will help a mother whose 3-year-old hits and bites other children? How can a teacher work most effectively with the child who has difficulty paying attention? What approach will help the painfully shy child in therapy? How should a pediatrician proceed with a child who vehemently resists being examined? This book seeks to answer these questions by describing individual differences in temperament in infancy and early and middle childhood and provides effective techniques for managing typical temperament-related behavior challenges that occur at each age and in different environments such as home, school, child care, health care, or therapy. Although temperament does not account for all problems or behaviors, it can help explain many; an understanding of temperament concepts offers professionals and parents an important basis for understanding and working with child behavior.

This book carries on the clinical work initiated by temperament pioneers Stella Chess, M.D., Alexander Thomas, M.D., and others and will help parents, educators, therapists, health care providers, and other professionals incorporate temperament concepts in their work with children. It provides an understanding of temperament theory, how temperament is manifested at different ages, and what behavioral issues are typical for certain temperaments. With this knowledge, strategies can be tailored to individual children based on their temperaments. Finally, applications are given for using temperament in different work settings. This book does not assess or diagnose any behavior disorders or learning disabilities, nor does it intend to substitute temperament strategies for the treatment of behavior disorders. It does suggest that temperament is a good starting point for working with behavior in order to prevent inappropriate labeling or misdiagnosis. If a more serious problem is diagnosed, temperament information is helpful background for other interventions, and temperament strategies can be used simultaneously with them.

TEMPERAMENT OR DISORDER?

When behavior such as tantrums, fearfulness, or aggression toward parents and peers seems unusual, frequent, extreme, or difficult to understand, parents and professionals often assume it is abnormal. As in Josh's case, the child's behavior may either control the family or cause constant battles, and standard parenting techniques may not work. Parents often seek answers from physicians, psychologists, and alternative practitioners. Physicians may find nothing of medical origin. Psychologists who do not understand temperament may mistakenly diagnose a behavior disorder such as attention-deficit/hyperactivity disorder (ADHD) and recommend child or family therapy. Alternative practitioners may identify the problem as a bodily imbalance and use a variety of treatments including herbs, supplements, special diets, or bodywork. In many cases, the behavior remains the same because it is related to the child's innate temperament. Parents feel discouraged, ineffective, and defeated. They can find no apparent reason to explain the child's behavior, even though they have explored several possibilities. Their pediatrician assures them that nothing is medically wrong. Discipline techniques learned from parenting books or classes usually have no lasting effect. Child therapy may not seem to produce any changes.

What accounts for a child who seems to explode for no reason, a child who refuses to talk in preschool, a child who defies discipline, or a child who hits or bites? How does one explain drastic differences in children who are members of the same family? Are these differences due to environment, gender, heredity, or parenting? Behavior results from a combination of factors. Many children's behavior is not problematic, but in the cases that are of concern, understanding children's temperaments gives professionals critical insights into extremely challenging behaviors. Temperament does not account for all behavior or difficulties, but knowing the effects of temperament on behavior can transform the way we view child behavior, support the interventions professionals use, and help prevent psychological misdiagnosis. Even when challenging behavior has a cause other than temperament, understanding a child's temperament can provide additional insight in dealing with the problem. Chapter 12 describes how to differentiate behavior disorders from temperament.

DEFINING TEMPERAMENT

Temperament is the constellation of inborn traits that determine a child's unique behavioral style and the way he or she experiences and reacts to the world. Most theorists agree that temperament refers to biologically based individual differences that are relatively stable over time (Goldsmith et al., 1987). In the definition used most often clinically, temperament defines *how* children behave in response to their environment and the people around them (Carey & McDevitt, 1995; Chess & Thomas, 1996), not why children do what they do (motivation) or how well they perform a task (abilities). Temperament accounts for the particular style in which children behave and determines what behaviors are typical for each child.

Behavior is influenced by many factors such as developmental level, environment, illnesses or disabilities, and events. For example, as a child proceeds through developmental stages, he or she experiences periods of equilibrium or disequilibrium (Berk, 2002). During periods of disequilibrium, a child may exhibit challenging or regressive behavior. Likewise, illness may cause a child to be quiet and lethargic or agitated, and a child who has an attention disorder behaves differently from a child with a social anxiety disorder. A stimulating or chaotic environment will produce different behaviors than a tranquil environment. Events such as a divorce, death in the family, or a new sibling also can cause behavioral changes.

Temperament influences how each factor is experienced. The following vignette describes how different children would approach a transition from riding a push toy to riding a tricycle.

• •

Cautious James looks at the tricycle with trepidation, and it takes him days to even sit on it. Outgoing, active Maggie races for the new tricycle and sits down, then tries again and again until she masters the pedals. Easily frustrated Brad sits on the tricycle and tries to make it go; when he is unsuccessful, he leaves. After several days and much frustration, he begins to accomplish his goal.

• •

Most likely, these children will achieve the developmental task of riding the tricycle, but they will do so in their own innate styles; they will follow a myriad of paths to reach the same goal. The definition of temperament, or how a child approaches a task, allows us to see the considerable range of children's behavior and expands our view of what is considered normal behavior. The way that an active, outgoing child responds to the environment differs from the response of a quiet, cautious child. Typical behavior for one child is not necessarily typical for another, yet both are "normal." Temperament by definition transforms the notion of how children *should* behave and, instead, speaks to each child's individuality.

Behavior is a function of the interaction between the individual and the environment and, therefore, a child's temperament must be understood within the context in which it is expressed. Temperament does not stand alone, but rather, responds to input from the environment. An active child does well in an environment that encourages movement such as a playground or an expansive yard, but may be disruptive when trying to sit quietly during a church service or story time at the library. A child who does not make changes easily excels in a preschool with a daily routine, but may have difficulty in free-play situations. Children who are sensitive can become overstimulated at the county fair and fall apart, but they do fine playing at a friend's house. The distractible child cannot pay attention in school when he is seated near the window by the busy street, but can focus when he sits in the front row near the teacher.

• •

Megan's kindergarten teacher, Ms. Roth, complained that Megan was noncompliant and disrupted the class, especially at circle time. Ms. Roth said she feared something was wrong because she had not seen behavior like this before. Megan's parents claimed that she had no difficulties in pre-school and that no changes at home had triggered the negative behavior.

Megan's parents consulted a temperament specialist who assessed her temperament and then observed her at school. A temperament as-sessment revealed that Megan was active, that she readily approached new situations and people, and that she was easily frustrated. This was very evi-dent during circle time, which came immediately after vigorous outdoor play. Megan was one of the most active children on the playground; she was in constant motion the entire time. When the whistle sounded, all ac-tivity ceased and the children were expected to line up and come inside to find their carpet square. The square defined their area of movement and they were to sit cross-legged, hands folded in their laps.

At the beginning of the observation of circle time, Megan sat as she was instructed at first. She raised her hand to report on the weather. The story began, and she listened. As she became more interested, she leaned forward to see the illustrations. Soon, she was off her carpet square and on her knees. The teacher reprimanded her. She sat still again. The story continued and she started to fidget as she lost interest and whispered to her neighbor. At this point, her hands were on her friend, not her lap, and Megan was giggling. She and her friend were then sepa-rated and moved to another part of the classroom. After that, Megan was quiet, but she became restless again as the story ended. By the end of circle time, 20 minutes had passed. She was not allowed to get up when circle time was over, but had to sit for 2 minutes and "practice" sitting still.

Megan's refusal to listen and follow directions was more indicative of her temperament than of noncompliance. Sitting in one position for 20 minutes following vigorous play may be too much for a child like Megan, who is active and sociable (described elsewhere as "approaching"). When she became bored, she could not persist with the long story.

The expectations at circle time were unrealistic for children with certain temperaments. A short "cool down" period before sending the students inside would help ease the transition from active play to sitting still. Once inside, allowing some movement during circle time such as marching in place to a song or playing rhythm instruments would help all of the children sit more quietly for the story. Breaking up circle time with more active participation would also help maintain the focus of children with low frustration tolerance. This sort of temperament information helped the teacher to realize that Megan was not being intentionally disobedient but that this was a reflection of her temperament style. Ms. Roth made changes to circle time that benefited all of the children, and Megan's behavior was rarely an issue after that.

• •

In this example, the school environment that required sitting for long periods of time was not right for the student's temperament. Fortunately, her teacher understood this and made adjustments. Teachers who do not realize the role that temperament plays in classroom behavior may attribute such behaviors to defiance, continue to reprimand these students, and sometimes even recommend them for suspension or expulsion. This type of situation or constant perception of wrongdoing may result in anxiety and lowered self-esteem for the student, as well as a miserable school experience for both student and teacher.

Once it is accepted that children differ in their responses to similar situations, parents, teachers, and clinicians can readily understand that the same strategy does not work with every child. The key is to learn how temperament traits combine to shape behavior and then determine which techniques best address particular traits. The concepts are effective, easy to use, and individualized to each child's unique temperament. After a child's temperament profile is established, many challenging behaviors can be addressed and resolved quickly.

THE HISTORY OF TEMPERAMENT

Temperament was not always readily accepted as a means to understanding and working with behavior problems. Luckily, since the 1980s, there has been an increase in research on and successful use of temperament concepts to work with children (Cameron, Rice, Hansen, & Rosen, 1994; Carey, 1994; Carey & McDevitt, 1995; Chess & Thomas, 1996; Kurcinka, 1991). Attempts to explain differences among people have been made since ancient times. The term *temperament* comes from the Latin word *temperare*: to mix, which implies that various influences work together to create behavior. The question of innate, biological differences between individuals has been discussed through the ages.

The ancient Greeks used a temperament model to explain behavior. Behavior was seen as a combination of biological differences in bodily fluids (i.e., blood, yellow and black bile, and phlegm), known as the four humors (Kagan, 1994). The particular balance of these qualities produced individual differences of emotionality, behavior, and health. The ideal temperament existed when the humors were in balance. When one of the four qualities was dominant, less ideal behavior was exhibited. The behavioral types explained by the four humors were *melancholic, sanguine, choleric,* and *phlegmatic.* The melancholic was morose and pessimistic; the phlegmatic was stolid, apathetic, and undemonstrative. The choleric type was ambitious, revengeful, shrewd, and quick to anger; and the sanguine person was optimistic, enthusiastic, and excitable. This fourfold theory of temperament continued through the Middle Ages and the Renaissance.

By the early 20th century, personality theory was beginning to evolve, and theorists began to study differences in emotional expression and the strength and speed with which feelings change (Eysenck, 1947). Child psychologist and physician Arnold Gesell (1928), who developed normative growth tables for infants and young children, strongly supported the role of heredity and focused on the biological and maturational aspects of psychological development. Gesell and his colleagues reported significant differences in the behavioral characteristics of infants that they believed were innate and separate from environmental influence (Gesell & Ames 1937; Shirley, 1931).

Even Sigmund Freud (1950), in his early writings, attributed temperamental differences to the amount of energy in the libido and the excitability of the nervous system; however, his later writings concentrated on the importance of early childhood experience as the primary force in behavioral development. This influenced psychological thought for a majority of the 20th century, and the importance of innate biological differences was largely dismissed.

Many psychologists rejected the idea of innate differences largely because of the influence of psychoanalytic theory. Learning theorists and behaviorists, much as they disagreed with Freud, believed that the infant was a tabula rasa, a blank slate on which experience inscribed its patterns (Berk, 2002; Locke, 1892). Because environmentalism in the 1950s considered early experience as the primary cause for behavior, and behaviorists believed that conditioning (Skinner, 1938) and learning (Bandura, 1977) explained children's conduct, the possibility of inborn tendencies was emphatically rejected.

The concept of individual differences generated the nature-versus-nurture debate in the latter half of the 20th century. Those taking a *nature* view (e.g., Lorenz, 1971) argued that genetics and biology account for differences, whereas those who supported the *nurture* side (e.g., Bowlby, 1969) stressed the importance of early environment—particularly the caregivers' role. Psychologists tended to favor nurture over nature until Chess and Thomas (1959) planted the seed that changed those views with their extensive study of individual differences in the 1950s.

CHESS AND THOMAS

Stella Chess, M.D., and Alexander Thomas, M.D., two psychiatrists from New York, found that their psychoanalytical training did not explain the differences in children that they observed in their practices. They had been taught that the environment and parents, particularly the mother, accounted for a child's behavior and the development of behavior problems, but these theories were not born out in their own practice. Chess and Thomas saw, on the one hand, children who had problems yet came from good environments and had sensitive, responsible parents. On the other hand, they also saw children who had no problems who came from a context of seemingly inadequate environments and parents. After noting in both clinical and personal settings how children responded very differently to similar situations and to similar parenting styles, Chess and Thomas began to realize that children's behavior was more than just a reaction to their environment at school and at home. They sought new explanations for children's behavior that would explain the individual differences that they observed.

In 1956, Thomas, Chess, and Birch initiated the landmark New York Longitudinal Study (NYLS; Chess & Thomas, 1959; Thomas, Chess, & Birch, 1968; Thomas, Chess, Birch, Hertzig, & Korn, 1963), which followed individuals from infancy through adulthood. They differentiated three aspects of behavior: the *what*, the *why*, and the *how* mentioned briefly in this chapter. The *what* refers to abilities and talents, or how well a person performs a task. The *why* is motivation, or in other words, which goals motivate a person. The *how* is the style in which a person does what he or she does, or the person's *temperament*. (Findings were described in Thomas et al., 1963.) With data from the NYLS, Thomas and colleagues (1968) identified nine temperament characteristics to describe a child's behavioral style:

1. Sensory threshold
2. Activity level
3. Intensity (sometimes called *intensity of reaction*)
4. Rhythmicity (sometimes called *regularity*)
5. Adaptability
6. Mood
7. Approach/withdrawal
8. Persistence
9. Distractibility

These traits (which may vary in order listed depending on the source) are discussed in detail later in this chapter and are summarized in

Table 1.1. Temperament definitions according to Thomas and Chess

Sensory threshold describes the level of stimulation necessary to evoke a response.

Activity level is the child's general level of motor activity when awake and asleep.

Intensity is the reactive energy of a response, whether happy, sad, or angry; how expressive a child is.

Rhythmicity determines the predictability of bodily functions such as appetite, sleep/wake cycle, and elimination patterns.

Adaptability describes how easily a child adjusts to changes and transitions.

Mood is the basic quality of disposition. It may be more positive (a happy or cheerful child) or more negative (a cranky or serious child).

Approach/withdrawal is the child's initial response to novelty: new places, people, situations, or things.

Persistence describes the ability to continue an activity when it is difficult or when faced with obstacles; "stick-to-it-iveness."

Distractibility is the ease with which the child can be distracted by extraneous stimulation; the level of concentration or focus.

Table 1.1. The varying degrees to which children exhibit the nine traits determine the children's temperaments, the "how" of children's reactions to their environment. The way these traits combine produce different patterns of behavior, and the possible variations are unlimited. Chess and Thomas's theory is used by most clinicians today and has influenced other temperament researchers, who are discussed later in this chapter.

EASY, DIFFICULT, AND SLOW-TO-WARM-UP

Although combinations of temperament traits are unlimited, three distinct patterns of temperament emerged from Thomas, Chess, and Birch's (1968) findings: *easy, difficult,* and *slow-to-warm-up*. Children labeled *easy,* who composed the largest group (40%), were characterized by regularity in bodily functions; positive mood; high adaptability to change and transitions; a positive approach to new people, places, and things; and mild intensity. Easy children quickly developed regular sleep and feeding schedules, were sociable to strangers, smiled and laughed easily, and adapted readily to new rules and transitions.

In contrast, some parents characterized their children as very difficult to deal with. (One parent went so far as to describe her child as "a mother killer.") Only 10% of the children fell in this category. The traits that identified these children were low regularity, initial withdrawal from anything new, slow adaptability, high intensity, and negative mood. Children described in this group had difficulty with sleep and feeding schedules and took an exceptionally long time to adjust to any change or transition, to which they reacted loudly and intensely. They experienced frustration that often resulted in temper tantrums and long periods of loud crying.

The third group, comprising 15% of the children, were described as *slow-to-warm-up*. These children were low in intensity and activity level, slow adapting, and withdrawing in new situations. They initially rejected any new places, people, or things, tended to be clingy, and when upset, were inclined to withdraw from the situation. They were often described as "shy" by parents.

The remaining 35% of the children who participated in the study by Thomas and colleagues (1968) had a combination of different characteristics and did not fall clearly into one of these three patterns. Their temperament characteristics might also have been challenging but not in the same way as the slow-to-warm-up or difficult groups. For example, children who are highly sensitive, low in persistence, and intense do not fit into any of these groups but can present different issues for parents.

Thomas, Chess, Birch, and Korn (1963) took an interactionist approach, which held that temperament represents only one aspect of child behavior and does not stand alone. They made it clear that temperament is a part of personality but does not define it because the effects of parenting style and other environmental variables determine how temperament characteristics are expressed. The child reacts to the environment, and the environment, in turn, responds to the child. For example, when the active child runs through Grandma's house and breaks a vase, Grandma puts all breakables out of reach for subsequent visits. The interaction is bi-directional. Therefore, temperament must always be viewed in terms of the context of the interaction.

GOODNESS OR POORNESS OF FIT

The interaction between child and environment is beautifully explained by the notion of *goodness* or *poorness of fit*. Goodness of fit is defined as the compatibility between the characteristics of the individual and the demands and expectations of the environment (Thomas & Chess, 1977). Poorness of fit occurs when incompatibility occurs. Working with a child's temperament rather than against it promotes goodness of fit, and the child experiences healthy psychological adjustment and positive relationships. Research confirms this idea: Establishing goodness of fit at an early age has been found to prevent the development of behavior problems (Cameron, 1978). A teacher of a highly active child helps illustrate goodness of fit.

• •

Mrs. Johnson notices that Amber is restless, fidgeting in her chair. Ms. Johnson calls her to her desk and asks her to run some books down to the library. After Amber returns, she is able to sit in her seat and continue her classwork because she has expended some energy.

• •

An active child who is given positive ways of expending his energy experiences a good fit with his environment. Poorness of fit can result in the development of behavior problems and unhealthy relationships (Cameron, 1978; Chess & Thomas, 1984; Thomas & Chess, 1980; Thomas, Chess, & Birch, 1968). When a child's temperament is not taken into consideration, he may become anxious, defiant, or out of control, or develop other behavior problems. For instance, a teacher who does not recognize John's need for movement and who expects him to sit still and be quiet works against his temperament. If she then punishes him by keeping him in from recess, the energy that originally made it difficult for him to sit still will come out in even more negative ways. Poorness of fit between temperament and behavioral expectations is further explored in Chapter 2.

To create goodness of fit requires first understanding a child's temperament and then determining suitable strategies to work with that particular child to create a positive environment.

HOW THE NINE TRAITS AFFECT BEHAVIOR

Each temperament trait affects behavior, and all people possess varying degrees of these traits. There are no good or bad traits, just as there are no good or bad temperaments. Depending on the environment, each trait can provide challenges or benefits. Some temperament traits, however, are more significant than others, individually and in how they combine to produce behavior. Following are some descriptions of the behaviors that are associated with each temperament trait (see also Table 1.2). These definitions tend to describe the extremes of the traits (high and low), but children can rate anywhere on the continuum. In subsequent chapters these traits are discussed in this order, primarily, but because traits vary in relevance to each issue, not every trait is mentioned in every section and terminology may vary.

Sensitivity   Highly sensitive children are like radios with the antennas up, only they are not picking up just one station but ALL the stations at once. Sensitive children may notice everything from the tag in their tee-shirt to the temperature of their milk. They often perceive minute changes in their environments. Because of this awareness, they can become easily overwhelmed or overstimulated, especially in busy environments. They perceive others' feelings and their own feelings may be easily hurt, but they are also very empathic and conscientious.

In contrast, the child who is low in sensitivity is not usually bothered by sand in his shoe or a playmate's critical remark. He may have difficulty picking up social cues or nuances and be unaware of the effects of his behavior on others. He is more likely to take risks because he is not as reflective or observant, and he is not slowed down by a slight injury. This child may not indicate that he is ill as soon as a sensitive child, so parents often do not know that their child has an ear or throat infection until it is found during a routine check-up. These children are often seen as being more resilient or physically "tough."

Activity Level   Active children have a great zest for life—their activity level propels them out into the world to explore and experience it. They are independent and insist on doing things themselves. They approach any task with their entire body and learn by doing, not watching. They go through the motor milestones earlier than less active children and excel at gross motor skills. Often in constant motion, they can exhaust parents and those who work with them. They dislike being confined and need positive ways to express their energy. They

Table 1.2. Example of behavioral differences by temperament trait

Trait	Low	High
Sensitivity	High tolerance to discomfort or pain	Sensitive to smell, sound, touch, and texture
	Difficulty tuning in to feelings	Illness, injuries, cause greater discomfort
	Difficulty reading social cues	Becomes overstimulated or overwhelmed
Activity	Prefers quiet activities	In constant motion, gets revved up easily
	Fine motor skills are more developed	Gross motor skills are more developed
	Moves at a slower pace	Hates being confined (e.g., car seats, stroller)
	Moves toward independence at a slower pace	Moves toward independence at a fast pace
Intensity	Is quiet, calm	Very loud, dramatic, has strong feelings
	Emotions are difficult to "read"	Expresses extremes of emotions
	Does not express emotions readily	Cries easily, laughs easily
Rhythmicity (predictability)	Unpredictable hunger, sleepiness, elimination	Predictable hunger, sleepiness, elimination
	Regular bedtime and mealtimes are difficult	Difficulty changing schedules
Adaptability	(Slow)	(Fast)
	Inflexible	Flexible
	Transitions and changes are difficult, even small ones	Makes transitions easily
	Takes time to adjust	Does not need a schedule
	Likes control, power struggles likely	Goes with the flow
Mood	(Negative/Serious)	(Positive)
	Fussy or cranky	Happy, smiles and laughs
	Serious	Content
	Negative	Positive
Approach/ withdrawal	(Withdrawal)	(Approach)
	Most comfortable with the familiar	Loves new things, people, situations
	Dislikes new situations, people, foods, and so forth	Leaps before looking
	Needs time to warm up to new things	Nothing is left untouched
Persistence	Easily frustrated	Labeled "stubborn"
	Wants adults around for assistance	Difficulty "letting go" of tasks once occupied
	Not inclined to practice a new skill or activity	Plays alone well
	Gives up easily	Not easily frustrated
Distractibility	Difficult to distract from activity	Easily distracted from an activity
	Has "tunnel vision" when absorbed in a task	Difficulty concentrating

have a tendency to become "revved up" and are hard to settle down when involved in highly active pursuits.

Low-activity children move more slowly. Sometimes this slowness is misinterpreted as intellectual slowness, but this is far from the case. They often excel at fine motor skills and generally prefer a task such as an art project to climbing a tree. Parents do not have to worry about these children running off in a crowd or jumping from a high play structure. Because of their low activity level, they are dependent on parents longer and content to "stay put." They move through the motor milestones more slowly than their active counterparts because they are in no hurry.

Intensity of Reaction   Intense children are LOUD and DRAMATIC. Their emotional highs are higher and their lows are lower, so that by others' standards they over-react to situations. They are expressive whether happy, sad, or angry, but for some children, intensity is revealed mainly in response to negative situations or feelings. Few have to guess how intense children are feeling. Many an intense child has done extremely well in the school drama program. Intensity colors how the other temperament traits are expressed and can be triggered by other aspects of temperament; for example, physical discomfort or too much stimulation can trigger intensity in a highly sensitive child.

Children who are low in intensity are quiet and subdued in their emotional expression. Their easygoing reactions can be a pleasure for parents who do not appreciate drama. Whereas an intense child might express displeasure through a tantrum, a low-intensity child expresses it with mild fussing. In fact, this child may have trouble expressing emotion, and it may be difficult to know how the child is feeling.

Rhythmicity   Children who are high in rhythmicity are very predictable in eating, sleeping, and elimination patterns. As the saying goes, you can set your watch by them. They easily adopt regular mealtime and bedtime schedules and have problems when the schedule changes, such as during daylight savings or when on vacation in different time zones. Their regular elimination patterns make toilet training easier. They are also more organized in their daily behavior than less regular children.

Children low in rhythmicity vary in sleep, eating, and elimination patterns from day to day. It is very difficult to establish regular mealtimes and bedtimes for these children, and potty training is less predictable. Daily behavior also tends to be more disorganized; for example, they have disorderly rooms, misplace possessions, and have fewer set routines.

Adaptability Highly adaptable children go with the flow. They handle changes and transitions well and can easily switch gears from one situation to the next. Their ability to easily adapt to different settings and new places make them good travelers. Adaptable children are easy to get along with and handle intrusions on their personal space well, but because they are so adaptable, they may be overlooked or "lost in the shuffle." Sometimes more controlling children can take advantage of them.

Slow-adapting children have a difficult time with changes, transitions, and intrusions. They like to know what to expect and when to expect it, so they resist any transition that occurs too quickly. A simple but unexpected request such as "Come to the table for dinner" may be met with a tantrum or stalling—anything to slow down the transition. Changes are also protested. Serving juice in the red cup instead of the usual blue cup or reading a different bedtime story can result in a meltdown. Children who are slow to adapt also dislike intrusions and may oppose almost anything, from someone getting into their space to having their hair brushed or ears examined. It can be hard for adults working with these children to understand why little things set off such large reactions. Control issues come up often because slow-adapting children try to control situations when they do not know what to expect. This is why slow-adapting children do well with structure and routines.

Mood Some children are more positive or negative in their outlook. Children who are positive in mood are happier and less easily upset. Negative children are fussier and may appear serious or irritable, but this trait is greatly affected by the other temperament traits and goodness of fit. A child who has an easier temperament is more likely to be positive than is a child with a more challenging temperament. This can be considered a *downstream trait* or one that is affected by other traits (Cameron, Rice, Hansen, & Rosen, 2000). For example, a child who is highly sensitive, slow adapting, and intense may have reasons to exhibit more negative mood than a less sensitive, adaptable, low-intensity child. Because of this downstream quality, many of the current temperament assessments have eliminated mood as a temperament trait (e.g., see the theories of Rothbart, Buss and Plomin, or Goldsmith mentioned later in this chapter).

Approach/Withdrawal   Approaching children are attracted by novelty. If it is new, they want to investigate it. They do not hold back from new people, places, or things. For this reason, they can be accident prone, especially if they are also active. They are sociable and outgoing and tend to be hands-on learners.

Withdrawing children need time to warm up to novel stimuli. They are hesitant with new people, places, and things, and they prefer the familiar. They are cautious and avoid risky situations. Anything unfamiliar is initially rejected. They are observers, not doers, and learn by watching. People often refer to these children as shy, but they can be quite outgoing once they are used to a situation or in familiar surroundings.

Persistence   Highly persistent children like to finish what they start. They also practice a new task over and over until they master it. For this reason they often have a hard time stopping an activity before it is finished to move onto another one (unlike the slow adapters who will not stop because they dislike the transition). This ability to stick with a thought or behavior is often described as "stubbornness" and may drive parents, caregivers, and teachers crazy. This same stubbornness when used to finish a project is a teacher's dream, however. Persistent children are able to play on their own and amuse themselves because of their excellent attention spans.

Children who are low in persistence have difficulty sustaining attention and may move from one thing to another, especially if they are unable to achieve their goal quickly. They are often overwhelmed by tasks that are difficult and tend to give up more easily than persistent children. Because obstacles and delays easily irritate them, they depend on caregivers to relieve their frustration, so they like to have adults nearby in case they encounter such a situation. For this reason, they often protest separations. This trait makes it easy for them to switch between activities, however.

Distractibility   Children who are highly distractible are perceptive. They notice everything from a person walking past the door, to the noise when the refrigerator turns on, to the leaves blowing on the tree outside and are often sidetracked by these distractions. This high perception makes it difficult for them to focus on one thing in busy environments, but gives them an excellent eye for detail. These children move from one activity to another not out of frustration, but because something else catches their eye.

Low-distractible children have excellent focus. In fact, once they are concentrating on something they block out all extraneous stimuli and do not attend to anything else. Nothing diverts them. This differs from high persistence in that a persistent child may be distracted but then returns to the task at hand, whereas the low-distractible child is not sidetracked. This ability to focus can make it difficult for them to be soothed once upset.

TEMPERAMENT TRAIT COMBINATIONS

The ways in which each trait combines with others reveals rich and complex patterns of behavior. Rarely does just a single trait determine a behavioral issue such as poor eating habits or reluctant toilet learning. The issues develop according to how the different traits work together (see Table 1.3). In Cameron's (2003) research, certain temperament combinations emerged: active, low frustration tolerance; intense, slow-adapting; sensitive, intense, withdrawing; intense, low frustration tolerance; active, slow-adapting; low activity, low frustration tolerance or slow-adapting; low activity, fast-adapting, high frustration tolerance.

Although the possibilities are endless, here are a few examples of how combinations may affect behaviors:

- The toddler who is distractible yet persistent may be easily redirected from the wall outlet but will return to it again and again.

- The active, approaching, but slow-adapting school child will dive headfirst into all the new activities on the school field trip but then fall apart at home later, because he is reacting to the change in his typical daily routine and the resulting extra transitions.

- The child who is low in sensitivity, low in persistence, and high in intensity may become easily frustrated by a task and then may express her frustration by banging her head on the floor. (The intense, easily frustrated child who is high in sensitivity is *not* likely to be a head-banger, however. Children with high sensitivity feel more pain.)

- The highly sensitive, active infant will awaken herself by her own movements in the crib.

Because there are a myriad of ways in which these traits combine, they must be considered together in order to get a more complete picture of behavior. Temperament combinations influence behavior patterns

Table 1.3. Examples of how children with different temperament combinations react to different situations

Issues	Temperament combinations		
	Active, fast-adapting	Intense, slow-adapting	Sensitive, withdrawing
Meals	Eats anything, resists sitting at table, prefers to "eat on the run," needs to snack often	Picky about food changes, resists a varied diet	Rejects new foods, is very particular about taste and texture
Toilet learning	Learns early and quickly	Resists strongly if pushed too fast	Learns slowly, dislikes novelty of using the toilet and may be fearful
Peer interactions	Makes friends easily, jumps into all activities	Wants to control the play, may be bossy	Watches before joining in, prefers one or two friends to many
Accident risks	Shows little fear, unaware of dangers	Returns repeatedly to off-limits activities	Cautious, avoids new dangers
Separations	Leaves parents easily	Slow to separate	Dislikes new caregivers
Learning	Learns by doing, a "hands-on" learner	Resists directions	Learns by observing

across different age ranges, as the chapters in Section II of this book illustrate.

OTHER TEMPERAMENT THEORISTS

Following Chess and Thomas's lead, others began to investigate temperament. Although investigations vary in attitudes concerning temperament, most researchers agree on several points: Temperament refers to a group of related traits, has biological roots, reflects behavioral tendencies rather than discrete behavioral acts, and is recognizable in infancy (Goldsmith et al., 1987). Theorists do not agree on the different temperament characteristics, temperament definitions, or how temperament relates to emotional behavior, however. Others question temperament stability over time and the specific temperament traits found in individuals.

The following temperament researchers—Buss and Plomin, Rothbart, and Goldsmith—have approaches to the concept of temperament that differ from the clinically based theory of Chess and Thomas. These are not the only other temperament theories; for example, Strelau (1983) based his theory on a Pavlovian model of central nervous system reactivity. The theories that follow are examined in this chapter because they are often referred to in the temperament research literature and are well-known and respected in the temperament field.

BUSS AND PLOMIN

Arnold Buss and Robert Plomin (1984) defined temperament as a set of inherited traits that appear early in life, are genetic in origin, and are stable over time. They identified three traits: *emotionality, activity,* and *sociability*. Each is independent of one another and provides a foundation for an individual's personality later in life. Emotionality involves emotional and behavioral arousal. Activity consists of tempo and amplitude of speaking and moving, duration of energetic behavior, and rate of response. Sociability is the preference for being with others rather than being alone and is measured by the attempts to make social contact, the number of affiliations, the amount of time spent with others, and social responsiveness. Buss and Plomin (1975) developed the Emotionality, Activity, Sociability (EAS) temperament survey to assess these dimensions.

Buss and Plomin maintain that temperament influences the environment more than the environment influences temperament (Goldsmith et al., 1987). In other words, an active individual seeks active, high-energy situations, whereas a less active person seeks more sedate activities. They acknowledge the concept of goodness of fit in the idea that a mismatch can occur between environment and child when another person's expectations do not take into account the child's temperament.

ROTHBART

Mary Rothbart defines temperament as individual differences in reactivity and self-regulation that are relatively stable, primarily biologically based, and influenced over time by heredity, maturation, and experience (Rothbart & Derryberry, 1981). *Reactivity* is the excitability of motor activity, affect, endocrine, and autonomic responses. *Self-regulation* designates processes that either enhance or inhibit reactivity. These include approach and avoidance, attention, behavioral inhibition, and self-soothing. Overall, temperament is observed at all ages in individuals' differing emotionality, activity, and attention (Rothbart, 1989a).

Rothbart and others developed questionnaires to assess temperament in infancy, toddlerhood, early childhood, early adolescence, and adulthood (Capaldi & Rothbart, 1992; Goldsmith, 1996; Rothbart, 1981; Rothbart, Ahadi, & Evans, 2000). According to these researchers, each age group has different temperament dimensions. In the Children's Behavior Questionnaire (CBQ), Rothbart, Ahadi, Hershey, and Fisher (2001) distinguished 15 dimensions for measuring child temperament. Three factor patterns from the CBQ were identified: *negative affectivity, surgency extraversion,* and *effortful control*. Negative affectivity includes scales of discomfort, fear, anger/frustration, sadness, and soothability (i.e., not easily soothed). Surgency extraversion contains scales of impulsivity, activity, approach, high-intensity pleasure, and shyness. Effortful control includes low-intensity pleasure, smiling/laughter, inhibitory control, perceptual sensitivity, and attentional focusing. This last factor is related to the development of attentional systems and involves children's capacity to focus and shift attention, their ability to inhibit action when necessary, and their response to reward and low intensity stimulation. According to Rothbart, individual differences in effortful control have important implications for attention and self-regulation. Children with innately greater capacities for self-control and the ability to sustain attention achieve self-regulatory skills at earlier ages (Ruff & Rothbart, 1996).

Rothbart emphasized that temperament changes with maturation, and that one dimension may change while others remain stable. She viewed this model as interactive because temperament exists within the person but is manifested within the environment and influences how a person experiences the environment. For example, a person with strong behavioral inhibition feels distress in a social situation in which he must interact with strangers, whereas an approaching individual finds such situations exciting and may even seek them out.

GOLDSMITH

H. Hill Goldsmith defines temperament as individual differences in experiencing and expressing the primary emotions (Goldsmith et al., 1987). He views temperament as emotional in that emotions regulate internal psychological processes as well as social behaviors. For example, some children are innately more fearful than others and their tendency is to be cautious in unfamiliar situations. Goldsmith acknowledges some degree of stability and believes that temperament dimensions form the foundation of later personality characteristics. In this theory, the term *emotionality* could be substituted for *temperament* (Goldsmith et al., 1987). Goldsmith developed the Toddler Behavior Assessment Questionnaire (TBAQ; Goldsmith, 1996) for children 18–36 months old. In the TBAQ, Goldsmith's temperament dimensions are activity level, joy/pleasure, social fearfulness, anger proneness, and interest/persistence.

OVERLAP BETWEEN THEORIES

The temperament theories mentioned here have some similarities and overlap in traits (see Table 1.4 for a comparison of temperament dimensions from the four theories just described). For example, Buss and Plomin's concept of sociability has qualities of Chess and Thomas's trait of withdrawal, Rothbart's concept of shyness, and Goldsmith's concept of social fear characteristics. Rothbart's anger/frustration trait has aspects of Buss and Plomin's emotionality scale and Chess and Thomas's mood scale. Chess and Thomas's persistence scale is related

Table 1.4. Comparison of temperament dimensions from four theories

Chess and Thomas	Buss and Plomin	Rothbart	Goldsmith
Sensitivity threshold	Emotionality	Positive anticipation/ approach	Joy/pleasure
Activity level	Activity	High intensity pleasure	Activity level
Intensity of reaction	Sociability	Smiling/laughter	Social fearfulness
Rhythmicity		Activity level	Anger proneness
Adaptability		Impulsivity	Interest/ persistence
Mood		Shyness	
Approach/ withdrawal		Discomfort	
Persistence		Fear	
Distractibility		Anger/frustration	
		Sadness	
		Soothability	
		Inhibitory control	
		Attentional focusing	
		Low intensity pleasure	
		Perceptual sensitivity	

to Rothbart's attentional focusing and Goldsmith's interest/persistence. Sensitivity threshold in Chess and Thomas's theory is related to Rothbart's perceptual sensitivity. All of these theories have an activity category. The differences lie in the actual dimensions of temperament, the individual definitions of temperament, the assessments used, and whether the theory is used primarily in a clinical or research context. The four theories and their major tenets are summarized in Table 1.5.

CLINICAL USES OF TEMPERAMENT

Temperament theorists recognize how both individual differences and the environment affect children's behavior and use temperament concepts to explain behavioral and physiological patterns and responses. Clinicians utilize temperament information to modify the environment and the way in which others respond to the child to encourage a better fit. Chess and Thomas emphasized the use of temperament in clinical settings. Although the theorists mentioned previously have expanded on and extended their research (see Goldsmith et al., 1987), clinicians still rely primarily on temperament as defined by Chess and Thomas. Their theory was developed within a clinical context and

Table 1.5. Comparison of tenets of four major temperament theories

Theorists	Definition of temperament	Major tenets
Chess and Thomas	Behavioral style: The "how" of behavior	Independent psychological attributes
		Different from motivation, abilities, and personality
		Interactional framework: Temperament interacts with motivation, abilities, and the environment
		Expressed as a response to an external stimulus, opportunity, expectation, or demand
		Affected by the context of the situation
		Not a personality theory
Buss and Plomin	A set of inherited personality traits that appear early in life	Genetic in origin
		Appear in infancy (during the first year)
		Excludes individual differences that are not personality traits
		Excludes personality traits that originate in the environment
Rothbart	Relatively stable, primarily biologically based individual differences in reactivity and self-regulation	Observed at all ages as individual differences in patterns of emotionality, activity, and attention
		Goes beyond behavioral style to specify individual's predisposition to particular reactions (e.g., distress, smiling, laughter)
		Not limited to emotionality, but includes aspects of orienting and activation that go beyond the emotions
		Temperament and personality overlap, with temperament providing the biological basis
Goldsmith	Individual differences in the probability of experiencing and expressing the primary emotions and arousal	Focuses on genetic and physiological determinants of temperament
		Emotional in nature
		Refers to behavioral tendencies rather than actual occurrences of emotional behavior
		Relatively stable
		Indexed by the expressive aspects of emotion
		Does not include cognitive or perceptual factors

Source: Goldsmith et al., 1987.

was first used in their own psychiatric practices. Chess and Thomas's nine temperament categories explain behavior in ways that are easy to understand and useful in developing concrete strategies.

Temperament can be used clinically in a number of ways. Temperament counselors are individuals who are trained to work specifically with parents and other professionals to help them understand children's temperament and temperament-related issues. They assess a child's temperament and then develop an individual behavioral plan for working with that child's temperament issues. Temperament counseling is practical and cost effective because many behavioral problems can be resolved in a relatively short time. Therefore, child-focused agencies, medical centers, schools, and mental health providers incorporate temperament concepts into their work or are developing their own temperament programs. Temperament counselors help parents or other professionals to assess children's individual traits and, based on the findings, determine interventions to solve behavior problems. Some teach temperament-based parenting classes or lead parent support groups, but many work in conjunction with other professionals such as pediatricians, nurses, psychotherapists, or educators. Early intervention has been shown to prevent behavior problems in adolescents. One study examined the effects of infant temperament on the development of psychiatric symptoms in adolescence (Teerikangas, Aronen, Martin, & Huttunen, 1998). Infants' temperament traits were assessed at 6 months of age, and a fussy, difficult temperament predicted psychiatric symptoms in adolescence. Those infants with difficult temperaments who underwent a family counseling program during the first 5 years of life (ten times per year) did not develop symptoms in adolescence. This early intervention protected temperamentally at-risk children from later problems.

THE ROLE OF TEMPERAMENT COUNSELING ACROSS SETTINGS

In a medical setting, the temperament counselor works alongside physicians and nurses, consulting on cases involving anything from toilet training and sleep issues to discipline and school problems or providing direct temperament counseling to families. Even if not working in a medical setting, physicians often refer behavior problems to the temperament counselor, especially if they are unable to address them adequately during a medical visit. Physicians who utilize temperament concepts in their practices find that they can provide specific advice for their patients and resolve behavioral issues more quickly (Carey & McDevitt, 1995).

In the educational setting, temperament counselors carry out classroom observations and suggest changes that will improve goodness of fit in the classroom for a particular child. They work together with teachers to address temperament-related classroom problems and how temperament affects the way a child learns. Counselors also may have parents and teachers complete a temperament assessment and then meet together with both parties to recommend strategies that will help the child function better at school and at home.

Temperament counselors can work as part of a therapy team, providing temperament information and behavioral strategies directly to the parent with the therapist. Or counselors may provide a temperament assessment and consult with the therapist, who then works solely with the client. The therapist uses the temperament assessment as part of a treatment plan.

Finally, parents may seek temperament counseling on their own. For parents reluctant to seek help from a professional for fear of the stigma attached or the possible labeling of their child, temperament counseling is a nonthreatening step toward managing problems, and behavioral problems often can be quickly understood and solved sooner. Because temperament is perceived as "normal," it has no negative associations that may intimidate parents. If a problem involves more than temperament, parents may then be much more open to taking the next steps to help their child.

Whatever the setting, the first step is an assessment involving an in-depth, age-appropriate questionnaire, interview, and/or child observation to determine the child's temperament profile. Chapter 3 will explain different temperament measures. The assessment is used to help explain children's behavior and ascertain which techniques will work best to remedy behavior issues. Children's environments must also be discussed, however, to determine goodness or poorness of fit before an individualized behavior plan is developed.

USING TEMPERAMENT CONCEPTS IN PRACTICE

Professionals who use temperament concepts in practice find that their work with children is enhanced. Physicians can approach a physical exam in a way that elicits better patient cooperation. A therapist takes a client's temperament into account when determining treatment options or when deciding if a problem is pathological. A teacher can use temperament concepts to decide on the most effective learning approaches. Parents have a way to organize their parenting behavior and often report positive results with children for whom it seemed "nothing worked." For example, children who are consistently noncompliant may simply be slow-adapting. Some may interpret this as a behavioral disorder needing psychotherapy, but when noncompliance is seen as related to the child's innate inability to adapt to changes or intrusions, it can be prevented or reduced easily using temperament strategies. Slow-adapting children feel the world is moving too quickly with its expectations so they refuse to comply in an attempt to slow down these demands. When clinicians help parents to work with low adaptability by preparing the child for changes, slowing down transitions, and utilizing consistent routines, they are able to obtain cooperation rather than instigate power struggles. This type of behavior need not be labeled or associated with a disorder (although sometimes it might be) or managed using psychotherapy (although this is called for in some instances).

Most Frequently Observed Temperament Combinations in Clinical Settings

Clinicians see certain temperament combinations more often than others. In 400 cases referred for temperament counseling in my HMO pediatric practice, infants, toddlers, preschoolers, and school-age children fit into one of five different temperament combinations: 1) low energy, high adjustability; 2) high energy, low adjustability; 3) low/average energy, low adjustability; 4) high energy, high adjustability; or 5) sensitive, withdrawing.

Table 1.6 shows some possible temperament combinations and their attendant traits. Figure 1.1 shows the percentages of members of each group (temperament combination) in this sample of 400 children (for all age groups). The highest incidence of cases (34.75%) seen by temperament counselors was in the high energy, low adjustability category, which included combinations of high activity level, high intensity, slow adaptability, and low persistence. These children might be

Table 1.6.   Temperament traits in various temperament combinations

High energy, low adjustability	Sensitive, withdrawing	Low/average energy, low adjustability	High energy, high adjustability	Low energy, high adjustability
Active, slow-adapting or intense, slow-adapting Active, low persistent or active, low persistent and slow-adapting	Sensitive, in-tense, and withdrawing or sensitive, withdrawing	Low/average activity and slow-adapt-ing or low/average intensity and slow adapt-ability and/or low persistence	Active and/or in-tense plus adaptable and/or ap-proaching	Low in in-tensity and/or low in activity Adaptable Approaching

considered similar to Chess and Thomas's "difficult" child. For example, Hermione, age 7 years, could be considered a difficult child. She is loud, dramatic, and has a strong opinion about everything. She prefers a daily routine and becomes very upset when her mother suddenly changes plans. Though her high energy propels her into new activities, she will attempt most tasks, but she becomes extremely frustrated if she cannot perform them perfectly. Because of her obstinate behavior, frequent frustrations, and dramatic reactions, her parents sought help in working with these behaviors.

Sensitive/withdrawing children were the second group seen most often (25.5%), and they are similar to slow-to-warm-up children. These children are shy, cautious, and highly sensitive to any stimulation. Consider Hank: He refused to interact with his peers at preschool. He cried when he arrived and his parents left, and during noisy free play periods would hide under the table. He refused to try new activities and liked to stay near one teacher. His teacher suggested that his parents seek help to aid him with these difficulties.

At 21%, the low/average energy, low adjustability group was the third-largest receiving counseling; they include traits of being strong-willed, easily frustrated, but not highly active or overreactive, like Harry. Harry's mother described him as "a whiner." Once he made up his mind about something he remained firm. He was not openly defiant; he would simply ignore his parents' requests. When attempting a new task, Harry would refuse help, but he would become increas-

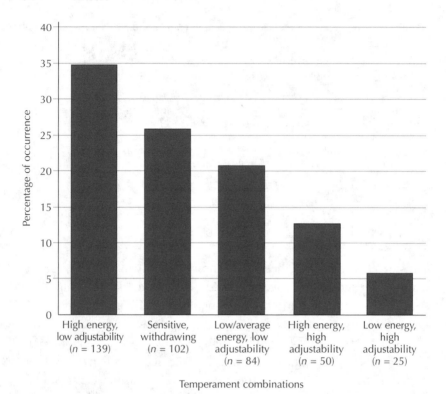

Figure 1.1. Percentage of children with temperament combinations for all age groups (highest to lowest incidence) referred for temperament counseling in Kaiser Permanente program (*N* = 400).

ingly frustrated and begin whining. Exasperated by this continual behavior, his parents wanted to learn how to handle his frustrations.

The high energy, high adjustability group is fourth (12.5%) in number. These children "get into everything" but adjust easily to changes. Traits of this group appear to be more problematic in the younger ages because no school-age children were in this group. Tate, age 2 years, had this temperament combination. He was constantly on the go and his caregiver was exhausted. He would run off during outings, get himself into precarious positions, and rarely want to rest. He was happy and flexible, but the caregiver worried about accident risks. She sought help to know how to keep him safe, yet not stifle his wonderful joie de vivre.

Parents of children who would fall in the low energy/high adjustability group (6.25%) were least likely to seek counseling. These are the "easy" children. For example, Monique, age 10 years, was a good student, easygoing, and agreeable with friends and adults. Her parents had no complaints about her behavior, but they were concerned because of her easygoing nature. They wanted her to learn to be a bit more assertive when needed and did not want anyone to take advantage of her, so they sought advice from their pediatrician.

In the pediatric sample of 400 children participating in the Kaiser Permanente program, the ages most often seen were infants (33%) and preschoolers (32%), followed by toddlers (24%) and school-age children (11%). This sample had a high number of infants because pediatricians referred infants as soon as they recognized a behavior issue to prevent these issues from escalating into later problems. The only gender differences found were in the high-energy, low-adjustability group, with almost twice as many boys falling into this category as girls.

Another sample of 208 children I observed in my private practice over 5 years mirrored the temperament combinations that were most likely to be seen for counseling, with most referrals in the high energy, low adjustability group (46.2%). The low energy, low adjustability group was next with 23.1%, followed by the sensitive, withdrawing group (19.7%). Low energy, high adjustability (5.7%) and high energy, high adjustability (5.3%) were the groups least likely to be referred. In this sample parents of the preschoolers were most likely to seek help (69%); next were toddlers (29%); then school-age children (12%); and last, infants (5%). Parents are less likely to seek help with infants unless their behavior seems extreme. Parents are more likely to seek help for their toddlers than for their infants, but many attribute problem behavior to the "terrible twos" and assume it will pass. Parents are most likely to seek help by preschool age, when the "terrible twos" have not subsided and discipline, aggression, or school problems are increasing. Parents often first seek help from their pediatrician, who may provide temperament information if trained to do so, or who may refer them to a temperament specialist within the practice or elsewhere. (See Figure 1.2 for a breakdown of children with various temperament combinations referred for temperament counseling, by age group.)

Each temperament combination has its own set of strengths and challenges. Different age groups also have different temperament-related issues. These issues sometimes overlap in the different groups, but each

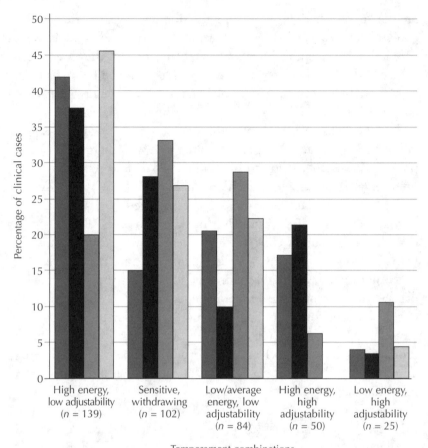

Figure 1.2. Percentage of children with various temperament combinations referred for counseling in Kaiser Permanente study, broken out by age group (*N* = 400). Not all age groups are listed every time if a combination is not problematic for that group. (Key: ■ = Infants, ■ = Toddlers, ■ = Preschoolers, □ = School-agers.)

issue is handled differently according to the child's temperament (see Table 1.7). Section II of this book discusses common temperament issues for each age range and suggests strategies for management.

When clinicians are familiar with the kinds of temperament challenges each group presents and know which age groups most often experience behavioral issues, they can plan the strategies they need to provide better services for their clients. Clinicians can provide effective strategies to help manage their clients' behavioral issues once they are familiar with the different challenges each temperament group presents and know which temperament combinations are most

Table 1.7.   Child behavior issues reported by parents for different temperament and age groups

Temperament group	Age		
	Infants	Toddlers/ preschoolers	Middle childhood

High energy, low adjustability	Sleep issues
	  Night waking
	  Irregular naps
	Resists intrusive child care procedures such as diaper changing, nail cutting
	Does not like transitions
	Resists restrictions
	  Dislikes high chair, car seat, stroller
	Feeding issues
	  Is slow to wean (won't take bottle)
	Vomits when upset
	Is easily overstimulated
	Has tantrums
	Has problems separating
	Is fussy
		Sleep issues
		  Resists going to bed
		  Sleeps with parents
		  Awakens frequently at night
		Is in constant motion
		Resists toilet learning
		Has difficulty with transitions
		Food issues
		  Is picky eater
		  Is slow to wean
		School issues
		  Has poor peer interactions
		  Is aggressive
		Discipline issues
		  Is noncompliant, talks back
		  Is stubborn, bossy
		  Engages in head banging
		  Has tantrums
		Has separation problems
			Sleep issues
			  Fights going to sleep
			  Won't sleep in own bed
			Transitions poorly
			Is aggressive
			Engages in destructive play
			Discipline issues
			  Is noncompliant
			  Has tantrums
			  Is disrespectful
			  Persists with off-limits activities
			  Lies to get by
			  Steals
			Food issues
			  Is a picky eater
			School issues
			  Demands attention
			  Is bossy
			  Is easily distracted
			  Lacks persistence with schoolwork
			  "Forgets" homework

Sensitive, withdrawing	Sleep issues
	  Awakens at night
	  Takes naps irregularly
	Food issues
	  Resists new foods
	  Is slow to wean
	Is fussy
	Has tantrums
	Is timid
	  Is clingy
	  Has separation anxiety
	Is sensitive to soiled diapers
	Dislikes transitions
		Sleep issues
		  Awakens at night
		  Will not sleep in bed
		Food issues
		  Only eats certain foods
		School issues
		  Has socialization problems
		  Does not participate easily
		Is easily frustrated
		Has tantrums
		Is stubborn
		Is timid
		  Is insecure
		  Experiences separation anxiety
			Sleep issues
			  Has difficulty falling asleep
			  Will not sleep alone
			Food issues
			  Is a picky eater
			Is timid
			Is often anxious/worried
			School issues
			  Is disorganized
			  Is easily frustrated
			Peer issues
			  Is argumentative
			Control issues
			  Has difficulty with transitions

(continued)

Table 1.7. (continued)

Temperament group	Age		
	Infants	Toddlers/ preschoolers	Middle childhood
Sensitive, with-drawing cont.		Resists toilet learning	Is lethargic
		Has poor peer inter-actions	Does not enjoy life
		Has difficulty with transitions	
Low/average energy, low adjustability	Sleep issues	Sleep issues	Sleep issues
	Resists going to sleep	Resists going to bed	Resists going to bed
	Awakens at night	Awakens at night	Awakens at night
	Protests routine changes	Sleeps with parents	Transitions poorly
	Separation issues	Won't stay in bed	Discipline Issues
	Wants to be near parents	Poor transitions	Is controlling
	Protests new child care providers or child care	Discipline issues	Is bossy
		Control issues	Is difficult
	Is slow to wean	Tantrums	Communicates poorly
		Bangs head	Is aggressive
		Aggressive	School issues
		Food issues	Has difficulty doing homework
		Is picky eater	Is disorganized
		School issues	Shows lack of interest
		Is antisocial	Has difficulty with separations
		Will not follow directions	Worries excessively
		Has separation problems	Has poor peer relations
		Toilet learning issues	Has a negative self-image
		Is timid	
High energy, high adjustability	Sleep issues	Sleep issues	School issues
	Awakens at night	Awakens at night and in early morning	Has trouble sitting still
	Is too busy to nap		Has difficulty com-pleting homework
	Is fussy when tired	Wants to sleep with parents	Tests limits
	Resists confinement	Toileting issues	
	Food issues	Is too busy to go to the bathroom	
	Is too busy to eat	Discipline issues	
	Toileting issues	Has tantrums	
	Resists diaper changing	Control issues	
	Discipline issues	Is stubborn	
	Is aggressive	Is aggressive	
		Resists limits	
		Is easily frustrated	
		Safety issues	

Temperament group	Age		
	Infants	Toddlers/ preschoolers	Middle childhood
Low energy, high adjustability	Sleep issues Has separation anxiety Awakens at night Food issues Won't take bottle Toileting issues Resists diaper changing	Sleep issues School issues Food issues Poor peer interactions	School issues Is ignored by teachers in large classrooms Expressiveness is limited May be victimized Is underappreciated intellectually

likely to experience difficulties. Parents can learn about their children's temperaments by reading temperament-based parenting books (see Appendix B), meeting with a temperament specialist, or taking a temperament-based parenting class. Teachers, child care providers, and other nonclinicians also can learn about temperament through reading, workshops, and classes and by meeting with other professionals who specialize in temperament.

SUMMARY

Since ancient times, the causes of individual differences have fascinated scholars. Some explanations have been simplistic or speculative, whereas others relied on observation or scientific study. In the nature versus nurture debate, some theorists embraced the idea that all behavior was learned and that a person's environment determined outcome, whereas others attributed behavior to innate biological differences and heredity. Most developmental psychologists now acknowledge an interactive viewpoint that recognizes inborn biological differences in conjunction with the effects of the environment (e.g., Kochanska, 1995; Scarr & McCartney, 1983; Seifer & Schiller, 1995).

The study of temperament takes the approach that innate individual differences combine with environmental influences. Children enter the world with unique temperaments. The Latin word *temperare,* which means *mixing,* is accurate because we can see how the child's innate temperament traits blend to produce a distinct individual and then combines with the environment to produce behavior. Knowing both the child's temperament and the environmental influences provides scholars and clinicians with powerful tools to describe, understand, and treat behavior.

Chess and Thomas laid the groundwork for understanding how individuals differ in their behavioral styles and how this understanding can be used clinically. Prominent researchers including Buss and Plomin, Rothbart, and Goldsmith continue to expand knowledge of what temperament is and how it affects behavior. The findings of all temperament researchers help parents and professionals achieve more success in their work with children and help children become better adjusted in their interactions with the world. Understanding the origin and evolution of temperament concepts and how temperament can affect children's behavior is only part of the explanation. The next chapter explores the interplay of temperament and the environment, the bi-directional quality of child–environment interactions, and how particular environments fit with particular temperaments.

CHAPTER 2

Goodness of Fit

Getting Along with Each Other and the Environment

• •

A story is told of identical twin boys who were separated at birth and adopted by two different families. The social worker assigned to monitor each adoption observed the two children closely as they grew. He was curious to see how the twins would develop separately and hoped to learn whether their differences stemmed from their environments or from a predetermined genetic disposition. When the twins were about 3 years old, the social worker asked one mother if she had any difficulty with her son.

"He won't eat a thing!" she replied.

The social worker looked over his records. Puzzled, he asked her, "His growth chart looks normal, and he seems to be gaining weight. You can't mean he doesn't eat. He seems healthy. Could you explain?"

"Well," the mom replied, "mealtimes are a real problem. He won't eat anything unless it has ketchup on it!"

This mother found her son's eating habits problematic because she thought he should appreciate his food the way that she prepared it, without additional condiments. She wanted him to eat as she did, without ketchup, and interpreted his insistence on ketchup as disobedience. This made mealtimes unpleasant as she tried to change her son's culinary preferences.

The social worker visited the other adoptive parents and asked how their son was doing.

"He's doing just wonderfully. We have no problems," was the reply.

"How about his eating habits? Does he eat well?"

"Oh, yes!" exclaimed the mother. "He eats everything with no problem, as long as it has ketchup on it!" This mother understood her child's reactions to food and had found a way to work with him. She accepted his use of ketchup and had created a "good fit" with her child.

• •

As discussed in Chapter 1, the concept of goodness of fit, developed by temperament pioneers Alexander Thomas and Stella Chess (1977) and discussed subsequently by others (e.g., Carey & McDevitt, 1995; Kurcinka, 1991, 1998; Turecki, 1985), is fundamental in understanding the broader concept of temperament. It explains how a child's temperament affects his or her relationships with other people, reactions to certain situations, and specific environments. This concept makes clear how forming a "good fit" with children supports raising healthy, well-adjusted individuals and creating smoother social interactions. Clinicians and others who work with temperament constructs aim to create a good fit for individuals with their environments and the people important in their lives.

Creating a good fit involves working *with* a child's temperament rather than working *against* it by trying to change it. Goodness of fit provides a neutral point from which to begin temperament counseling without blaming the child or the parent for challenging behavior. It helps parents and those working with children to understand the context in which behaviors occur. Certain temperaments respond to certain environments, discipline techniques, and ways of communicating more positively than they do to others. Like finding the jacket that fits just right, finding the techniques that fit best with a particular child makes life more comfortable.

DEFINING GOODNESS OF FIT

Goodness of fit exists when the demands and expectations of the environment are compatible with a person's temperament, abilities, and other characteristics (Chess & Thomas, 1986). Poorness of fit occurs when there are inconsistencies and dissonance between environmental demands and the person's capabilities and characteristics. When harmony exists between the individual and the environment, optimal development can occur (Chess & Thomas, 1992). Goodness of fit is most important in relationships between children and significant adults, such as a parent, teacher, physician, child care provider, or relative. Children's reactions to similar environments vary, and the ways in which adults respond to these reactions can create either a good or a poor fit. Adults who recognize how a child responds to certain situations can adjust their reactions to the child and help to establish a good fit and build positive interactions. They can help children to become more self-aware and to make appropriate modifications in their behavior, which benefits both child and adult. Adults who fail to understand and work with children's reactions risk creating a poor fit, which can lead to negative adult–child interactions and poor adjustment.

When a mother cuts the tags from her sensitive child's tee-shirt, she creates goodness of fit. When a teacher allows an active child to expend excess energy, he creates goodness of fit in the classroom. This is not to say that an adult must give up all control of the situation or meet a child's needs at the expense of other needs. Figure 2.1 illustrates the equal nature of support and structure within the construct of goodness of fit (Cameron, 1994).

GOODNESS OF FIT BETWEEN CHILDREN AND ADULTS

When a child exhibits challenging behavior at home, school, or child care, the problem could be a lack of goodness of fit between an adult (or adults) and the child. Professionals can help adults understand the child's temperament and how it influences the challenging behavior. This involves reframing the perception of the child's behavior to recognize temperament's influence and then determining how to best cope with it. Goodness of fit can then be established by changing the way in which the adult interacts with the child or by modifying the child's environment.

Goodness of fit also encourages positive self-esteem and self-awareness in children because when it occurs, children are recognized for who they *are* rather than what they *do*. When goodness of fit is present, fewer problems occur, and those that do occur are generally less intense and often easily solved. For example, a highly active child

Providing support	While	Providing structure
Meet the needs of child's temperament	While	Meeting parent and family needs
Meet the needs of child's temperament	While	Meeting school and child care needs
Meet present needs	While	Anticipating future needs
Show appreciation for child's individuality	While	Avoiding being controlled

Figure 2.1.   Creating goodness of fit by working with the child's temperament and the environment includes goals of both support and structure. (*Source:* Cameron, J. [n.d.])

who has to sit for long periods at his desk will often fidget or bother his neighbor, which creates a disruption in the class. The teacher can create a good fit and reduce the disruption by giving the child a task such as collecting homework papers, which allows the child to expend excess energy. The child who is highly persistent and low in distractibility can become so engrossed in his work that he does not hear the teacher's instruction to stop and move on to another subject. A teacher who does not understand his temperament may think he is disobedient, but the teacher who creates a good fit will give him advance warning of the change and then help him put closure on his project before going to the next task.

Poorness of fit results in negative interactions and power struggles between child and adult because expectations do not fit with the child's temperament. The child may see her behavior as "bad," even though the behavior occurs because of temperament. For this reason, a poor fit can negatively affect self-esteem and increase a child's negative behavior. Temperament-related behavioral issues can escalate into behavior problems and psychological maladjustment can occur when children and adults experience a poor fit (Chess & Thomas, 1999).

• •

Kimmy, a very active 5-year-old, was always on the go. She preferred loud, active play and would not sit still for very long. Her parents understood this and provided many opportunities for active play. They had a large yard with a play area and often went to the park or on bike rides.

These activities helped Kimmy release energy after a day at school or before quieter activities when she had to be still. Kimmy had a good fit with her family and her environment because she was able to expend her energy as needed.

. . . .

Jed, who was as active as Kimmy, lived in a small apartment with parents who were not active people. They preferred quiet activities and constantly admonished Jed to "sit still and settle down." This poor fit led to constant power struggles and a confrontational parent–child relationship because active Jed had nowhere to release his energy. He often would release energy in negative ways by jumping on furniture or running through the house. The more his parents tried to inhibit his activity, the more energy he seemed to have.

. . . .

How the environment is structured is important to goodness or poorness of fit, but the interaction of two different temperaments also plays a part. As illustrated by the story of Jed, less active parents may find it difficult to understand the energy needs of an active child. The expectation that a persistent parent has for a less persistent child may be to start a task at the beginning and not stop until it is completed, a poor fit for the child's temperament, which needs tasks to be approached in smaller parts. The spontaneous, adaptable mother who loves doing things at a moment's notice creates a good fit when she realizes that such spontaneity wreaks havoc with her slow-adapting son. So she creates a good fit when she carefully plans their outings together and lets him know the plan beforehand. She can still enjoy her spontaneous nature when she is alone or with her other spur-of-the-moment friends.

Poorness of fit does not always result from the interaction between opposite types. A child who is slow-to-warm-up and low in energy may struggle in a classroom led by a teacher with a similar temperament type who has trouble reaching out to less assertive, less active children who do not make their needs known, for example.

Table 2.1 includes several examples of goodness of fit strategies for each temperament type.

GOODNESS OF FIT BETWEEN CHILDREN AND THEIR PEERS

The way in which children interact with their peers also reflects goodness or poorness of fit. Some children get along better with certain children than with others because of their temperament styles. Parents who understand goodness of fit between children can consider the children's temperaments when planning play dates or social events, working with sibling behavior, or enlisting the child in extracurricular activities. For example, the parent who enrolls his very active son in a

Table 2.1.   Examples of goodness of fit strategies by temperament characteristic

Temperament characteristic	Strategies
Sensitivity	Providing a quiet retreat for the highly sensitive child who reacts to noise
	Helping the low-sensitivity child notice social cues
Activity level	Providing energy outlets for the highly active child
	Giving the low-activity child extra time to complete a task
Intensity	Remaining calm when responding to a high-intensity child's outburst
	Encouraging the low intensity child to express emotions through art or writing rather than verbally
Adaptability	Warning a slow-adapting child of an upcoming change
	Being aware of the needs of an adaptable child who may not express them
Regularity	Allowing the irregular child to read books for 15 minutes before "lights out" when she is not tired at bedtime
	Knowing that the regular child is always hungry at the same time (e.g., 11:00) and being prepared with a snack wherever you are at that time
Approach/withdrawal	Taking the highly approaching child to the children's Discovery Museum, rather than the antique furniture show
	Visiting the new school and meeting the new teacher before the withdrawing child starts school
Persistence	Having the low-persistence child take breaks while learning to ride a two-wheel bike
	Telling the highly persistent child that she has only 10 minutes to color before bedtime, then letting her put closure on the activity before stopping
Distractibility	Giving the highly distractible child only two instructions rather than four
	Making eye contact with the low-distractibility child when giving instructions

watercolor class creates a poor fit for his son who has difficulty sitting still as well as for the other children who enjoy quiet projects. This child would do much better on a soccer team. The parent who understands that Emily needs more time to become acquainted with a new babysitter than her sister Joan helps to create a good fit when she allows an extra half hour before leaving the children. The child care provider who knows that a child is sensitive to noise and light and finds a dark, quiet place for her to nap away from other less sensitive children is creating a good fit. The teacher who seats the distractible child near the front of class where there are fewer distractions creates a good fit. The pediatrician who allows the slow-to-warm-up child to inspect the otoscope and then looks in the teddy bear's ears before examining the child's ears creates a good fit. Other ways in which parents, teachers, physicians, and child care providers use temperament information to establish goodness of fit are examined in Section III of this book.

• •

Dirk, a very persistent child, had a less persistent friend come to his house for a play date. They began to build an elaborate Lego castle. Soon the less persistent playmate became frustrated with the activity and wanted to play something else. Dirk had no intention of doing anything else until the castle was complete, and he refused to play another game with his friend. The play date was a disaster. Dirk's mother noticed that her son's style conflicted with certain children and devised a strategy for future play dates. Before a less persistent child visited, she and Dirk would agree on some activities that could be completed relatively quickly. The activities that could last indefinitely were put away. Dirk could fulfill his need to complete an activity, yet the activity was brief enough to prevent frustration in the other child. This strategy worked very well and ensured a good fit between Dirk and less persistent playmates.

• •

Children with the temperament cluster of high intensity, low rhythmicity, slow adaptability, high activity, and negative mood (considered by some to be "difficult" children) typically struggle with relationships with peers, parents, and other adults, which often establishes negative behavior patterns in the child. They like to control play because of their slow adaptability, have the possibility of becoming aggressive because of their high activity and intensity levels, and do not fit well into routines because of their irregularity. They do not transition well from one activity to the next and have problems following directions. These children are more at risk for exhibiting behavior problems (Caspi, Henry, McGee, Moffit, & Silva, 1995; Oberklaid, Sanson, Pedlow, & Prior, 1993; Sanson, Smart, Prior, & Oberklaid, 1993; Thomas, Chess, & Birch, 1968). Children rated as more controlling and inflexible also have problems with sibling and peer interactions because of their difficulty with the give and take of everyday relationships (Billman & McDevitt, 1980; Stevenson-Hinde & Simpson, 1982). Those assessed with low self-control are more aggressive toward peers (Rothbart, Ahadi, & Hershey, 1994). The highly sensitive child who plays with an intense, less sensitive child can get feelings hurt more easily than when she plays with another child who is calm and equally sensitive. Two highly active children can escalate in energy until both are out of control. Knowing how these children react can inform the best approach to setting up social experiences at home or at school to create goodness of fit. Temperament guidance used at an early age promotes goodness of fit and can prevent many of these problems.

GOODNESS OF FIT IN THE COMMUNITY

Creating goodness of fit in places such as classrooms, child care facilities, extracurricular activities, and doctors' and therapists' offices benefits the community and also increases awareness of individual differences in temperament. The specifics of using temperament concepts in these settings are covered in more detail in Section III of this book.

Children who experience good fit in the classroom have greater academic success (Caspi & Silva, 1995; Hegvik, 1989; Keogh, 1989, 2003; Pullis, 1989; Rothbart & Jones, 1998), and certain temperament traits are likely to lead to success more easily than others. For example, adaptable and persistent children with low intensity and low activity levels have higher scores in math and reading than children who are slow to adapt, active, and not persistent (Keogh, 2003; Martin, 1988a).

Children with more challenging temperament traits, however, can also succeed in math and reading with the right support and the right fit. The teacher who provides appropriate energy outlets for the active child, who pairs the less persistent child with a more persistent child, who has a quiet corner where the highly sensitive child can retreat, and who gives the slow-adapting child ample time and warning for transitions in the classroom creates a good fit for each of these children. Good fit in the classroom lays the foundation for successful learning experiences for all children.

A basic understanding of students' temperaments can also help child care providers. Fearful children respond with more stress to full-time, center-based child care than do fearless children, and children who are more negative and more active than other children exhibit more negative behavior toward peers and adults as the day progresses (Crockenberg, 2003). Knowing this, parents may opt for shorter days or smaller home-based care, depending on the child's temperament. Child care providers can use this information to help these children decrease their levels of stress as the day proceeds by modifying the environment and providing ways to relieve stress.

Temperament concepts can help physicians and other health care providers with their patients. Health care providers can use temperament techniques to understand their patients and manage current medical issues (Cameron, Hansen, & Rosen, 1989; Carey, 1982a, 1985, 1994). For example, the pediatrician who examines a slow-to-warm-up child knows to move slowly, to describe the process first, and to give the child time to become familiar with the new procedures. The nurse who understands temperament knows that the intense child will react loudly and forcefully to an injection, whereas the less intense child will react with a slight whimper. Besides knowing how to approach a patient, health care providers can use temperament information (perhaps kept in a child's profile, chart, or file) to give the parent more concrete advice on issues such as sleeping, eating, giving medication, following treatment procedures, and other medical concerns.

Finally, in psychotherapy, the therapist who understands a client's temperament is more likely to know the best approach for treatment options and also the best ways to communicate with a particular client (Cameron, 1978; Chess & Thomas, 1986). Therapists can vary their approaches according to the client's temperament. For example, the therapist working with a slow-adapting child creates a good fit by approaching any changes in treatment or therapy more slowly and steadily than he would for a fast adapter.

THE CHILD AS AN ACTIVE PARTICIPANT

The child is an active participant in the caregiver–child relationship (Rutter, 1982). Although infant temperamental characteristics are not the only cause of parental behavior, they may influence the caregiver–child relationship. Kaye (1982) pointed out that different infants have different effects on caregivers. Extremely difficult infants may elicit negative reactions from some parents, which in turn increase the infant's difficulties. When parents do not understand why their infant fusses and cries excessively, they may respond negatively or use inappropriate techniques to attempt to quiet the infant. When a child's cycles are easy to anticipate and interpret, however, the parents' behavior is more consistent, which creates easier and more effective communication. Similarly, studies have found that mothers of "difficult" infants were less responsive and interacted less with them than did mothers of infants who were not rated as difficult (Campbell, 1979; Crockenberg & Smith, 2002).

Many parents and professionals do not have the proper temperament information and react negatively toward children with more challenging temperaments. They may interpret a child's behavior as defiance or rudeness rather than as a temperament-based reaction. How a child initially reacts to the teacher, physician, or parent (because of temperament) determines how these adults respond to the child in turn. For example, a sensitive, slow-adapting child who withdraws from novelty is likely to refuse to interact in new situations. This may trigger a negative response in the parent, who pushes the child to join in. This causes further withdrawal in the child. The child's temperament influences the parent's behavior just as the parent's temperament influences the child's behavior. The child has a good fit with the parent who prepares him or her beforehand for a new experience and then allows the child time to get used to it. The adult who can anticipate a child's reaction by knowing the child's temperament acts accordingly.

Children with easier temperaments elicit more positive responses from their environment and have an easier time getting along in the world. These children seem to "go with the flow," relate better at home and at school, and do better socially. Children with more difficult temperaments are more likely to contribute adversely to interactions (Barron & Earls, 1984; Billman & McDevitt, 1980; Milliones, 1978; Thomas, Chess, Birch, & Korn, 1963; Thomas, Chess, & Birch, 1968; Webster-Stratton & Eyberg, 1982). One study showed that the more difficult the child is, the more the mother is anxious and both outwardly and inwardly irritable (Stevenson-Hinde & Simpson, 1982). Interactions are a reciprocal process with the individual characteristics of one person influencing the behavior of the other.

Sometimes the parent's temperament hinders good fit. For example, a parent whose temperament is low in sensitivity may have difficulty noticing a child's subtle behavioral cues. This makes it difficult to respond appropriately to the child, especially if the child does not make her needs obvious. The ways in which parent temperament contributes to goodness or poorness of fit is discussed further in Chapter 7.

PARENT SENSITIVITY

Parents who are sensitive to their child's individual differences can establish goodness of fit. Learning how their child reacts to her surroundings and knowing what can trigger different responses helps parents become more sensitive. It may be harder for parents of a difficult child to establish goodness of fit than for parents of an easy child. It may also be more difficult for a parent who is low in sensitivity to pick up subtle cues. Also, children who are very low in intensity and also low in sensitivity are less expressive and may not exhibit cues as clearly as the more intense, sensitive child. Assessing a child's temperament with the help of a professional or by careful observation can help the parent become more sensitive to the child's needs. Assessing temperament is discussed in Chapter 3.

Sensitive parents

- Learn about their child's temperament
- Notice and can interpret their child's cues
- Know situations that can cause problems
- Anticipate how the child will react to certain circumstances
- Understand what behavior is appropriate for the child's developmental level
- Keep expectations realistic according to age and temperament
- Are flexible but firm when necessary
- Behave in a consistent manner

Sensitive parents understand their child's temperament and work to read and interpret a child's signals, however subtle or unique, and then work with those signals. They know when an active child needs to expend energy or when a very sensitive child has had too much stimulation. They understand the situations and events that trigger an intense reaction. They know how the child reacts to his environment, and they guide the child accordingly in a consistent, timely manner. Sensitive parenting takes into account the child's temperament, developmental stage, and current situation. Parents are flexible according to the child's needs yet maintain a suitable level of control. They understand what is typical for the child's developmental level and do not expect more advanced behavior. They make their expectations for appropriate behavior clear and gently but consistently guide their child toward acceptable behavior. Sensitive parenting creates goodness of fit and promotes healthy adjustment.

THE ROLE OF ATTACHMENT

Sensitive parenting has often been associated with healthy parent–child attachment (Seifer & Schiller, 1995). Attachment refers to the affectionate bonds that develop between caregivers and infants that endure across time and situations (Ainsworth, Blehar, Waters, & Wall, 1978). Attachment theory (Bowlby, 1982) is based on the idea that a child's early experience with a caregiver forms the basis for later relationships and strongly influences the child's concept of self. Attachment theorists agree that all infants become attached regardless of the kind of care they receive but that the quality of care determines the kind of attachment that is formed. An infant who receives inconsistent, rejecting care still becomes attached to the caregiver; however, the attachment is insecure and the child expresses anxious or avoidant behavior (for a complete discussion of attachment theory see Bowlby, 1973, 1982, 1988).

Attachment between child and caregiver is frequently assessed with a laboratory procedure called the Strange Situation, developed by Mary Ainsworth (Ainsworth, Bell, & Stayton, 1971). The Strange Situation consists of eight 3-minute episodes in which the mother and child enter the laboratory together and go through a series of increasingly stressful events during which the child is placed with the parent alone, a stranger alone, and by him- or herself. During these time periods, trained raters determine the security of the child's attachment based on his or her reactions to separation and reunion. The child's security of attachment rates either as insecure (anxious/avoidant or anxious/resistant); secure (Ainsworth et al., 1971); or disorganized, disoriented (Main & Solomon, 1990) depending on how the child reacts to separation from and then reunion with the caregiver in the Strange Situation. The security of attachments predicts the child's behavioral outcome.

Caregivers of securely attached children provide sensitive, responsive, and consistent care and offer a secure base for exploration. Securely attached children are more cooperative and compliant (Londerville & Main, 1981), better adjusted, more socially competent, and have fewer behavior problems than insecurely attached children (Arend, Gove, & Sroufe, 1979; Erickson, Sroufe, & Egeland, 1985; LaFreniere & Sroufe, 1985). Children who are insecurely attached or disorganized tend to have parents who provide inconsistent, insensitive, or neglectful care.

Sensitive parenting fosters a secure attachment between a child and caregiver, just as it contributes to goodness of fit. But what role do attachment and temperament play in a child's development? This controversial question has puzzled child psychologists, although most theorists now recognize the role of both nature and nurture. In the past, attachment theorists placed more importance on the role of the environment and caregiving, and temperament theorists stressed the importance of innate biological differences; however, more recent research indicates that both constructs contribute to a child's behavior (e.g., Seifer & Schiller, 1995; Susman-Stillman, Kalkoske, Egeland, & Waldman, 1996). Being sensitive to the child's temperament may influence the attachment relationship.

TEMPERAMENT AND ATTACHMENT

The debate between the temperament theorists and the attachment theorists lies in the role that temperament plays in attachment assessment (e.g., Kagan, 1982; Sroufe, 1985). Temperament theorists argue that a child's temperament could influence his or her reactions to the Strange Situation. A child who is temperamentally inhibited or fearful will react differently to a new setting such as the Strange Situation than a child who has an approaching, active temperament. This can affect the attachment ratings (Calkins & Fox, 1992). Jerome Kagan (1982, 1984) suggested that assessments like the Strange Situation might reflect the infant's temperamental responses to a stressful situation. He found that infants who are highly stimulated by unexpected changes in the environment are more likely to be classified as insecurely attached (resistant) during their first 2 years of life than infants who are not easily stimulated. Fearful infants react very negatively to separation during the Strange Situation, display heightened proximity seeking or clingy behavior, and resist the parent's attempts to soothe them during reunion episodes (Thompson, Connell, & Bridges, 1988).

Conversely, attachment theorists usually dismiss temperament, saying it has little relevance in the child's attachment security and arguing that attachment is a relationship that exists above and beyond the effects of temperament (Belsky & Rovine, 1987; Sroufe, 1985; Vaughn, Lefever, Seifer, & Barglow, 1989).

Because temperament influences how a child behaves in certain settings, the more active, approaching child is more likely to exhibit exploratory behaviors in the Strange Situation. Conversely, temperament traits such as fear (Rothbart, 1981), withdrawal, or slow-adaptability (Thomas et al., 1963) could influence how strongly the child reacts to an unfamiliar adult as well as the transitions that occur during the assessment. Likewise, temperament traits such as soothability and distractibility determine the ease and time it takes to soothe the child when distressed during separation from the mother. A child's sensitivity, persistence, and orientation are also related to the quality of interactions with both people and objects during the parent's absence (Seifer & Schiller, 1995).

Temperament and attachment may be related in two important ways (Seifer & Schiller, 1995). First, temperament might influence the interpretation of the attachment assessment. As mentioned before, the behaviors of an inhibited, fearful child in the Strange Situation may replicate those of an insecurely attached child, yet be entirely temperament-related. Second, a child's temperament may influence parent–child interactions that are important in the development of attachment during the first year of life. The infant who is innately "difficult" will affect the responses of the parent. If parent–child interactions do influence the development of the attachment system, an understanding of temperament can lead to developing more secure attachments with "difficult" children. For example, parents of a child who is intense, negative in mood, low in adaptability, and difficult to soothe are less likely to experience a positive, mutual interaction or be successful in helping the child with self-regulation—both of which are important to the development of a secure attachment. Understanding the child's temperament characteristics can help the parents work with these traits to create a better fit and more sensitive parenting.

The mother's temperament also affects her reactions to her child. Mothers of securely attached infants rated themselves as more adaptable, whereas mothers of insecurely attached infants considered themselves more reactive and less adaptable in new situations (Weber, Levitt, & Clark, 1986). Social support also helped mothers create secure attachments, particularly with difficult infants (Crockenberg, 1981). Difficult infants were more likely to be classified as insecurely attached when their mothers did not have the social support of friends or family. However, difficult infants whose mothers had social support networks were less likely to be rated as insecure. In addition, "easy" babies were unlikely to develop insecure attachments even in unfavorable social situations because they were safeguarded by virtue of their own temperaments.

The bi-directional quality of the caregiver–child relationship must be considered when interpreting child behavior. The relationship described by attachment is determined by the quality of care and the caregiver's sensitivity to the child's needs. The child, through virtue of innate biological differences or temperament, experiences the environment and people in different ways and, in turn, elicits responses from those around him or her.

SUMMARY

Goodness of fit describes a relationship just as attachment does. The caregiver who is sensitive to the child's individual differences, who can read the child's cues, and who responds to the child's needs in a fitting manner creates goodness of fit and, in doing so, also promotes a secure attachment. A relationship is formed in which the child can depend on the caregiver to respond consistently and sensitively. Each knows what to expect of the other.

When working with caregivers or other adults in the child's life, the concept of "goodness of fit" provides us with a starting point for understanding behavior and making changes. Once there is a good fit, positive relationships incorporating reciprocity promote healthy adjustments. Goodness of fit begins from the neutral position of working with an individual's innate temperament rather than against it.

CHAPTER 3

The Temperament Profile

Your Guide to Behavior

- -

The parents of 4-year-old Annie called their pediatrician because Annie woke up several times each night and had difficulty going back to sleep. After looking at her medical chart, the doctor realized that Annie had had sleep difficulties since infancy. He asked if there had been any changes at home: Had either of them gone on a business trip? Had Annie's bedtime routine changed? Was there any marital discord? The parents said that no changes had occurred at home and also explained that there were no changes at preschool or child care. They went on to say that as Annie had gotten older, her night waking had increasingly disrupted their sleep, especially when she came into bed with them. They wanted help in coping with the problem. They explained some of the strategies they had tried, such as letting her cry, taking her back to her own bed repeatedly, and threatening punishment. Unfortunately, none of these techniques had worked—the parents just ended up giving in.

After exploring the sleep issue thoroughly with the parents, the pediatrician said, "In order to give you advice about what will work best with Annie, I'd like to assess her temperament. I have observed Annie in my office and know about her behavior at home from what you have told me, but I'd like you to complete a temperament questionnaire so that I can see her temperament profile. Then I can give you more accurate advice for helping her to sleep through the night."

- -

Many professionals find a temperament assessment such as a questionnaire helpful in determining the right strategies for a particular child. A temperament assessment is an effective first step in working with a child's behavioral issues when a parent specifically seeks help. It gives the parents and the clinician important insight on the child's behavior and provides a concrete tool to help them better understand the child's temperament. An assessment may also be used later after the clinician has tried some possible strategies but found that they do not work as well as expected, or it may be used in conjunction with other behavioral techniques, such as an incentive system. With a particularly challenging child, a temperament assessment can provide the professional with important insights on the child's characteristics, explain why behaviors are occurring, and help in deciding which strategies will be most effective.

Most professionals use a questionnaire such as a parent report to evaluate a child's temperament; however, some clinicians prefer to combine methods. In addition to a questionnaire, professionals may implement such strategies as observations and parent interviews to obtain a complete temperament evaluation and avoid misdiagnosis or inappropriate labeling. Pediatricians, health care providers, teachers, child care providers, therapists, and others who have been trained to use temperament in their practices often are qualified to use the available temperament assessments (see Appendix A for a list of temperament assessments). Professionals who have not had temperament training but want to use an assessment can work with temperament counselors who can conduct and interpret the assessments. The temperament profile provides parents and clinician with a list of the child's ratings on the different temperament traits, showing which traits significantly affect the child's behavior. According to James Cameron, clinical psychologist and temperament researcher,

> When you buy a new car you get an owner's manual that explains how the car runs and what it needs for maintenance. Parents don't get an owner's guide with their children. A temperament profile is the parents' "owner's manual." It tells them what "model" they have, what they can expect, and what is needed for optimum maintenance.
> (Cameron, 1992)

OBTAINING DATA: TYPES OF ASSESSMENTS

Temperament assessments include interviews, naturalistic or laboratory observations, and questionnaires. The assessment chosen depends on the professional's clientele, his or her preference and setting,
and which method works best in a particular situation. On the one
hand, teachers may find observation useful because they have many
opportunities to observe a child's behavior and reactions throughout
the day. On the other hand, a health care provider who spends only
brief periods of time with each patient might find a questionnaire to be
most efficient. A psychotherapist might combine the practices of observing the child in the play room, interviewing the parents, and having
the parents complete a questionnaire. Each method has advantages
and disadvantages, so temperament professionals must determine which
strategy or combination works best for them. Descriptions of different
assessment methods follow.

INTERVIEW

An interview is a person-to-person conversation used to obtain information on a child's temperament. Clinicians who work with young
children interview one or both parents and sometimes a child care
provider. Those who work with older children or adolescents may
choose to interview them directly, instead of, or in addition to, interviewing the parents. In a structured interview, the interviewer asks a
series of specific questions and records the subject's answers. An unstructured interview asks more open-ended questions and can change
direction depending on the subject's answers or the information the
interviewer seeks.

Initially, in the landmark New York Longitudinal Study (NYLS),
temperament pioneers Thomas, Chess, and Birch (1968) used extensive parental interviews to assess temperament. Some clinicians still
use this method when they want to delve deeper into issues or want
to ask about different types of situations. For example, if the interviewer asks, "Does your child have difficulty sitting still?", the interviewer can then find out exactly when and where this behavior tends
to occur. Both structured and unstructured interviews provide the flexi-

bility to explore issues that might not be covered on a questionnaire. Interviews are also useful when questionnaires are not available, when a parent or teacher is not amenable to completing a questionnaire, or with parents who have disabilities or who face language or literacy barriers. Parents who are completing a great deal of paperwork for other child evaluations may prefer an interview assessment to lessen the amount of paperwork. Clinicians who are trying to isolate very specific areas of temperament may find the interview useful. For example, a child who is highly sensitive physically to very particular sensations may have his sensitivities described in more detail through an interview than by a questionnaire. Interviews can also reconcile differences between behavior in different situations such as home and school. The interviewee can describe in detail behaviors and situations in each context.

Although interviewing has many advantages, professionals should keep in mind that interviews are time consuming and can be inconsistent. The interviewer must spend a large amount of time to obtain enough information to make an adequate assessment. Interviewers may not gather the same amount of information from each person interviewed because people vary in the amount of detail they volunteer when answering questions. Parents may present biased information about their children and answer questions for social desirability, especially if they find the questions or the interview situation uncomfortable (Bates, 1989; Dantrock, 2000). Cultural differences may also affect the interview process. Behavior is interpreted differently in various cultures, and certain temperament characteristics may be valued in one culture and not another (Hanson & Lynch, 2004). The interviewer's own opinions and prejudices (interviewer bias) may affect how the interviewer interprets the interview.

NATURAL AND LABORATORY OBSERVATIONS

Natural observations, which take place in the child's natural environments such as home, school, or child care, can provide valuable information about child temperament. For example, a child's activity level, intensity, or tendency to approach or withdraw from situations can be easily seen during a natural observation, which is typically conducted without the child's knowledge that she is being observed. A parent may report that a child "has an attention problem," for example, but a knowledgeable observer may see that the child is only distractible in a noisy, busy environment. Natural observations are particularly valuable when focusing on a child's specific behaviors, such as inattention during circle time or aggression against peers at recess. For example, Kiera had a difficult time attending to the story at circle time but could focus for long periods on an art project. Nate got along well with his peers in the classroom, but reacted aggressively to intrusions of his space at recess. Observations help clarify when and where specific behaviors occur.

Similar to interviews, the disadvantage is that observations can be very time consuming. In order to obtain a reliable assessment it is necessary to observe the child in different activities such as during play or meals or with peers over an extended period of time, and this may take many hours of observation at different times and in various situations. Because of the time involved, observations can also be expensive if the observer is being paid at an hourly rate. Measurement error can occur because of the observer's limited objectivity. The emotional state of the mother, child, and observer may affect the observation, and the lack of normative comparison data makes it difficult to standardize observation assessments (Prior, 1992). The context of the observation can affect the data, as well. For example, observations at a child's home may elicit behaviors that differ from those the child exhibits at school because of the different activities involved in each setting. The child may also be more aware of an observer at home than at school. When Kaiser Permanente filmed children for a series of temperament videos, the presence of the cameraman affected the children's behavior. The children were very aware that they were being filmed and modified their typical behavior. Several mothers remarked that their children had never behaved so well.

A laboratory observation provides a more artificial context than a naturalistic observation, but the examiner can present children with specific situations and stimuli and record their immediate responses (Prior, 1992). The highly structured environment of a laboratory assessment can create advantages. For example, this style of observation takes less time than its naturalistic counterpart and enables the examiner to give the child a series of situations that measure temperament.

Examples of this are Goldsmith and Rothbart's (1992) Laboratory Assessment Battery (LAB-TAB), Kagan and Snidman's (1991b) assessment of inhibited and uninhibited behavior (see also Kagan, Snidman, & Arcus, 1998), or Matheny's (2000) play assessment of infant temperament. In these and other laboratory assessments, however, the sterile environment limits the ability of the observer to assess the context and range of the child's temperament characteristics. The child may also exhibit atypical behavior in laboratory assessments because of the novel situation. For example, a child who has the temperament characteristic of initially withdrawing from novelty may refuse to participate in the laboratory assessment and hide behind his mother for the entire session. A child who is active, approaching, and intense may be so excited about the novelty that she bounces from one task to another without completing any of them.

Observational data prove to be most valuable when used to supplement questionnaire data. Some clinicians or temperament counselors first have parents complete a temperament questionnaire, and then the counselors observe the child either in a structured setting or at home to corroborate the questionnaire findings. For example, one temperament counselor found that parents had rated their daughter as very active on a temperament questionnaire, but when the counselor observed her in a typical play situation, she had a balance of quiet and active play, which indicated that her activity level was average. Such misinterpretation may be due to the rater's own low activity level in comparison with the child's or the rater's limited contact with other children who are more active.

Questionnaires can help professionals know where to start in the observation process. Clinicians and teachers can observe temperament when they know what to look for. Figure 3.1 is an example of an informal questionnaire listing behaviors to observe that fall in the extremes of each trait when a standard questionnaire is not available.

Researchers debate the consistency between parent observation ratings, laboratory observation data, and home observation data. Some found limited correlations among the three measures (e.g., Bates, 1989; Rothbart & Goldsmith, 1985), whereas others found greater consistency that showed that temperament can be assessed in different situations by both parents and impartial observers (e.g., Matheny, Wilson, & Thoben, 1987).

Low sensitivity	High sensitivity
❏ High tolerance of physical sensations or pain ❏ Not sensitive to others' feelings ❏ Does not notice social cues ❏ Feelings are not easily hurt	❏ Bothered by many physical sensations: tastes, smells, sounds, touch, texture ❏ Low tolerance for illness or injuries ❏ Easily overstimulated or overwhelmed ❏ Feelings are easily hurt
Low activity	**High activity**
❏ Prefers and excels at fine motor skills ❏ Prefers quiet activities ❏ Moves at a slower pace ❏ Moves toward independence slowly ❏ Can sit quietly for long periods	❏ In constant motion, gets energized easily ❏ Prefers and excels at gross motor skills ❏ Has difficulty sitting still ❏ Dislikes car seats, strollers, or any confinement ❏ Has difficulty slowing down for a quiet activity ❏ Moves toward independence quickly
Low intensity	**High intensity**
❏ Is difficult to "read" ❏ Quiet, calm ❏ Does not express emotions readily	❏ Very loud, dramatic, has strong feelings ❏ Expresses extremes of emotions ❏ Cries easily, laughs easily, overreacts
Fast-adapting	**Slow-adapting**
❏ Flexible ❏ Makes changes and transitions easily ❏ Not bothered by intrusions ❏ Goes with the flow	❏ Inflexible ❏ Has difficulty with transitions or changes ❏ Dislikes intrusions of any kind ❏ Bossy, wants to control situations ❏ Does best if forewarned of a change or event
Approaching/curious	**Withdrawing/hesitant**
❏ Very outgoing and sociable ❏ Likes new things, people, situations ❏ Leaps before looking ❏ A "hands-on" learner	❏ Prefers anything that is familiar ❏ Holds back with new situations, people, things ❏ Very cautious ❏ Learns through observation
High persistence	**Low persistence**
❏ Can be "stubborn"—does not give up ❏ Wants to complete tasks once occupied ❏ Plays alone well ❏ Not easily frustrated	❏ Becomes easily frustrated ❏ Likes to have adults nearby for assistance ❏ Not inclined to practice a new skill or activity ❏ Gives up easily ❏ Does not play well alone
High distractibility	**Low distractibility**
❏ Easily sidetracked from an activity ❏ Has difficulty concentrating on a task ❏ Notices everything going on around him or her ❏ Easy to redirect	❏ Difficult to distract from activity ❏ Has excellent focus when absorbed in a task ❏ Difficult to calm when upset ❏ Tunes out extraneous stimulation

Figure 3.1. Sample checklist for observing temperament in children.

QUESTIONNAIRE: PARENT OR TEACHER REPORT

Because of the limitations of interviews and observations, clinicians have developed parent and teacher report questionnaires to assess temperament. Noted pediatrician William Carey and colleagues developed the Carey Temperament Scales (CTS; Carey & McDevitt, 1978; Fullard, McDevitt, & Carey, 1984; Hegvik, McDevitt, & Carey, 1982; McDevitt & Carey, 1978; Medhoff-Cooper, Carey, & McDevitt, 1993) to measure temperament from early infancy though middle childhood. These scales comprise five questionnaires based on Chess and Thomas's interview and categories from the NYLS: the Early Infant Temperament Questionnaire (EITQ), for infants ages 1 to 4 months; the Revised Infant Temperament Questionnaire (RITQ), for infants ages 4 to 8 months; the Toddler Temperament Scale (TTS), for children ages 1 to 2 years; the Behavioral Style Questionnaire (BSQ), for children ages 3 to 7 years; and the Middle Childhood Temperament Questionnaire (MCTQ) for children ages 8 to 12 years. Initially, Carey developed the questionnaires for use in pediatric practice, but now a variety of professionals use them in other settings. Cameron and Rice (1999), for example, adapted the CTS and developed their own questionnaires for infants, toddlers, and preschoolers (see a later section in this chapter on the Cameron-Rice Profile). Professionals routinely use the Carey Temperament Scales in their practices to help provide responsible clinical care (Carey, 1992). Other questionnaires based on the NYLS dimensions, such as the revised Dimensions of Temperament Survey (Windle & Lerner, 1986), cover early childhood through young adulthood and have a self-report version for adolescents and young adults.

The advantage of using a questionnaire to generate a temperament profile is that it gives stakeholders such as clinicians, parents, and educators information to guide their approach toward the child. The temperament profile provides a concrete way for parents to visualize their child's temperament. It helps the professional explain children's behavior to parents and helps them realize what influences children's reactions. The profile also helps parents realize how their own responses can affect their child's behavior. Parents more frequently follow recommendations once they realize their responsibility for the child's behavior relies mostly on their reaction to the child's temperament, which the temperament profile helps substantiate.

Professionals usually prefer using parent-report questionnaires for assessments because (unlike interviews and observations) they cost very little, are easy to administer, and generate a great deal of information about behavior across a variety of situations. However, some researchers have questioned the accuracy of parent-report questionnaires (Kagan, 1998; Seifer, Sameroff, Barrett, & Krafchuk, 1994). They claim that parents may be biased and that they do not have a normative base of reference. Different parents may interpret questionnaire items differently, and their ratings may not reflect the child's typical behavior in all settings. Others in the field note that parents are good reporters because of their ability to observe a wide range of their children's behavior in various settings and to describe subtle variations of behavior that might not be apparent to other observers (Mangelsdorf, Schoppe, & Burr, 2000; Rothbart & Bates, 1998; Teglasi, 1998). When parents are asked the right questions in an appropriate way, their responses are of moderate to high validity (Carey, 1982b). Even though parent-report measures may have a subjective component, they provide valuable information about child functioning that cannot be found elsewhere (Guerin, Gottfried, Oliver, & Thomas, 2003; Mangelsdorf et al., 2000). Bates and Bayles (1984) found that mother-rated temperament assessments are not dominated by subjectivity but do measure inherent child characteristics. For example, parents can report on sleeping and eating patterns that only they can observe. Temperament consists of behavioral tendencies that are influenced by situations, experiences, and others' behavior, so temperament measurement depends on context. Caregivers possess an extensive database of child behavior in numerous contexts from which to draw.

Other temperament theorists have developed questionnaires based on their definitions and dimensions of temperament (e.g., Buss & Plomin, 1984, Goldsmith & Campos, 1982). For example, Rothbart's Infant Behavior Questionnaire (1981) measures the dimensions of activity, distress over limitations, fear, duration of orienting, smiling and laughter, and soothability (see Tables 1.4 and 1.5 in Chapter 1 for a comparison of different theorists' temperament dimensions). Psychologists use these various questionnaires in psychological research but not often in clinical work. Other questionnaires developed for teachers (e.g., Keogh, Pullis, & Cadwell, 1982; Martin, 1988b) are used clinically and also in educational research. Appendix A provides a comprehensive list describing temperament questionnaires available for clinicians, researchers, and teachers.

Combined Assessments: Modified Interviews with Questionnaires

Some clinicians use a modified interview format when reviewing a child's questionnaire temperament profile with parents and/or teachers. As they discuss temperament traits, the clinician probes further to attain more specific information. The following vignette illustrates this practice.

• •

A mother completed a questionnaire to understand why her young son Tyler acted out at home and at school. He had become noncompliant and aggressive, which she considered atypical behavior for her son. The profile revealed no extreme scores except for moderately slow adaptability, but this by itself did not explain Tyler's extreme behavior. The counselor asked if there had been any major changes in the boy's life, and his mother said there were none. Further questions revealed that there *had* been a change, however. Tyler's aunt was going through a divorce and had moved in with the family for a while, but the mother did not consider this a major change because he loved his aunt and she visited their house frequently before the divorce. Tyler's mother was trying to help her sister through this stressful time and did not think her sister's visit affected her son directly because she believed it did not concern him. However, Tyler's adaptability was low enough that having another person living in the house—even though she was familiar—had triggered his acting-out behavior. His sensitivity to this change and the stress it created in the household led to his noncompliance—his attempt to exert some control over the changes he perceived. If the clinician had counseled strictly from the questionnaire data, he would have missed this fact. A child's behavior becomes clearer once the professional knows the child's temperament and how the environment affects it.

• •

School and child care are two environments in which children often experience temperament-related problems. When both educators and parents complete temperament questionnaires to address a school problem, their combined views provide a more complete evaluation of the child and the means to work on the problem behaviors both at home and at school. For the most reliable results in locating the source(s) of problem behavior, each party should complete a temperament questionnaire designed to elicit accurate information, however. Because some questions on parent questionnaires do not pertain to school or child care environments, educators cannot answer them accurately, just as parents cannot answer questions strictly related to the classroom. Questionnaires developed specifically for teachers, such as the Teacher Temperament Questionnaire–Short Form (Keogh et al., 1982) or the Temperament Assessment Battery for Children, Teacher Form (Martin, 1988b), provide an accurate view of child temperament in the classroom.

Once the questionnaire is completed and scored, the resulting profile organizes temperament information into an understandable context that prevents inappropriate labeling of the child. The professional uses the profile to discuss the child's temperament traits and how they interact to produce the child's behavior. When combined with interview questions either before or during the discussion of the profile, an even clearer picture of the child's temperament emerges.

CREATING THE PROFILE

Temperament questionnaires help the rater clarify the child's behavior in a variety of contexts. The CTS (e.g., Carey & McDevitt, 1978; Fullard, McDevitt, & Carey, 1984; Hegvik et al., 1982) or the Cameron-Rice questionnaires (1999) are often used clinically with parents. The statements or questions describe how the child behaves and responds to many different activities and situations. The individual who completes the temperament questionnaire must spend a substantial amount of time with the child in order to provide an accurate rating. Questions pertain to each temperament category and are written to include both high and low directions for scoring. The items in both assessments are rated on a six-point scale of frequency of occurrence, ranging from *al-*

most never to *almost always*. The following are some typical items from a questionnaire:

- The child wakes up about the same time each morning.
- The child's first reaction to new surroundings is to explore.
- The child continues to play with objects after being told to stop.
- The child adjusts easily to changes in his/her routine.
- The child is sensitive to noises.

More examples of statements from temperament questionnaires related to various temperament types are given in Figure 3.2.

After the caregiver or teacher has completed the temperament questionnaire and it has been scored, the temperament profile shows the

---

Sensitivity
When going outdoors the child seems to notice whether the temperature is hot or cold.
The infant reacts even to a gentle touch (startle, wiggle, laugh, cry).

Activity level
The child runs to where the child wants to go.
The child fidgets when a story is being read to him/her.

Intensity
The child reacts strongly (cries or complains) to a disappointment or failure.
The child laughs hard when watching a cartoon or comedy.

Regularity
The child spontaneously wakes up at the usual time on weekends and holidays.
The amount the child eats at each meal is predictable.

Adaptability
The child is slow to adjust to changes in household rules.
When told it is time to leave, the child gets ready to go without much complaining.

Mood
The child is pleasant at bedtime.
The child becomes angry with playmates.

Approach/withdrawal
The child avoids new guests or visitors.
The child is willing to try new things.

Persistence
The child will keep returning to a difficult toy until mastering it.
The child says he/she is "bored" with his/her toys or games.

Distractibility
The child seems not to hear when involved in a favorite activity.
The child stops an activity because something else catches his/her attention.

Figure 3.2. Sample items from temperament questionnaires.

child's rating on each scale. The CTS can be hand scored or computer scored. Figure 3.3 illustrates a computer-scored profile for 9-year-old "Amy" from the MCTQ (Hegvik, McDevitt, & Carey, 1982), completed by Amy's mother. Amy's parents sought a temperament assessment because of what they perceived to be Amy's noncompliance and intense reactions at home. Her temperament profile provides the clinician with insights on Amy's behavior and helps determine the strategies for working with the behaviors during the counseling session.

THE CAREY TEMPERAMENT PROFILE

To create a Carey Temperament Profile for an individual, the ratings generated from the questionnaire for each scale are averaged, and this generates the profile results. The CTS include a mean or average for children in the designated age range (in Figure 3.3, Amy's profile falls in the age range of 8–12). The numbers 1–4 on either side of the mean on the top of the profile show standard deviations—how far the score

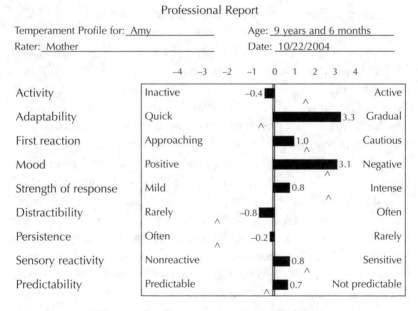

Figure 3.3. Sample professional report from a Carey Temperament Profile. Participant is in the middle child age group. Results show that the child scores high on gradual adaptability rather than quick adaptability and tends to be negative, rather than positive, in mood, among other things. (From Hegvik, R.L., McDevitt, S.C., & Carey, W.B. [1982]. Middle Childhood Temperament Questionnaire. *Developmental and Behavioral Pediatrics, 3*, 197–200; adapted by permission). (Key: ∧ = general impressions of caregiver, indicating agreement or disagreement with scores.)

deviates from the mean. The bar graph indicates the child's score for each category, and a number by each bar shows the standard deviation. A score of 0.0 indicates exactly average for the age. At the end of each bar, the exact standard deviations are indicated. For example, 0.8 for strength of response represents 0.8 standard deviations from the mean.

The scores that fall to the right of the mean—such as high activity, slow adaptability, high intensity, high sensitivity, and low persistence—tend to be more difficult areas of temperament than the scores to the left of the mean, although some scores that fall to the left may also present challenges, such as high persistence and high approach. Temperament counselors using this type of profile should point out to parents that any score of 1.0 or greater will be more likely to affect their child's behavior. The CTS dimensions clarify the traits' meanings for parents by relabeling approach/withdrawal as *first reaction,* intensity as *strength of response,* thresholds as *sensory reactivity,* and rhythmicity as *predictability.*

Parents' General Impressions   Assessments such as the Carey scales allow parents to offer their general impressions of their children. This "general impressions" feature allows parents to give their view of the child based on one question per category, such as "the amount of physical motion during daily routine" (Behavioral Style Questionnaire, McDevitt & Carey, 1975–1995). On the profile, the general impressions are compared with the questionnaire results and can be useful to the professional because they show where the parent agrees or disagrees with the questionnaire score or where the parent may misinterpret the child's temperament. The professional report of the CTS indicates the parents' general impression as a carat mark (∧). General impressions are based on a list of nine ratings, each pertaining to one temperament trait. For example, the rater rates activity level—the amount of physical motion during daily routine—on a scale of 1=*very inactive* to 6=*very active* and rates approach—responses to new persons, places, and events—on a scale of 1=*not hesitant* to 6=*very hesitant.* Agreement between the score and general impressions indicates that the parent understands the child's temperament trait and agrees with the rating. For example, when the general impression shows that the parents rate the child as withdrawing and the questionnaire score also indicates high withdrawal, then the parent impression of withdrawal recognizes the child's withdrawal.

Sometimes the general impression differs from the questionnaire score. For example, if a parent's general impression indicates that a child is fast adapting but the questionnaire score shows that the child is slow adapting, this may mean that the parent does not recognize the child's slow adaptability, and this could be the cause of some of the child's behavior difficulties. It may also mean that the parents' general impressions reflect the child's true behaviors that have not been revealed by questionnaire items or that one recurring event intrudes so much on the family that it distorts the overall general impressions. For example, a child's recurring high-intensity reaction at bedtime may cause the parents to rate the child as *high intensity* in their general impressions because they have the most difficulty with this issue, when, in fact, bedtime is the only time the child truly exhibits high intensity. Other discrepancies occur because parents may rate their child as they would like to see him or because they really do not understand certain aspects of the child's temperament. At other times, the difference occurs because a parent is in denial about a trait. This conflict often reflects an area of real difficulty for the parent or the impressions reflect the parent's temperament: Intense parents tend to give more extreme general impressions.

Issues of Behavioral Concern   Many temperament professionals include a blank page with the questionnaire on which the rater can list behavioral issues of concern (e.g., "At school and the playground she will not try anything new"; "Has temper tantrums when she doesn't get her way"). This lets the clinician know what kinds of challenges or difficulties the rater has with the child. He or she can then begin to relate these issues to the child's temperament and decide which behaviors to focus on when counseling the parents. Often, the issues of concern provide additional information about the child's behavior not covered in the questionnaire. Then, during the counseling session, the rater can give specific examples of behaviors and when they occur or can clarify questions answered in the questionnaire.

Interpreting the Carey Temperament Profile   A clinician would read Amy's profile (shown in Figure 3.3) as follows: Amy's activity level (−0.4) is about average for her age, and this indicates that she has the ability to play actively but can also sit quietly. Her most extreme score was on adaptability (3.3), and this indicates that this trait presents the most issues. She has difficulties with any change or transition and will react strongly if she is not prepared beforehand or does not have time to adjust. The first reaction score shows that she is cautious (1.0), so she will initially withdraw from new situations or people. Her negative mood score (3.1) indicates that she is serious or irritable in disposition. Her strength of response (0.8) can be intense. Because of negative mood, the intensity would most likely show up in negative situations or when she is upset. She is not particularly distractible (−0.8), which indicates that she has a good ability to focus but that she may also have a hard time moving on when concentrating on an activity. Average in persistence (−0.2), Amy can focus well on some tasks and not on others, depending on the task and her level of interest. Her sensory reactivity score (0.8) indicates that she is fairly sensitive and certain areas of sensitivity may cause more notice than others. Her predictability (0.7) indicates that she may be consistent in some behaviors or biological patterns and not in others.

Several discrepancies can be found in the general impressions and questionnaire scores in Amy's profile. For example, Amy's mother sees her as much more active than the questionnaire score indicates. Perhaps she finds Amy's active periods difficult or maybe because she has low energy, Amy's average activity level seems high. When general impressions and questionnaire scores are different but in the same direction—for example, Amy's mother views her as slightly more cautious than the questionnaire score—there is less concern than when the ratings are in the opposite direction, as in the adaptability scale. Amy's mother sees her as fast adapting, although the questionnaire score reveals slow adaptability. This shows that her mother may be missing Amy's cues that she is slow adapting, and the mother's expectations concerning Amy's ability to adapt do not fit with Amy's level of adaptability. The professional working with the family should explore these discrepancies.

When the counselor discusses this profile with the caregiver, he or she can also explore the slightly higher than average scores to see if anything in particular stands out. For example, the parents may divulge that although Amy is not sensitive to physical sensations she gets her feelings hurt very easily or that although she is persistent with most tasks, she is easily frustrated with math, which she finds difficult.

Going back to the behavioral issues of concern, this is how they would relate to Amy's profile as fours areas of concern:

1. *At home, Amy is angry, easily upset, and reactive. Her parents do not know what will upset her.*

2. *She refuses to do what is asked of her.*

3. *She is overly sensitive about what her parents say.*

4. *Although she is well behaved outside the family, she is the opposite with her parents and siblings.*

To understand how these issues relate to the profile, Amy's quickness to anger and her parents' inability to know what will upset her can be explained by her slow adaptability and her high intensity. Because her parents see her as faster adapting, they may be making sudden, unexpected requests that result in her angry reactions and refusal to comply. Her parents may interpret her unwillingness to comply as disobedience rather than her difficulty with changes and transitions. Slow adaptability can also explain why she behaves differently with family and with others. Slow adapters often use up their self-control at school or in other situations and have little adaptability left at home.

At school, because of the daily routine, Amy knows what to expect and finds it easier to comply. Lower distractibility may also contribute to noncompliance because it causes her to focus so completely when engaged in a task that she does not hear her parents' request or has difficulty disengaging. This, combined with the low adaptability, makes it extremely difficult for Amy to stop what she is doing and comply, which could possibly contribute to her negative mood score. She is sensitive in her reactions to what her parents say, so she may be more emotionally sensitive than physically sensitive.

Because of her high intensity, she reacts strongly whenever her slow adaptability or emotional sensitivity are triggered. Knowing why

Amy responds the way she does will help the counselor explain to her parents how to work with her adaptability, intensity, sensitivity, and distractibility to create a better fit and avoid problems. Section II of this book gives details on which strategies work best for certain temperament traits.

THE CAMERON-RICE PROFILE

The Cameron-Rice questionnaires (adapted from the Carey questionnaires) used to derive the Cameron-Rice Profile (1999), have versions available for infants, ages 4–11 months; toddlers, ages 1–3 years; and young children (early childhood category), ages 3–5 years. The scales and subscales for infant, toddler, and early childhood are shown in Table 3.1.

Similar to the Carey Profile, the Cameron-Rice Profile uses standard scores in graph form to display a child's rating (see Figure 3.4) but has slightly different categories than the CTS (as seen in Figure 3.3). The solid vertical rule in the middle designates the mean and the black horizontal bar originating at the mean on the top line of the scale indicates the questionnaire score. Each vertical dashed line to the right or left of the mean represents one standard deviation above or below the mean. The small rectangle located on the second line of each scale indicates the rater's general impression.

The scores that fall to the right of the mean are more often associated with temperament-related difficulties than the scores located to the left of the mean; however, for certain scales, high or low scores can also be associated with issues or problems. For example, high or low scores in either approach or withdrawal can cause problems: The highly approaching child can be at risk for accidents, and the withdrawing child can be fearful. The same is true for high or low scores of distractibility or sensitivity. For example, a low-distractible child can focus well on a task but may have difficulty moving on to other activities once focused; a child who is low in sensitivity may not notice certain social cues and behave socially inappropriately in certain situations.

The Cameron-Rice Profile for Sam, a 5-year-old boy, displayed in Figure 3.4, shows that, according to the general ratings, Sam is average in sensitivity, average in distractibility, active, moderately high

Table 3.1.   Cameron/Rice Temperament Questionnaire scales and subscales

Infant	Toddler	Early childhood
Sensitivity	**Sensitivity**	**Sensitivity**
(No subscales)	To small differences	To change
	To distractions	To novelty
		To texture/temperature
Movement	**Movement**	**Movement**
(No subscales)	When self-control is not expected	When self-control is not expected
	When self-control is expected	When self-control is expected
Reactivity	**Intensity**	**Intensity**
Movement reactions to child-care procedures	Positive	Positive
Intense reactions to child-care procedures	Negative	Negative
Intensity of other reactions	In new situations	In new situations
Regularity	**Regularity**	**Regularity**
Sleep patterns	Sleep	Sleep
Feeding	Meals	Meals
Activity		Bowel movements
Adaptability	**Adaptability**	**Adaptability**
To restrictions and intrusions	To intrusions	To intrusions
To change	To transitions	To transitions
To transitions	To change	To change
N/A	**Approach or withdrawal**	**Approach or withdrawal**
	Personal	Personal
	Impersonal	Place
		Preferences
Frustration tolerance	**Frustration tolerance**	**Frustration tolerance**
(No subscales)	Positive persistence	Positive persistence
	Negative persistence (after being told to stop)	Negative persistence (after being told to stop)
		Distractibility
		(No subscales)
Soothability	**Soothability**	**Soothability**
(No subscales)	(No subscales)	(No subscales)

From Cameron, J., & Rice, D. (1999). Cameron-Rice Temperament Questionnaires. Retrieved from http://www.preventiveoz.org; adapted by permission.

Scales

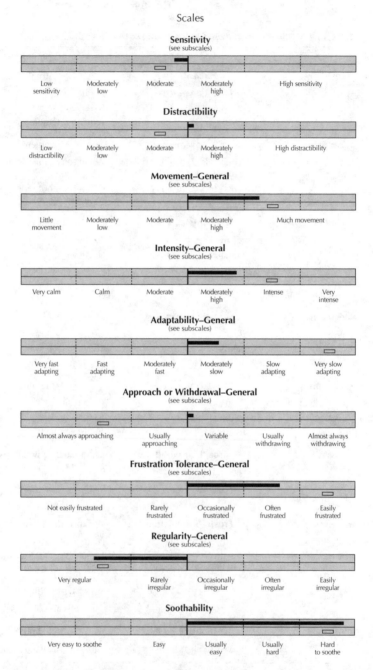

Figure 3.4. Sample Cameron-Rice Profile from a preschool questionnaire. Results show that the participant is active, often frustrated, and scores high on "hard to soothe." (From Cameron, J., & Rice, D. [1999]. *Cameron-Rice Temperament Questionnaires*. Retrieved from http://www.preventiveoz.org; adapted by permission.)

in intensity, moderately slow-adapting, average in approach or withdrawal, often frustrated, very regular in bodily functions, and hard to soothe. This profile explains certain aspects of Sam's behavior, but the subscales must be examined to gain a complete understanding of Sam's temperament.

Several categories of the Cameron-Rice Profile have subscales. The subscales provide clinicians with a clearer view of a child's temperament by breaking a trait into different aspects and may help clinicians to pinpoint the types of situations in which the traits affect the child's behavior. Figure 3.5 provides an example of a subscale for approach or withdrawal.

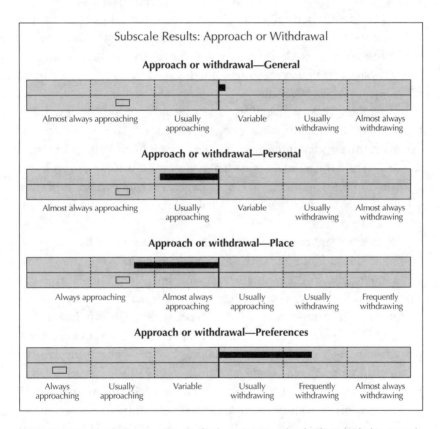

Figure 3.5. Example of a Cameron-Rice preschool questionnaire subscale. This individual is approaching with people and comfortable in new places but withdraws when presented with new things such as new toys or food. (From Cameron, J., & Rice, D. [1999]. *Cameron-Rice Temperament Questionnaires*. Retrieved from http://www.preventiveoz.org; adapted by permission.)

INTERPRETING THE SCALES AND SUBSCALES

The subscales pinpoint specific areas of temperament in the Cameron-Rice Profile. Sensitivity has three subscales: sensitivity to change or novelty, texture, and temperature. According to the rater's scores on these subscales, it appears that Sam is average in sensitivity to change and novelty, so changes or novelty in his environment do not bother him any more than the average child his age. He is less sensitive to taste and texture, so physical stimuli bother him less than average for his age group. Sam rates average on distractibility, which has no subscales. Depending on his interest in a task or activity, he stays focused or becomes sidetracked as much as other children his age.

Movement when self-control is not expected and when it is expected divide the movement subscales. Sam has high activity when control is not expected and also when others expect him to control himself. Sam is very active in most situations and also has difficulty remaining still when necessary.

Positive intensity, negative intensity, and intensity in new situations define the intensity category. Sam's scores fall in the average range on the positive intensity subscale but are high on both the *negative intensity* and the *intensity caused by new situations* subscales. So, with this information one can ascertain that Sam reacts calmly when things are going his way but if upset or in a new situation, he can be loud, dramatic, and over-reactive.

Sam's general adaptability appears moderate; the subscales show that he is slow-adapting to intrusions, average-adapting to transitions, and moderately slow-adapting to changes. Intrusions entail any event that unexpectedly encroaches, interrupts, or interferes with what a child is doing; for example, Sam might object strongly to his hair being brushed or his nails being cut, an immediate request, a loud noise, or a playmate getting into his space or taking his toy. Transitions involve moving from one activity to the next, and changes include variations in rules and routines and discrepancies between expectations and reality.

Sam appears average in the approach or withdrawal scale, but the subscales explain that he actually is very approaching to new people and places, but withdrawing in terms of preferences such as new foods or new clothes. His slow adaptability to change could add to this withdrawal because new preferences also entail changes. (Refer again to Figure 3.5 for an example of Sam's approach/withdrawal subscale.)

Sam is often frustrated. Positive persistence and negative persistence define frustration tolerance. Sam rates near average in positive persistence, the ability to persist on his own in the face of obstacles or delays. His negative persistence explains that he usually persists when told to stop. Sam resists strongly when frustrated by parental limits.

Regularity scores indicate that Sam exhibits regularity with sleep patterns, eating, and bowel habits. His parents should have no issues in this area as long as these routines are maintained.

Soothability has no subscales, but Sam appears to be very hard to soothe when upset. When something triggers his intensity, he remains upset and his parents cannot easily calm him.

General Impressions for Sam   The parents' general impressions show no extreme differences from the questionnaire scores except in adaptability. In this area, Sam's parents see him as more slow-adapting than is indicated by the score on the questionnaire. They also see him as almost always approaching. The subscales confirm these general impressions because he is slow-adapting to intrusions and also very approaching with people and places. The area of adaptability may be a particularly difficult one for Sam's parents, and that is why their general impressions are lower than the questionnaire score. Sam's parents listed five areas of concern:

1. *He gets very aggressive when he's upset. He hits and screams at his parents and other kids.*

2. *He has tantrums when angry, when he doesn't get his way, or if something happens that he doesn't like.*

3. *He becomes overly excited at birthday parties, holidays, and special events.*

4. *He has difficulty dealing with new surroundings.*

5. *When he is frustrated or disappointed, he does not cope in a socially acceptable way.*

Sam reacts physically because of his high activity level. This tendency, combined with his high negative intensity, fuels aggression or tantrums when he becomes upset. His intensity is triggered by an unexpected change or intrusion (slow adaptability), frustration (low frustration tolerance), or a new situation (intensity in new situations). Once triggered, his intensity can develop into a tantrum that does not resolve easily due to his difficulty being soothed.

Sam becomes overexcited at certain events because of his high activity and intensity. He is intense in new situations and, as he becomes stimulated, he can spiral out of control. He approaches new people and places easily, so this, combined with his high activity level, propels him into new situations where he then has the potential for intense reactions.

RECOMMENDATIONS BASED ON THE PROFILE INTERPRETATION

Once the professional knows how the child's temperament affects the issues of concern, he or she can determine the most effective solutions. For example, in Sam's case the clinician, practitioner, or professional can indicate which areas of temperament trigger his tantrums and aggression and then work on methods to prevent the triggers. Sam's parents could begin by warning him before changes occur and planning together for new situations so that Sam knows what to expect and what is expected of him. They can monitor his activity level and intensity and have him take breaks before escalating out of control, and they can prevent unwanted intrusions by avoiding unstructured situations with large numbers of people. The clinician would not expect the parents to institute all possible suggestions but would help them prioritize their concerns and work on one or two issues at a time. In each case, how a child's unique temperament affects his behavior determines the behavioral plan.

OTHER TEMPERAMENT SURVEYS USED CLINICALLY

Some temperament questionnaires based on Chess and Thomas's temperament dimensions found variations on the nine categories. Assessments also vary in terms of audience or use: One assessment is used with school-age children; others are for teachers to measure temperament in the classroom (e.g., Keogh, 1982; Martin, 1988b); and another is an informal assessment that can give parents, teachers, or clinicians a quick view of a child's temperament.

SCHOOL-AGE TEMPERAMENT INVENTORY

The School-Age Temperament Inventory (SATI; McClowry, 1995a) was developed for use with 8- to 12-year-old children. Factor analysis of the nine dimensions established from the NYLS revealed four primary dimensions: activity, approach/withdrawal, task persistence, and negative reactivity. Activity in this case refers to general motor activity. Approach/withdrawal refers to a child's first reaction to new people or situations. Task persistence relates to a child's ability to stay with a task even if he or she is interrupted, and negative reactivity describes a child's tendency to react negatively to inconveniences and life situations that he or she encounters.

The SATI temperament survey consists of a 38-item parent report. The assessment can be scored by hand (McClowry, 2003) or online by computer (http://www.nyu.edu/education/nursing/insights/). The child's scores are tabulated and compared with average scores to generate a high medium or low score in each of the four categories. Temperament traits that are considered most challenging for parents are high negative reactivity, low task persistence, withdrawal, and high activity. The book *Your Child's Unique Temperament* (McClowry, 2003) also provides strategies for working with the child's temperament.

TEACHER TEMPERAMENT QUESTIONNAIRE–SHORT FORM

The Teacher Temperament Questionnaire–Short Form, developed by Keogh and colleagues (1982), identified three factors from the NYLS dimensions. Factor One, *Task Orientation,* is composed of activity, distractibility, and persistence. Factor Two, *Personal/Social Flexibility,* is made up of adaptability, approach/withdrawal, and positive mood. Factor Three, *Reactivity,* is composed of intensity of response, sensory threshold, and negative mood. The teacher rates each statement on the 23-item survey on a 6-point scale of frequency from *hardly ever* to *almost always.* The psychometric analyses of the Teacher Temperament Scale show that this is a reliable instrument for teachers to assess children's temperament.

The scale can be scored by hand; when working with parents and teachers, Keogh used a profile approach, charting the scores to make a horizontal graph of the scores on each dimension.

> We do not try to show how a given child's profile compares norma-tively unless a score is really extreme. Rather, we emphasize the varia-tion within each child's profile, hopefully identifying the strengths and weaknesses. We also present the child's scores on the three factors (mean value of the particular dimensions which make up each factor); for ex-ample, a child might be high in Task Orientation (Factor One) but low in Personal/Social Flexibility (Factor Two). The emphasis is on in-child individual differences rather than between child differences. (Personal communication, July 25, 2003)

INFORMAL TEMPERAMENTS

Some clinicians want to have an immediate impression of a child's temperament without taking the time to have parents complete a for-mal questionnaire. They can obtain a "quick view" of temperament by having parents give their impressions with a short survey that covers the nine categories (see Figures 3.6 and 3.7 for examples of quick view surveys for a child and caregiver). These forms do not give the de-tailed information that a formal questionnaire provides and should not be used as a replacement. It is beneficial when parents have not had time to complete a lengthy questionnaire or when a clinician suspects temperament as the cause of a problem and wants an on-the-spot snap-shot of the child's temperament. A similar survey can be used to get an idea of a parent or caregiver's temperament when examining good-ness of fit between the adult and child's temperaments.

SUMMARY

The temperament assessment provides professionals with a means to understand, describe, and work with child behavior. Observations and interviews can provide a general picture of the child's tempera-ment but may not reveal temperament in various contexts. Tempera-ment profiles that result from clinical temperament questionnaires pro-vide a concrete illustration of the child's temperament traits. This can

A Quick Survey of a Child's Temperament

Sensitivity: How does the child react to sensory stimulation? Is he or she sensitive to textures, tastes, noises, odors? Is the child overwhelmed easily? Do the child's feelings get hurt easily?

1	2	3	4	5
Low				High

Activity: Is the child energetic, active, and always on the go or quiet, moving at a slower pace and more interested in quiet activities? Does he or she prefer fine motor or gross motor activities?

1	2	3	4	5
Low				High

Intensity: How does the child react to the world? Does he or she tend to be loud, very expressive, and dramatic? Or more calm, subdued, and quiet?

1	2	3	4	5
Low				High

Regularity: How predictable is the child on a day-to-day basis with eating, sleeping, and other daily patterns? Is the child's daily behavior generally more predictable or unpredictable?

1	2	3	4	5
Predictable				Unpredictable

Approach/withdrawal: Is the child more hesitant with new situations, people, or things? Or does he or she dive right in, appreciating and seeking out novelty?

1	2	3	4	5
Approach				Withdrawal

Adaptability: How well does the child adapt to transitions and unexpected changes? How flexible is the child? Can the child shift gears quickly or does he or she need time to adjust?

1	2	3	4	5
Fast				Slow

Persistence: How well does the child persist with a task? Does he or she tend to stay with a task until completed or become frustrated and quit if it is too difficult or boring?

1	2	3	4	5
High				Low

Distractibility: Is the child easily distracted by the surrounding activity, noise, or stimulation? Does the child become so focused on an activity that all else is blocked out?

1	2	3	4	5
Low				High

Mood: Is the child's tendency to be happy and positive or more serious and negative? Does the child tend to focus more on positive or negative events?

1	2	3	4	5
Positive				Negative

Figure 3.6. An example of an informal survey to elicit temperament information about the child.

General Impressions of Caregiver Temperament

Sensitivity: How do you react to sensory stimulation? How sensitive are you to textures, tastes, noises, odors? Are you overwhelmed easily? Do your feelings get hurt easily?

1	2	3	4	5
Low				High

Activity: Are you energetic, restless, and always on the go or are you more sedate, moving at a slower pace?

1	2	3	4	5
Low				High

Intensity: How intense are your reactions to the world? Do you tend to be loud, very expressive, and dramatic? Or are you more calm, subdued, and quiet?

1	2	3	4	5
Low				High

Regularity: How predictable are you on a day-to-day basis with eating, sleeping, and other daily patterns? Are you generally more predictable or unpredictable in your daily behavior?

1	2	3	4	5
Predictable				Unpredictable

Approach/withdrawal: Are you more hesitant and cautious with new situations, people, or things? Or do you dive right in, appreciating and seeking out novelty?

1	2	3	4	5
Approach				Withdrawal

Adaptability: How well do you adapt to transitions and unexpected changes? How flexible are you? Can you shift gears quickly or do you need time to adjust?

1	2	3	4	5
Fast				Slow

Persistence: How well do you stick with a task? Do you tend to stay with an activity until completed or do you become frustrated and quit if you find it too difficult or boring?

1	2	3	4	5
High				Low

Distractibility: Are you easily distracted by the surrounding environment or do you become so engrossed in an activity that you don't hear or see anything around you?

1	2	3	4	5
Low				High

Mood: Is your natural tendency to be happy and positive or more serious and negative? Is the cup half empty or half full for you?

1	2	3	4	5
Positive				Negative

Figure 3.7.   An example of an informal temperament survey to elicit temperament information about the caregiver.

help the caregiver or professional working with the child to see the temperament or temperament combinations more clearly and understand which traits contribute to the child's behavioral issues. Whether clinicians choose a questionnaire, interview, observation, or a combination of methods, the resulting temperament information offers effective tools for understanding and working with problem behavior. Many professionals will not attempt to give advice or determine appropriate behavioral interventions without first obtaining a temperament profile. When used with other clinical methods, the temperament assessment is part of a complete clinical evaluation of the child.

Looking at Temperament Through Childhood

CHAPTER 4

Infants

Unique from the Beginning

● ●

A physician giving a tour of a neonatal intensive care nursery stopped at one of the incubators. "And this," he said, pointing to a tiny infant attached to various tubes, "is Red Sonja. We call her that because, even for her size, she is the loudest baby in the entire nursery." This infant was already showing her individuality.

● ●

Any nurse who works in a newborn nursery will confirm that all babies are different from the start in terms of temperaments. During infancy, more developmental changes take place than during any other time in life. Between birth and 2 years of age, an infant goes from being a totally dependent newborn to a toddler who is able to talk, walk, and think independently. An individual's specific temperament traits determine, to a large extent, how these new abilities are manifested.

Most researchers in the field of temperament study children's temperaments beginning with infancy because temperament is most directly observable during this stage (Goldsmith et al., 1987). As children mature, behavior becomes more complex, and it is more difficult to distinguish temperament from other behavior patterns. Noted pediatrician and author T. Berry Brazelton (1984), for example, observed indications of temperamental differences manifested in infants through the administration of his Neonatal Behavioral Assessment Scale. For one, he found that infants react differently to various stimuli. Some neonates, acutely sensitive at birth, already have strong reactions; others do not. Similar to some adults, some infants have the capacity to shut out extraneous stimulation; others become increasingly agitated.

ASSESSMENT IN INFANCY

As discussed in Chapter 3, temperament is typically assessed using interviews of adult caregivers, naturalistic or laboratory observations or procedures, and parent report questionnaires (Birns, 1965; Brazelton, 1973, 1984; Brazelton, Nugent, & Lester, 1987; Matheny, Reise, & Wilson, 1985; Medhoff-Cooper, Carey, & McDevitt, 1993; Rothbart, 1986). Although temperament can be measured in early infancy (before 4 months of age), assessments are conducted most often after the age of 4 months, when an infant begins to show set behavior patterns. (A comprehensive list of available infant temperament assessments is found in Appendix A.)

TEMPERAMENT TRAITS AND INFANT BEHAVIOR

During infancy, the predominant behavioral issues revolve around sleeping; feeding; separating from caregivers; fussiness; and daily tasks such as bathing, dressing, and diapering (Cameron, Hansen, & Rosen, 1989). Particular temperament characteristics and combinations of characteristics result in specific behaviors. For example, infants identified as "difficult" by caregivers exhibit frequent crying and, in general, are fussier (Bates, 1980). Highly active and intense infants react more loudly and negatively to a greater number of stressful events (e.g., hunger, separations, changes in the environment) than do those with "easier" temperaments (Karraker, Lake, & Parry, 1991). A discussion of various temperament characteristics and the infant behaviors associated with them follows.

ADJUSTABILITY

Cameron and colleagues (1989) found that slow-adjusting, slow-adapting, and withdrawing infants who were also low in regularity had sleep,

eating, and sensitivity issues, whereas infants low in persistence or easily frustrated had more separation and dependency issues. The slow-
adjusting infants had difficulty with falling asleep and getting back to
sleep without a bottle or nursing and a tendency toward night waking.
They also experienced unpredictable hunger and were more likely to
refuse to try new foods, and they were shy with strangers. The easily
frustrated infants had difficulty playing by themselves for any amount
of time and cried more often when left with a child care provider than
did infants who were higher in frustration tolerance. Consider the story
of Katie.

• •

Katie's mother complained that her infant daughter acted fussy most of
the day. Nothing she did seemed to help, although she tried many different techniques: rocking her, taking her for walks, putting her in a swing,
and playing music. A temperament assessment revealed that Katie was
slow-adapting and sensitive. Trying many different methods to calm her
presented Katie with too many transitions. She needed less stimulation
and more reliable routines. Following the assessment, her mother set up
a daily routine where she changed Katie's diaper first thing in the morning,
gave her a bottle, dressed her, and then fed her breakfast. A walk and a
nap followed a short playtime. She offered Katie lunch at the same time
each day, and another playtime preceded the afternoon nap. Katie's
mother then established similar routines for late afternoon, dinner, and
bedtime. When Katie needed calming, her mother used quiet methods
such as rocking and soft singing. Katie's fussiness decreased measurably
after her mother established these consistent, daily routines that reduced
overstimulation.

• •

ACTIVITY AND INTENSITY

An infant's activity and intensity levels predict the child's assertiveness
and risk for accidents. Parents soon realize how easily an active baby
can tumble off of the changing table. The research of Cameron and col-

leagues (1989) confirmed Thomas, Chess, and Birch's (1968) results showing that these traits contribute to safety issues; that is, active, intense infants were at more risk for accidents than their less active peers.

Escalona (1968) also studied the impact of activity level. Among 1- to 3-month-old infants, those who were less active showed more tactile exploration and fine motor activity than did highly active infants. These less active infants tended to focus more on faces; be engaged in more nonnutritive sucking; and at 4–5 months, be engaged in more self-directed activities and self-exploration. Even at 6–8 months of age, these infants continued to direct more attention to their own bodies than to their surroundings.

In comparison, active infants engaged in more behaviors directed toward inanimate objects. By 6–8 months, active babies made more noise and covered more space in their movements than did less active babies. Active infants moved around more whether asleep or awake. They also exhibited more complex behavior and directed more attention to their surroundings than did the less active infants.

DISTRACTIBILITY

Distractibility in infancy relates to how easily an infant can be soothed (Cameron, Rice, Hansen, & Rosen, 1994; Carey & McDevitt, 1978). An infant's ability to refocus his attention helps him to be soothed and helps in regulating stimulation (Rothbart, 1989c). In her lab, Rothbart found that watching an adult blow bubbles calmed distressed infants. As the infants focused on the bubbles their heart rates declined and they calmed down. Infants who have difficulty redirecting their attention are more difficult to soothe and fussier (Strauss & Rourke, 1978).

Soothability levels can be observed when a hungry infant can be distracted temporarily while waiting to be fed. But that same distractible infant can also be difficult to feed because he will attend to any external stimuli while eating. Many a nursing mother has experienced the pain of having her distractible baby turn to follow a sound or sight without releasing her nipple.

APPROACH/WITHDRAWAL

The approach/withdrawal dimension is associated with the way an infant responds to novel experiences. *Approach* in an infant relates to smiling and laughter when exposed to new experiences, people, and objects. One way to measure this concept is to record how quickly an infant reaches for and grasps new objects (Rothbart, 1988).

The opposite of approach is withdrawal. Withdrawal can be observed in early infancy when the infant becomes fussy or turns away when presented with new stimulation, which might be anything from a new toy to a visiting grandparent. Researchers associate withdrawal with the later development of inhibited behavior (Kagan, 1994; Kagan, Reznick & Snidman, 1987). Thomas and colleagues' (1968) assessment of this dimension includes both distress to novelty and the infant's orientation toward or away from it. Issues associated with withdrawal include separations, sensitivity to new environments and people, and feeding issues, particularly around weaning or new foods (Cameron et al., 1989).

TEMPERAMENT AND DEVELOPMENTAL ISSUES

Each child develops sequentially. An infant learns to roll over before she can crawl and to crawl before she can walk. But the timing of these developmental milestones varies greatly, and individual differences in temperament contribute to how a child proceeds through motor, cognitive, and social development. The next section discusses the effects of temperament traits on these areas of development. Then, temperament influences on typical behavioral issues that occur in infancy are explained.

MOTOR SKILLS

Activity level can affect the rate of motor development. Active infants move around more frequently because their high activity level propels them out into the world. They soon discover that they can move from one place to another by rolling, scooting, wriggling, and crawling. One mother reported that her daughter was not very active. "At 6 months, Zoe has just started to roll over," she said. "She is more content to sit in her infant seat and watch the world around her. Her sister, Jenny, was much more active and rolled over at 4 months. She sat by herself and then crawled at 5 months and walked at 9 months." Active babies go through the motor milestones earlier than less active infants. They focus on and excel at gross motor skills. For this reason, motor development involving large muscles and movement occurs first. Fine motor skills come later.

The opposite is true of low activity infants. They focus more on fine motor skills and develop their gross motor capabilities later. Parents concerned about their infant's motor development can gain insight by examining the child's activity level. They may notice that although their baby may not quickly acquire gross motor skills, she may excel at fine motor skills. For example, at 13 months, Ellen had not started to walk. The pediatrician found nothing physically wrong and advised a temperament assessment. The assessment showed that Ellen was low in activity and low in persistence. She was easily frustrated and did not practice using large muscle skills, and therefore her walking was delayed. Her mother was aware that her fine motor skills had developed early and that Ellen "just didn't seem interested in moving much."

The way in which other temperament traits interact with activity level can further affect an infant's motor development. High sensitivity can slow down an active infant. Because sensitive infants have a lower pain threshold, the ensuing bumps, scrapes, or bruises that come with mobility can delay their attempts at locomotion. Sensitive infants will not practice crawling or walking, for example, if the attempts result in a painful experience. Conversely, active infants who are low in sensitivity are not slowed down by slight injuries and they tend to carry on despite falls or bumps. This may contribute to even earlier motor development.

Persistence also affects motor development. Persistent infants have better focus of their attention, practice new skills more frequently, and do not become easily frustrated. For example, a persistent infant learning to roll over will practice it again and again until he has accomplished it. When he is learning to crawl he will not be daunted by falling forward as he attempts to maneuver his arms and legs and will try until he succeeds. If he is also highly sensitive, however, the bumps and bruises may slow him down a bit. Infants low in persistence are easily frustrated at learning new motor skills and are more likely to give up after an unsuccessful attempt at rolling over, crawling, or walking, as seen in the story of Ellen. For this reason, they expect parents to be their vehicle of mobility and may not go through the motor milestones quite as early as more persistent infants.

Withdrawing infants may resist a new skill because of their preference for the familiar. This may slow down the acquisition of motor skills. Hesitant 15-month-old Andres resisted any activity that involved climbing, for example. Other infants in his baby gym class would climb the small slide or crawl up the steps to get to the jumping platform. Andres would stop, raise his arms to his mother, and cry until she carried him to the top.

In contrast to withdrawing infants, approaching infants will attempt a new skill even if it seems beyond their capabilities. Nine-month-old Vanessa loved to climb. When her mother briefly left the family room to answer the telephone, she heard Vanessa shriek. She ran back into the room to find her daughter standing on top of the television set, clinging to the entertainment unit. Approaching Vanessa had no fear of climbing any object.

COGNITIVE DEVELOPMENT

Aspects of temperament can influence an infant's cognitive development, as well. For example, an approaching infant will be attracted to novelty, which contributes to exploration and curiosity conducive to cognitive development, and persistent infants learn new skills more quickly by practicing them. Temperament ratings have been found to correlate with certain scores on the Bayley Scales of Infant Development (Bayley, 1969). Newborns who have higher ratings of orienting rate higher on Bayley mental test scores at 3–12 months of age (Matheny, 1989). Infants with sustained attention; positive mood; easy adaptation to ongoing changes; and approachability to new people, places, and objects had higher mental test scores in the Infant Behavior Record of the Bayley Scales.

Language Development   Temperament effects on cognitive development can also be observed in language development. Infants begin to babble at approximately 2 months of age and say their first word around 1 year of age (Berk, 2002). Infants who are adaptable, soothable, positive in mood, higher in persistence, and who have positive affect (i.e., the display of feelings and emotions through facial expressions; similar to positive mood) at 13 months have better language production at 20 months than infants without these traits (Dixon & Smith, 2000). Language development is discussed in greater detail in Chapter 5.

Ability to Separate from Caregiver　Cognitive development is also related to how an infant responds to separations. All infants experience separation anxiety, beginning as early as 6 months and increasing until approximately 15 months. In order to be less distressed by separations, infants must develop object permanence (i.e., the understanding that objects still exist when they are out of sight), which begins around 7–8 months (Berk, 2002; Landy, 2002). Temperament influences the extent to which an infant feels distressed by separations. Kagan and colleagues (1987) noted that inhibited children have more extreme responses to separations than do uninhibited children. Researchers at Kaiser Permanente found that temperament affects separation anxiety (Cameron et al., 1989). "Easily frustrated infants who depend on parents to reduce any frustrating situations they encounter may have more extreme reactions to separations than infants who have a higher frustration tolerance" (J.R. Cameron, personal communication, August 11, 1999).

Other temperament traits can contribute to separation difficulties. Infants with low activity levels do not separate from parents as easily as do active babies. (A high activity level propels the infant away from the parent to explore the environment.) Less active infants do not have that desire to explore as much, so they would rather stay with parents. They tend to be dependent on parents longer than active babies.

A less adaptable infant has difficulty with transitions and changes. When the change involves being separated from a parent and staying with a different person, the infant reacts negatively and takes more time to adjust. Infants familiar with the caregiver because of regular visits adapt more quickly. They also make a better transition when parents implement a goodbye routine.

Similar reactions occur in withdrawing infants who have difficulty with novelty. It will take time for a withdrawing infant to accept any new experience or people (Chess & Thomas, 1987). Infants who are withdrawing usually have difficulty separating from parents to go to a new caregiver until they become familiar with the new person. A withdrawing infant who is also slow-adapting responds more strongly to separations because he is reacting to the change or transition as well as to the novelty of the situation.

Easily frustrated infants do not usually spend much time playing by themselves when left alone by a parent (Cameronet et al., 1989). Because these infants do not have the frustration tolerance to persist on their own, they cannot handle the frustration of separations. They learn early on that parents help to reduce frustration, and they like to have parents nearby in case they encounter a frustrating situation. They object to even the most minor separations. Parents complain that they cannot put their baby down or go into another room without loud protests. When parents respond without fail, these children become even more dependent and less likely to separate. Therefore, for easily frustrated children, it is helpful for parents to establish regular times when the child remains nearby but on his own. For example, each time Dad washes the dishes, he places Nathan nearby with some toys but does not hold or play with him until the task is finished. Dad may talk to Nathan but that is the extent of the interaction. If Dad does this consistently, Nathan will soon learn to amuse himself during that time, which will increase the boy's frustration tolerance.

Soothability does not directly affect the separation as much as it affects the response to separation. An easily distracted infant can be readily soothed. When a separation occurs, the distractible infant can usually be diverted with no trouble. The less distractible infant will not easily have his attention diverted once upset, however.

Intensity affects the degree to which the infant protests a separation. An intense infant can make a difficult separation even more difficult with loud screams of protest. Unfortunately for caregivers, an infant will be more difficult to appease if he or she is also low in soothability or high in persistence.

TEMPERAMENT AND BEHAVIORAL ISSUES

Temperament affects infants' daily behavior. How easily an infant goes to sleep, if she wakes at night, how well new foods are accepted, and reactions to daily caregiving tasks can be greatly influenced by an infant's temperament. Temperament also determines the best way to work with these issues. The descriptions of the most common issues that parents report in infancy and the strategies that work for each different trait are summarized below.

Sleep Issues

For many exhausted parents, having their baby take regular naps, go to sleep at night, and sleep through the night are important goals. One mother reported, "Gina has a hard time getting to sleep at night. I have to nurse her to sleep and then she wakes two or three times a night and wants to be nursed again. I didn't mind initially, but now she's 8 months old and we need our sleep." An understanding of Gina's temperament could help resolve these sleep issues.

Researchers have associated infant sleep difficulties with "difficult" temperaments (Carey, 1974; Weissbluth, 1982, 1989a, 1989b). Infants rated "easy" develop more mature patterns of sleep, sleep through the night sooner, and require less soothing and other interventions than those rated "difficult" (Keener, Zeanah, & Anders, 1988). Difficult infants may also sleep less than easy infants: According to a study by Weissbluth (1982), difficult infants slept 9.6 hours at night and 2.7 hours during the day at 5 months of age, whereas easy infants slept 11.7 hours at night and 3.7 hours during the day. The organization of an infant's sleep/wake patterns incorporates the temperament characteristics of rhythmicity, activity level, sensitivity, and soothability (Carey, 1974; Keener et al., 1988).

The development of sleep patterns in infancy follows a predictable path. At first, an infant sleeps only a few hours at a time in a random pattern. Night sleep becomes more organized at approximately 6 weeks of age when the infant sleeps in 4- to 6-hour stretches in the evening, whereas day sleep patterns develop at 3–4 months of age (Weissbluth, 1989). After about 4 months of age, more regular rhythms are established and the infant goes through various sleep cycles from light sleep to deep sleep. When these patterns do not develop, sleep problems can occur including short duration of sleep and abnormal day or night sleep schedules (Weissbluth, 1989). This causes an increase in cortisol levels and is associated with crying, fussing, and higher arousal (Tennes, Downey, & Vernadakis, 1977), which makes it increasingly difficult for an infant to fall asleep and establish regular sleep patterns. The more difficult an infant's temperament, the more likely that a negative sleep cycle will occur. Also, the more difficult an infant's temperament, the more likely that the infant will sleep with the parents. A study of 204 2- through 4-month-old infants found that 85.8% of them slept alone, 8.3% slept with one parent, and 5.9% slept with both parents (Kelmanson, 1999). The infants who slept alone were more positive in mood and more persistent than those who shared a bed with parents. The infants sharing a bed with both parents were rated the most negative in mood and the most difficult. Identifying which temperament traits contribute to sleeping difficulties helps parents know which techniques will be most effective because different temperament traits contribute to different sleep problems.

Irregular Infants   The trait of rhythmicity (regularity or predictability) is an especially crucial ingredient in healthy sleep patterns. Infants with high rhythmicity are almost always ready for naps or bed at the same time, whereas low rhythmicity prevents infants from developing regular sleep patterns. When infants do not become tired and fall asleep on a regular schedule, parents never know when their infants will sleep. When parents allow infants to set their own sleep schedules, the infants become sleep deprived and behavior worsens (Weissbluth, 1989b). If parents establish routines for nap and bedtime at the same time each day and discount protest crying, low-rhythmicity infants can become accustomed to a schedule. Infants who also are intense will increase their crying and not settle down easily, so parents may have to take this into consideration when helping them establish a sleeping pattern. According to Weissbluth (1989a, 1999), parents may want to wait until their infant is 3, 4, or 5 months old to structure sleep habits because this is when sleep rhythms become better established.

• •

Stevie, 8 months old, seemed to have no set patterns for sleeping. His parents tended to have erratic schedules, so Stevie slept whenever he felt like it. He woke often during the night, and the entire family suffered from lack of sleep. Their pediatrician advised Stevie's parents to establish a daily sleep routine. They began to put him to bed around the same times during the day and night. They set up simple routines around naptime and bedtime. They put him down for a nap within an hour after his lunch and a story. At night, after his bath, they rocked him, and sang him a song and after 2 weeks, Stevie's sleep improved. With time and consistency, more regular sleep patterns were possible.

• •

Sensitive Infants   Highly sensitive infants are acutely aware of sounds, light, and touch. Sensitive infants are easily awakened by any noise, whether it is a truck rumbling past the window, a floor creaking, or the doorbell ringing. When sensitive infants sleep in their parents' bedroom, nighttime noises such as snoring or bed creaks can wake them. An infant who is very sensitive to temperatures may awaken if she becomes uncovered and is cold or if she is taken out of her crib for a feeding and is put back into a cold crib. New bedding, as well, may bother a touch-sensitive infant. The infant who reacts to light may have a more difficult time napping during the day. Likewise, at night the headlights of a passing car can disrupt a sensitive infant's sleep. These sleep issues can be addressed by manipulating the sensory experiences that create the problem. Working with sensitivity is a matter of determining what the infant reacts to and reducing or removing the cause.

A small fan or device that creates a low, monotonous sound (i.e., white noise) can often mask unwanted noises. If the infant is sleeping in the parents' room and their night noises awaken her, moving her to a quiet room can help. Infants who react to temperature do better in winter with blanket sleeper outfits, which keep them consistently warm because they cannot be kicked off like blankets can. Cribs can be kept warm when the infant is removed for nursing by using a sheepskin or other soft, warm cloth. A heating pad can be used to warm the crib when the infant is taken out and then removed just before the infant is returned to his bed. Likewise, new bedding or pajamas can be washed several times before use to ensure that they are soft. Blackout shades can eliminate light. Elaine Aron (2002) described devising a tent of blankets that fit over her son's crib to block out stimulation. The tent was used at home, and whenever the baby slept in a new place, it provided a comforting and familiar environment to help him fall asleep.

Active Infants   Highly active infants have their own sleep issues. They may move around so much during sleep that they wake themselves up. They sometimes roll into the crib's side or become wedged into a corner. If they are also sensitive, they are likely to wake up. Active infants resist bedtime because they do not want to miss anything. Putting an active infant to bed while guests are present is difficult if she wants to be a part of the action, but using something to mask noise may be helpful. While learning new motor skills such as crawling, active infants may practice in their sleep and wake themselves up. One mother observed her active daughter, who had been working on crawling during the day, wake herself up by crawling in her sleep and bumping her head on the end of the crib.

Many parents have used bolsters to keep an active baby from moving too much. A foam wedge or rolled-up towel or receiving blanket under the sheet on either side of the infant can serve as a bolster to help to prevent excess movement. Once an infant starts to stand, however, she can use bumpers as a booster to climb out of the bed, so they can become a hazard.

Slow-Adapting Infants   An infant's degree of adaptability can present another set of sleep problems. For the slow-adapting infant, the issues include difficulty making the transition to sleep initially and getting back to sleep once awakened. This infant will take longer to learn to fall sleep alone than one who is more adaptable. Parents of slow-adapting infants need to be consistent and persistent.

The slow-adapter often depends on a transitional object or routine to fall asleep. This may be a mother's breast, a bottle, a pacifier, or rocking, all of which involve the caregiver. Any such habit, once established, takes time and consistency to break, so parents must take this into consideration when establishing a transitional object.

Because these infants depend on rituals, using routines at bedtime helps them fall asleep. After going through the bedtime routine, putting them in the crib before they are completely asleep allows them to fall asleep on their own. Parents can also transfer the transitional object from themselves to a blanket or stuffed animal. Charlotte held Miranda's favorite teddy bear with her while she sang and rocked her each night before bed, for example. As Miranda snuggled close to the bear in her crib, it reminded her of the warm, loving ritual with her mother.

Low-Persistence Infants   An infant's low persistence or low frustration tolerance can be a factor in sleep problems and can affect his daytime behavior. A sleep-deprived infant is less persistent and has a shorter attention span during waking hours. Low persistence is also correlated with shorter naps (Weissbluth, 1989a).

An infant's low frustration tolerance can be associated with separation problems and this can affect sleep behavior (Cameron et al., 1989). As mentioned previously, an easily frustrated infant soon learns that parents help reduce frustration by helping him overcome obstacles. For this reason, low-persistence infants like to have parents nearby when they are going to bed. If a low-persistence infant was rocked or nursed to sleep and then put in his own bed, when he awakens later he may protest if he finds he is alone because he expected the parent to still be there. The infant becomes frustrated without a parent to help him go to sleep. This differs from slow adaptability in that the sleep issue is one of separation rather than transition.

The best way to increase frustration tolerance is by building it gradually, allowing the low-persistence infant to play independently a bit more each day. Increasing independence during the day can help the infant become more independent at night. Encouraging the infant to use an attachment object also helps him to fall asleep or remain asleep when the parent is not near. A transitional object that has the parent's scent can help when the infant wakes during the night. Holding the transitional object with the infant during feeding accomplishes this. When the infant transitions into light sleep, the parent's scent can give the illusion that the parent is nearby, helping the infant go back to sleep.

Intense Infants   Intensity influences the ways in which the other traits are expressed. In terms of sleep, it affects the way in which an infant reacts to sensitivities, transitions, separations, and other factors related to sleeping habits. Parents often react to the extreme response of their intense infants. When an intense infant cannot get back to sleep, parents assume something is terribly wrong because of the strength of the responses, which might include crying inconsolably or worse ("I tried to let Jonathan cry himself back to sleep but he became so upset that he vomited," a parent might say of such an infant). Parents find such behavior very disturbing and respond intensely and immediately, doing whatever it takes to calm their child. Responding in a calm, consistent manner before the intensity escalates helps to manage such strong reactions.

One mother developed a strategy for naps.

> We live in a condominium development, so all of the units are very close. I wanted to work on a naptime routine for Kai but he is so intense and loud that I was worried about being reported to Child Protective Services. I spoke to my neighbors to prevent any misunderstandings, and also put a sign on my front door that said: 'Nothing is wrong—Kai is just working on a new naptime routine.' I found the neighbors were very supportive.

When parents accept their infant's intensity—that in most situations nothing is wrong; their baby is just very expressive—it helps them to anticipate most loud dramatic reactions to minor changes.

Sleep and Temperament Combinations   When an infant experiences sleep problems, more than one temperament trait may be causing them. Depending on the infant's temperament traits, parents can combine techniques used for each trait involved. For example, sleep strategies for an active, sensitive, slow-adapting, and low-persistence infant might include using bolsters to minimize nighttime movement and establishing a bedtime routine with a transitional object. Parents and caregivers can also help by being consistent and introducing new techniques slowly that will help establish new sleep patterns. The left-hand column in Table 4.1 lists each temperament type with its attendant sleep issues. The right-hand column presents solutions for infants of each type to help them get a good night's sleep. Caregivers can look at strategies for various types in children with strong combinations.

Table 4.1. Temperament issues and solutions regarding sleep habits in infancy

Temperament trait	Temperament issues	Temperament-based solutions
High sensitivity	Wakes from noise, light, touch, movement	Provide a dark, quiet place to sleep and white noise to mask night noises.
	Has difficulty sleeping in new places	Take along familiar bedding or toy if sleeping in new place.
	May not fall asleep if overstimulated	Keep stimulation low before bedtime.
High activity	Has difficulty slowing down before bedtime	Engage in quiet time rather than active play before bedtime.
	May not appear tired and can get into a negative sleep cycle	Have a bedtime routine and regular bedtime (earlier rather than later).
	May wake up from movement in sleep	Use bolster to prevent waking from movement.
High intensity	Cries loudly; parents tend to respond quickly	Respond calmly and quietly.
	Difficult to settle	Be patient but firm and consistent with responses.
Low rhythmicity/ regularity	Not predictable in waking and sleeping	Try to establish regular nap and bedtimes.
	Tired at different times each day/resists a regular schedule	Use routines and rituals to help child take naps or go to bed.
Slow adaptability	Has difficulty falling asleep	Establish a bedtime routine.
		Use a transitional object to help baby go to sleep.
	Experiences night waking	Respond consistently when baby wakes.
	Takes longer to adjust to a new sleeping pattern	Allow time to adjust to any change.
	Experiences setbacks with any illness or change	Be consistent.
Withdrawal	Experiences difficulty sleeping in new places	Take familiar objects when sleeping in a new place.
	Resists a new bed, new sheets, new room	Allow the child time to warm up to new sleeping situations.
Low persistence	Has separation issues; may wake at night and want parent, if alone	Try to put baby to bed awake.
		Use soft music so baby feels less alone.
	Depends on parent to help get back to sleep	Use an attachment object with Mom's scent.

Feeding

Feeding issues often begin early in infancy with the introduction of a bottle or new foods or weaning from breast-feeding. If these issues are not handled appropriately, patterns can be established that create eating problems during the toddler ages and beyond. Knowing their infant's temperament helps parents understand how the infant will respond to different feeding issues and how to address these concerns most effectively. Table 4.2 provides a summary of some of the major temperament traits and how they influence an infant's reactions to feeding and eating.

Sensitive Infants   "George refuses anything but breast feeding. He will not take a bottle under any circumstances," a mother reports. George may be showing early gourmet tendencies but, more likely, his preference indicates a temperament trait—sensitivity. High sensitivity makes a child exquisitely aware of differing textures in a bottle nipple versus a breast nipple, varying food temperatures, and taste differences. Parents of sensitive infants who gradually introduce new tastes and textures find that their babies accept different foods more readily. For example, an infant will accept a bottle more quickly if the nipple is very soft and the contours are similar to that of the breast. One mother reported that it took a while to find a bottle nipple that was soft enough for her sensitive infant but that once she had, the infant accepted it much more readily than the bottle with the harder nipple.

Solid foods present another problem. Taste and texture differences affect sensitive infants. A sensitive infant will more readily accept pureed, bland foods over thicker, more flavorful foods. Parents can help their infant accept new flavors by adding a small amount to an already enjoyed flavor and then increasing the amount of the new food. Likewise, sensitive infants may protest foods that have an unfamiliar texture. For example, an infant is more likely to accept the texture of cereal for the first time if it is diluted almost to a liquid—similar to the milk or formula she likes. The thickness can be gradually increased. Some sensitive infants may always prefer bland foods with little texture, and parents can respect this by removing the infant's por-

Table 4.2. Temperament issues and solutions regarding feeding habits in infancy

Temperament trait	Temperament issue	Temperament-based solutions
High sensitivity	Reacts to tastes, textures, smells, and food temperature	Gradually introduce foods of different tastes, textures. Keep food temperature and flavors moderate.
High activity	Does not want to stop to eat	Have nutritious snacks available and provide often during the day.
		Feed when hungry.
	Stands up in highchair	Provide suitable ways to use energy.
	Has difficulty sitting at table	Do not expect infant to sit for long periods.
Low rhythmicity/ regularity	Not always hungry at mealtimes Various amounts of food eaten	Have healthy snacks ready for later (or save meal).
		Encourage child to sit with family for a short period.
		Do not expect child to eat if not hungry.
Slow adaptability	Refuses changes involving new or different foods, including different presentations of usually accepted foods	Introduce a different food when child is not extremely hungry.
		Serve the new food regularly so child adapts to it.
		Serve the new food with an accepted food.
Initial withdrawal	Initially rejects any new food	Use gradual familiarization.
		Serve the new food often. Introduce new foods when child is not extremely hungry or is in a fun situation (e.g., picnics).
High persistence	Gets "locked in" to likes and dislikes	Do not become involved in power struggles. Present the food and disengage from protests.
		Do not make mealtime a battleground.
High distractibility	Has difficulty eating because of constant distractions and interruptions	Limit distractions.
		Turn on answering machine. Allow no television, no toys at table.
		Help child stay focused on task at hand.

tion before seasoning it for the rest of the family and making sure it is smoothly pureed. Other sensitive infants eventually grow to enjoy more flavorful foods with different textures. Using the right utensils with sensitive children is important, too; the feeling of a hard spoon may assault a sensitive infant's mouth, so a spoon with a soft rubber "bowl" might be preferable.

Slow-Adapting Infants A slow-adapting infant who has been breastfed will protest the *change* from the breast to bottle more than the *texture* difference. A routine will help him to adjust to the bottle. Giving the infant the bottle at the same times each day, when he is not too hungry, will increase acceptance. It may also help if a caregiver other than the mother initially gives the bottle to the infant because the infant will expect the breast from the mother. Weaning from the breast directly to the cup may be easier for the slow-adapting infant because it will present the infant with one less change than weaning to the bottle before the cup.

Slow-adapting infants do not like change, and solids present a big change from the breast or bottle. Offering the same food in the same manner each day and at a time when the infant is not extremely hungry can help ease the transition to solids. Also, repeatedly presenting the infant with just one or two new foods will help the slow-adapting infant gradually accept different foods. Parents need to be persistent when introducing a different food to their slow-adapting infant. It may take many attempts for the infant to accept the food, and parents should be cautioned to not give up too quickly.

Withdrawing Infants A withdrawing infant will reject the new bottle initially, but will accept it once she becomes familiar with it. The more often she experiences the bottle, the more familiar it becomes, so a parent should offer it daily. The same goes for introducing new foods.

The withdrawing infant prefers the familiar, so she will protest any new food. One mother mixed all new foods with applesauce, a well-liked flavor, and then gradually decreased the amount of applesauce. Another technique involves offering the same new food daily until the infant becomes familiar with it.

Distractible Infants   Distractible infants do not usually have trouble accepting new or different feeding arrangements or foods (unless the infant is also sensitive, slow-adapting, or withdrawing). The most common problem with feeding a distractible infant is that too many things are competing for the infant's attention and drawing him away from eating. This infant is interested in everything around him and will stop eating to investigate. Parents usually find it easier to feed distractible infants in quiet surroundings with little activity in order to complete mealtimes in a timely fashion. Parents may even use distractions in a limited way by offering their infants a toy, getting him to smile, and then slipping the spoon in the child's mouth. (Distractible infants are good candidates for the "Here comes the choo-choo" feeding method.)

Active Infants   Caregivers may find feeding active infants in highchairs problematic. These infants, who are in constant motion, do not like to be confined. Active infants will readily practice their standing and climbing skills at mealtime; however, standing up in the chair presents an accident risk. Making sure that the infant is put into the chair when he is truly hungry and then serving or feeding the food immediately helps him to focus on the food. Using a chair that hooks onto the table can help, because the infant feels more a part of the family. Allowing the infant to take short breaks to expend energy also helps him sit longer. Active infants often like to share control and may resist being fed with a spoon. Caregivers find that giving an infant his own spoon or a cracker to hold while being fed prevents him from grabbing the spoon or resisting.

Active infants also enjoy "experiencing" their food, which can mean rubbing it in their hair, squishing it in their fists, or finger painting with it on the table or highchair tray. When they are finished eating, they are likely to signal their completion by dumping the remaining food on the floor or throwing their dish across the room. This may benefit the family dog, but parents are not appreciative. Feeding the active infant when she is truly hungry prevents playing with the food, and removing the food at the first sign of completion prevents messes.

EVERYDAY TASKS

Besides coping with separation, sleep, and feeding issues, caregivers must learn to manage the everyday care of their infants. Seemingly simple tasks such as bathing, diapering, dressing, or putting the infant into the car seat or stroller can become challenging with babies of certain temperaments. Table 4.3 includes strategies for working with some of the major temperament traits in order to ease daily tasks in infancy.

Bathing, Diapering, and Dressing Bathing, diapering, and dressing can present daily problems for parents of sensitive infants. Sensitive infants are acutely aware of the change in temperature when being changed or undressed. Being placed into a warm bath is another assault to their senses. Because of their profound sensitivity to temperature, sensitive infants react to the warmth of the water and the sensations produced by wetness. Techniques that better accommodate such an infant's sensitivities include undressing her in a warm place (put-

Table 4.3. Temperament solutions regarding daily living tasks in infancy

Temperament trait	Bathing, diapering, dressing	Riding in car seat or stroller
Sensitive	Undress or diaper in a warm place.	Use soft padding for stroller or car seat straps.
	Use moderate bath temperature.	Use shade to block sun in car.
	Go slowly.	Pull rather than push stroller to decrease wind in face.
		Use backpack or front pack.
Active	Use floor for dressing or changing.	Have special toys for car or stroller.
	Let older infant stand for dressing or changing.	Use a backpack or wagon instead of stroller.
	Have older infant "help."	Take breaks during long car or stroller rides.
	Have a special toy to play with during dressing changing.	
Slow-adapting or withdrawing	Use routine when performing daily tasks.	Use a ritual to get into car seat or stroller.
	Work with baby's movements to decrease intrusions.	No fast transitions—prepare infant first.
	Signal changes with words or songs.	Bring familiar toy or blanket.

ting her on a warmed towel or a sheepskin), finding just the right temperature for the water, and waiting for her to get used to the water before being bathed. If the infant reacts to the bath because of her sensitivity to new experiences, once she becomes familiar with the bath she will enjoy it.

Slow-adapting infants also react to diapering and dressing because these usually entail a transition from and also an intrusion on whatever activity they were previously enjoying. Dressing at the same time each day as part of a routine increases the infant's acceptance. Working with—rather than against—an infant's adaptability makes dressing and diapering seem like less of an intrusion. One parent found that it helped his baby when he sang different songs to indicate dressing, diapering, and bathing. Soon, the baby associated each event with its own song. This allowed the infant to know what to expect and created a ritual for each task.

Active infants resist dressing and diapering and move continually during the process. As they become more mobile, they do not want to stop for diaper changes. They make a game of escaping, and when the caregiver begins changing the diaper or dressing, they resist by rolling around and flipping over. This makes the chore maddening, not to mention dangerous if the infant is on a changing table. Changing the diaper on the floor makes it easier. Parents also can make diapering or dressing part of a routine that includes a special toy that appears only at that time. Later, once active children start to walk, they often do not want to lie down and be changed. Caregivers find that they can gain cooperation by letting children stand during the diaper change. Placing a few diapers where a child can reach them and asking her to go and get one helps her expend some energy so she can stand or lie still more easily for the change. Bath time can be energizing, so parents or caregivers may decide to bathe their active infants during the day rather than just before bed so that the child is not too revved up to sleep.

Using the Stroller and Car Seat   Active infants hate to be confined. They protest being strapped into the car seat or stroller. Because the car seat is a safety must, an infant should have no choice in this matter. If he does not want to sit in the seat, parents can try diversions such as special toys for the car or favorite music; however, they often simply have to persist. Regular stops during long car rides are a necessity for the active infant to release energy.

Sensitive infants may react to the feel of the seat. The straps can cause discomfort, so soft fabric or padding can be used to soften them. They also react to bright sunlight in their eyes or loud noises such as sirens or other traffic noise. Shades can be placed on automobile windows to prevent direct sun, and infant sunglasses can also be purchased, although some sensitive infants might react negatively to the way the glasses feel.

The slow-adapting infant resists making the transition into the car seat. Using a ritual to get her into the seat can help. For example, gathering the diaper bag and a special toy while she watches prepares her for what comes next—being picked up and put into the seat. Caregivers might also try singing a familiar song or saying the same thing each time the infant is placed in the seat to help with the transition. One father noted that the most difficult part of riding in the car seat for his slow-adapting son was the stop and go of city traffic. The infant would scream each time the car stopped at a traffic light. "I ran more yellow lights trying to keep the car moving and avoid the screaming," he said.

Withdrawing infants react to the car seat when it is new. Once it becomes familiar, they accept it without protest. A caregiver may want to bring along a familiar toy or blanket to ease an infant's reaction to the novelty of the seat. For parents of intense screamers, earplugs and perseverance will eventually persuade even the most persistent infant that when in the car, he must be in his car seat.

Strollers present a different problem. Once an active infant can crawl or pull herself up, she may not want to ride in the stroller. She may accept riding in a specially designed infant "backpack" more readily. Another option is pulling the infant in a wagon if convenient, provided she is safe and secure. For an active infant, attaching special toys to the stroller and allowing the infant to take breaks to crawl or walk or be allowed to push the stroller when possible makes the stroller more acceptable.

Sensitive infants who do not like the wind in their face may prefer having the stroller pulled rather than pushed. Similar to the techniques for helping an infant get used to a car seat, caregivers can make the stroller more comfortable for sensitive infants. Some sensitive infants prefer a back or front infant carrier to the stroller. When caring for an infant who has several challenging traits, combining the techniques for each trait minimizes the hassles of everyday tasks.

THE IMPORTANCE OF APPLYING TECHNIQUES EARLY

Many temperament issues arise in infancy. Parents may feel that they are normal stages through which the infant will pass, and so they wait for further development to take care of the problem. Clinicians often hear, "I thought he'd grow out of it." Infants with challenging temperaments often do not "grow out of it." Temperament issues that are not recognized and addressed early in infancy can escalate into problems later on. The following example illustrates how common problems during infancy can continue into the toddler years if temperament is not understood and worked with early.

• •

Emma was a colicky infant with a very loud cry who was difficult to soothe. Her parents, Susan and Kurt, were loving parents who were sensitive to her needs and responded immediately when she cried. They were frustrated because they found it difficult to establish any routines or schedules for Emma. Susan found that nursing calmed Emma, so she offered her daughter the breast whenever she needed comfort or soothing. Emma did not sleep well at nap or bedtime and she awoke often at night. Her exhausted parents finally took Emma to bed with them so they could get more sleep. Still, she awakened often, but nursing on her mother's breast helped her fall back asleep. Susan and Kurt waited for Emma to outgrow this stage of infancy and establish more regular sleep and feeding schedules but the behavior did not improve, and this pattern continued into Emma's toddler years.

By the time Emma was 2½, she still had never slept through the night, and her parents became increasingly exhausted. Emma had grown into a toddler tyrant, controlling Susan, Kurt, and the household. She was demanding during the day and night, and she would begin screaming intensely when she did not get her way. Little would soothe Emma when she became upset except nursing.

When Susan consulted with the temperament counselor, her main concerns were getting Emma to sleep through the night, to stop having tantrums, and to wean from the breast. Emma still nursed on demand and slept with her parents. After her 11:00 P.M. bedtime, she would wake every hour or two to be nursed back to sleep. Susan also used nursing throughout the day whenever she needed to comfort or calm Emma. Susan was fatigued, and Kurt was frustrated.

Emma's intensity factored into her control over the family. When she did not receive what she wanted and screamed loudly, Dad and Mom, being sensitive, could not stand the screaming and usually acquiesced. Because her parents catered to her demands, exhausting behavior patterns developed from her challenging infant temperament: highly intense, highly active, highly sensitive, extremely slow-adapting, initially withdrawing, and low frustration tolerance.

The counselor knew that Susan and Kurt, sensitive to screaming and permissive in their parenting style, would have difficulty following through with any fast, strict methods, so they would need to work on one issue at a time. This would also provide slow-adapting, withdrawing Emma with fewer new changes. The counselor began by talking about ways to prevent some of Emma's intense outbursts. Susan needed to recognize her toddler's slow adaptability and prepare her for any transition by talking about it first and giving her time to make the change. Transitions had to be predictable and consistent. Consistency helps a slow-adapting infant accept change, so Susan had to establish daily routines. Because Emma was running the show, she had no definitive routines, so the counselor suggested putting in place a simple routine that would be followed each night before bedtime. The goal at this time was not to get Emma to sleep alone but simply to establish a bedtime routine. Susan also began to work toward a general daytime routine in which certain activities happened within certain times of the day. For example, morning would be reserved for errands and active playtime, whereas afternoon would be the time for quiet activities at home and naptime.

The counselor also discussed Emma's sensitivity and asked Susan to watch for cues that revealed when Emma felt overstimulated. These cues vary from child to child and might be anything from a change in tone of voice to becoming fidgety or rigid in body posture. Susan was to introduce into the routine an hour of quiet time each day to reduce extraneous stimulation, to watch for events that triggered intense responses, and to remain as calm as possible when responding. When a tantrum did occur, Susan and Kurt were to hold firm instead of giving in.

Susan returned to counseling 3 weeks later. She and Kurt had started a bedtime routine for Emma. It was not consistent yet, but evenings were a bit better and Emma seemed to be beginning to accept bedtime. Emma was still waking and nursing at night as well as during the day. Susan had noticed that before a tantrum occurred, Emma seemed restless and became whiney; however, she was not able to prevent Emma's tantrums and they had not diminished. Susan attributed this to the fact that Kurt hated to hear Emma cry and often encouraged Susan to nurse her to stop the crying.

Susan wanted to address the weaning issue next. The counselor asked her to keep track of how many times she nursed Emma during the day and night. After Susan knew the number of times she nursed, she would eliminate some of the daytime nursing by only breast feeding at routine times and offering different soothing techniques at other times.

When Susan returned 2 weeks later, she was smiling. "I was nursing Emma 13 times in 24 hours and I'm down to 7 times!" She had also noticed that Emma "spaced out" when she had too much stimulation, so Susan had started scheduling a quiet time for her. The counselor advised her to eliminate two more daytime nursings, to be more consistent with the bedtime routine, and to make bedtime 15 minutes earlier to begin to work toward a more reasonable bedtime.

At the next appointment, Susan reported that Emma was waking every 3 hours, which was an improvement, but that she still had to be nursed back to sleep. Susan and Kurt had succeeded in getting her to bed earlier and the bedtime routine was going more smoothly. The counselor suggested that they continue the routine at naptime, using Emma's bed, and encourage Emma to sleep in her own bed at naptime to get her accustomed to it. At this time, the goal was only to get Emma more accustomed to being there. Susan was to soothe her back to sleep without nursing, if possible, but to nurse her if necessary.

After 2 weeks, Susan reported that Emma now napped in her own bed and no longer protested beginning the nighttime routine in her bed. Now, to prepare Emma to sleep through the entire night in her bed, Kurt or Susan would sit next to her while she fell asleep. If she woke up and came into their room, one of them would put her back into her bed after she had nursed. The counselor stressed the importance of consistently following this routine.

Two weeks later, Susan said that Emma slept in her own bed and awoke only twice a night. Emma's quiet room, free of other people, played a part in her waking less frequently. Susan also proudly reported that she nursed Emma only three times during the day: when she woke in the morning, before naptime, and before bedtime. When Emma asked to nurse at other times, she was offered a drink in a cup or directed to another activity. If that did not work and Emma melted down into a tantrum, her parents ignored it. Susan said that tolerating the noise had initially been very difficult and that Kurt would take a walk when he could not stand listening to it. But with consistent handling, the number of daily tantrums had decreased. They were now ready to eliminate the nightly nursing.

Susan and Kurt knew they had to respond to Emma's waking in the same way each night. They decided to try to settle Emma in her crib by gently rubbing her back. If her crying escalated, they would take her out of the crib, offer her a drink of water, rock her until she calmed down, and put her back into her bed. If the crying resumed, they would go in after 10 minutes, tell her it was time to sleep, turn on a lullaby tape, give Emma her teddy bear, and leave, letting her cry it out. They felt comfortable with this plan and were convinced that they could do it.

Susan called the counselor after the first night and said she was not sure they could go through with this plan. Emma had screamed off and on all night. They were all exhausted. The counselor told her that they had to be consistent and to continue if they wanted it to work, knowing that it was not going to be easy. The counselor also pointed out the progress they had made in other areas.

Susan and Kurt returned to the counselor 3 weeks later with good news, describing the first week as "hell." Emma would scream for as long as 2 hours before falling asleep exhausted, then wake again around 5 A.M., at which point she would scream until they got up to calm her. After about 10 days of sleep deprivation, they started nursing her at 5 A.M. when they were too weary to try anything else. They feared establishing negative habits, so they decided on a different tactic that would provide them all with more sleep. They told Emma that she could come to their bed when it was "almost morning" and beginning to get light, but that there would be no nursing. If she asked to be nursed, she would be put back in her own bed. It took about 5 days to establish this but they reported that now, when Emma awoke, she came in to their bed with them, snuggled in, and fell asleep for a few more hours. This satisfied both parents.

The complexity of Emma's case revolved around her challenging temperament evident from infancy and her parents' overly permissive parenting style. By gradually establishing routines and consistent responses that fit with Emma's temperament, Susan and Kurt solved the sleep and weaning problems and greatly reduced Emma's tantrums. Had her parents understood how her temperament contributed to her behavior in infancy and had begun to work with it then, they could have prevented the problems that continued into her toddler years.

SUMMARY

Temperament affects an infant's motor, cognitive, and social-emotional development. Knowing how temperament affects development helps parents and clinicians know what to expect and helps them know that development is on track for a particular child. Common problems with sleep, separations, and daily tasks can be planned for and carried out by using temperament concepts. When parents or caregivers know an infant's temperament, they can approach these problems with greater understanding and plan effective strategies for each child. In this way, parents can effectively address the current problems and prevent them from becoming bigger issues in the future.

CHAPTER 5

Toddlers and Preschoolers

Energy, Expression, and Exploration

Cammie is an active, intense, slow-adapting toddler. Her temperament makes the challenges of toddlerhood especially difficult for her mother. "Cammie is into everything and is always testing limits," Cammie's mother told the temperament counselor. "She is in constant motion, looking at me and smiling as she misbehaves. She has tantrums when I tell her 'no' or try to discipline her. She won't slow down to go to bed, and sometimes she is up until 11:00 P.M. She wants me to lie beside her and rub her back until she falls asleep, which can take more than an hour. I'm exhausted all of the time and sometimes give in just to get some peace."

Toddlers are all about expression, exploration, experimentation, ego-centricity, and energy. For caregivers, this can equal exhaustion. The amount of these qualities a child exhibits is influenced by temperament. Toddlers not only are learning about the world around them, but also they are becoming more independent, differentiating themselves from others, and determining how much control they have over their environment. The development of self-regulation, language, and cognitive and motor skills characterize this age.

In contrast to toddlers, preschoolers are more composed. Their increased motor abilities facilitate autonomy and self-help skills. Their growing vocabulary and the use of language allow more effective communication. Maturing cognitive skills and boundless imaginations expand children's play with an increase in make-believe as they try on new roles and identities. They are increasingly able to delay gratification and understand the feelings of others, leading to empathy and better peer interactions (Landy, 2002). Impulse control increases during the preschool period and is related to the ability to focus attention (Rothbart, 1989b; Ruff & Rothbart, 1996).

DEVELOPMENT AND TEMPERAMENT

As children move from infancy to toddlerhood and the preschool years, the ways in which they acquire autonomy, social skills, and motor and cognitive skills are influenced by their individual temperaments. The temperament traits that helped define them as infants continue to have an effect on their development and behavior and on those around them.

AUTONOMY

Autonomy is central to the developing toddler, and temperament shapes a child's drive for independence. Active, approaching children tend to be independent earlier than their less active peers. Their activity level propels them outward to explore and experiment. Their curiosity and manipulation of the environment is often misinterpreted as misbehavior as they try to understand how their world works and what effect they have on it.

Children who are less active are dependent longer and, because they are less likely to explore and experiment, are content to remain near their parents and focus on their immediate surroundings. Being sensitive or withdrawing increases these tendencies. Sensitive children move toward autonomy more gingerly because they are so acutely aware of everything around them. Any reaction that they perceive as too loud, too frightening, or too overwhelming will slow their steps toward independence. Some sensitive toddlers prefer a quiet corner to exploring new territory because it limits their encounters with overwhelming stimuli (Aron, 2002). Withdrawing children are hesitant to explore new situations and cautiously stay within familiar territory, increasing their dependence on familiar caregivers. Persistent children repeatedly practice new skills and continually test parental limits. If their persistence is tempered with high activity and intensity, they are driven toward independence at high speed. Children who are low in persistence move toward independence steadily as long as they do not encounter frustration. They may remain dependent on parents, who help them overcome obstacles or frustrations. Intense children assert their autonomy loudly, dramatically, and forcefully.

MOTOR SKILLS

Temperament affects timing and sequence in the development of fine and gross motor skills. As in infancy, active toddlers learn motor skills more quickly than their less active peers and prefer gross motor skills that use their large muscles. Less active children develop fine motor skills first, preferring activities that require small muscle coordination.

The persistent child acquires new skills quickly, through continuous practice. Parents who worry about their active, persistent children getting hurt as they climb up the slide or down the stairs are better off teaching them to perform such skills safely rather than restraining them from attempting such skills at all. A low-persistence child does not practice new skills readily if they cause him frustration and, therefore, he achieves mastery more slowly. The withdrawing child is cautious: He is likely to stick with the familiar and therefore acquires new skills more slowly than the approaching child.

As children develop their motor skills, the possibility of accidents increases. A study at Kaiser Permanente (Hansen, Rosen, Cameron, Rice, & Kristal, 1991) examined the relationship of temperament to accidents and found that children who are active, intense, and approaching had more motion-related accidents such as falling, bumps, and cuts because of their tendency to "go for it." The second group was average in activity, lower in adaptability, and less persistent, and they had more self-inflicted accidents such as ingesting hazardous materials. The third group was persistent, adaptable, distractible, positive in mood, and less active. They had more accidents involving "other inflicted" harm, such as being hurt by a sibling or knocked down by a dog. Another study found that children who were more withdrawn, less adaptable, and less attentive were more prone to unintentional injuries (Irwin, Cotaldo, Matheny, & Peterson, 1992). Schwebel and Plumert (1999) found that children who were low on inhibitory control and more extraverted had more accidents because they tended to overestimate their physical abilities. Chapter 10 discusses in more detail the kinds of accidents children of various temperaments are more likely to have.

COGNITIVE AND LANGUAGE DEVELOPMENT

Cognitive skills rapidly increase during the toddler and preschool years as children begin to engage in pretend play, experience an increase in symbolic representation, and communicate better. Language skills greatly increase, and temperament affects language acquisition. Adaptability, positive mood, and high persistence at 13 months predicted advanced language production and comprehension at 20 months (Dixon & Smith, 2000). "Duration of orienting," which is similar to high persistence and low distractibility, predicted better language production at 21 months (Dixon & Shore, 1997). Children who approached people readily, were very cooperative, minimally fearful, and positive in mood at age 2 were advanced in language acquisition and development at age 7 (Slomkowski, Nelson, Dunn, & Plomin, 1992).

Until language is understandable, communication can be very frustrating for both child and caregiver. Children who are low in frustration tolerance become particularly upset when caregivers do not understand them. For example, a child who cannot make his needs known may become angry. If the child has high intensity, he may express his anger with a tantrum. One child would become so frustrated when his parents did not understand him that he would bang his head on the floor. Children who are active, intense, and low in persistence react strongly when they are unable to communicate. Head banging and biting are common reactions that cause great concern for parents, but these behaviors decrease as the child communicates better.

Language contributes to self-control and anticipation. From 18 months through 4 years, children increasingly use words to help them regulate their behavior (Krakow & Johnson, 1981). For example, when Sophie was 1 year old, she used to delight in tearing pages from books. Her mother would take them away and say, "Don't tear the book!" At about 18 months she would shake her head "no" and then tear the book anyway. At 2 years old she would take a book, say, "No tear book," and then carefully turn the pages.

SOCIALIZATION

The ability to regulate emotions and behavior improves as children get older and are able to recognize and understand others' emotions. In order for empathy to occur, a child must be able to feel the emotion and to inhibit behavior (Rothbart, 1989). Without these skills, socialization is difficult.

A child who is low in sensitivity is less likely to react to another's hurt and may not easily pick up social cues of another's distress. Two-year-olds who are unreactive and who exhibit little affect show less empathy to an unfamiliar adult in distress than do more reactive children (Young, Fox, & Zahn-Waxler, 1999). Highly sensitive children readily feel these emotions and are more empathic than less sensitive children.

Persistence is related to attention, and as attention increases, so does the ability to control impulses (Krakow, Kopp, & Vaughn, 1981; Mischel, 1983; Ruff & Rothbart, 1996). Being able to shift attention and inhibit action is related to higher levels of empathy and guilt and lower levels of aggression (Rothbart, Ahadi, & Hershey, 1994). Thus, persistent, adaptable children who are low in intensity develop impulse control faster than intense, slow-adapting, easily frustrated children.

Active children play harder, louder, and with more endurance than less active children. With high activity the likelihood of aggression, tantrums, impulsivity, and externalizing behavior problems increases (Guerin, Gottfried, Oliver, & Thomas, 2003; Rothbart, 1989; Rutter & Garmezy, 1983; Stevenson-Hinde & Simpson, 1982). Active children often stretch the limits, are disobedient, try to be the center of attention, and exhibit more externalizing behavior problems than less active children (Buss, Block, & Block, 1980; Guerin et al., 2003). When they are in busy, exciting situations, their activity level may escalate and they may spiral out of control. They do not slow down, but keep going, often long after parents and other playmates have stopped.

Children who are withdrawing, highly sensitive, or inhibited present other socialization issues. These children do not readily engage in social situations and their behavior is characterized by prolonged clinging, staying close to the mother, not talking, not joining in play, and retreating from novel events (Kagan, 1994). Often called *shy,* these children have difficulty making friends and are distressed by any new situation. Playgroups, child care, or preschool often present adjustment problems for them. They withdraw in these situations and do not readily seek out playmates, often preferring to play alone. (See *The Highly Sensitive Child* by Elaine Aron [2002] for a complete description of the issues faced by these children.)

TEMPERAMENT AND BEHAVIORAL ISSUES

Toddlers and preschoolers repeatedly demonstrate certain temperament-related issues. The problems encountered most often by professionals working with families with children of this age are tantrums, discipline, toilet learning, eating and mealtimes, sleeping, peer relations, aggression, and school or child care issues. Other problems such as vomiting on cue or head banging occur in children of certain temperaments.

TANTRUMS

As toddlers struggle for autonomy, the frequency of tantrums increases, and some children are particularly prone to tantrums because of their temperament. Tantrums occur most often in children who are active and highly intense because these children express their emotions in a more physical way; however, other temperament traits can trigger high intensity and result in tantrums. For example, in a highly sensitive child, being overwhelmed by the environment, becoming overstimulated by too much activity, or feeling physical discomfort can trigger a tantrum. Similarly, if a child is high in activity level, being confined for too long can result in pent-up energy bursting out in a tantrum. For children who are slow to adapt, an unexpected change, too many transitions, an intrusion, or the lack of choice can result in a meltdown. Even a "quiet" child, one who is temperamentally withdrawing, can fall apart if forced into a new situation or approached by new people. A child with low frustration tolerance may become frustrated by an obstacle or delay or by having to deal with a separation. One who is highly persistent may refuse to let go of an idea or behavior or may resist being forced to stop something before completion.

Each of these traits alone can trigger a tantrum. Children with several of these traits have multiple triggers, and the triggers can be cumulative: The more triggers there are, the more likely an explosion will occur. The following example illustrates this.

• •

Jason is a sensitive, active, intense, slow-adapting, frustration-intolerant child who went to the State Fair with his parents. First, the car ride to the fair was confining. When he finally arrived, Jason had to wait in line for various amusements. Then, there were numerous transitions between activities and the intrusions of people bumping into one another on the crowded midway. Jason looked forward to the Ferris wheel, but he was disappointed to find that it was broken and out of service—an unexpected change. During the ring toss he missed the target, which frustrated him. All of this, punctuated by the loud music, pungent smells, heat, dust, and bright lights, caused Jason physical discomfort and overstimulation. These factors, combined with no nap, hunger, and novel foods, created a recipe for disaster. Jason's parents, who do not understand their child's temperament, believed that they were giving Jason a wonderful experience, and so they were upset about the ruined family outing.

• •

The prevention of tantrums requires knowing a child's temperament. In the State Fair scenario, decreasing the number of triggers could have prevented a meltdown. The following are some suggestions that Jason's parents could implement the next time they go to the fair or another outing to avoid tantrum triggers:

- Make sure that Jason has a good night's sleep the night before the outing to increase his adaptability and frustration tolerance and decrease sensitivity.
- To minimize confinement, break up the car ride by stopping occasionally to let Jason release pent-up energy.
- Choose a day when lines are shorter, such as midweek.

- Decide beforehand what rides to go on or attractions to see to limit the number of transitions and to know what to expect.
- Take breaks in quiet places throughout the day to reduce stimulation.
- Make it a shorter, rather than a longer, outing to prevent burnout.
- Take along nutritious and familiar snacks rather than eating only fair food.
- Plan a very quiet, routine day at home the following day.

Some tantrums are delayed reactions, especially in children who are active or approaching but also slow-adapting. A child with these temperament traits appears to be adaptable because her activity level or love of novelty propels her into new situations. But, after a certain number of transitions, the child's adaptability is drained and one more transition produces a meltdown. Parents often miss the signs of low adaptability in active or approaching children. Once they learn the delayed reaction pattern, they can determine how many transitions the child can handle. One mother observed, "I know when I pick Nick up from school that I can do no more than three errands with him or I will pay for it later, or even the next day." A child who has had an unusually busy day with many transitions may wake up the next day "on the wrong side of the bed." Being aware of how many transitions the active, slow-adapting child can handle will prevent meltdowns and make behavior more predictable.

When a child's intensity begins to escalate, parents and other caregivers can head off the child's tantrum by intervening early with calming activities such as blowing bubbles or water or clay play. If the child's intensity goes even higher, parents may prevent the outburst by helping the child physically release the energy by such activities as kicking a ball, swinging, running, or jumping. If the intensity escalates too far, a tantrum is inevitable. If the trigger is not recognized in time or if the intensity has escalated to a high degree, then the child has to go over the top to come back down again. When this occurs, the child needs a place where he can release his emotions safely.

What begins as an occasional temperament-triggered tantrum can become a behavior pattern if it produces the desired results for a child. Parents tend to respond quickly to intense children because they express their emotions so forcefully. Realizing that intense children are often loud and very expressive helps caregivers to react calmly and deal with the issue at hand. Caregivers can learn not to give in, over-react, or become angry, but instead to respond in a consistent and neutral manner. Some children recover from a tantrum more quickly if left alone. When leaving the child, adults can tell her that she needs to calm down and that they will be available in the next room if needed. Another child may need the caregivers to help him contain his tantrum. These children benefit from having adults hold them, which allows them to calm down. It may take a trial of both meth-ods to see which works for a particular child. In general, active chil-dren do not like confinement, so the holding method only exacer-bates the tantrum. After a tantrum, labeling the trigger can help a child manage himself in the future. In Jason's case, his parents could say, "Missing that target was very frustrating for you." Table 5.1 in-cludes common triggers for each temperament type and some strate-gies for preventing these triggers. Table 5.2 includes some cues of escalation of temper to watch for in children with various tempera-ment traits.

How Children of Different Traits Respond to Discipline

Temperament affects the internalization of limits and rules. According to the developmental literature, children internalize rules in two ways, by feeling the optimal amount of arousal and by experiencing posi-tive parent–child interactions (e.g., Kochanska, 1997a, 1997b; Mac-coby, 1984, 1992). Punishment produces arousal that the child associ-ates with actual or potential misconduct. When the optimal amount of arousal is felt, internalization takes place. Gentle discipline that de-emphasizes power promotes optimal arousal, whereas harsh, power-oriented discipline results in much higher arousal and interferes with internalization. Internalization also occurs through positive, coopera-tive interactions between parent and child, in which parent and child become colleagues going after the same goal.

Sensitive, Withdrawing Children   Kochanska (1995) found that sensitive, withdrawing children benefit most from gentle, psycho-logical discipline. Even a harsh word can reduce these children to tears

Table 5.1. Some temperament triggers for tantrums and ways to prevent triggers

Temperament type	Temperament tantrum triggers	Behavior strategies
High sensitivity	Overstimulating environment	Keep stimulating situations to a minimum.
	Being overwhelmed	Take quiet breaks to reduce stimulation and prevent becoming overwhelmed.
	Physical discomfort	Manage physical discomfort when possible.
High activity	Confinement	Break up confinement, such as long car rides, with active play.
	Pent-up energy	Provide ways to release energy each day.
Low regularity	Hunger	Have snacks available for unpredictable hunger.
	Fatigue	Ensure sleep and naps, especially before active events.
Slow adaptability	Intrusions	Prepare for necessary intrusions (e.g., child care procedures) and limit unnecessary ones.
	Transitions	Make time for transitions and use routines.
	Unexpected changes	Prepare child for changes.
Withdrawal	New situation, new child care provider	Plan for new situations and people.
	New experiences	Avoid "sink or swim" methods for new experiences. Take new experiences in smaller parts.
Low persistence	Frustration	Watch for escalating frustration and take a break.
		Use segmentation for frustrating tasks.
	Delays	Prepare for delays if possible, use redirection for lengthy delays.
High persistence	Limits	Set limits early and put closure on an activity before stopping it.
	Being told "no"	Use the word "stop" instead of "no."

Table 5.2.　Possible cues of escalation leading to tantrums

Changes in body language (e.g., rigidity, facial expression)
Changes in voice tone (e.g., volume, whiney)
Agitation, pacing back and forth
Becoming "locked in" to a behavior or idea
Sudden withdrawal from a situation

because harsh discipline creates fear and anxiety. These children respond well to reasoning and to induction (learning the effects of their behavior on others). They are empathic and achieve internalization more quickly than active, strong-willed children. When sensitive, withdrawing children are alone, they are less likely than their more outgoing peers to do things they have been told not to do (Kochanska, 1997b). This may be because of their tendencies to avoid taking risks and to avoid criticism, but it also may be attributed to their ability to inhibit behavior.

Fearless Children　For fearless children (active, approaching, adaptable), a parental show of power results in anger, resentment, and noncompliance. These children benefit from mutually positive, reciprocal parent–child interactions, which motivate the children's cooperation with the parent. Parents who discuss the problem with the child and decide on a solution or appropriate discipline together eliminate unnecessary power struggles. These children also benefit from having an admired role model whom they can imitate.

Caregivers often find it difficult to discipline children with challenging traits such as high activity, high intensity, low adaptability, low frustration tolerance, or negative persistence. For these children, caregivers need to

- Work on only one or two issues at a time; too many issues can be confusing for the child and may make the parent appear inconsistent
- Have clear and consistent rules that the child understands
- Incorporate choice and collaboration
- Institute routines regarding tasks and discipline
- Provide incentives that are appropriate for the child's temperament

STRATEGIES FOR COPING WITH
TEMPERAMENT-RELATED BEHAVIOR ISSUES

Depending on temperament traits or the combination of temperament traits, several different strategies may be employed to improve children's behavior.

Consequences Discipline is most effective when carried out in a calm, firm, and consistent manner. Some children are slower to respond to a new approach, so caregivers must resist the urge to stop or switch methods too early. A slow-adapting or negatively persistent child will take longer to accept a new rule or routine. Often, parents say they tried one technique, then another and another, but nothing worked. Trying many different techniques without giving a child time to adjust presents him with too many changes. When parents understand that their slow-adapting child may take weeks or even months to comply, depending on his level of adaptability, they can persist with one strategy. Once he "gets" the rule or routine, he will follow it exactly.

Time-Outs Though power-assertive discipline does not work well with challenging children, "time-out" can be effective. Time-outs can be used proactively as a "cool down" time for highly active or intense children. This is not a form of punishment but it breaks the pattern of negative behavior. When the child's negative behavior begins to escalate, the parent suggests that the child should "take a break" or redirects her to a calmer activity. This prevents out-of-control behavior and a parent–child power struggle, but it must be used before the child has escalated to the point of noncompliance.

The "1–2–3 Magic" method (Phelan, 1995), a strategy that combines counting down and time-out, works particularly well with slow-adapting or persistent children. When a child misbehaves, the parent gives a warning by counting, "That's 1." If the misbehavior continues, the parent says, "That's 2." If it still continues, the parent says, "That's 3; time-out" and the child is given a time-out, alone in her room or another safe place away from the parent. This approach works well because it does not ask the child to comply immediately but instead, gives the child two chances to control her behavior. The child knows what to expect and the parent can be consistent.

Loss of Privileges   Another type of discipline that is effective for some children uses loss of a child's privileges. This works when the privilege is something that the child values and will miss.

• •

Time-outs did not work with persistent, active, intense, 4-year-old Tad. His aggressive behavior got to the point that his parents had to develop a new strategy. They identified his most important possession: his collection of toy vehicles including cars, trucks, and boats. They explained that each time he displayed one of three aggressive behaviors—hitting, kicking, or pushing—he would have to choose one of his vehicles and they would dispose of it. As his fleet dwindled and only his most prized vehicles remained, his behavior significantly changed. Finding what has meaning to the child is part of a significant consequence.

• •

Incentives   Incentives work well with most children, especially those who are slow-adapting. Whereas a consequence takes away their control, an incentive motivates them to maintain control and to have the control to obtain the incentive. Parents and children determine the incentives in advance, so a child knows exactly what behavior is expected in order to receive the reward. The level of persistence determines what schedule of incentive will be most effective for children of any temperament. Children who are low in persistence have a difficult time sustaining behavior over long periods of time. Because they are frustrated easily, they need small, frequent, and immediate rewards. Low persistence children respond to the strategy of focusing on only one behavior and having several opportunities to succeed during the day. For example, if Kayla has difficulty keeping her hands to herself, that could be chosen as the focus behavior. If she can keep her hands to herself at circle time, when waiting in line to go outside, and during lunch, she will be rewarded after each event. She has three opportunities to succeed, and if she fails at one, she still has two more chances. For low-persistent Kayla, this is much more effective than being rewarded once for keeping her hands to herself all day.

Children high in persistence are able to work for long-term incentives. Because they are able to persevere, they can inhibit or maintain a behavior over a longer period of time in order to receive a reward. Highly persistent Carmen can work for one daily reward and also maintain the behavior to achieve a larger weekly reward with no problem.

Discussion Rather than Confrontation   Challenging children can respond to confrontation by shutting down, ignoring, or fighting back. Children who are slow-adapting or persistent react negatively to commands and directives. The slow-adapters believe commands take away their control and strongly resist them. Persistent children become "locked in" against the directives and become negatively persistent, doing exactly the opposite of what they have been instructed. Instead of issuing an immediate directive, then, parents can discuss problem behaviors at a neutral time. Choices produce more cooperation than commands, and with strong-willed, active, intense children directives must come "through the back door."

Indirect Approaches   Direct approaches such as commands or directives often become control issues with slow-adapting or negatively persistent children. They benefit from indirect approaches because they can process the information gradually and not feel as though they have lost control. One indirect approach involves storytelling.

• •

John was aggressive during free play. Time-outs did not work, and lectures caused him to shut down. His parents learned that using stories was more successful than talking to him directly about his behavior. One time his mother told him, "When I was little there was another girl, Camilla, who would tease me at school. I got into trouble because I would fight with her, but one day when she teased me I moved away from her and asked the teacher for help. Soon she stopped teasing me." No overt connection was made between the story and John's behavior. At this point, seeds were being planted in John's mind. John's mother revisited the story the next day with a thoughtful comment, "I wonder if what worked for me and Joan would work for you and Ben at preschool." She avoided saying "You should do what I did with Joan" because this would be another command that would be met with resistance.

• •

Another indirect technique is to enlist the child's help by asking for the child's advice regarding an issue similar to the one in which the child is having difficulties: "A friend told me about a little boy who grabs her daughter's toys. She asked how to help this boy share, but I didn't know. You are about same age. Can you think of something that might work for him?" Children often come up with wonderful suggestions: "Tell him he can play with one of her toys if she can play with one of his." Caregivers should resist the urge to say something like, "You should try that when you don't want to share." Instead, the caregiver might comment that this is a great idea and later ponder out loud, "I wonder if your idea would work when Julie wants to play with your toys." Again, "back door" communication is more effective with slow-adapting or negatively persistent children than a direct or confrontational method.

Toilet Learning

Toilet learning is an issue that is highly charged for parents and can cause many battles. Parents are especially eager for toilet learning if their child is going into a preschool that only accepts potty-trained children. But the child must be ready for this step toward independence or she may exert her control. Events such as the birth of a sibling, a move, or a separation or loss may influence toilet learning, as does the child's temperament. Often, several different temperament traits contribute to the issue and must be considered in determining a strategy. Table 5.3 lists issues for children of each temperament type regarding toilet learning as well as strategies to help them through the toilet learning process.

• •

Bart, 4 years old, had learned to stand at the toilet for urinating but refused to have a bowel movement there because he said it did not "feel right." He insisted on using a diaper, and he would stand behind the drapes

Table 5.3. Toilet learning and temperament

Temperament type	Temperament issue	Behavior strategies
High sensitivity	Reacts to the feel of underpants, toilet seat, painful bowel movement	Avoid tight underpants and wash them to soften them. Practice wearing underpants to get used to them. Use child-size potty; it may be more comfortable. Keep child's bowel movement soft with diet.
Low sensitivity	Does not notice the feeling of the need for elimination	Help child notice the feeling after elimination before expecting him to notice the need to eliminate. Have routine times to use the toilet throughout the day.
High activity	Will not stop to use the toilet	Establish routines to use the toilet before outdoor play and throughout the day. Enlist an older peer to be a model for training.
Low regularity	Has no set elimination time	Help child become aware of elimination cues. Be prepared for inconvenient bathroom needs (portable potty, dry clothes).
Slow adaptability	Resists the change from diapers to underpants or to the toilet, and the transition of stopping a task to use the toilet	Transition gradually from diapers to the toilet. Take one step at a time and allow time to get used to each change. Create a routine for using the toilet but do not insist on success. Use choices. Be patient.
Initial withdrawal	Initially rejects the novelty of potty training, the new feeling of underpants or toilet seat, the flushing sound	Use gradual familiarization, allowing the child time to become familiar with each new aspect of toilet learning before proceeding to the next.
Low persistence	Becomes frustrated and overwhelmed with all the steps involved in toilet learning; finds it easier to stay in diapers	Break toilet learning into smaller parts and work on one part at a time. Play an active role at first and then gradually give the child more responsibility for the task.
All temperaments	Can be intimidated by the process because it involves several steps	Make certain child is developmentally ready.
	Wants the ultimate control	Do not create a power struggle.

in the family room for privacy to have his bowel movement. Bart was sensitive and slow-adapting. He was accustomed to standing to have his bowel movement, not to the way it felt to sit down to have them. Standing behind the drapes became his routine for having a bowel movement.

Bart, being slow to adapt, benefited from a gradual approach to toilet learning. First, his parents suggested that he stand in the bathroom instead of behind the drapes to have his bowel movement. He gradually agreed to this. The next step was to get him to sit on the potty and have his bowel movement with his diaper still on. Eventually, he was able to use the potty and then the toilet without a diaper.

• •

Sensitive Children   Sensitive children dislike the feel of wet or dirty diapers, and this can be an advantage to toilet learning. However, they are also more sensitive to the way the potty chair or toilet seat feels than are other children. If it is too cold or too hard, they may resist. Making the seat as comfortable as possible helps. One mother used a commercially available soft toilet seat to help her son accept sitting on it. Sensitive children also react to the way underpants feel. The elastic around the waist may be tight or the fabric or tag scratchy. New underpants can be washed several times and tags can be removed to make them less irritating to sensitive skin. Caregivers can also have the child try on new underpants at certain times during the day, for example, after bath time, to help the child become used to how they feel.

Constipation presents another problem for sensitive children. If a bowel movement is painful, children may be reluctant to try having one again, which causes them to retain their stools. This can lead to encopresis and ensuing medical problems. A sensitive child's pediatrician should be consulted after any sign of bowel retention. Highly sensitive children's bowel movements need to be soft and regular.

Low-Sensitivity Children   Children low in sensitivity often have difficulty recognizing their own bodily cues and are not aware of the feeling of fullness that accompanies the need to evacuate bladder or bowel. One mother said her low-sensitivity 3-year-old would urinate while wearing underwear and be oblivious to the fact that he was making a puddle on the floor. The feeling of wet or dirty pants does not bother low-sensitivity children, so they are less inclined to use the toilet to avoid that feeling. The first step is having the child notice *after* she has already "gone," and then she can start to recognize the feeling before going, although this will take time. Routine toilet times throughout the day can aid learning. Once the child recognizes the feeling of bladder or bowel fullness, she can begin to try to use the toilet.

Active Children   Active children are too busy playing to stop and use the toilet. When they do realize that they must "go," it is often too late, and accidents occur on the way to the bathroom. Even when caregivers notice that the child is fidgeting in a way that indicates she needs to use the toilet, the child will often deny it until it becomes a power struggle. Caregivers can establish a routine in which the child tries to use the toilet before going out to play and at regular times throughout the day before she is engaged in active play. For this and other temperament types, it can be helpful to chart the times that the child has a bowel movement and urinates; this helps the caregiver make a routine whereby the child is encouraged to go to the bathroom when he is most likely to go. Because active children also move toward independence earlier than do less active children, this quest for autonomy can cause them to want to use the toilet earlier like their already trained peers. Having children observe older friends or siblings who use the toilet can encourage them to emulate the behavior to "be like the big kids."

Irregular Children   For the irregular child, elimination time varies each day. Caregivers can plan more easily for the regular child who always eliminates at the same time by suggesting that he or she sit on the potty then. Again, keeping track of toileting times for a few days can help determine the best time to use the potty. Irregular children need to first become aware of their internal cues. Their ability to do this will depend on their level of sensitivity. Once they recognize their bodily needs, they can let parents know of their need to use the potty, but because they have irregular temperaments, this can happen anytime and anyplace. One parent carried a small, portable potty in the trunk of her car just for those unpredictable, out-of-the-way occasions.

Slow-Adapting Children   Resistance to toilet learning for slow-adapting children has to do with *change* and *control*. A slow-adapting child does not like the change from diapers to underpants or to the toilet, or the transition involved in stopping an activity to use the toilet. The child must get used to one change at a time. The caregiver can begin by replacing the child's diapers with disposable underpants, then with cloth underpants. A toilet routine is helpful if the caregiver does not insist on success. Deciding with the child when she will sit on the potty—for example, when she wakes up, before lunch, and after school—sets the routine. Providing the child with special books to look at when sitting helps with the transition, also. Giving the child choices such as "Would you like to sit on the potty or the big toilet?" or "Which book would you like to look at while you try?" can give this child a sense of control. With the slow-adapting child, the key is to take one step at a time, with the child's help, and not turn the process into a power struggle. Slow-adapting children must feel that they have some control and that their caregivers are not dictating their toilet habits. If the child chooses to exert his control by *not* using the toilet, caregivers can plan on a long disagreement.

Withdrawing Children   A withdrawing child reacts poorly to the novelty of potty training. Wearing underpants is a new experience. The potty chair is not familiar and the toilet makes strange, loud noises and flushes away what the child has produced. A withdrawing child must be familiar with a situation before he is comfortable enough to proceed, so the learning must happen in stages, much as with a slow-adapting child. The child must become familiar with each new aspect of toilet learning before proceeding to the next in order to feel comfortable and be successful. Encountering unfamiliar bathrooms when away from home is also problematic for the withdrawing child and also for the slow-adapter, who reacts to novelty and different appearance. Sensitive children notice each change and are often bothered by the odors. Parents can discuss with the child how bathrooms differ before going to a new one. Also, the child can visit a new bathroom when she does not have to use it in order to become familiar with it for next time.

Low-Persistence Children Toilet learning consists of several frustrating events for a low-persistence child. First, the child must recognize the urge to "go," then he must get to the bathroom in time. He must remove his pull-up or underwear, sit down on the toilet or potty, and release the urine or feces. Next, he must wipe; deposit the paper in the toilet; pull up his underwear, then his pants; flush; and wash his hands. The process comprises so many parts that the low-persistence child becomes overwhelmed and frustrated trying to complete all of the steps. For these children, it is far less frustrating to remain in diapers and have caregivers help. Breaking toileting into smaller components and working on only one part of the task at a time makes it more attainable. With low-persistent children, parents play a very active role in toilet learning at first and then gradually give the children more responsibility.

As mentioned, toilet learning involves several steps for children, and this is true regardless of temperament type. Children must be developmentally ready, must not be experiencing any major changes, and must not be sternly pressured by parents or caregivers. When these conditions are met, temperament provides the additional information to create successful toilet learning.

FOOD ISSUES

Parents often are concerned about eating habits and may attempt to persuade children to eat more or to try new foods. This can result in a power struggle. A child soon learns that food is an emotional issue for parents. Eating, like toilet learning, is an area in which a child has much control; she cannot be forced to eat if she does not want to. Temperament influences how a child behaves at mealtimes, how new foods are accepted, and what he eats (Chess & Thomas, 1987). When a child has a combination of challenging traits, food issues can be complex. Table 5.4 lists food issues and behavior strategies for coping with various temperament traits.

Table 5.4.   Food issues and temperament

Temperament type	Temperament issue	Behavior strategies
High sensitivity	Reacts to tastes, textures, smells, and food temperature	Gradually introduce foods of different tastes, textures. Keep food temperature and flavors moderate.
High activity	Does not want to stop to eat	Have nutritious foods available to "graze" on during the day.
	Has difficulty sitting at table	Expect child to sit with family for a short time. Provide suitable ways to expend energy (e.g., getting more napkins).
High intensity	Has strong reactions to likes or dislikes	Teach appropriate expressions: for example, to say "No thank you," instead of screaming, "I hate beans!"
	Talks loudly	Practice using a quiet voice.
Low regularity	Not always hungry at mealtimes	Don't expect child to eat if not hungry.
	Eats various amounts of food	Child can be expected to sit at table with family for a short time. Have healthy snacks ready for later (or save meal).
Slow adaptability	Refuses changes involving new or different foods, including different presentations of usually accepted foods	Discuss foods to be served before a meal. Introduce a different food when child is not extremely hungry. Discuss similarities of the new food to a liked food. Serve the new food regularly so that child adapts to it. Use choices.
Initial withdrawal	Initially rejects any new food	Use gradual familiarization. Serve the new food often. Introduce new foods when child isn't extremely hungry or is in a fun situation (e.g., picnics, with a friend). Serve new foods along with familiar foods.
High persistence	Gets "locked in" to likes and dislikes	Don't become involved in power struggles. Set up expectations before child locks in. Present the food and disengage from protests.
High distractibility	Has difficulty eating because of constant distractions and interruptions	Limit distractions. Turn on answering machine; turn off television; do not allow toys at table. Help child stay focused on task at hand.

Sensitive Children   Sensitive children react to foods on a number of levels, and each food must meet their highly selective criteria in order to be consumed. One mother reported: "My son cannot stand the smell of certain foods. He sometimes reacts by gagging and occasionally throws up. He notices a disliked odor from food that was cooked in the house yesterday. Once he gets past the smell, it's the texture. God forbid if there are lumps or if any foods touch on the plate! Then he reacts to temperature—if it is too cold or too hot. And finally, his food cannot be seasoned."

Parents of a sensitive child may have a difficult time meeting all of his criteria in putting a meal on the table, but they can respect some of the child's preferences without cooking separate meals for him. Their goal is not to cater to all of the child's sensitivities but to offer at least one or two acceptable foods. Caregivers will be most effective if they attempt to broaden the child's tastes very gradually, whether they are working on tastes, textures, colors, or presentation. Because this child is so aware of slight differences, enlisting the child in food presentation so he can make it the way he likes it may help the food seem more appealing and, subsequently, it will be more acceptable.

Active Children   Active children often have difficulty with stopping an activity long enough to eat and sit still through a meal. An active child prefers to graze throughout the day, so caregivers can provide nutritious foods that she can eat "on the run." Parents can set limits on what and where eating is allowed but they must reduce their expectations at mealtime. Parents can expect a toddler to sit a short time and then to run off some energy before coming back to the table. If the child seems fidgety, they can give the active child appropriate reasons to leave the table such as picking up a napkin or getting another spoon in the kitchen.

High-Intensity Children   Children with high intensity react to foods, mealtimes, and eating with extreme passion: love or hate, ecstasy or tantrum. Modulating the intensity is key. When intensity begins to rise, redirection can avert further escalation. Parents who know temperament triggers can manage them to prevent outbursts. Practicing a softer table voice and appropriate expression of intensity also helps. As the toddler becomes older, his ability to self-regulate increases and he can learn to say, "No, thank you" instead of melting down when he sees beets, for example.

Irregular Children   Irregular children are not hungry at the same time each day, so setting regular mealtimes is difficult but not impossible. A toddler or preschooler with an irregular temperament can be expected to sit at the table for a short time but should not be made to eat if she is not hungry. Some parents reheat dinner or provide a nutritious snack later if their children complain of hunger. Parents do not have to be short-order cooks but can plan for what foods are allowed if their child does not eat at mealtime. If meals are provided only at consistent times each day, the child may develop regular eating habits over time.

Slow-Adapting Children   Issues for slow-adapting children involve difficulty with transitions such as stopping an activity to come to the table, accepting new foods, and experiencing changes in dinner routines. Coming to the table is a transition and should be handled with preparation and consistency. Slow-adapters will meet the request, "Dinner is on the table, come and eat" with extreme resistance if it happens too suddenly, but a routine such as giving two warnings and having the child wash his hands can make the transition go smoothly. The following vignettes about two slow-adapters illustrate other issues.

• •

"Jenna had a complete meltdown at the table," her mother noted. "She came to the table fine, but when I dished up her spaghetti, she threw herself on the floor screaming, 'I wanted chicken!'"

• •

"Albert has very limited food choices and likes only one brand of macaroni and cheese. This brand had a new dinosaur-shaped pasta and because Albert loves dinosaurs, I served it. He had a fit and refused to try it!" said Albert's frustrated father.

• •

Anyone can have expectations that do not match reality, but slow-adapters let go of their hopes more slowly—and more loudly if they are also intense. Because her mother did not tell her the menu, for some reason Jenna came to the table thinking of chicken. When her expectation was not met, she could not adapt. Slow-adapting children need to know what to expect once they are at the table. Caregivers can discuss meals each day. Some parents find having a weekly menu plan prevents problems with their slow-adapting children's expectations.

Slow-adapters also do not like any changes in the foods that they are used to. If a change is made, as it was in Albert's case, it should happen gradually. The child should be prepared beforehand; even with preparation, the food may not be accepted at first.

Withdrawing Children Withdrawing children resist new foods. Gradual familiarization is the key to getting withdrawing children to try new foods. They prefer foods that are more familiar and are more likely to try new foods that they repeatedly encounter (Sullivan & Birch, 1990). They are also more likely to try a new food when they are not tired or hungry. When a child has a friend who likes a variety of foods, this can also entice the child to try something new. Children tend to emulate the eating patterns of people they admire, both adults and peers (Birch, Zimmerman, & Hind, 1980). Sharing control by letting a child serve himself or by having him assist with the preparation helps to familiarize the child with new foods.

• •

Nicole would only eat plain pasta without sauce. Her mother took a gradual approach, putting a spoonful of sauce on the plate and being careful it did not touch the pasta. At first, Nicole protested, but she got used to seeing it on her plate. Each time pasta was served her mother moved the sauce closer to the pasta. One day it touched the pasta, and again, Nicole protested. Gradually the sauce was put on top of some pasta, then on more pasta until Nicole was eating her pasta with the sauce.

• •

Sleep Issues

Resisting bedtime, falling asleep, and awakening at night are problems for many toddlers and preschoolers and are especially common in children ages 2–5 years old (Crowell, Keener, Ginsberg, & Anders, 1987). One survey found that 42% of 12- to 35-month-olds resist bedtime and 35% wake up at night (Johnson, 1991). The relationship between temperament and sleep problems is well established. Toddlers who have more difficult temperament traits have more sleep problems than do children with easier temperaments (Atkinson, Vetere, & Grayson, 1995; Sadeh, Lavie, & Scher, 1994; Schaefer, 1990; Weissbluth, 1999). In another study, in describing their children mothers reported a relationship between less sleep and less adaptability (Sher, Epstein, Sadeh, Tirosh, & Lavie, 1992). Other data indicated that children 5.7 years old on average who were diagnosed with sleep problems not only had more negative emotionality but also were more disruptive during the day. Children with disrupted sleep patterns had more negative adjustment in preschool (Bates, Viken, Alexander, Beyers, & Stockton, 2002). When sleep problems are treated, daytime behavior improves considerably (Minde, Faucon, & Faulkener, 1994).

Falling asleep is an issue for sensitive, active, irregular, slow-adapting, withdrawing, and low-persistence children. Many of the same strategies that applied in infancy still apply in early childhood, but there are some new twists on old problems and strategies.

Sensitive Children   Just as in infancy, physical discomforts or overstimulation cause the sensitive toddler or preschool-age child to have difficulty falling asleep. White noise, temperature adjustments, soft sheets and pajamas, and black-out shades or night lights help control the physical environment. Most important at this age is preventing overstimulation. A very busy day or too much activity before bed makes it difficult for the sensitive child to go to sleep. One child explained, "My body wants to go to sleep, but my mind won't let it!" Regular quiet times and limited stimulation during the day and evening leads to peaceful sleep. Sensitive children are more likely to have night fears from seeing something frightening in daily life, on television, or in a book. Caregivers can keep frightening images away from children whenever possible to prevent this kind of overstimulation. Claire, for example, could not fall asleep knowing that the book with the picture of the scary witch was on her bookshelf. Her father had to move it into the garage.

Active Children   An active child does not want to stop playing to sleep. One father said that his active daughter fought sleep for fear of missing something because to her, "sleep is boring." Energetic children are like fast cars with no brakes. The more active these children are, the more tired they become, and the harder time they have slowing down. Roughhousing or exciting television before bed stimulates them, and noise outside their bedroom makes it difficult for them to fall asleep. A bedtime ritual that slowly applies the brakes helps the active child to decelerate: A warm bath, a hypnotic book, whispering, dim lights, and slow songs can create a quiet interval before bedtime that allows the child to settle down to fall asleep.

Of course, some children will try to get up and leave the bedroom even with a quieting down time, which makes parents resort to creativity. Three-year-old Sheeva would not stay in bed at bedtime. Her parents used a gate at the door to keep her in her room. At first she protested, but as she became used to the gate, shutting it helped her contain her activity and became a necessary nightly ritual when her parents said goodnight.

When an active child awakens during the night, parents may find it helpful to implement a "less is more" strategy in trying to get her back to sleep. If there is too much interaction, the child becomes wide awake and difficult to get back to sleep. Each time she awakens, parents can guide the child back to bed in the same way with the message that it is time for sleep.

• •

Five-year-old Gretta was very active at night and would kick off the covers and then get cold. She would go to her parents to cover her up. Her father talked with her during the day about pulling the covers back up herself, and drew her a picture showing each step to get back to sleep. Each night before bed they looked at the picture and practiced pulling up the covers after kicking them off. They tucked the picture under her pillow. When she woke up and asked her parents to cover her, her father would tell her to look at the picture. Soon she was able to pull up the covers herself, but she made certain the picture was under her pillow each night.

• •

Irregular Children   For children who are irregular in their sleep patterns, an evening and bedtime routine greatly encourages a regular bedtime and sound sleep. Some irregular children will ultimately adapt to the schedule. If not, parents can establish a "bedroom time" when the child must be in bed but can look at books for a while before the parents turn the lights out.

Slow-Adapting Children   Routine is the key to getting slow-adapting children to sleep. These children will try to postpone bedtime by dawdling, wanting "just one more story" or making "curtain calls" after being in bed. Any routine established during infancy and toddlerhood is more difficult to change as the child grows older. For example, the child whose parents lie down with him each night will soon refuse to fall asleep any other way. If he wakes up in the night, he will need the parent to lie down again in order to fall back asleep. To help the child learn to fall asleep alone, the routine cannot be changed too rapidly. He will do best with one change at a time and enough time to adjust before the next change occurs. If the child is also intense, parents can expect long and loud protests with each change.

Helping a child fall asleep alone requires first telling the child that instead of lying down with him, the parent will sit next to him and hold his hand until he falls asleep. This talk should be done early in the day, not immediately before bedtime. Protests are normal but, with consistency, the child will make the adjustment. At bedtime, steps to make these small changes might include sitting on a chair next to the bed but not touching the child, moving the chair farther away from the bed, and eventually moving it outside the room. The child will then gradually get used to falling asleep alone. This takes time and commitment, but these gentle changes are easier for parent and child in the long run than expecting the child to do it all at once. Night waking is another issue for slow-adapters.

• •

Trent, an active, slow-adapting 3-year-old, would wake at night and come into his parents' bed. He slept soundly but disrupted his mother's sleep with his movements. His parents put Trent's Superman sleeping bag on the floor next to their bed and told him that he could be near them but not in the bed because he disturbed his mother's sleep. He protested loudly, but after I week he would slip into his sleeping bag without disturbing his parents. His parents gradually moved the sleeping bag farther from the bed and eventually back into Trent's room.

• •

Withdrawing Children   Withdrawing children have difficulty falling asleep in new situations. The unfamiliarity of sleeping in a motel or campground or staying in a new bed at Grandma's house can cause sleeplessness. Even the feel or smell of new sheets, rearranging the bedroom furniture, or moving from a crib to a bed disrupts sleep. Bringing familiar things from the child's own bed on vacation or when visiting makes it easier. When a withdrawing child moves from the crib to a bed, parents can move the new bed in a few days before taking the crib down to help the child feel comfortable.

Low-Persistence, Slow-Adapting Children   Low-persistence, slow-adapting children can be resistant to going back to sleep after waking at night because they have a difficult time doing things on their own and are not flexible.

• •

Low-persistence, slow-adapting, intense Vanessa had trouble sleeping through the night. She would wake at night to use the toilet. She would walk past her bathroom to her parents' room and announce that she had to "go potty," use their bathroom, and then insist that they tuck her in her bed. Her father would get angry and demand that she go back by herself. This triggered her intensity, making it harder to get her back to sleep. Her mother took the gradual approach, knowing that it was too frustrating for Vanessa to go back to bed alone. Her mother told her that she would walk Vanessa back to her room but that she would have to tuck herself in. Once Vanessa accepted that step, her mother walked to her doorway and watched her get into bed. Gradually she decreased the distance she walked with Vanessa, until the night came when her mother did not get out of bed and called out to Vanessa, "Go back to bed and tuck yourself in." At this point Vanessa decided it was too much work to go all the way to her parents' room and began to use her own bathroom without waking her parents.

• •

Naps   Toddlers typically still take naps, but many preschoolers begin to give up their daily nap anywhere between 3 and 5 years of age, much to their caregivers' chagrin. Active, slow-adapting, sensitive, or easily frustrated children need naps to replenish their energy, adaptability, and frustration tolerance. As fatigue increases, adaptability and persistence decrease. Sensitive children are easily overstimulated when they become tired. Active or approaching children do not want to stop for naps, but without rest, their energy escalates further.

Paradoxically, good naps start with a good night's sleep. A good night's sleep improves a child's adaptability and frustration level and makes it easier for him to settle down for a nap the next day. As with bedtime, a quiet period and naptime routine is necessary. A sensitive child needs quiet and dark in order to fall asleep, which can be difficult during the day. If the child refuses to nap, he can have a quiet time and rest while watching a calming video, listening to music, or looking at books. The rest time should be in a quiet, calm place for a specified amount of time. Knowing that he does not have to sleep may allow the child to relax enough to fall asleep anyway.

VOMITING ON CUE

Intense children can become so upset that they vomit, which may become intentional. The example of Ayesha illustrates this practice.

• •

Eighteen-month-old Ayesha would not go to sleep at night. Her parents decided to let her cry it out, and she became so worked up that she vomited. This distressed her parents so much that they did everything they could to prevent it from happening again. Ayesha discovered that she could make herself vomit, and she began to use this new power. Riding in the basket in the grocery store at age 3, she would say, "Mama, I want cookies." When her mother said, "No, we are not buying cookies," Ayesha would begin to gag and her mother would race to the cookie aisle to prevent any mess in the store.

• •

This pattern is typical of intense, easily frustrated children, and their parents often accommodate them to avoid it happening. Parents can learn to stop this pattern early. They must remain calm and plan ahead by having bowls, airsick bags, and towels at hand. Once the child realizes this behavior has no power, it soon disappears.

HEAD BANGING

Children who are active, high in intensity, and low in frustration tolerance may become so frustrated that they bang their heads. These children often are also low in sensitivity. Children who are high in sensitivity, intense, and easily frustrated may bang their heads, but they stop quickly because of the pain and usually do not repeat the action. One father exclaimed, "Jordan becomes so frustrated when she cannot do what she wants that she bangs her head on the floor over and over again. I am afraid she'll seriously hurt herself." Parents and caregivers are alarmed when such behavior occurs and they try to do whatever they can to stop it.

Head banging, like vomiting, biting, and hitting, often begins in the toddler period, when the toddler lacks the verbal skills to express frustration and negotiate solutions. At that time, the head banging is typically nonmanipulative, so that is the time that parents need to start working with this behavior. If children consistently get strong reactions, they may use these behaviors when they want attention or to get what they want. When parents realize that these behaviors are temperament-related, they can respond in a calm, consistent manner. They monitor frustration, provide breaks with activities to let off steam, redirect the child when frustration mounts, and encourage the child to use words and channel intensity in more physically appropriate ways. If the child reaches the point of head banging, the parent can calmly move the child to area where he will not hurt himself, such as onto a thick carpet, or place a pillow under his head. It is important that the parent does not give in, overreact, and punish the child in response to this behavior. When intensity has decreased and the child is calm, parents can encourage him to use words and plan for better ways to express frustration in the future. Calm, consistent responses are key to eliminating head banging and to ensure that it does not become intentional and manipulative.

TEMPERAMENT AND SOCIAL ISSUES

Toddlers and preschoolers are learning valuable lessons about socialization. Children are gaining new self-regulation skills and learning to interact in group situations. The issues of sharing, taking turns, and controlling aggression are fundamental. Caregivers are concerned about the child who is aggressive as well as the child who seems shy and hesitates to interact with others.

SHARING AND TAKING TURNS

Children who are sociable and outgoing and who have good self-regulation skills are better at sharing, taking turns, and showing empathy toward peers than are children who have low self-regulation skills and high emotional intensity (Eisenberg et al., 1993). Children who are active and intense react physically and tend to rush into play situations, taking what they want. Caregivers must talk about sharing and turn-taking before play in order to help these children stop, observe, and evaluate the situation before rushing in. Mary Sheedy Kurcinka, in her book *Raising Your Spirited Child* (1998), described this as the "stop, look, and listen" technique.

AGGRESSION

Handling aggression involves knowing the temperament triggers, minimizing them, watching for cues of escalation, and controlling the environment. Aggression in toddlers decreases with language development and increased self-regulation, but active, intense children are likely to have difficulty using words instead of action. Intrusions, unexpected changes, frustration, and too much stimulation can elicit biting, hitting, or pushing.

Biting   Biting is very upsetting for caregivers, but it usually decreases once the child has language, though some children continue to bite because it feels good. Stella Chess (personal communication, 2001) tells of an intense, approaching child who would happily greet her father with a big bite on any exposed body part. Biting also causes a big reaction and is a way for slow-adapters to take control. Another kind of biting is situational and occurs only in certain contexts.

• •

Tina and Joey, both 3 years old, wanted the same toy and had it in a tug-of-war grip. Persistent Tina knew she would lose it if she took her hands off of the toy, so she bent over and bit Joey's hand. He let go. Tina had bitten three times in 2 months but only when other means were ineffective. Biting was not a regular response for her.

• •

Children who are low in frustration tolerance may bite when they become frustrated. If a child with low frustration tolerance is incited, he may bite another child. If he is frustrated because he cannot achieve a goal, he may bite himself. For all biters, caregivers must establish a "No biting people or other living things" rule. Parents can label for the child the feelings that trigger biting, and the child can be encouraged to use words instead of teeth. These strategies, combined with a simple, firm consequence such as an immediate time-out, usually discourage the behavior. If toddlers seem to enjoy the physical sensation of biting, parents can provide appropriate objects such as apples and teething toys when a child attempts to bite. Parents can also monitor rising intensity or frustration, redirect activity, take breaks to reduce frustration or intensity, and use an incentive for self-control. All of these teach impulse control. For the situational biter, biting can be prevented by an immediate consequence, an explanation of how biting affects others, and later, role playing that recreates the biting incident. One mother provided her daughter with a "biting bracelet," a rubber teething ring that she wore on her wrist. She instructed her daughter to "bite the bracelet" whenever she felt like biting someone.

FREE PLAY

Free play—with its lack of structure and many unexpected intrusions, changes, and transitions—often leads to problems for children of different temperament types, especially slow-adapting children. When children also are active and intense, they try to control the situation and often resort to aggression. During free play there is also more opportunity to get revved up, frustrated, or have intensity triggered. Active children have problems with getting too revved up and reacting physically—they become rougher until someone gets hurt. Intense children also react quickly, loudly, and sometimes physically (especially if they are active). Children who are easily frustrated and active are likely to react aggressively to frustration.

Free play can be structured by giving the child a task such as helping to get out play equipment or helping a younger child with an activity. Monitoring rising intensity and redirecting the child also prevent aggression.

Slow-adapting children often have an agenda when they play. If another child's agenda differs, aggression may occur. Preparing these preschoolers for a play date helps prevent problems. First, the caregiver and child put away the toys that the child is not willing to share. Then, they discuss possible play activities. For example, if Alsana is bent on playing "store," her mother can ask what other games might be fun in case her friend wants to play something else. This gives Alsana time to consider and adjust to other possibilities. Discussing options and the possible sequence of play helps children know what to expect. These children also need time for transitions as they move from one activity to the next. Caregivers can prepare a child for a play date and provide the necessary transitions when activities change.

When the friend arrives, a structured activity that does not involve competition or taking turns eases the transition. This can be followed by free play and another structured activity if needed. If a child has difficulty with impulse control or aggression, a shorter rather than longer play date is best. This also gives the child a better chance for social success. The length of play dates can be increased as the child becomes able to handle it.

INTERACTIONS DURING PLAY

In a play date, the other child's temperament is an additional consideration. Two active children can rev up and become out of control. Two slow-adapters may engage in constant power struggles. Two intense children can create ear-splitting play that disintegrates into a fight. A persistent child may insist on staying with one activity when his less persistent companion is ready to change activities. A less sensitive child may easily upset a very sensitive one.

Breaking the Pattern of Aggression   When activity and intensity levels escalate, breaking the pattern of escalation prevents aggression. As intensity increases, adaptability decreases and so does the possibility for impulse control. Children often provide cues that they are escalating, but parents may miss the cues of overstimulation or escalating intensity. Active children become increasingly wild. One child may clench her fists, whereas another changes the tone of her voice.

• •

"Ken gives me no cues that he is about to explode. It just happens," one mother claimed. When she looked for cues, however, she said she noticed that each time 4-year-old Ken started to escalate, he would pace back and forth. Once she identified the pacing she could redirect him to a calmer activity or a "cool down." In this case, she had him blow up a balloon. This caused him to breathe deeply and helped calm him. She knew her tactic was successful when, one day, Ken had a friend over who started to become agitated. Ken said to him, "I think you need to blow up a balloon!"

• •

Deep breathing works well to decrease escalating intensity, but preschoolers may not respond positively to the directive, "Take a few deep breaths." Blowing up a balloon (for older preschoolers) or blowing bubbles facilitates deep breathing and also provides a positive redirection for children.

Finally, managing the aggression of a slow-adapting, low-frustration-tolerance, intense child involves controlling the environment and creating goodness of fit. Such a child does better in play situations with fewer children because there are fewer intrusions. If the child's preschool or child care has little structured time, there are more possibilities for intrusions, frustrations, and unexpected changes that can trigger aggression. Such a child will do better in a structured setting.

To avoid aggression, caregivers can

- Plan the play date beforehand with the child
- Monitor the play
- Provide structure for the play
- Watch for signs of increasing intensity
- Manage the environment according to the child's temperament
- Take into consideration the playmate's temperament

SHYNESS OR SOCIAL INHIBITION

Whereas some children have the tendency to behave aggressively, others have the opposite problem. Children identified as inhibited or shy have temperament characteristics of withdrawal, sensitivity, and low intensity. They are quiet and subdued in social situations, offer fewer spontaneous comments, and smile less frequently (Kagan & Snidman, 1991a; Kagan, Snidman, & Arcus, 1998). They tend to keep to themselves and stand back and watch rather than join in play. Many prefer solitary play. Often, more uninhibited children dominate them socially.

Research shows that mothers who continually protect these children from minor stresses or are overly solicitous make it more difficult for the child to engage in social interactions or unfamiliar situations (Arcus, Gardner, & Anderson, 1992; Arcus & Kagan, 1995). Mothers who are firm, who do not overreact to fretting and crying, and who make age-appropriate demands help inhibited children become less fearful (Arcus, 2001).

Parents can encourage children who stay on the periphery and have problems making friends by planning play dates with children of

Caregivers can help a socially hesitant child by

- Helping the child move into a new play situation, then gradually retreating
- Not protecting the child from new experiences but providing support to help the child feel comfortable
- Planning play dates with children of similar or slightly more outgoing temperament
- Helping the child establish a friendship outside of school or child care

similar or slightly more approaching temperaments. A less withdrawing playmate can gently push a shy child to try new activities. Establishing a friendship outside of child care or preschool can help develop a connection when in the group setting, and one positive social interaction can encourage the development of another. Mollie had a hard time making friends at preschool, for example, so the teacher suggested that her mother arrange a play date with Aidry, who was slightly more outgoing. Soon Aidry and Mollie became friends, and Aidry's friend Deanna would also join in their play at school.

Parents and teachers can help withdrawing children develop friendships by staying with them, helping them gradually move into a play situation until they become engaged in an activity, and then slowly retreating.

Morning Routines

Getting the children up in the morning, ready, and off to where they need to be (e.g., child care or preschool) without incident is a common problem.

Five-year-old Tim is slow-adapting, irregular, intense, and distractible. All of the steps between waking up and getting into the car are transitions, so each requires adapting. He is not hungry after he wakes up because he is irregular, and he plays when he should be dressing because he is distractible.

"Mornings are a nightmare," says Tim's mother. "Tim hates to wake up, so I try to let him sleep as long as I can, which means that we have to get ready and out of the house quickly to get to work and school on time.

I end up dragging him out of bed kicking and screaming. He dawdles getting dressed and ends up playing in his room. Often I can't get his hair or teeth brushed and he won't eat breakfast. Getting into the car is a fight, and I'm in tears by the time I drop him off."

Tim needs a morning routine and fewer distractions. After talking with Tim, they decide to pick out his clothes the night before to save time in the morning. His mother began waking him up earlier rather than later so that he would have more time to get ready. They created a morning routine that included getting dressed in the bathroom, where there are fewer distractions, and taking a bagel in the car when he is not hungry at breakfast.

• •

When morning routines vary from day to day, power struggles are likely because the child does not know what to expect. Instead, a family can plan a morning routine with few elements and display it on a chart with pictures for the nonreaders. Each morning the family can look together at the daily calendar so there are no surprises.

For the slow-adapter, getting up is a major transition. Parents can help by waking the child up 15 minutes earlier than necessary and allowing her to lie in bed awhile. A suggestion such as "You can listen to three songs on your Barney tape before it's time to get up" provides a time frame as well as a ritual for waking up. Parents need not expect a cheerful conversation when the child first gets up.

The irregular child does not wake up at the same time each day. What time the child went to bed, if he had a nap, or how much activity he had during the previous day influences his sleep patterns. Regulating these variables may help. For example, if a child stays up later at night because he has had a nap, he may have difficulty waking up. Eliminating naps helps him to go to bed on time so he can wake up earlier. If this does not make a difference, a waking-up ritual can help him know when it is time to get up.

Sensitive children are particular about how clothes feel. They insist on wearing only one outfit or having their shoes tied repeatedly until they feel "just right." Parents can encourage their sensitive child to pick out and try on the clothes they buy or buy only clothes that they know are comfortable for her. They can also place limits on their responses to other sensitivities: "I will tie your shoes only three times and then you must live with it or wear your Velcro shoes."

Low-persistence children want parents' help with dressing because they get frustrated easily. Parents can agree to help with some of the dressing and gradually give their child more responsibility for dressing herself.

• •

Sanyu at 4 years old was low in persistence and sensitive and refused to dress himself. He stood limply as his mother dressed him. He complained that "the buttons were hard" and "the sleeves were tight." His mother solved the problem by having him choose all of the clothes that were comfortable for him. The others were put away. Each night they chose an outfit for the next day. In the morning, Sanyu could choose two pieces of clothing to put on himself and his mother helped with the rest. Later he was expected to put on additional pieces of clothing, until eventually he was dressing himself.

• •

STARTING CHILD CARE OR PRESCHOOL

Beginning child care or preschool is a major step for toddlers and preschoolers. Parents want the best experience for their child and have certain expectations about how the child will succeed. Well-meaning parents may choose child care or a preschool that has excellent qualifications, but it may not be the right fit for their child's temperament. Schools also have certain expectations of their students depending on their philosophy and curriculum. Knowing a child's temperament helps caregivers choose the child care or preschool that best suits their child and helps make the transition as smooth as possible.

Each child responds differently to beginning child care or preschool. The active, approaching child dives right in and barely says good-bye to his parents. If he is also slow-adapting, he still dives in, but a few days later he may have a delayed reaction and protest going to school because after the newness wears off, he realizes that this is a permanent change. Withdrawing, sensitive, or slow-to-warm-up children initially respond with hesitation and unease. Withdrawing children can take anywhere from 2 weeks to 2 months or more to adjust to the school, depending on their level of withdrawal. The more often the child attends school, the more quickly he becomes familiar, and once familiar with the school, teachers, and children, he is fine. Illness or vacation may start the process again, however. A slow-adapting child protests the transition of going to school, the changing activities, and the different routines. This child may protest going to and leaving school: It is the transition she protests, not the school. Once she learns the routines, incidents rarely happen until another change occurs.

CONSIDERING TEMPERAMENT IN SELECTION

A caregiver who considers temperament when choosing a preschool or child care can help the child adjust. Children who are sensitive and withdrawing may do better in a small family home child care than a large, busy child care center. They need a warm, nurturing environment, and a family home child care becomes familiar more quickly than a center. These children can also flourish in a formal preschool as long as it is small in size and predictable in structure.

Slow-adapting children do better in smaller settings that have daily routines and structure than in large facilities with many children, many transitions, and large amounts of free play. They need to know what to expect from the routine, the rules, and the teachers. These children have difficulty with too many day-to-day changes and need consistency. Laurie, for example, had problems in her cooperative preschool because of the change of parent workers each day. The schedule changed from month to month, and sometimes parents switched days in order to fit their changing schedules. Even though all of the parent workers enforced the same school rules, their styles varied in doing so. Laurie became increasingly noncompliant in response to these changes.

Active children need schools that embrace their high energy and provide opportunities for them to practice large motor skills. A large playground with play structures that allow them to use their large muscles suits these children. They need a balance between active play and calm activities so they can adequately release energy but also learn to slow down and focus on tasks involving finer motor skills. Too many quiet activities and too much sitting still cause problems for them. These children flourish with teachers who are skilled at monitoring escalating energy and can redirect it when necessary.

If problems do develop in child care or preschool, looking at the fit between a child's temperament, the school's environment, and the teachers will help parents and teachers decide the best approach. Teachers who understand the child's temperament may work well with the parents to establish a better fit, but in some cases a change of school is necessary.

• •

Jade was sensitive, intense, slow-adapting, withdrawing, and easily frustrated. At 2½ years old, she was the youngest of three children. She was a challenge from infancy, unlike her two older sisters who had easy temperaments. Jade was demanding and the family revolved around her, trying to appease her so she would not "melt down."

The issues her mother, Liz, presented to the temperament counselor were Jade's extreme tantrums and her noncompliance with most requests. This made bedtime, mealtimes, dressing, family outings, and daily life often unbearable.

At Jade's temperament consultation, Liz and the counselor discussed the hallmarks of 2-year-old behavior: negativity, tantrums, egocentricity, and autonomy. Jade's temperament made these qualities even more extreme. Liz took home the assignment of noticing what triggered the tantrums, watching for early cues of overstimulation. Because of Jade's slow adaptability, Liz would introduce more structure each day and prepare her for any changes. But Jade's high intensity would make it difficult for her parents to be consistent.

Liz decided to focus on dinnertime as a first issue because Jade's tantrums often ruined dinner for the entire family. The plan was to have an afternoon quiet time to reduce Jade's stimulation and renew her adapt-ability for dinnertime. Liz would prepare Jade for dinner by describing the menu and stating her positive expectations for Jade's behavior. She would count down the time before dinner to help Jade put closure on any cur-rent activity. Liz would create a simple routine for coming to the table, such as turning off the television and washing her hands.

The following week, Liz reported that Jade had sat at the table and they had had one good meal, but in general, dinner was still difficult. Liz had noticed that Jade's low adaptability played a large part in triggering tantrums, and this information helped Liz prepare Jade for transitions; however, there were still problems. When it was time to turn off the tele-vision and come to dinner, for example, Jade refused even though she had been prepared well in advance. Liz decided to give the choice, "Do you want to turn off the television, or should I?" If Jade again refused she would be told, "I see that you have chosen to have me turn off the television."

When Liz returned to the temperament counselor in 2 weeks, din-ners were going more smoothly and choices were beginning to work, but there were still tantrums over other issues such as clothing. Jade preferred to go naked because of her high sensitivity. When she did dress she would wear one of only three outfits that were much too large for her, and she would not wear socks. When Liz pointed out to her, "Other children wear clothes that fit and socks with their shoes," Jade replied, "I'm not like other children." Clothes were an issue in which she and Jade could share control while working on lessening the tantrums. Liz decided to let Jade wear clothes that did not fit and go without socks, concentrating instead on being consistent in other areas.

Gradually the routines, choices, and consistency made life easier. Then, a big change occurred. Jade, now age 3, began preschool. Huge issues reappeared. First, when her uncle visited, Jade refused to get dressed for an outing to a park for a picnic. Liz finally took her naked in the car and brought clothes to the park. Jade refused to get dressed and stayed in the car screaming. The car was next to the picnic site and her parents took turns watching her and asking her to get dressed and join them. She refused and the picnic hurriedly ended. Next they went to the beach. By this time, Liz was exhausted and the parking lot was not close enough to leave Jade in the car, so Liz allowed her to play naked on the beach.

Jade's need for control led to her having tantrums. A new school, a house guest, and novel activities were more changes than Jade could handle. She tried to regain control in the area of clothes. She continued to wear only three outfits and no underpants or socks. But two of the outfits were loose-fitting dresses, and Jade had no modesty as she climbed on the monkey bars or sat spread-legged. When Liz asked her if other children went without underwear at school, Jade replied, "No, but I do." Sometimes she refused to dress at all in the morning. Liz tried several tactics to make her wear clothes: rewards, time-outs, and forcefully dressing her, but all resulted in tantrums.

The counselor encouraged Liz to persist with one tactic because of Jade's slow adaptability. The plan was that Jade would help pick out clothes the night before because this had worked in the past. If she rejected the clothes the next morning, she could get dressed in any outfit she chose by the time that Liz was dressed and ready to go downstairs. If Jade was not dressed by that time, Liz would dress her in the clothes she chose the previous night. After 1 month, Jade was getting dressed most of the time but still not wearing underwear. Liz decided that Jade could practice wearing underwear 2 days a week and receive an incentive for doing so.

Two months later, the clothes issues were much better. Jade had worn underwear for 4 days and then had stopped, announcing that she would wear it "when I'm 4." Her birthday was 3 days later and, like she promised, she began to wear underwear.

By then, Jade's meltdowns had decreased significantly. She was getting dressed and wearing underwear. She sat at dinner. The issues that came up could be explained and managed more easily. Liz was having an easier time being consistent and preventing problems by planning ahead for Jade's temperament. The family no longer revolved around the possibility of Jade's meltdowns.

• •

SUMMARY

Toddlers and preschoolers go through many physical, cognitive, emotional, and social changes. How they navigate these changes depends on their temperaments. For example, active children go through motor milestones more quickly than do less active children, and persistent children will stay with a cognitive task until they learn it. Children approach independence, language acquisition, and peer relationships in individual ways. Children who are approaching tend to separate easily from their caregivers, and children who are active and intense may have problems with aggression. Common issues such as discipline, toilet learning, food and mealtime issues, sleep problems, tantrums, and peer relationships become clearer when the child's temperament is considered. Temperament helps parents and clinicians understand why these issues occur and how to prevent behavioral issues by controlling the environment or working with the child. If temperament-related problems do develop, they can be effectively managed. Caregivers who use the child's temperament as their guide find that the typical issues they encounter are understandable, and that with understanding comes solutions. As children move from early childhood into middle childhood, using temperament concepts makes the transition easier.

CHAPTER 6

School-Age Children

Learning, Working, Making Friends

• •

Jeff, 9 years old, is a good student who conscientiously approaches each
assignment. When he begins a task, he stays with it until it is complete
and he follows all instructions precisely. He is a teacher's ideal student,
but he has problems with his peers. In cooperative learning activities he is
very set in his ideas on how a project should be done. He is quick to criticize when others do not follow directions or when someone views them
in a different way. On the playground he is bossy and insists on playing by
his rules. For these reasons, his classmates do not like to play with him.

• •

Emily is a social butterfly at school and has numerous friends. She is
happy and playful and enjoys the give and take of socializing. She loves
working with other classmates and does better in collaborative efforts
than with individual work. In class she is easily distracted, notices what
everyone else is doing, and would rather talk with her neighbor than do
her work. Consequently, her schoolwork suffers, and the teacher often
reprimands her.

• •

Amir is the most athletic in his class and prefers physical education to
math and reading. He is pleasant and sociable with his peers, and his ath-

letic abilities make him popular on the playground. He does best in subjects that involve interactive learning or field trips, but when a subject is difficult he resorts to being the class clown and derails the lesson. Amir gets poor grades in the subjects that require sitting still and attending.

• •

These three school-age children have three different behavioral styles that affect their school and peer interactions. Jeff is average in activity level, low in distractibility, slow-adapting, and persistent. Emily is highly approaching and distractible. Amir is active and low in persistence, especially if the task involves quiet learning such as reading and math.

Middle childhood is sometimes called the latency period, but school-age children are anything but latent. Many motor, cognitive, and social-emotional changes take place during this time. Gross motor and fine motor skills improve as children gain balance, flexibility, agility, and coordination. Thought becomes more flexible and better integrated; self-understanding and empathy increase. Children's self-regulation skills improve along with their understanding of complex emotions. Temperament influences the development of these skills. Children with "easy" temperaments develop self-regulation skills more quickly than do those with more challenging temperaments (Chess & Thomas, 1986). Kochanska, Murray, and Coy (1997) found that fearless children (i.e., active, approaching, low in inhibitory control) have more problems controlling their behavior than do children who are more fearful or withdrawing. The children who are temperamentally more fearful internalize the ability to inhibit their behavior and develop self-regulatory skills sooner than do their fearless counterparts.

At this age children spend less time with families and considerable time with peers. They also have more opportunities to play or work on their own (Berk, 2002). One study found that children interact with peers more than 40% of their day between the ages of 7 and 12 (Barker & Wright, 1951), and they become increasingly skilled at social problem solving. Classrooms, playgrounds, and peer groups are the main contexts in which children learn to evaluate themselves and form self-concepts. Self-esteem drops initially during the early school years as children begin to compare their skills with others

(Berk, 2002). As they realize their own skills and where they excel, self-esteem increases.

TEMPERAMENT AND DEVELOPMENTAL ISSUES

Differences in temperament affect the developmental courses of children across childhood in behavioral, intellectual, academic achievement, and environmental areas (Guerin, Gottfried, Oliver, & Thomas, 2003). According to Caspi (1998), temperament's influences on development are seen in six ways at this age:

1. The ways in which children learn
2. The reactions that children elicit from others
3. How children perceive the environment
4. How children compare themselves and others and the effect this has on self-concept and self-esteem
5. The situations children choose to engage in
6. The ways in which children manipulate their environments and how they attempt to shape others' behaviors

Temperament influences the ways in which children learn. In the school setting this effect is even more evident than in early childhood. For example, children differ in their levels of distractibility and persistence and some children are more receptive than others to incentives and consequences. Children who are withdrawing tend to learn through observation, whereas those who are active and approaching learn by doing.

The reactions that children elicit from parents, teachers, friends, and others differ according to the children's temperamental traits. For example, intense, active children are physical in their reactions and may elicit aggressive responses from peers. Teachers often rate highly active children as having inappropriate behavior (Guerin et al., 2003). Teachers' attitudes tend to be more positive toward children who are less active and higher in persistence than those who are active and distractible. They tend to view children who are persistent, adaptable, and less active as harder workers (Guerin et al., 2003).

How children perceive the environment influences their experience of events, situations, and people. For example, approaching children perceive a large, noisy party with new people as exciting. They are drawn to new experiences and delight in meeting new people. Withdrawing children perceive the same event as uncomfortable and anxiety producing. They retreat from novelty and avoid meeting new people. Different temperaments produce different perceptions of the same situation.

Temperament influences the comparisons children make between themselves and others, and this affects self-concept and self-esteem. Initially withdrawing children are aware that they are more uncomfortable meeting new people and going into new situations than highly sociable children, for example. When they see the ease with which approaching or active children manage social situations, they may feel inadequate, and this can affect their social self-esteem.

Temperament influences the situations children choose to engage in. For example, an active child might choose to join the soccer team, whereas a low activity, persistent child might prefer the chess club. Likewise, children most often choose friends who have similar temperament types and, hence, similar interests.

Temperament influences the ways in which children manipulate their environments and how they attempt to shape others' behaviors. Persistent children will be relentless in their attempts to change another's point of view, whereas slow-adapting children may ignore the request to make a transition. Temperament in middle childhood is a significant part of children's developing personalities.

TEMPERAMENT AND SOCIAL ISSUES

Social expectations are greater in middle childhood than they are at younger ages. Because children spend increasingly more time with peers, friendships take on new meaning and children seek peer acceptance. Friendships for an "easy" child are comfortable and rewarding, but for a slow-to-warm-up child making friends can be stressful and complicated (Chess & Thomas, 1987). Children who are active, intense, and slow-adapting, may find friendships difficult because they like to be in control and have the potential for intense, physical reactions.

Successful social interactions require flexibility, complex thinking, and processing. Kenneth Dodge's (1985) model for social information processing described the steps that a child must take for a successful social interaction. According to Dodge, the child must first *perceive* the social cues, *interpret* the meaning of the cues, *search for responses* to the cues, *choose the best response*, and *enact the response*. For example, Alan goes out on the playground and sees a group of children playing softball. He notices that there are three children playing: one pitching, one batting, and one in the outfield (perception). He sees that the outfielder is alone and that everyone is taking turns (interpretation). He wants to play, so he decides that he could do one of two things: run in and try to catch the ball or ask between hits if he could play outfield too (response search). After the batter hits the ball over the outfielder's head, Alan chooses the latter; he decides to run up to the group and say, "Hey, can you use another outfielder?" (response choice). He does this, the group agrees, and he takes his place in the outfield (response enactment).

The sequence of events in Dodge's model could be quite different depending on the child's temperament. If a child is low in sensitivity and does not pick up social cues easily, he tends to join play without attempting to decode the social cues. If he comes closer and the children see him, he might not notice a posture that says, "Go away." The other children may reject him, admonishing that there is no room for another player, which he probably has not considered. If he is also persistent, he keeps trying to join the play no matter how many times he is rebuffed. Eventually the other children may avoid him on the playground, disliking his pushy behavior.

Another child who is active, approaching, and intense may see the ball in the air and run up and grab it without evaluating the situation and the possible responses. An active, intense, and slow-adapting child may rush into play without evaluating the situation; she is acting on expectations that she will be welcomed by the others. When her expectations differ from those of the group, the child may react aggressively. A sensitive, withdrawing child may notice the appropriate cues and know the appropriate responses, but may hold back and not approach an unfamiliar group. A low-persistence child may enter the peer group appropriately and begin to play, but if the game is difficult he may become frustrated and not want to continue. If he is also intense, he may overreact to the frustration. The distractible child may miss certain cues because her focus is elsewhere, or she may enter into play with no problem but then notice another activity and leave to pursue that.

PLAY

During middle childhood the structure of play evolves from symbolic to play with rules. Organized sports are popular and provide an opportunity for children to learn to work together and follow rules. At recess or on the playground, children engage in free play in which they can practice social as well as physical skills.

Temperament influences the kinds of play that children choose. A low-activity, persistent child chooses to build and paint model airplanes while an active, persistent child builds a tree house. Slow-adapters choose play in which the rules aren't clear-cut or in which they can orchestrate the activity. Free play continues to present problems for them if there are unwanted intrusions or too many unexpected changes. Sensitive, withdrawing children tend to engage in more solitary play, or they choose quiet play with just one or two friends. Distractible children move quickly from one activity to another. Everything catches their attention. Children who are low in persistence may become frustrated by play that they find too challenging, and they may quit to pursue easier activities.

Team Sports   Many children are involved in team sports, and temperament influences which organized sport suits a child best. Slow-adapting children often have problems with team sports such as soccer or basketball, which are characterized by constant give and take and fast, unexpected changes. Eric, an active, slow-adapting 8-year-old, was kicked off his soccer team because of his aggressive behavior. If a teammate missed a goal, if the ball was not passed to him when he wanted it, or if the coach took him out to give another player a chance, he would yell, swear, and kick whatever was nearby. After Eric had exploded several times, the coach asked him to leave. Children such as Eric will experience success with a sport in whch they have more personal control. They tend to enjoy sports such as gymnastics, swimming, or martial arts in which the competition is more predictable and they are competing with a personal record rather than with a team. Horseback riding is another sport that suits active, slow adapters because of the actions of riding and learning how to control as well as work with the animal. Active children do best with quick-moving sports. Sports like softball or swimming are slow and have too much waiting to satisfy them.

Kate, an active, distractible 10-year-old, got into trouble on her softball team. When she was in the outfield she would act silly or toss her glove in the air while waiting for a hit to come her way. When she was waiting her turn at bat, she often bothered her teammates. She complained that she was bored. After a disastrous softball season, her parents signed her up for basketball. Kate excelled. The game was fast-paced, so she was in constant motion. When she was on the bench, she watched the high-energy game with interest.

Besides taking temperament into account when determining what sport is best for a child, parents must be aware of the goodness of fit between the coach and child. Sensitive, withdrawing children will wilt with a harsh coach, whereas an intense child will get into shouting matches with an equally intense coach. Slow-adapters will resist commands from a rigid coach and walk all over a coach who does not give clear instructions.

LEARNING AND SCHOOL

Each year, school-age children face the challenge of new classrooms, teachers, classmates, and curricula. More is expected of them in terms of social behavior, and they must follow new rules and routines. Slow-to-warm-up children have initial difficulties with each new experience and are often labeled "anxious" by teachers, but they do adjust when given time and encouragement (Chess & Thomas, 1989). Once teachers realize that these children need time to become familiar with new situations and people, they can help them gradually become comfortable with novel experiences.

Slow-adapting children have difficulty adjusting to changes involving different teachers, routines, and classrooms, and they continue to have difficulty each time they are presented with an unexpected event such as a substitute teacher or a pop quiz. Teachers and peers often perceive "difficult" children (active, intense, slow-adapting, irregular, negative mood) as immature because of these children's quick and explosive natures (Chess & Thomas, 1987).

As children spend more time in academic environments, the importance of attention increases. Barbara Keogh (1982, 1986, 1989, 2003) identified the most important characteristics in school functioning as task orientation (high persistence, low distractibility, and low activity level), personal-social flexibility (high adaptability, approachability, and positive mood), and reactivity (high intensity, low threshold, and negative mood). In a typical school population, 10%–20% of children have low task orientation, which can be perceived as attention problems (Carey & McDevitt, 1995). But poor task orientation can also reflect a child's temperament rather than an attention disorder. For example, Randi's high distractibility caused her to notice everything around her and not focus on her classwork. When her teacher allowed her to sit in a different desk, away from classroom activity, she could focus better. Although her inattention could appear to be disorder-related, it was actually temperament-related and solved by managing her environment. In their book *Coping with Children's Temperament,* Carey and McDevitt (1995) provided a complete overview of temperament and attention disorders.

Task orientation and attention can also relate to the teaching style, curriculum, and classroom environment. For example, a sensitive child may have difficulty attending to schoolwork in a classroom that is noisy or that has walls covered with brightly colored artwork. A withdrawing child may have problems staying on task with a teacher who is very approaching and who insists on trying new projects. A curriculum that includes lessons with hands-on experiences for approaching children as well as observational tasks for more hesitant children provides positive task orientation for children of different temperaments.

The way a child reacts to testing, class assignments, and homework also depends on temperament. Withdrawing or sensitive children may experience anxiety before testing, which affects the test results. Although the child may know the testing material well, the testing format produces such apprehension that the child cannot recall the answers correctly. Sensitive children may also react to the environment. A noisy or cold room, an uncomfortable chair, or an illness will negatively affect a child's testing results. Active children have difficulty sitting through a test, especially a lengthy standardized test. Temperaments should also be taken into account when giving class assignments and homework because children have different capabilities in terms of focus, task orientation, and activity level. Various temperament types and how they affect children in learning environments are given in Table 6.1. Class assignments and homework are discussed in more detail later in the chapter.

ROLE OF TEMPERAMENT IN SELF-CONCEPT/SELF-ESTEEM

Children develop positive self-concepts when they successfully master society's social and task demands at each age. Peer groups, classrooms, and playgrounds are the main contexts in which children evaluate themselves (Harter, 1986). The feedback children receive from people important in their lives also influences self-image. Children whose temperaments fit well with the environmental demands and expectations have more self-confidence than children who cannot meet the expectations of others because of their temperaments. NYLS children who experienced stress when they could not meet parental demands because of temperamental characteristics suffered feelings of inadequacy, expectations of failure, and a negative self-concept (Chess & Thomas, 1987).

Table 6.1. Effects of common temperament traits on learning

Trait	High	Low
Sensitivity	Physical discomfort affects performance	Is unaware of how their behavior affects others
	Is overstimulated by too much noise	Does not notice subtle nuances of teacher or learning tasks.
	Overreacts to criticism, discipline, or failure	Misses small errors in work
Activity	Has difficulty sitting for long periods	Prefers sedentary activities
	Rushes through work quickly	Does work very slowly (sometimes mistaken for intellectual slowness)
	Lacks fine motor skills (e.g. handwriting, drawing)	
	Prefers activities that use large muscles	Has difficulty with gross motor skills (e.g., physical education)
Intensity	Expresses feelings loudly	Is quiet
	Excels at drama	Difficult to "read"
	Is enthusiastic	Internalizes when upset
	If upset, can be physical or aggressive	Does not readily express emotion to teacher or peers
	Overreacts when upset or happy	
Predictability	Behavior is predictable	Behavior is unpredictable
	Is organized	Is disorganized, misplaces possessions
	Has a neat desk	Has an untidy desk
	Pays good attention to homework	Attention to homework varies
Persistence	Stays on task until completed	Does not stay on task if difficult
	Has difficulty stopping an activity before completion	Plays class clown to avoid work
	Has long attention span	Has short attention span
	Tends to be a perfectionist	Is overwhelmed by complex or long tasks
Adaptability	Is flexible	Does well with routines
	Follows instructions easily	Needs clear rules and instructions
	May have needs overlooked	Needs time to change from one activity to the next
	Goes with the flow	Does not like classroom changes
		Needs preparation before a change or transition
Approach/ Withdrawal	(Approach)	(Withdrawal)
	Difficulty keeping hands to self	Has difficulty starting new activities
	May be impulsive (if also active)	Has difficulty with unfamiliar curricula
	Is sociable, outgoing	Does not join easily into new groups
	Is a hands-on learner	Learns through observation
Distractibility	Has difficulty focusing on one task	Has an excellent ability to focus
	Is easily sidetracked by extraneous stimulation	Has difficulty moving on when engaged in a task
	Needs eye contact when given directions	Needs eye contact when given directions

Quentin's mother was concerned about her 10-year-old son's risky beha-vior with friends, his poor self-esteem, and his lack of responsibility. He was easily influenced by peers and had recently taken a dare to ride his bike on the highway. When reprimanded for misbehavior he would ad-monish himself, which Quentin's mother believed reflected low self-esteem. She had high expectations and strict standards for his behavior. She expected him to keep his room tidy, help with chores, and take care of his pets; however, Quentin rarely met her expectations. He did not fol-low through with chores, was disorganized and messy, and forgot to feed his dog. When his behavior did not improve despite his mother's increas-ingly restrictive discipline, this made her annoyed and critical.

Quentin's temperament profile revealed high activity, approacha-bility, and low persistence. Because he was overwhelmed by the many tasks and expectations his mother presented, he either did the job halfway or tried to avoid it altogether. He got little praise from his mother and felt he was, in his terms, "a screw-up."

When Quentin was with peers, however, the approval and admira-tion he got when he accepted risky dares raised his social self-esteem. The temperament counselor helped his mother decrease her expecta-tions and focus only on a few major chores. His mother discussed these with Quentin and they agreed on a time for completion. They broke chores into manageable parts to prevent overwhelming him. She learned to praise him for the parts he did accomplish, which encouraged him do more, and she looked for positive behavior to reinforce. With these changes Quentin completed more of his chores and his compliance im-proved. As he received more praise and less criticism from his mother, his self-concept also improved. His risky behavior decreased as he received more positive responses at home.

School-age children shift from defining themselves through ex-ternal characteristics to defining themselves through internal characteristics. Rather than describing themselves by hair and eye color and what they like to eat, as they did in early childhood, they now describe themselves in terms of social characteristics and social comparisons (Harter, 1999). Children's use of psychological characteristics in self-definitions increases (Aboud & Skerry, 1983). These can include temperament definitions: "I'm shy in a crowd of new people," "I have these big reactions!" "I hate it when plans change." As children become more aware of their temperaments as they grow up, they use these descriptions in defining themselves and they see their temperamental differences as positive and "normal" for them.

Self-esteem is tied to self-concept. By age 8, children have formed at least four areas of self-esteem: academic, social, physical, and athletic (Berk, 2002). Temperament plays a part in the development of all types of self-esteem, even the physical. For example, two children might be equally attractive, but one might have generally negative mood and think she is not attractive while the other child has positive mood and thinks she is attractive because, in general, she's more positive about everything. Children who have temperaments that are conducive to learning and studying have high academic self-esteem. A child who is active, low in persistence, and distractible, however, may have difficulty settling down to a learning task and may be less successful than his more persistent, focused counterparts. If the teacher does not understand this child's particular behavioral style, and if the child has not learned how to approach a task given these traits, his schoolwork may suffer and so will his academic self-esteem.

Similar to children with academic self-esteem, outgoing and sociable children have good social self-esteem, and those children who are active and who excel at gross motor skills usually have high athletic self-esteem, whereas those with opposite traits often have lower self-esteem in these areas.

EFFECT OF TEMPERAMENT UNDERSTANDING ON SELF-ESTEEM

Children who do not understand their temperaments may see themselves as different from other children and decide that there is something wrong with them:

- "Everyone likes that loud music except me, and they laugh at me when I cover my ears."

- "Sharon loves scary rides, but I'm just a chicken."
- "I'm always blowing up and getting angry. Other kids don't do that."

If other children point out these differences in a negative way, social self-esteem suffers, because children place so much importance on what peers think at this age. When children understand their temperaments, they learn how to enhance their strengths and work with their limitations.

Children can learn to reframe their temperament characteristics in a positive way. The statements above can be positively reframed as:

- "I just like other types of music. When the music is too loud, I go to a quieter area or get involved in another game. I don't cover my ears anymore, and the kids don't laugh."
- "Sharon loves scary rides and I don't; we just like different things."
- "I feel things very intensely, in a good way sometimes, too. I try to stay away from situations that make me get angry. If I do get angry, I try to calm myself or get the anger out in a positive way such as running or swinging."

Other ways to couch temperament traits in a positive light might include statements such as

- "I'm shy in a crowd of new people, but after I get to know someone I have fun—it just takes a little time."
- "I have these big reactions, and my drama teacher appreciates my passion!"
- "I hate it when plans change, so I use schedules and keep track of plans ahead of time."

COMMUNICATING WITH CHILDREN ABOUT TEMPERAMENT

Ideally, caregivers, teachers, and other child specialists talk with children about their typical responses and reactions. Validating how children feel from a young age is important in building self-concept and self-esteem. For younger school-age children, simple observations such as "I know it's hard for you to stop drawing and get ready for bed now," or "You feel very frustrated when you can't fasten your skates," give them ways to label and understand their feelings rather than simply reacting.

To help facilitate temperament understanding of
middle childhood, parents
and others working with a
child must initially

- Learn about the child's
  temperament traits
- Begin to manage the
  behaviors by working
  with the challenging
  traits, modifying the environment, and adjusting
  their responses to the
  child
- Give the child appropriate
  feedback about her tem-
  perament ("It's hard for
  you to stop a project once
  you start")
- Suggest a way to work
  with the challenging trait
  ("I'll give you a 10-minute
  warning before it's time
  to stop")

In middle childhood, children can increase their understanding of temperament traits and how different people have different temperaments. As children can better understand themselves, they need even more temperament information because they can modify their behavioral responses to help them through difficult spots or to plan ahead to make difficult situations easier.

When a child has a problem to discuss, using a temperament perspective in the discussion can normalize the problem and help the child to find solutions. If the problem involves peers or family members, such a conversation could begin with the parties involved and a discussion of each individual's temperament, noting which individuals have similar or different traits and how the traits might work with or against one another. The temperament counselor can discuss the traits in a nonjudgmental way, and humor can be used as people give examples of their traits. For example, when Mary identifies herself as intense, the counselor might comment, "So, everyone knows for certain when you're happy or upset!" Often, family members will also point out a humorous aspect to a trait. Next, the participants identify the problem and the temperament traits that might contribute to it. The group develops a strategy that takes everyone's temperament, needs, and feelings into consideration and devises a plan that everyone can live with, writing it down to prevent any confusion or future questions.

For example, parents working on a family problem such as completing the daily chores might use a temperament perspective to address the issue by

- Describing the problem from each person's point of view
- Identifying each family member's temperament

- Discussing how each person reacts to the problem according to their temperament
- Writing down possible solutions according to the different temperaments involved
- Determining the best way to solve the problem, taking each person's temperament into consideration

• •

Ted and Dawn have not been completing their chores, which is making their parents unhappy. The family determines that Dad is persistent, Mom is intense, Dawn is distractible, and Ted is slow-adapting. Each individual's particular traits determine his or her reaction to the housekeeping: Dad insists that the chores be done immediately from start to finish, Mom gets very upset and yells when the chores are not done. Dawn has difficulty completing her chores because she is easily sidetracked, and Ted becomes upset when he is expected to do his chores without delay. To solve the issue they determine a schedule so that Dad will know when the chores will be done. The schedule helps Ted to plan ahead for doing his chores. Having a regular chore schedule helps prevent Mom's yelling, and she gives Ted and Dawn a warning before it is time to do the chores. Mom also makes a short list of Dawn's chores to help her from becoming sidetracked. Knowing how family members' temperaments interact can help determine a plan that works for all. This method can also be used in classroom, child care, or other child-centered situations.

• •

Tally at age 6 was active, intense, slow-adapting, and low in persistence. Her mother sought temperament counseling for problems in discipline, noncompliance, and outbursts. With help she received from the counselor, Tally's mother put in place the typical strategies for slow adaptability: routines, warnings, time for transitions, and consistency. These helped Tally manage her behavior to a certain extent, as did breaking down tasks at home for chores and schoolwork. At school Tally did well and did not have the outbursts or strong-willed behavior that her mother reported at home.

When Tally was 8 years old, her mother returned to counseling because of daily power struggles. She requested that Tally come with her to the sessions, and one of the first things that the temperament counselor did was to show Tally her earlier temperament assessment. They discussed each trait and how it affected Tally's behavior, and then they discussed her mother's temperament, determining which traits were shared between the two and which traits were different. The fact that they were both intense explained why shouting matches often developed over Tally's failure to do chores. Tally's mother was adaptable and Tally was not, however, so her mother often expected fast responses to her directions that Tally could not give her. Looking at the differences in their temperaments, they could understand how their arguments quickly developed. They came up with a plan that took into consideration both of their temperaments: Chores would be done each day at a certain time. The routine appealed to Tally, and the fact that it would get done— although not at a moment's notice—appealed to her mother. They mapped out a plan for when chores would be done and consequences for when they were not.

At age 10, Tally's control issues resurfaced. She was reacting to relatively minor incidents at home and "blowing up" at her mother when she became frustrated. Tally realized that this was because of her high intensity. In counseling she talked about her successful interactions at school. Even though she had to manage many transitions and frustrations, she did not have problems there. The counselor asked Tally to describe her strategy for avoiding her triggers at school. Tally thought for a minute. "When I get upset at school, I get one of my friends to chase me and the intensity goes away," Tally said. The counselor suggested that Tally probably was using up all of her adaptability at school, leaving none for when she came home. It was clear that she needed some "down time" after school to restore some of her adaptability, but this alone would not guarantee that no more blow-ups would occur.

Tally discussed ways that she could release her intensity at home instead of blowing up at her mother. First, she worked on noticing early stages of rising intensity, then she identified ways that she could release her intensity. She came up with an acceptable way for her mother to suggest that it was time to release some intensity: At the first sign of escalating intensity, Tally's mother would say, "Maybe you need a break." When Tally heard this she would assess her level of intensity and then tell her mother how she would release it: "I think I'll go for a run." They tried this for a while and it worked most of the time, as long as Tally's mother gave her her cue on time. If Tally's mother waited too long for the reminder and allowed Tally's intensity to rise, Tally would lock in, refuse to accept the reminder, and blow up. When things had calmed down, they would discuss what went wrong. Tally really began to understand what made her "tick." After a while Tally's mother did not have to remind her to take a break because Tally could recognize the rising intensity and announce that she was taking a break.

The last time Tally and her mother came into counseling, Tally was 13. She described some difficulties she was having with another student. The student would "push Tally's buttons" and Tally would eventually explode. She asked the counselor, "Do you think it's because of my slow adaptability or my high intensity?" Tally was clearly thinking in temperament terms and using her knowledge to regulate her behavior.

• •

Children who understand their temperaments can work with the issues that come up in a concrete way. They can plan to avoid potentially volatile situations and learn the best way to handle undesirable feelings and reactions.

MIDDLE CHILDHOOD BEHAVIORAL ISSUES

DISCIPLINE

In middle childhood, parent–child relationships change. Children spend considerably less time with their parents. Parents' expectations for compliance are greater as children's responsibilities increase. If parents

Parents seeking compliance from their slow-adapting or negatively persistent child can

- Use requests rather than demands
- Use routines and rituals with requests (e.g., garbage is always collected before dinner on Tuesday)
- Share control: Let the child take part in devising a plan
- Help the child put closure on one activity before starting the next

If the child is also intense, stay calm and help the child stay calm when intensity begins to escalate.

• • • • • • • • • • • • • • • •

have developed a warm and loving, firm and consistent style of parenting, child-rearing actually becomes easier. If the parenting has been permissive or overly strict, then parenting may become more difficult, especially with children who have challenging temperaments. Parents, temperament counselors, and parent educators mention noncompliance and not listening as discipline issues that they often cope with at this age. Selecting effective consequences is also an issue if what worked in early childhood no longer has an effect on behavior.

Noncompliance, or refusing to do what is asked, often is associated with slow adaptability or high negative persistence. When high activity and/or high intensity are added to the mix, noncompliance can include acting out, aggression, or tantrums. Tantrums, typical for toddlers and preschoolers, are no longer acceptable in middle childhood but can still occur in the active, intense, school-age child. Children are no longer small enough to be physically made to take a time-out, and parents may fear that a reprimand will trigger intense reactions.

A slow-adapting child may meet any unexpected demand made by caregiver or teacher with a resounding refusal and increasing intensity. If the adult counters with intensity, tempers escalate quickly. As in early childhood, the adult can avoid this by using requests instead of demands and by letting the child know about the task ahead of time. Sharing control is even more important now than in early childhood, and slow-adapting or negatively persistent children must be part of the solution. For example, because children of this age should have more responsibilities in the family, chores are often an issue. Parents should involve children in deciding how and when the chores will be completed and what consequences will follow if the chore is not completed.

Coregulation, a model in which parents supervise behavior while allowing children moment-by-moment decision making, is essential at this age and grows out of a mutually cooperative relationship between parent and child. This mutually cooperative relationship is associated with the internalization of conscience in children with challenging temperaments (Kochanskab, 1997).

• •

Eleven-year-old Connor resisted most requests and let his chores go undone. When his parents, Jack and Sue, admonished him, he yelled at them and refused to comply. This made Jack angry, and he would yell at Connor and demand obedience. Tempers escalated until Connor was in tears, Jack was enraged, and Sue completed the chore herself. This pattern had gone on for several years.

Jack and Sue sought help from a temperament counselor. Connor's temperament assessment revealed that he was high in activity, distractible, intense, and low in persistence. The counselor pointed out that Jack's intense response to Connor increased his son's intensity and decreased any possibility of compliance. She advised Jack and Sue to pick a neutral time to discuss with Connor three chores that he could complete. Any more than three chores would be difficult for him because of his high distractibility and low persistence. Together they would agree on when and how the chores would be done and create a chore chart. They also would agree on an incentive for completing the chores. This created a routine that would fit with his distractibility, break up the tasks, and also prevent arguments about expectations.

The counselor told them that it might take a while for Connor to "get with" the new program but to persist and to use some built-in incentives. Because of Connor's low persistence, they were to choose chores that were not too difficult and ones that could be left unfinished without a problem. For example, Jack and Sue knew they would not let the dog go hungry, so feeding the dog was not a good chore for Connor, but he could collect and empty the household garbage each week and pick up his games and personal belongings each day. They were also instructed to break up chores into smaller parts to prevent frustration. Both the garbage and straightening up tasks could be broken into steps. Providing a chart that outlined the chores and helped Connor break them up helped keep him on task and focused. They discussed with Connor how to make the chores into a game—a sort of "beat the clock" that took advantage of his high activity level. He agreed and came up with another way to make picking up fun, by tossing certain toys and his dirty clothes into baskets and counting 2 points each time he hit the target.

When they returned to counseling a month later, Jack and Sue said that chores were going better. It took Connor almost 3 weeks to start doing his chores regularly. As an incentive he earned extra time playing computer games. Progress was disrupted whenever Jack's intensity escalated, but this reinforced the need for calm and consistency.

• •

Children who do not listen to their parents tend to be lower in activity level and intensity than children who are intense and active and openly defy their parent. This does not mean that intense, active children never ignore parents. In fact, ignoring may be the first level of defiance before things intensify. Children may not listen because the request felt "too fast," and ignoring the request slows down the need to respond quickly. Ignoring can also be a means of maintaining control, or when the child has the trait of low distractibility he may be so intent on another activity that he really does not hear.

The first step in fostering listening is to find out under what circumstances a child does not listen and which temperament trait this behavior is related to. A slow-adapting child will ignore requests that involve unexpected or fast transitions and will try to exert control by se-

Parents of children who are very distractible and low in persistence will attain better compliance by

- Not expecting the child to do too much at once
- Giving the child a short list of requests to help keep him on track
- Using a chart to help the child keep on task
- Breaking the tasks up into smaller parts
- Making the request when the child does not have other matters to attend to
- Using an incentive for completing the task

• • • • • • • • • • • • • • •

lective hearing. A child low in distractibility will not hear if deeply absorbed in another activity, a persistent child will combine all three (ignoring a fast request, not hearing if involved, and trying to control the situation so he can complete the activity). Once the cause is determined, the temperament type provides the guidelines for selecting the solution.

BEHAVIOR PROBLEMS THAT AFFECT PEER RELATIONSHIPS

Aggression Peer interactions become more prosocial in middle childhood, and physical aggression declines (Rubin, Bukowski, & Parker, 1998). When aggression does not decline, children are at risk for peer rejection. In one study, rejected children had lower adaptability, higher

Parents who want their child to have better listening skills can

- Determine when the child is not listening and how it relates to temperament

- Warn the child before a task is expected so that she will have time to adjust to the request

- Have the child help determine the routine to move from one activity to the next

- Put closure on one activity before moving on to the next

- Make eye contact when giving instructions and ask the child, "What did you hear me say?"

activity levels, higher distractibility, and lower persistence (Walker, Berthelsen, & Irving, 2001). Highly active children are especially prone to aggression if they are also high in intensity. If they are also low in adaptability, the many unexpected changes and intrusions that occur during unstructured time such as recess can trigger aggression. If a child is low in sensitivity, he may not pick up important social cues or he may misinterpret another child's intention. When aggression does occur, providing structure during free play helps. If this is not possible, a child must learn to identify what triggers her intensity, to prevent or manage the triggers, to identify increasing intensity, and to use appropriate outlets. Parents can work with the child at home to help her identify escalating intensity.

Robby had difficulty monitoring his intensity. Because he was low in sensitivity, he did not notice the cues until his intensity reached the point of no return and he could not control it. At a neutral time, Robby's parents suggested an experiment. They had him put his hand on his heart to check his heart rate when he was calm, and then again when he was excited. The difference was obvious even to him. When his parents noticed his intensity escalating, they would have him check his heart rate. If it was racing, he knew he needed to calm down.

● ●

Once children can identify their rising intensity, they can use calming activities such as taking a few deep breaths, reminding themselves to stay calm (self-talk), swinging on swings, or bouncing or kicking a ball. Or they can learn to remove themselves from the situation that is creating the reaction. Learning this takes time, and each step must be worked on separately before the child can identify and manage the triggers and then modulate the intensity.

Adults can help children with aggression by

• Identifying the situations that trigger aggression

• Helping the child recognize what triggers the intensity

• Helping the child identify his or her own cues of rising intensity such as increased heart rate, tone of voice, or body tension before the intense reaction

• Discussing alternative reactions with the child such as using words; breathing deeply; counting to 10; swinging on swings; or some other repetitive, calming activity, or just walking away

Shyness   Shyness is another area that presents problems in establishing peer relationships. Children who are highly sensitive and withdrawing are often perceived as aloof and socially awkward. These children have difficulty regulating emotion, experience social anxiety, and withdraw if faced with social challenges (Rubin, Stewart, & Coplan, 1995). The more difficulty they have interacting, the harder it becomes to be successful with peers. Boys have more problems related to shyness than do girls because in our society it is more acceptable for girls to be shy, and peers may label shy boys as "sissies" or "crybabies." With a highly sensitive and withdrawing boy or girl, it is necessary to approach so-cial fears one at a time in order not to overwhelm the child. Because the sensitive child often expands on a fear and carries it to extremes, parents can help the child break the fear into smaller parts and deter-mine which are real and which have been exaggerated.

• •

Richard feared starting fourth grade at his new school. He told his parents that he did not want to go because he did not know anyone. His anxiety increased as the first day approached. Richard's parents asked him what he was afraid of. He said that he was afraid that at recess he wouldn't know how to play the games and all of the children would laugh at him. His parents helped him to break down the parts of the first day at school into steps: Step one would be going into the classroom, step two would be meeting the teacher, and step three would be finding his desk. Then they planned together how to make each step comfortable. When they discussed recess, they listed all of the games he had played successfully at his old school. He agreed that if he did not know a game he would ask to watch the other children play before he joined in. Planning for each part of the day and discussing ways to handle his fear of recess helped Richard decrease his anxiety. It helped that Richard soon met a boy who was also new and they became friends.

• •

A friendship outside of the classroom with a classmate, possibly of a similar temperament, can create an alliance inside the classroom. Par-ents can use role play or toys to help the child practice social greetings and join play situations. For example, Sam wanted some help with his shyness regarding the headmaster, who greeted Sam each day at school. Sam, who was hesitant and sensitive, would look down and walk past her. At home, his father practiced the greeting with Sam in steps. First, he role played being greeted by someone new and giving a nod of his head, then making eye contact. Sam then got used to making eye

Adults can help the sensitive, withdrawing or shy child by

- Breaking up fears or anxieties into parts and determine which parts are real and which are exaggerated
- Discussing only one fear at a time
- Making a plan to handle each fear as it occurs
- Encouraging a friendship with a classmate
- Role playing difficult situations
- Talking about new experiences in terms of similar past, successful ones

• • • • • • • • • • • • • • • •

contact with a slight nod of his head. Then he added a smile. After practicing each step at home, Sam would carry out the greeting at school. Eventually he could look, smile, and wave, and say "good morning" to the headmaster.

Children who are shy often develop just one or two close friendships, so it is unrealistic for caregivers or teachers to expect more. These children also avoid social events and are more comfortable in familiar situations than new ones, so they prefer to have a friend come to their home rather than go to an unfamiliar house. Painfully shy children may benefit from small social competence groups. These are usually led by therapists and contain a small number of children with similar issues. They provide social skills exercises in a safe environment so that these children have more positive peer interactions.

• •

Rachel had been invited to birthday sleepovers from the time she was in first grade, but she was afraid to go. Her parents respected her feelings but were concerned that she did not participate in these "normal" social events. Finally, in fifth grade, after much deliberation and anxiety, she decided to go. She took her favorite stuffed animal and pajamas with her, and her parents told her that if she decided not to stay, they would pick her up. On the way to the party she burst into tears, worrying, "What if I can't fall asleep?" "Don't worry," her mother replied. "No one sleeps at slumber parties." This assurance assuaged her worry, and Rachel made it through the night. Because she knew that she did not have to sleep and that she could go home if she wanted to, Rachel was the first to fall asleep. Getting through that slumber party made the next one easier and more enjoyable.

● ●

BEHAVIORAL ISSUES OVER HOMEWORK

Homework creates problems at home for parents as well as children. Children who have trouble with homework often have temperament traits of high or low activity level, low persistence, high distractibility, and slow adaptability. If they are also intense, this colors how they express their distaste for homework. Highly active children have difficulty settling down to do homework after being in school all day and have difficulty sitting still to do it. Children low in activity complete the work slowly. Children low in persistence are often overwhelmed by the amount of work and frustrated if the work is difficult or tedious; they therefore give up easily. Children who are highly distractible have problems focusing on homework, especially if it is demanding or boring. Children who are slow-adapting have a hard time making the transition to homework and resist being told to "do it now"; thus, power struggles result.

The following are some strategies, also summarized in Table 6.2, to use with children with various types of temperament traits.

Sensitive Children   Sensitive children need to decompress after the stimulation of the school day. A quiet time before beginning homework helps. This is especially necessary if something upsetting has happened at school. Because they are sensitive to their surroundings, these children will react more to discomfort than their less sensitive peers. They require a comfortable place to do their homework. Caregivers can keep in mind the child's sensitivities when deciding what best suits the child. Whether the child is sensitive to noise, smells, light, or touch will determine when, where, and how the child does his homework. For example, Arnie, sensitive to noise, odors, and clothes, chose to change into his comfortably soft sweat suit before beginning homework. He liked to work as far away from the kitchen as possible because he disliked cooking smells. His younger brother and sister could

Table 6.2. Some strategies for homework problems according to temperament traits

High sensitivity	High activity	Low adaptability	Low persistence	High distractibility
Schedule quiet time after school and before homework Have a comfortable place to work Break up overwhelming tasks Work with child's area of sensitivity	Release energy before starting Take time to settle down Take regular breaks to expend energy during long projects Use active forms of learning	Have a transition time to start homework Establish a routine for doing homework; involve child in setting the routine Use incentives for completing work	Help child get started Break up homework into smaller parts Be available for help but gradually give child more responsibility for work Use organizational tools Have child take a break when frustrated	Establish a quiet work space Schedule homework when there are fewer family distractions Make a list of tasks Check in to see that child is on task

be noisy, so his parents set up a work space for him in the basement, away from the after-school racket created by his siblings.

Active Children   Active children need to expend some but not too much energy before sitting down for homework. If they become too active, they take longer to settle down. "Settle down time" should be built into active children's homework routines because it is difficult for them to go quickly from active play to sitting still. They also often need a snack because they burn a great deal of energy during the day, and this creates a transition to help them settle down and begin work. During long projects these children need to release energy periodically to allow them to sit still and continue. When possible, using active forms of learning helps the active child expend energy while she learns. For example, the child can learn to do addition or subtraction problems by using beans, or before writing a book report she can act out a favorite scene from the book. The more learning can be "hands on," the better active children respond. With low-activity children who proceed slowly, caregivers must allow them enough time to finish the work and help them set realistic goals for completion.

Slow-Adapting Children   Slow-adapting children do best when there is a routine for doing homework. The child must have definite homework time, and because control is also an issue, the child must be involved in setting that schedule. The routine should not begin too late because as children become more tired, they become less adaptable and more likely to battle about homework. Slow-adapting children also need time to transition from school to home to homework time. An after-school routine can help. It is best if the routine can be the same each day, but this is not always possible because of extracurricular activities. Caregivers and children can agree on a time, write down the homework schedule, and institute an incentive to establish the homework routine. Caregivers can use small, meaningful incentives to encourage the child to complete homework. The child can help decide on the incentives; for example, once the child completes his homework, he can play a computer game or shoot baskets.

Low-Persistence Children   Parents need to provide more initial assistance to children who are low in persistence, and then they can gradually give the child more responsibility for tasks. This process might include going over the homework with the child, agreeing on what needs to be done, and making a plan for completion. Parents also take an active role at first in seeing that the homework is done. They may have to sit with the child to help him get started and then be nearby for questions. Gradually, caregivers can reduce their presence as the child is able to work more on his own. For example, low-persistence Adair always did her homework at the kitchen counter while her mother prepared dinner. Her mother could oversee the progress and be available for questions while not being too involved.

The low-persistence child needs to take breaks to keep frustration from mounting. Parent and child should establish break time before beginning, because the low-persistence child may have difficulty returning from a break to a tedious task, especially if he is also distractible. Frustrating assignments can be divided into parts, and a clock and a timer can be good tools for designating work time and break time. Organizational tools such as calendars, Post-its, and dry erase boards help children stay on task and arrange assignments so that they are not overwhelming. Children feel control if they help choose the tools to manage their work.

Distractible Children   Distractible children need quiet work spaces free from extraneous stimuli. Doing homework in their bedrooms can work for a distractible child if there are no other distractions, but, if she is also low in persistence, it may be difficult to persevere in a room full of toys, away from any help. Parents may need to check in with the child to make sure she is staying on task. Making a list of homework assignments and using other organizational tools can help the child stay focused.

• •

Nine-year-old Chris had problems in the classroom with attention and on the playground with peers. The teacher claimed that he disrupted the class with his antics as class clown and had problems following instructions and finishing work. At recess his peers found him bossy and often did not want to play with him because he lost his temper when things did not go his way. Homework was a constant battle between him and his parents, Barb and Rudy. It was a fight to get him to sit and begin and even more difficult to get him to finish. Chris complained that there was too much homework and it was too hard. If his parents did not sit nearby and help him with each assignment, Chris would not finish. His parents tried having him do homework at different times each day, they tried punishments and rewards, and they tried ignoring the problem. Nothing worked. Chris took more than 2 hours each day to get the work done—and then it was not done very well. Rudy believed he should just sit down, get through it, and be done with it. "In the time he takes whining about it, he could have it done," he asserted. Tempers escalated and the teacher complained of unfinished, poorly done work.

After the teacher expressed concerns about Chris's behavior in the classroom and with peers at a parent–teacher conference, Chris's parents sought help from a local temperament program. A temperament assessment revealed that Chris was low in persistence, distractible, slow adapting, active, and intense. The temperament counselor worked with Chris's parents on homework issues and with the teacher around school issues. Together they worked on the peer issues. In talking with the teacher, the temperament counselor found that Chris's class clown behavior usually occurred during math, his most difficult subject. In the afternoons his attention seemed to wane, and he had more trouble staying on task. As for the peer issues, some days were better than others but there were still altercations, particularly when a game did not go his way.

Because of Chris's slow adaptability, the temperament counselor decided to work on only two issues: homework and his class clown behavior. The approach would be to set up routines to address his slow adaptability, to break up the work because of low persistence, to gradually decrease parental support, and to provide breaks for his high activity level. The temperament counselor believed that getting a handle on homework would give Chris techniques he could use in class during seat work. Rudy's attitude that "Chris should just sit down, get through it and be done with it" did not fit with Chris's low persistence. Further discussion revealed that Rudy was very persistent in contrast to Chris, which made it hard for him to understand that Chris could not stick with an assignment from start to finish without stopping. It was clear that Chris needed breaks to decrease frustration and segmented homework to decrease feeling overwhelmed. Chris and his parents set up a homework routine. Chris was to begin work each day at the same time after school, following a half-hour of free time and a snack. The homework was divided into weekly and daily assignments. At the beginning of the week Rudy would help him to organize the week's work. Each day Barb helped him organize the daily work. She would sit with him to keep him on track and help him to break assignments into steps. For example, Chris broke up a page of math problems by placing a piece of paper over all but the problems he was working on. Chris also used a timer, setting it for 15 minutes of work on one of his assignments. When the buzzer sounded he could take a break, but because Chris was also distractible, he set the timer for a 3-minute break. Then it was time to return to work for another 15 minutes. This gave Chris some control over the work. At first Rudy or Barb had to help Chris organize his work and sit with him, but as the timer became a routine, they could check in with him only at breaks. Eventually, the timer became Chris's monitor and his parents could let him work alone.

To help Chris follow directions, the teacher gave the instructions verbally and then wrote them on the board. This helped Chris stay on track because he often missed the verbal instructions due to his distractibility. The teacher placed his desk in the front row, away from the window, to cut down on visual distractions. Before a desk assignment, the teacher made sure Chris could move around in order to expend some energy, such as collecting papers, erasing the board, or getting up with the entire class to stretch.

In math class Chris became overwhelmed, and his class clown behavior was a way for him to avoid a difficult task. The teacher established an incentive program to keep Chris on task during math. When he worked without disrupting others he received a paper showing a green light. If he disrupted the class, he got a red light. If he had to be warned about his behavior but then controlled himself, he got a yellow light. At home his parents rewarded the green lights with extra time on the computer. Chris was encouraged to break up classroom math tasks as he did at home by covering all but the problems he was doing. He was also assigned a "math buddy," a student Chris liked who did well at math, and whom he could ask for help when he did not understand a problem. His class clown behavior began to decrease.

The counselor addressed the peer issues once the homework and class clown behavior was improving. Chris's parents encouraged a friendship outside of class with a boy who was adaptable and easy for Chris to get along with. This helped ensure a compatible peer for play at recess. Rudy and Barb monitored Chris's intensity at home and worked with him on identifying situations and feelings that triggered it. They coached him to recognize rising intensity and to expend it in constructive ways such as riding his bike, kicking his soccer ball, or running, rewarding him when he succeeded. This helped him with intensity at school. His teacher helped him to identify the games that gave him the most trouble and he stayed away from those as much as possible. The teacher instituted another "green light" incentive program to encourage cooperative behavior and appropriate expression of his intensity. Although there were still problems, his peers were not avoiding Chris as they had before, and because he was able to better regulate his behavior and emotions, he was becoming a better student.

SUMMARY

School-age children have made great strides in their cognitive, social, and physical abilities, and their temperaments contribute to the ways in which these abilities are expressed. Whereas younger children need parents and other adults to help them manage their behavior and regulate their emotions, school-age children are increasingly gaining the capability to manage and regulate themselves. When school-age children understand their temperaments, they begin to realize why they behave in certain ways. With this knowledge they can learn how to avoid difficult situations, modify their reactions, and get along better in school, home, and social environments.

Middle childhood is a time when children are developing more self-control. They spend more time at school and with peers and less time with parents, so it is natural that many of the issues of this age have to do with school, learning, and peers. Because the relationship with parents is changing from early childhood, discipline takes on a different structure. Parents are sharing control more with their children and are able to use reasoning more effectively than before. Children with challenging temperaments need clear, consistent limits and if this has been in place since early childhood, discipline actually becomes easier. If not, working with temperament and setting consistent rules is still effective, but may take longer because caregivers and teachers may be new to this type of interacting and it may be different from what the children are used to.

Because of increased cognitive skills, children are refining their self-concept. Talking to children about temperaments helps them to understand and manage their reactions and behavior better. It also helps them understand differences in others better and provides a basis for learning to improve familial and peer relationships. With understanding comes increased self-regulatory skills and higher self-esteem. Temperament awareness also helps children know their strengths and gives them ways to work with weaknesses. And it provides a nonjudgmental way for everyone in the family to understand each other. Thus, the transition to adolescence is smoother.

Using the Temperament Perspective

CHAPTER 7

Working with Parents

• •

Ginny and Rob came to the temperament counselor with concerns about their 3-year-old son. Ginny explained, "Pierce has always been a challenge. As an infant I could not soothe him easily. He hated having his diaper changed, being dressed, or having a bath, and his terrible twos started at 18 months. He resisted anything new and was so sensitive to changes. Any upset resulted in a tantrum. He still has tantrums and can react aggressively. We are worried that if this behavior continues, he will have no friends, fail in school, and become a real problem in adolescence."

Rob explained that their other children, Anne and Brendan, did not behave this way, and he and Ginny were worried that they had done something wrong. Rob said, "When Pierce was 8 months old, I had to go on a long business trip and it was really hard on Ginny; maybe that made Pierce's behavior worse. I was always a very active parent before that trip. Maybe the separation affected Pierce's attachment. I also worry because my Uncle Tim has schizophrenia, and I heard that he was always 'odd' as a child. What if Pierce inherited that?"

Ginny added, "In my third trimester I drank champagne when we celebrated Rob's promotion. I thought it wouldn't hurt. I know it's bad to drink at all during pregnancy—maybe that affected Pierce. We've tried everything to work with his behavior but nothing helps. It must be our fault or maybe there is something wrong with him."

• •

Parents often seek explanations for their child's problematic behavior when it seems different from that of siblings or other children. They have never encountered a child quite like theirs. At first they assume that the child's behavior is their fault, that they are not good parents. After trying different strategies with no success, they may believe that the problem lies within the child, perhaps a recessive gene for mental illness or a behavior disorder. But a child's behavior is dependent neither on parents' ability nor on the child's genetic make-up alone. Parenting factors influence the child as child characteristics influence parenting. This chapter discusses parenting factors that affect behavior, including parent characteristics, parenting styles, and the effects of temperament on parenting. The discussion continues with differences between parents and ways to provide effective parent guidance to help manage child behavioral issues.

PARENTING INFLUENCES

Different psychological theories propose different parenting techniques for managing child behavior and attaining positive parent–child interactions. A psychoanalytic approach (Freud, 1940), for example, would contend that children form a superego from internalizing their parents' values and that behavior stems from early experience with the parents. Difficulties might be explained by the parent or child's unresolved conflicts or subconscious drives, and the psychoanalyst would help parents resolve these issues. A professional using a cognitive developmental approach (Piaget & Inhelder, 1969) would suggest that parents use discipline or control techniques appropriate for the child's developmental level and examine the ongoing interactions the child has with his or her environment. Professionals advocating a social learning theory (Bandura, 1977) would examine how children learn behaviors through observation and modeling and might recommend that parents model appropriate behavior. Those using a behaviorist approach (Skinner, 1974) would focus on how the child is conditioned to behave in a certain way and would recommend the use of positive and negative reinforcements and punishment. Proponents of a temperament perspective would examine how individual temperament characteristics affect behavior and then seek to create a good fit between a particular child's temperament and his or her environmental contexts.

Belsky (1984) pointed out that factors influencing parenting stem from within the parent, within the child, and from broader social contexts. The parents' characteristics and upbringing affect their parenting. Mature, psychologically healthy parents promote optimal child functioning with attentive, warm, and responsive caregiving. The child contributes his or her own individual characteristics to the relationship, especially temperament traits that make parenting more or less challenging. Temperamentally difficult children can negatively affect parenting functioning (Bates, 1980). Difficult children may elicit less sensitive parenting than easy children because parents have a hard time knowing how to respond appropriately to them. Parents cannot easily read a difficult child's cues or know what triggers the child's negative behavior. After trying many different techniques to no avail, the parent may become discouraged and less involved in attempting to manage negative behavior.

The social context also affects the physical and psychological health of both parent and child, influencing parental functioning. Parents under stress have difficulty dealing with a temperamentally challenging child. For example, the parent who is unemployed and worrying about how to pay the rent and buy groceries may find it more of a challenge to cope with a difficult child than a parent who does not have such stresses. When parents must focus on meeting basic human needs, they are less likely to focus on creating a "good fit" or using techniques specific to a child's temperament. As a result they may respond to their child's difficult behavior with harsh punishment, inattention, or by giving in to the child's demands.

Parents are better able to handle an irritable infant when they have a strong support system (Crockenberg, 1981). When they have the support of friends, relatives, and others in the community, parents are less punitive and restrictive than when there is no support available (Coletta, 1979).

• •

Carol, a single mother of active, intense, slow-adapting, easily frustrated Chloe, often felt at her wits end when trying to manage her daughter after a hard day of work. On particularly difficult days she would call her sister, Bev, or her best friend, Janet. One or the other often would take Chloe for a few hours. This gave Carol a chance to relax, regroup, and prepare for her time with Chloe. Carol could better handle Chloe's behavior when her stress level was reduced.

PARENTING STYLES

Baumrind's landmark studies (1966, 1971) have documented the effects of parental control and warmth on children's behavior. She identified three parenting styles:

- *Authoritarian.* Authoritarian parents exhibit high control and low warmth, attempting to shape children's behaviors with a set of absolute standards. They discourage give and take with their children and often use physical punishment. They expect children to listen and not question or talk back, and they respond to any deviance from their strict rules with punishment such as a spanking.

- *Permissive.* Permissive parents have low control and high warmth, making few demands and allowing children to regulate their own activities as much as possible. They use little punishment. They love their children dearly and have difficulty providing any discipline. They have an "anything goes" attitude and their children are often out of control.

- *Authoritative.* Authoritative parents display high control and high warmth. They encourage give and take with their children, expect self-directing behavior, and guide by explaining the reasons behind their directives, using nonpunitive discipline when necessary. They discuss problems with their children, listening carefully to them and considering what they say. When they need to apply discipline they do so firmly and fairly; however, discipline does not include physical punishment.

Maccoby and Martin (1983) identified a fourth style, uninvolved or neglectful parents, who rated low on control and low on warmth. They are not involved with the child and more concerned with their

Authoritarian parents	Permissive parents
Low warmth, high control	High warmth, low control
Authoritative parents	**Neglectful/Uninvolved parents**
High warmth, high control	Low warmth, low control

Figure 7.1. Matrix of parenting styles showing salient characteristics of warmth and control. (*Sources:* Baumrind, 1966, 1971; Maccoby & Martin, 1983.)

own lives, sometimes to the point of neglect. Figure 7.1 is a matrix that provides a snapshot of each of these parenting styles.

How Children React to Parenting Styles

Children of authoritarian parents typically lack self-esteem, may struggle with poor academic success, are not independent, and tend to react with hostility toward peers when frustrated. Children of permissive parents behave immaturely, have little impulse control, are defiant and demanding, and are easily frustrated by school tasks. Children of authoritative parents are self-confident, self-controlled, follow directions better, interact more, and in general are better adjusted than children of other parenting styles (Baumrind & Black, 1967; Denham, Renwick, & Holt, 1991; Ghosh, 1995; Steinberg, Lamborn, Darling, Mounts, & Dornbusch, 1994). Children of uninvolved or neglectful parents have the poorest adjustment of all and display poor emotional regulation, less social competence, less school achievement, and more behavior problems than the others (Kurdek & Fine, 1994). The ways in which children respond to a particular parenting style depends on their temperaments. A child with an easy temperament has fewer problems with permissive or authoritarian parenting styles than children who have more challenging temperament traits (Braungart-Reiker, Garwood, & Stifter, 1997; Harris, 1998).

Cultural Effects on Parenting Styles

Culture affects parenting styles and discipline practices. The authoritative parenting style is more successful in some cultures than in others (Baumrind, 1997; Steinberg, Dornbusch, & Brown, 1992). In Caucasian and Latino populations, authoritative parenting is related to higher child competence, but for Asian Americans and African Americans this is not always the case. These cultures view authoritarian discipline as a sign of concern on the parents' part (Landy, 2002). In Asian American cultures, strong peer support seems to balance the effects of harsh authoritarian discipline. In the African American culture, mild physical discipline may be viewed as parental caring, and in dangerous, violent neighborhoods, strict enforcement of rules helps to keep children safe (Baumrind, 1997).

OTHER PARENTING STYLES

Chess and Thomas (1987) describe six different parenting styles that they have encountered in their clinical work: *secure, insecure, intimidated, over-interpretive, victimized,* and *pathological.* Although different from the parenting styles of Baumrind (1971) and Maccoby and Martin (1983), some similarities can be found.

Secure parents feel confident in their responsibilities as parents. They can change if they make mistakes, and they see parenting as a self-fulfilling endeavor. These parents are similar to authoritative parents in that they can work with their child to improve parent–child interactions. Unlike authoritarian parents, they can recognize their mistakes and change the methods they use.

Insecure parents feel that parenting is an ordeal and any difficulty with the child is their fault. They fail to recognize temperament as a factor. For example, they believe that their child's tantrums are due to their inadequacies as parents rather than to a temperament trait such as low frustration tolerance.

The intimidated parent, like the permissive parent, cannot say "no" and stick to it. These parents may feel guilty for spending little time with the child because of work schedules, or the parent may not want to deal with the child's loud, intense reactions, so they give in to the child's demands.

The over-interpretive parent creates complex psychological explanations for the child's behavior. For example, the parent might interpret a child's slow-to-warm-up behavior as an anxiety disorder.

Victimized parents follow all parenting instructions diligently to guarantee a healthy, well-adjusted child, yet they may still experience problems because of the child's temperament. For example, the active child who constantly explores and resists sitting quietly interferes with the parents' plans of having a predictable household. They feel that the child deliberately tries to antagonize them, and they feel anger rather than understanding.

The pathological parent has a psychiatric problem that interferes with parenting. For example, a depressed mother who has difficulty responding to her child's cues and a low-intensity child who is not very expressive may have particular problems getting needs met.

Not all parenting styles are equally effective in child rearing. Parents who are flexible and willing to learn different methods can change their style to fit better with their child. Authoritative or secure parents have an easier time making necessary changes that fit best with their child's temperament; authoritarian parents have a more difficult time doing this. Their philosophy of children obeying immediately does not fit with slow-adapting, persistent, or intense children. Permissive or intimidated parents have difficulty setting limits and following through, especially with slow-adapting, persistent, or intense children. Flexible children can adapt to many different approaches. They are not likely to come to blows with authoritarian parents nor do they try to control permissive parents. Temperamentally challenging children engage in power struggles with authoritarian parents and tend to control permissive parents.

Clinicians and other professionals can work more effectively with parents when they understand the interaction between child temperament and parenting styles, and they are less likely to attribute problematic behavior to pathology. Professionals can determine a parent's parenting style by discussing how the parent approaches discipline and sets limits. They can examine the kinds of interactions the parent has with children during limit setting and learn about the parent's philosophy of child rearing. Parents who have a rigid, firm style of setting limits likely take an authoritarian stance, whereas parents who have difficulty setting limits and sticking with them are typically permissive. When temperament professionals explain to parents how certain parenting styles interact with certain temperaments, parents can consider moderating their styles to accommodate a better fit with their child's temperament. Parents are less likely to misinterpret the child's behavior as their fault or as intentional when they know about this interaction. With the clinician's help they can work on creating a positive match between their parenting style and their child's temperament by gradually shifting to a more or less rigid parenting style according to their need.

CHILD TEMPERAMENT AND PARENTING STYLES

Children interact with each parent in a unique way, according to their temperament and to the parents' styles. Kochanska (1995) examined the relationship between different parenting styles, child temperament, and compliance. She categorized parenting styles into *gentle guidance, controlling,* and *forceful,* and examined which style promoted internalization and compliance with fearful, anxiety-prone children and fearless, non–anxiety-prone children. Fearful children internalized self-control better with mothers who used gentle discipline than with those who used harsh methods. Nonfearful children complied and internalized best with parents who were patient and understanding and who worked with the child to achieve mutual goals rather than those who used harsh or gentle discipline (Kochanska, 1995).

Parents of fearful children often feel that they must protect them from potentially upsetting situations. When the child reacts negatively to new situations and people, some parents shield them from any novelty. Arcus (2001) showed that highly reactive infants whose mothers protected them from minor stresses and placed few limits on them became increasingly inhibited as toddlers, whereas mothers who set firm limits helped their highly reactive infants become less inhibited. Overprotective parents may cause children to be submissive or dependent and prevent them from acquiring essential coping strategies (Rubin, Burgess, & Hastings, 2002; Rubin, Hastings, Stewart, Henderson, & Chen, 1997). When parents of fearful children showed acceptance, provided adequate limits, and discouraged behavioral withdrawal, they helped their children move toward independence (Belsky, Rha, & Park, 2000; van Bakel & Riksen-Walraven, 2002). Children who are sensitive or fearful may have increased anxiety with harsh or authoritarian parents (Aron, 2002; Kochanska, 1995); however, extremely reactive infants became inhibited regardless of the extent of maternal limit setting (Arcus & Gardner, 1993).

Being very shy or inhibited can cause a child to exhibit with-drawing behavior, but parents who deride or criticize a child in front of others can also cause social withdrawal and poor self-concept (Bar-ber, Olson, & Shagle, 1994). In one study, when participating mothers were psychologically controlling or derisive, their already inhibited toddlers became socially reticent at age 4 (Rubin et al., 2002). Fearful fourth- and fifth-grade boys whose parents used harsh discipline had higher incidences of teacher-related aggression than either fearful chil-dren with gentle parents or fearless children with harsh parents (Colder, Lochman, & Wells, 1997). This supports Kochanska's (1995) findings that fearful children do better with gentle parental discipline.

The ways in which parents respond to their difficult children de-termines the kinds of behavior that their children develop. In another study, mothers who could successfully read and respond to their tem-peramentally difficult 9-month-olds' cues reported that when their chil-dren reached the age of 2 years old they had developed good self-control (Feldman, Greenbaum, & Yirmiya, 1999). Children with difficult tem-peraments are less compliant than those who have easy temperaments, and, in turn, noncompliant children elicit less-supportive parenting (Mirsky, Dodge, & Schiller, 1999). This indicates that temperament characteristics may affect a child's behavior, how the child processes socialization messages, and the methods that parents employ. For ex-ample, slow-adapting children may not comply with parents who ex-pect immediate responses because these children cannot make transi-tions quickly. In response to this noncompliance, parents may then use harsh means to get what they want or they may disengage, depending on their parenting style.

Children who are resistant to control or strong-willed are, in tem-perament terms, negatively persistent, slow-adapting, and intense. These children have greater difficulty with either permissive or authoritarian parents. When they have permissive parents who set few limits, these children tend to control the household because they are allowed to regulate their own activities. They also resist the control of authori-tarian parents and become increasingly noncompliant, which results in power struggles and the possibility of harsh punishment.

Certain parenting styles combined with particular child tempera-ments can result in behavior problems. First and second graders who scored high in irritable distress (similar to negative mood) and who had psychologically controlling mothers (e.g., verbally controlling) developed internalizing behavior problems such as anxiety, whereas similar children who had hostile mothers (e.g., intimidating, aggressive, antagonistic) developed externalizing problems such as acting out and aggression. Children who had difficulty controlling their behavior and had hostile mothers also demonstrated externalizing behavior (Morris et al., 2002). Children resistant to control acted out, had aggressive behavior, and were more likely to develop behavior problems later if their mothers exerted little control than those who had mothers who implemented higher control (Bates, Pettit, Dodge, & Ridge, 1998). Bates and colleagues commented that if parents are consistent with their limits, this may reduce early unmanageability in their children. With nonresistant children, the use of parental restriction predicted an increased number of behavior problems whereas the use of few restrictions predicted fewer problems. The effects of any negative parenting can accentuate difficulties with children who are temperamentally vulnerable or challenging.

Harris (1998) concluded that parenting style can produce changes in the child's expression of temperament traits. She found that high-energy infants who had authoritarian parents became more moderate in their energy as toddlers than did infants of other parents. Slow-adjusting toddlers became increasingly aggressive if they had authoritarian parents, whereas slow-adjusting infants with authoritative parents became more adaptable by toddlerhood. Harris's findings suggest that highly energetic children require the firm limits that authoritarian parents provide, but slow-adjusting children need the patience, understanding, and boundaries of authoritative parents.

EFFECTS OF PARENTS' TEMPERAMENTS ON CHILDREN

Parents also must consider their own temperaments in relation to their children's. As Chess and Thomas pointed out, "The child's psychological development is not determined by the parents' style alone, or by the child's style alone, but by the match or mismatch between the two" (1987, p. 53).

Layne, a spontaneous, fun-loving parent, tried to make life interesting for Alena, her 5-year-old daughter. She would announce, "Today we are riding our bikes to school instead of driving." Alena would howl in protest. After a day at the beach, Layne would decide spontaneously that a pizza and a movie might be fun and Alena would collapse in a tantrum. Layne could not understand why Alena would protest these enjoyable activities. Alena was slow-adapting, whereas Layne was highly adaptable. When Layne learned of their differences, she understood Alena's reactions. Layne had difficulty suppressing her spontaneous nature, but she learned to prepare Alena for changes and to keep daily life routine.

Steven insisted that his son Mikos complete a chore from beginning to end. Mikos took a very long time and used a circuitous route to finish. He often became frustrated by the chore. Steven approached his work with focus that did not wane until he completed the task, no matter how long it took. Steven was highly persistent, and Mikos was distractible and not persistent. Steven was relieved to learn that their differences had to do with temperament and did not reveal an attention problem. He now understood that Mikos would approach tasks differently than he did but could still get the job done when he did the chore in parts.

Parental expectations for behavior must correspond to the child's temperament. When parents expect more than the child is capable of, it can cause anxiety, defiance, or acting out, depending on the child's temperament. Parents who have similar temperament traits as their children can also have problems. For example, an intense child who has an intense parent becomes increasingly intense as the parent's intensity rises. If the parent also is authoritarian in parenting style, this combination can result in harsh punishment. If the parent's style is permissive, the child's intensity may dominate the parent, who then retreats from setting limits.

A mismatch between parent and child temperament can cause battles and frustration, as well. Combined with parenting style, the mismatch increases. If Layne is permissive, she will give in to Alena's protests and feel victimized or insecure. If Steven is authoritarian, he will insist that Mikos finish as he expects him to, punish him if he does not, and become involved in numerous power struggles. Once Layne and Steven understand the interplay of their parenting styles, their own temperaments, and their children's temperaments, they see that they are being neither victimized nor defied. They can then adjust their typical reactions to create a better fit with their children. Layne did this by becoming more structured with her daughter and saving her spontaneity for her friends, and Steven became less rigid about tasks, allowing Mikos to do them in parts and to take necessary breaks.

PARENTS WHO HAVE DIFFERENT PARENTING STYLES

Ideally, parents present a united front with their children. But parents with different parenting styles often disagree about how to handle an issue. This confuses children about discipline and causes them to test limits, ignore requests, or try to control the situation in an attempt to make sense of the parental differences. In one study, conflict between parents led to children's acting-out behavior (Emery, 1982). In another study, different parenting styles affected children's ability to concentrate (Kaplan, 1991). Specifically, when preschoolers experienced differences in their parents' warmth, their ability to focus attention was compromised.

Parents who differ in parenting styles often disagree when they have a temperamentally challenging child. If one parent is permissive and the other is strict, they may blame each other for the child's behavior. The permissive parent believes the difficulties arise because the strict parent is too rigid, while the strict parent thinks the permissive parent's tolerance causes the problems. Each begins to compensate for the other's behavior. The strict parent becomes firmer and the permissive parent more accommodating. Soon they are polarized and far away from any possibility of a united front.

Besides becoming polarized, parents of temperamentally challenging children sometimes go from one extreme of parenting to another. The permissive parent may accommodate his or her child until pushed to the limit and then suddenly react as an authoritarian. One mother explained, "I try to be patient, but then Zara gets me to the point that I explode or sometimes punish her. Then I feel horrible, apologize, and let her do what she wants because I feel guilty." This "flip-flop" parenting is particularly detrimental for children who need structure and clear limits. When they do not know what to expect, they continually test their parents to see where they stand.

Based on an idea by James Cameron and our work with hundreds of children and their parents, my colleagues and I came to define parenting as a continuum with both parenting extremes, authoritarian and permissive, on either end and with the authoritative style in the middle (Kristal, Neville, & Renner, 1994). Once parents identify which end of the continuum most characterizes their styles, they can begin to move more toward the middle. The clinician can help parents acknowledge their parenting differences and what changes they must make in order to gradually move toward the middle and approach their children's behavioral issues together. Authoritarian parents can learn what they must do to become more accommodating, and permissive parents can identify ways in which they can become more structured.

PARENT GUIDANCE

The relationship between children and their parents is crucial to children's healthy social and emotional adjustment. Parents and other caregivers have numerous opportunities each day to interact with children in warm, accepting ways (Maccoby & Martin, 1983) and to convey expectations for appropriate behavior. Clinicians can provide guidance to help parents understand temperament issues, change their interactions with their children, and thereby change the child's behavior. Besides clinicians, a wide range of professionals such as educators, physicians, nurses, and child care providers can utilize the parent guidance model in which the child's temperament is assessed, advice is individualized to each child's temperament, and the goal is to achieve goodness of fit (Chess & Thomas, 1986). Parent guidance increases competence and can prevent the development of problems when used

Parent guidance can be very effective when

- Parents can see the effects of temperament on their child's behavior
- Clinicians acknowledge the parents' successes as well as areas needing improvement
- Clinicians illustrate clearly where goodness and poorness of fit exist
- Parents acknowledge goodness and poorness of fit in the child's environment
- Clinicians provide clear behavior strategies that parents can easily follow
- Parents are willing to adjust their responses according to the child's temperament
- Parents recognize the role their own temperament plays in interactions
- Parents closely follow the strategies suggested by the clinician
- Parents realize that change may not occur immediately—it takes time and perseverance

• • • • • • • • • • • • • • •

before negative behavior patterns have set in.

Parents often have many issues they want to work on. Together the parents and the clinician typically choose one or two issues, and the clinician provides a behavior plan for parents depending on the child's temperament (at this point the clinician may talk to the parents about their temperaments or may decide to wait until later, depending on each individual case). The parents implement the suggested behavior strategies and after 2 or 3 weeks, they meet again with the clinician to report on their progress. The clinician can fine-tune strategies as needed or begin to work on additional issues. Parent guidance makes parents therapeutic allies in their child's treatment—colleagues going after the same goal. Because parents can implement interventions on a daily basis, any significant amount of positive parental change has a profound effect on the child (Chess & Thomas, 1986). Beneficial changes occur quickly, which encourages parents to continue their efforts and also prevents the need for long-term, expensive treatment. If psychotherapy is needed, concurrent parent guidance can expedite treatment.

ENSURING SUCCESSFUL PARENT GUIDANCE

Clinicians first assess the child's temperament through a temperament questionnaire, observation, or both. They then interview the parents to obtain a history of the behavior issue. After they complete the assessment, the clinician provides parent guidance. Chess and Thomas (1986) summarized six steps for clinicians to ensure successful parent guidance:

1. *Assure the parents that nothing is wrong with the child but that the fit between child and parent determines the behavioral issues.* The clinician can refer to the assessment and explain how temperament relates to the child's behavior and how such behavior is typical for a child with these temperament characteristics.

2. *Identify the areas of poor fit between child and parent or the environment and provide strategies to create a good fit.* The clinician and parents can examine the environment(s) in which the behavioral issues take place and determine the goodness or poorness of fit. It helps to find areas in which parents have a good fit with the child so that the parents realize they can succeed. Focusing only on poor fit can be counterproductive.

3. *Help the parents set priorities as to which behaviors to work on.* For parents of children with very challenging temperaments, choose an issue with which they will most likely have success. Once they realize they can successfully manage a problem, they will readily undertake the next issue.

4. *Individualize the guidance for each child and family.* Even with children who have similar temperaments, parent guidance will vary according to each parent's needs and situation.

5. *Outline an overall plan but advise parents to begin with only one or two issues.* Parents will have more success if they do not undertake too many issues. The more difficult the child's temperament, the fewer issues the parents should attempt. They will find it easier to be consistent and they will become less frustrated if they purposefully work on only one or two problems.

6. *Schedule a follow-up session to fine-tune strategies and continue with the outlined plan.* At times a strategy will work for a while and then need modifying, especially with slow-adapting children. Clinicians can help parents make the necessary strategy changes to achieve success and continue to work on the issues.

In addition to these six steps, counselors can also help parents identify their parenting style and learn about their own temperaments. Because

Parent guidance is not effective when

- Parents believe the child must change
- Parents do not recognize the child's temperament
- Parents expect the clinician to "fix" the problem
- Clinicians do not make clear where goodness and poorness of fit exist
- The behavior strategies the clinician suggests are vague or are not easy to follow
- Parents refuse to adjust their responses according to the child's temperament
- Parents do not stick with behavior strategies long enough for change to occur
- The problem is more than temperament

• • • • • • • • • • • • • • • •

parents often feel guilty and question their abilities, counselors should gradually address these issues separately. Explaining the child's temperament first removes the guilt from the insecure parent, creates understanding for victimized and over-interpretive parents, and helps establish control for the intimidated parent. While explaining the profile, the clinician can explore similarities and differences between child and parent to get an idea of the parent's temperament. Parenting style becomes apparent when discussing approaches to discipline. Parents leave the session with a better understanding about themselves as well as their children.

WHEN PARENT GUIDANCE FAILS

Parent guidance is not always successful because parents sometimes do not follow advice due to their parenting styles or temperaments. One authoritarian parent told the counselor, "When my parents told me to do something, I did it, no questions asked. I expect the same of my son, temperament or not." There was little the counselor could do to change his mind because he expected the child to accommodate his needs. In contrast, a permissive parent has problems setting limits or acting consistently. One parent said, "I know I should stick to what I say, but I can't stand to hear her cry." Both these parents have difficulty following advice if it goes against their parenting style.

Parental temperament can also negatively affect the outcome of parent guidance. Slow-adapting parents have trouble altering their usual responses because they have difficulty with change. They need to make small changes and work on only one issue at a time. Low-persistence parents become frustrated when they do not obtain quick results and may give up too quickly when trying an approach. They also have problems working on too many things at once, so breaking up what they need to do and taking one part at a time encourages success. Intense parents need to learn to tone down their reactions, especially if they have an intense child. This takes time and they must learn to identify what triggers their own intensity. Distractible parents get sidetracked from their behavioral goals, so focusing on one or two issues with few instructions works best. Sensitive parents may take difficulties personally or they may have trouble with particularly loud, intense children. One pediatrician recommended earplugs to help sensitive parents get through tantrums. Encouragement and reassurance helps these parents to look for small successes and know that they are on the right track.

Chess and Thomas (1986) outlined six issues that may account for the failure of parent guidance. Specifically, they noted that a child's behavior will not change

1. If parents make no change in their behavior

2. When a parent refuses to see his or her style as a poor fit, believes the child should accommodate to his or her behavior, and does not cooperate, as with the authoritarian parent

3. When a parent accepts all the recommended strategies and agrees to undertake them, but for one reason or another never uses them

4. If the parent expects the clinician to fix the problem, does not want to do any work, and may request medication to change the child's behavior

5. If the parent does not listen to the clinician and decides that nothing can be done to change the child's behavior. One parent told her husband after a temperament consultation, "That's just the way Alma is. We can't change her."

6. If the problem is more than temperament or is not temperament related. This may be the case when parents do make changes but the child's behavior does not change. These parents need a referral to another professional such as a physician or child therapist for further assessment, and other approaches might be needed.

Sena's son George, 5 years old, had sleeping problems. He frequently said he was scared to go to sleep and howled in protest when his parents put him to bed. He would wake several times each night and call out for his parents. His mother usually ended up sleeping with him because he did not want to be alone. His parents turned to temperament counseling for help. George's father, Hank, said he thought George was too old for "this nonsense" and should be locked in his room at night. Sena noted that George was an anxious, sensitive boy and needed reassurance. George's temperament profile indicated high sensitivity, high intensity, and slow adaptability.

The temperament counselor outlined a simple plan that established a bedtime routine, provided George with some support using a transitional object, and gradually gave him more responsibility for getting back to sleep on his own. The routine appealed to Hank because it was structured. Sena had difficulty with it because George resisted a different routine, but he eventually appeared to accept it.

After three sessions nothing had changed. The bedtime routine had not been established because Sena found it hard to stay on track. Hank became more rigid about bedtime and Sena worried about George's fears. They became increasingly polarized and hostile. The temperament counselor knew that if each parent could move slightly closer to a middle-ground approach, they could make effective changes. But neither parent would shift views and nothing changed due to their differences in parenting style and their own temperaments. Hank was persistent to the point of rigidity, and Sena's low persistence made it difficult for her to follow through. Sessions dissolved into bitter arguments between them. Temperament counseling failed to solve the sleep issue. The counselor suggested that they see a marriage counselor before trying parent guidance again.

Parent guidance also fails when parents wait too long to address issues.

• •

Fran and Paul came to the temperament specialist for help with their 12-year-old daughter Anna, who was argumentative, noncompliant, and negative. Fran said that Anna had been strong-willed since she was 2 years old but Fran had thought she would outgrow it. Things had only become worse, and Fran described a typical incident: When Fran told Anna that breakfast was ready, Anna came to the table and said, "Breakfast is not ready, there is no cereal in my bowl." Fran said, "You just have to pour in the cereal and milk." Anna would insist that breakfast was not ready and that her mother had lied. The more Fran tried to explain her point, the more Anna argued until Fran would dissolve in tears and eventually apologize to Anna. Paul described similar interactions with Anna. Both parents said they always tried not to upset Anna and consequently set very few limits.

Anna's temperament profile showed slow adaptability, high persistence, and high intensity. The counselor suggested techniques for working with her adaptability such as establishing rules and routines at home with Anna's help, and having incentives for following the rules and consequences for ignoring the rules. The counselor then made a follow-up appointment.

When Fran and Paul returned, they reported that no change had occurred and they were having difficulty putting any techniques into effect because of Anna's resistance. They described several new behavioral incidents and wanted the counselor to meet with Anna to make her understand that she had to change. But this was no longer a temperament problem. The negative behavior patterns that had developed over the years had turned into a family systems problem and made family therapy necessary. If Paul and Fran had started working with Anna's temperament at age 2, they might have prevented the need for family counseling at age 12.

• •

For the most part, parent guidance provides fast, effective ways of managing behavior when parents are willing to work together and make changes to improve fit. It can prevent problems by helping parents know what to expect. Once parents understand how temperament affects behavior, they can prepare for potentially problematic situations and prevent behavioral triggers. They can address current problems by using strategies that fit with the child's temperament. And, when treatment is needed, parent guidance can shorten treatment time when used in addition to therapy. For example, if Anna's family were to work with a therapist, the temperament counselor could still help provide specific strategies for working with Anna's problematic behavior. Knowing that Anna is slow-adapting could help both the counselor and therapist understand the need to go slowly with change, and the temperament counselor could provide specific strategies for working with breakfast-time problems.

Thus, clinicians can provide temperament guidance in various ways. Many parents prefer individual parent guidance, as described previously. Most issues can be resolved in two to three sessions (Chess & Thomas, 1986). Temperament counselors working in private practice or in medical centers reported that one to three sessions resolved 95% of cases (J.R. Cameron, personal communication, November 15, 1999).

In summary, a temperament specialist talks to the parents about the child's problems and explains about temperament and parent guidance. If the problem sounds temperament-related, the specialist gives the parents a temperament questionnaire to complete. After scoring the questionnaire the counselor schedules an appointment to discuss the results with the parents and devises an individualized behavior plan for the family. After the parents have begun the plan, they schedule a follow-up session in which the counselor modifies the plan as needed or addresses other issues. The length of guidance depends on the extent of the problems. Parents who have long-standing problems or who want ongoing support may need several sessions.

• •

Thea's 7-year-old daughter Maya was unmanageable. Problems had increased as Thea had developed a pattern of accommodating Maya's fears and demands. Now Maya had sleep issues, and her parents and child care provider were having discipline problems with Maya. Because of Maya's reactions to anything new and Thea's difficulty with consistency, the counselor decided bi-weekly sessions would be best so that they could get into a regular routine. They worked slowly on each issue, giving Maya time to adjust to new limits and Thea time to practice consistency. Maya's child care provider came to several sessions to create consistency between home and child care. After four sessions, the fit between Maya's behavior and the expectations of her mother and her child care provider improved considerably. Thea decreased her appointments to once a month for 3 months, then to every 6 weeks, until finally she only came in on an as-needed basis.

TEMPERAMENT PARENTING PROGRAMS

Parenting programs are a cost-effective way to prevent the development of behavior problems. They have proven effective in reducing behavior problems, especially for children with conduct disorders (O'Dell et al., 1982; Webster-Stratton, Hollingsworth, & Kolpacoff, 1989). They have been used successfully with families in medical settings (Gross, 1995; Melvin, 1995) and with inner-city families (McClowry, 1995b; McClowry & Galehouse, 2002). Temperament-based parent programs through family agencies, community organizations, and medical centers offer temperament assessments, consultation, and education. Services range from parenting classes and support groups to training programs for parents, Internet support groups and bulletin boards, and programs for at-risk children. Parents of challenging children learn of these programs through pediatricians, therapists, schools, child care providers, friends, or advertisements (including telephone directories under the categories of parenting, social services, or counseling).

SUPPORT GROUPS

Parents of temperamentally challenging children find support groups valuable because they often have felt alone (Turecki & Tonner, 2000). Being with other parents who experience similar problems offers a sense of security and camaraderie. These groups also provide a chance for parents to share knowledge about strategies that have worked with their children. Some groups focus on specific temperament types, such as parents of "spirited" children (Kurcinka, 1998a, 1998b) or highly sensitive or inhibited children (Aron, 2002). Other groups encourage the involvement of parents of children with any temperament type or types, even if the children vary greatly. This gives parents a chance to see the broad range of temperaments, and they often come up with innovative strategies for parents whose children differ from their own.

Facilitators set up support groups depending on their style, the mix of participants, and the groups' goals. Some groups are highly structured, whereas others have little structure. For example, one educator runs a group for parents of "spirited" children in which sleep problems are the focus and parents keep detailed sleep journals on their children. Another group tackles any issue that comes up. Parents in these support groups feel a special bond to one another because of their similar parenting problems, and many continue to meet on their own after the group has ended.

Turecki started one of the first support groups for parents of difficult children in The Difficult Child Program at Beth Israel Medical Center in New York (Turecki, 1989). Parents involved in his program found support groups extremely helpful in learning to deal with a difficult child (Turecki & Tonner, 2000). Sheeber and Johnson (1994) based their group parent-training program on the goodness of fit concept to help parents develop an understanding of their child's temperament and increase goodness of fit between parent and child. The group met weekly for $1^1/_2$- to 2-hour sessions for 9 weeks. During the group's first few sessions parents discussed their experiences and concerns about parenting a difficult child. Subsequent sessions centered on teaching parents techniques for managing temperament-related problems. At the end of each session, parents decided on the techniques they would use during the coming week. They discussed how those strategies had worked at the beginning of the next session. Mothers who participated in the parent training experienced increased parenting competence and better satisfaction with their parent–child relationship, and they reported that their children had fewer internalizing and externalizing behavior problems as a result.

Another facilitator described her group, which had six members who met once a week for $1^1/_2$ hours for 8 weeks. She accepted parents into the group who had children about the same age with challenging temperaments. Prior to the first session, each member completed a temperament questionnaire, and during the first session the group discussed the profiles and listed all of the issues they wanted to address. At the start of each meeting the facilitator briefly addressed the week's topic and how it related to temperament but kept the sessions loosely structured, providing ample time for discussion. The group also discussed the parents' temperaments in relation to their ability to carry out strategies and their goodness of fit with their children. At the end of each meeting, the group decided which issue to focus on for the next meeting depending on the group's need.

Another group met every week in a child care facility for children of toddler and preschool age. The parents began each meeting by playing with their children to help them adjust to separating from their parents. The children were left with child care providers when the parents went into an adjacent meeting room for discussion. The playroom had a one-way window so parents could observe their children during the class while the group leader pointed out aspects of child behavior, development, and temperament.

Although this was an example of a very sophisticated group that incorporates child observation and child care, other parenting groups offer child care so that parents can attend easily. Parents who lack child care or single parents who want to attend a night group without leaving their child at home need on-site child care or may need to enlist support from friends or family members.

Parent groups and parenting classes reach a large number of people at one time. Organizations that do not have the time or budgets to provide individual parent guidance can use groups or classes as a cost-effective way to disseminate temperament information. The classes also provide support for the participants who may feel alone in managing their challenging children.

Different kinds of temperament programs provide various services for parents. Three types of parenting programs provided by Kaiser Permanente, for example, are preventive programs, consulting programs, and parenting classes.

Preventive Programs Preventive programs help parents understand their young children's individuality before any potential problems arise. The age groups served by Kaiser's programs included infants ($4^{1}/_{2}$–12 months old), toddlers (12 months–$2^{1}/_{2}$ years old) and preschoolers (3–5 years old). Parents complete a temperament questionnaire and receive information concerning their child's temperament by mail, through the Internet, by telephone, or in person. Preventive programs aim to educate parents about behaviors that are typical for their child's temperament and provide anticipatory guidance for issues that may occur. Parents may receive individual counseling and temperament information if they request it, and individual or telephone follow-up is provided as needed.

Consult Programs Consult programs provide counseling for parents who currently have temperament-related problems with their children (from infants through age 12) or who seek to understand their children better. Parents are usually referred to such a program by a professional or they seek it out on their own. After completing a temperament questionnaire on their child, parents are provided with individual consultation with a temperament counselor in person or by telephone. Parents then receive a profile and an individualized behavioral program and follow up as needed.

Parenting Classes Parenting classes and groups provide temperament information through an educational format on various subjects such as discipline, limits, temperament, and socialization. A temperament questionnaire is used and follow-up groups and classes are provided as needed. Temperament-based parenting classes teach basic parenting skills in a classroom setting from a temperament point of view. Class formats vary. Usually a series of classes covers various subjects. Temperament-based classes range from drop-in classes of single sessions, each dealing with different topics, to 4- to 8-week series. Some classes require students to complete temperament questionnaires on their children, and others do less formal assessments or merely discuss the concepts. Some classes focus on certain temperament types or ages while others focus on any child at any age. For example, Temperament-Based Parenting Classes developed for Kaiser Permanente (Kristal, Neville, & Renner, 1994) are a series of six classes that cover basic temperament concepts, goodness of fit, parenting style, discipline, setting limits, communication, and socialization. Parents commit to all six classes, which last 2 hours each with homework each week. Lecture, group activities, and videos make up the class format.

PARENTS AS TEMPERAMENT SPECIALISTS

One unique community-based program, The Temperament Program, had mental health professionals train and supervise parents in providing temperament information to other parents (Smith, 1994). Parents were hired and trained as temperament specialists based on their parenting experience, their capability to help others, and the fact that they had a difficult child of their own. Because the trained parent specialists had the advantage of understanding other parents' situations, they could help the parents build strategies around the child's unique temperament and could make referrals to professional resources when necessary.

Parents entered the program because of concerns about their child's behavior. Many parents of difficult children have had negative experiences with professionals who provided generic parenting advice that did not work, so this parent program provided a bridge between parents and professionals. The temperament specialist met weekly with one or both parents for 45 minutes. Program length varied according to need, with some parents completing it in 4 weeks and others needing as much as a year.

The program consisted of four phases. The detailed assessment of phase one included a child behavior inventory, a parent interview, assessment strategies, and parent exercises. Phase two strengthened the parent–child relationship by identifying the child's strengths and exploring the fit between the parents' temperaments and expectations and the child's individual needs. In the third phase, the temperament specialist determined a plan to manage the presenting issues, helped parents work out parenting differences, and provided emotional support. If necessary, the specialist made referrals to other services or consulted the child's teachers or other professionals involved with the child. The final phase provided follow-up to the parents when new issues arose.

A review of program outcomes showed parental satisfaction: 93% of participants found the program helpful and 88% reported that they used the concepts often (Smith, 1994). This program went on to develop a temperament training curriculum, Temperament Talk (Goodman, Zukin, Tyler, & Shick, 1995). This course trains facilitators to work with parents, individuals, or groups and can be used in the workplace.

INSIGHTS into Children's Temperaments: An Intervention for Children, Parents, and Teachers

A program called "INSIGHTS into Children's Temperaments" (McClowry, Snow, & Tamis-LeMonda, 2004) provides interventions for disadvantaged minority children, their parents, and their teachers. The program aims to change the interpersonal dynamics between children and caregivers in order to improve goodness of fit, reduce behavior problems, decrease parental distress, and increase children's self-perceptions. INSIGHTS seeks to prevent conflict between children and adults and negative behavior patterns by changing the underlying perceptions about what causes behavior.

INSIGHTS consists of three integrated parent, teacher, and children's programs. Parents and teachers meet separately for 2 hours a week for 10 weeks with trained facilitators who lead sessions that include instruction, videotaped vignettes, role playing, discussion, and homework. The videotapes show children with different temperaments reacting to daily situations and strategies that teachers and parents can use in managing issues.

The children's program uses puppets to represent different temperaments: Coretta the Cautious hesitates with new situations and people and warms up slowly; Gregory the Grumpy reacts negatively to change, gets upset easily, and is very active; Frederico the Friendly is social and eager to try new things; and Hillary the Hardworker is industrious but also can be stubborn. Children learn in the classroom about themselves and about problem solving through dramas involving the puppets. Stories using the puppets portray how children of various temperaments react differently and provide the children with skills to handle difficult situations and relationships. When compared with an attention control group, INSIGHTS was effective in reducing the behavior problems of children who were at diagnostic levels of disruptive disorders and for children whose behavior problems were below diagnostic levels (McClowry et al., 2004).

ON-LINE PARENTING GROUPS

On-line computer parenting groups provide another resource for parents to connect with each other and get information about their temperamentally challenging children. This approach overcomes geographical boundaries when parents have difficulty attending groups. In addition, parents can participate at their convenience and they do not need child care in order to attend. An on-line temperament group gives parents another way to counteract their feeling of isolation. Those with time, motivation, and familiarity with the Internet will find these groups most useful.

Kaiser Permanente tested an on-line parenting group and studied the feasibility of this format (Cameron et al., 2002). Two temperament counselors moderated the pilot group of 36 parents from four different facilities. All parents had temperamentally challenging children, the majority being high energy and low adjusting. All had previously attended a parenting class or seen a temperament counselor. Prior to registering for the group, parents had provided descriptions of their child's temperament or a temperament profile and had received advice tailored to their child's individual temperament.

The site had three initial topics for participants: how to navigate the site, current behavioral problems, and positive family interactions. Parents received help with specific issues but also could comment on improvement or successful strategies. They could post a question or comment and receive information from a moderator or feedback from a parent who had coped with a similar issue. These issues generated sub-topics such as sleep for the moderators to address. Moderators also shifted the discussion when necessary and introduced general developmental information. Parents also could search for specific issues and read past advice and discussions.

Some parents were very active participants, posting many issues and comments. Others posted nothing but viewed the issues and advice. The follow-up data showed that 89% of parents found the advice from moderators helpful and 62% said the discussion group provided them with information and support that they could not get elsewhere.

Those who used the online discussion group the most reported high satisfaction, whereas those who participated least were less satisfied.

SUMMARY

Parents benefit from temperament information whether they receive it individually from therapists or temperament specialists, in support groups, parenting classes, or on-line discussion groups. All venues provide opportunities to discuss children's behavioral issues as they relate to temperament and parenting style and provide methods for working with temperament-related behavioral issues. They all can change ineffective or dysfunctional parent–child patterns. All temperament guidance resources offer parents support and increase competence by developing individual behavior strategies to enhance parent–child relationships. Parents understand themselves better by learning about their own temperament and parenting style. They learn how their children respond to their environments according to their temperaments. Parents can then change their assumptions about the causes of problem behavior and change their responses, thereby improving goodness of fit.

CHAPTER 8

Temperament and Child Care

· ·

Mariam started attending child care when she was 6 months old. Her parents had carefully chosen a child care center with a large caregiver-to-child ratio, loving care, and an enriching environment. Yet, 4 months later, she still cried when her parents left and fussed most of the day unless one particular caregiver held her. She did not nap regularly and woke easily, and she protested feeding except from one caregiver. This made it difficult for her to fit into the center schedule. She did not easily accept procedures such as diaper changes or being washed after eating. The center explained that they could not provide one-to-one care for Mariam when they had other children to tend to. Although on average, 15 infants attended the center, the number varied because not all children attended each day. Likewise, the caregivers changed in the morning and the afternoon, and some worked part time and others full time.

Mariam's parents liked the center and needed the child care, but Mariam was not adjusting. They sought answers in a temperament evaluation, which showed Mariam to have high sensitivity, low activity level, low frustration tolerance, and slow adaptability to intrusions and transitions. Because of her high sensitivity, noises from the other infants woke her during naptime and she became overstimulated easily from the activity surrounding her. A low activity level contributed to her dependent behavior, whereas low frustration tolerance explained her problems in separating from her parents. She wanted a caregiver to hold her to help her manage any obstacles or frustration she might encounter and to buffer her from overstimulation. Being slow-adapting, Mariam reacted negatively to the change in caregivers and children each day. This explained her preference for one particular caregiver and her protests against the intrusions of child care procedures. Even though the child care center provided an enriched, nurturing environment with a small enrollment, it was not a good fit for Mariam considering her temperament.

After 6 months at the center, Mariam still had not adapted, so her parents found a small family child care setting with one consistent caregiver and only two other children who attended each day. Her parents arranged their work schedules so that she spent less time in child care. With these changes she adjusted to the new child care program after 2 months.

• •

CHILD CARE TODAY

The need for child care for infants and children continues to increase as the work force includes more and more parents. In the 1950s 12% of women worked outside of the home. By 1985 the number increased to 50%, and in 2000 more than 78% of women ages 25–34 were in the labor force (U.S. Bureau of the Census, 2000). In 1996, 4.74 million U.S. children age 5 years or younger spent 20–60 hours each week in child care settings (U.S. House of Representatives Committee on Ways and Means). Sixty-five percent of preschool children have mothers who are employed. Of the 3- and 4-year-olds who are in child care while their parents work, more than half spend time in child care outside their own home (Berk, 2002).

Researchers have studied the effects of child care on child adjustment because of these high usage rates (e.g., McGurk, Caplan, Hennessy, & Moss, 1993; NICHD Early Child Care Research Network, 1998; Scarr, 1998; Zigler & Hall, 1994). Initial findings indicated that the more time children spent in child care, the lower their social competence and psychological adjustment. One study of 200 third graders who spent more than 30 hours per week in child care since their first year of birth showed that they had more noncompliance, lower academic achievement, and more negative peer relationships than other children (Vandell & Corasaniti, 1990). Children who spent more time in child care during their first 5 years experienced less positive socialization and higher maladjustment than children who spent less time in child care (Bates, Marvinney, Keyy, Dodge, Bennet, & Pettit, 1994; Belsky, 1990). These findings indicate that spending 20–30 hours per week in child care beginning in infancy and continuing into early childhood can lead to poor social-emotional adjustment.

Other studies have shown that the quality of care determines outcome more than the number of hours spent in child care (Field, 1991; Phillips, Scarr, & McCartney, 1987). High-quality care can lessen the negative effects of early, extensive child care. Children attending high-quality centers exhibited more compliance, more self-control, and better peer relations than children in low-quality centers (Howes & Olenick, 1986; Howes, Phillips, & Whitebook, 1992). The NICHD Early Child Care Research Network (1998) found that quality of care predicted social competence and behavior problems in children from 2 to 3 years of age, with higher quality of care accounting for higher social competence and fewer problems. They also found that children who had less stable child care arrangements had more problem behavior and noncompliance than did children with stable child care. They concluded that higher quality child care across the first 3 years of life predicted fewer behavior problems and more compliance. Therefore, the quality of child care has become an important issue in establishing public policy and in considering child outcomes.

A large study of 120 U.S. child care centers in three states evaluated children's social adjustment by examining child and family characteristics and quality of child care (McCartney et al., 1997). Results revealed that family and child characteristics had significant effects on adjustment, and quality of child care had small but statistically significant effects on social adjustment. A 4-year follow-up study found no long-term effects of differences of child care quality on school-age children's social, emotional, or behavioral adjustment in children from ordinary homes. For children who come from disadvantaged homes or who are at risk, the quality of child care may play a more significant role (Scarr, 1998).

Child care programs such as Project Head Start provide an enriched preschool environment as well as nutritional and medical services for children who are disadvantaged and at risk and services for parents that include parenting and child development programs. Children who attend these programs score higher in academic achievement and social adjustment than children in other child care programs (Berk, 2002; Head Start Bureau, 2003; Weikart, 1998; Zigler & Styfco, 2004).

This chapter discusses how children's temperaments affect the child care experience and which kinds of child care setting fit best with certain temperaments. Much of the information is also applicable to preschools.

HOW TEMPERAMENT AND CHILD CARE TRAITS INTERACT

Besides the number of hours spent in child care and the overall program quality, a child's characteristics also contribute to positive or negative outcomes. Children described by their mothers as difficult had more behavior problems and less social competence in child care than did easier children (NICHD Early Child Care Research Network, 1998). Children rated by parents and teachers as having difficult temperaments behaved more aggressively in child care (Billman & McDevitt, 1980). Quality of care interacts with child temperament, and even children with reasonable temperaments were shown to be more aggressive in low-quality child care than in high-quality care (Volling & Feagans, 1995). Also, in low-quality child care settings, fearful toddlers and preschoolers had a higher risk of having few friendly encounters with peers, whereas high-quality settings protected them from this risk.

Most of the research on temperament and child care focuses on theoretical issues rather on than practical applications (Carey & McDevitt, 1995). For example, researchers compared caregivers' and mothers' temperament ratings and found positive correlations in the way each viewed children's temperament (Northam, Prior, Sanson, & Oberklaid, 1987). Other researchers (Zigler & Hall, 1994) looked at how temperament affected a mother's decision to return to work and found that mothers of easy infants were as likely to return to work as stay home because the babies' flexibility made either choice a good option. In fact, more employed mothers rated their infants as easy than did unemployed mothers (Lamb, Chase-Lansdale, & Owen, 1979). Mothers of difficult infants were less likely to go back to work, however, because they felt their infants required maternal involvement that they could not receive in child care (Chess & Thomas, 1987; Galambos & Lerner, 1987).

Temperament affects a child's adjustment to child care (Klein, 1980; Nelson, 1987; Zajdeman & Minnes, 1991). According to teachers' ratings, positive mood best predicted child adjustment to child care. Cheerful, happy children had the most favorable reactions to child care and adjusted easily. An examination of activity level, the second predictor, revealed that highly active children adjusted poorly to child care (Zajdeman & Minnes, 1991).

Approach/withdrawal also predicted child care adjustment in that approaching children liked new experiences and easily adjusted to child care. This study showed that active, withdrawing children with negative mood most likely have difficulty adjusting to child care.

Anderson-Goetz and Worobey (1984) suggested using temperament concepts in child care as a tool to gain insight into children's behavior and social interactions, to improve child observations, and to aid in program and activity planning. Even though little research exists concerning applying temperament strategies in child care situations, some educators have described temperament tactics for working with children in child care (Anderson, 1994; Neville & Johnson, 1998). For example, allowing a slow-adapting child more time to get ready or being empathic to his difficulties helps the child move through the day with fewer problems (Anderson, 1994). Or allowing a cautious child to sit on the sidelines and watch an activity before joining in makes him feel confident to try it (Neville & Johnson, 1998). When considering the child's adjustment to the child care setting, care providers benefit from knowing the relationship between the child's temperament and the child care environment.

TEMPERAMENT TRAINING FOR CHILD CARE PROVIDERS

Staff members' or child care providers' training, knowledge, and skills affect the quality of child care programs (Cost, Quality, & Child Outcomes Study Team, 1995; Whitebook, Howes, & Phillips, 1989). Zigler and Hall (1994) proposed that child care training should include information that would enable child care staff to work with children of different temperaments. In its 12 principles of child development and learning, the National Association for the Education of Young Children (NAEYC; Bredekamp & Copple, 1997) included individual differences in temperament among other factors to consider in decisions about curriculum and child interactions.

Despite such encouragement, few early childhood education texts include information about temperament and few training materials for child care workers exist (Franyo & Hyson, 1999), although a few programs are in place. Far West Laboratory (1993) includes two training sessions in their program for caregivers, and the California State Department of Education (Childcare Video Magazine, 1990) produced a video for caregivers entitled *Flexible, Fearful, and Feisty: The Different Temperaments of Infants and Toddlers.*

Franyo and Hyson (1999) developed a temperament training workshop for child care providers from 14 child care centers. They found that 42.5% of participants had received some temperament information in a college course, 38% had taken a workshop, and 34.9% had read a book or article on the subject. But despite their exposure to the concept, they had very limited knowledge of temperament. After the training the participants responded positively, with 97% stating that the workshop had effectively increased their temperament knowledge. They enthusiastically accepted the concepts because of "increased understanding of the children and increased ability to meet individual needs" (Franyo & Hyson, 1999, p. 345). This study indicates the need for temperament training to help caregivers effectively nurture children's individual differences. Training in temperament concepts, then, benefits early childhood educators and child care providers and plays a role in high-quality child care.

DIFFERENT TYPES OF CHILD CARE, DIFFERENT TEMPERAMENTS

Parents have different options in the kind of child care they choose. In any setting, they seek child care that provides nurturing care, a safe environment, and toys and activities that are developmentally appropriate. They also consider how time is structured with teacher-directed and child-initiated activities.

TYPES OF CARE

Child care can consist of extended family or relatives who look after the child in their homes or in the child's home, in-home caregivers such as nannies or caregivers who work in the child's home, family child care provided in a caregiver's home to small groups of children, or center-based care. Each has advantages and disadvantages for children of different temperaments. Healthy adjustment depends on the kind of child care combined with warm and sensitive caregiving and a good fit with the child's temperament.

Extended Family or Relative Care Many parents leave their children with family members because they believe that the child will receive more loving care from them than from outside care. Other times they choose this method because of financial constraints or because this fits with cultural expectations. This type of care varies according to the time family members have to devote to child care. If one or two family members provide care on a consistent basis, this can work well for infants who are sensitive, easily frustrated, withdrawing, or who have difficulty with change. The familiar caregivers and setting makes the separation from parents easier and prepares the child for future child care experiences.

Other families choose to have several family members share the care depending on which relatives are available on a particular day. Parents may not know from day to day who will care for their child or children. This unpredictable kind of care presents children with numerous changes. Easy, flexible children typically cope better with this type of fluctuating caregiver schedule than do children with challenging temperaments, but having many caregivers involved in care can be confusing for any child.

Unstable child care arrangements are associated with problem behavior and noncompliance with child care providers (NICHD Early Child Care Research Network, 1998). Often, different family members have different parenting styles or philosophies on child rearing and discipline. With difficult children this inconsistency can elicit negative behavior and possible power struggles as the child attempts to determine the limits or tries to adjust between caregivers' styles. Slow-to-adjust children will also react negatively to the changing caregivers and environments. Slow-adjusting children who also are sensitive or those who require consistency will find it especially difficult to manage the changes, which can result in negative behavior at home or with the caregiver. For families who must use several different family members to provide care, setting up consistent days for each caregiver and then going over the schedule each day with the child will help provide structure for children who thrive on routine. Parents who enlist the help of many different family members should also meet with them regularly to discuss child rearing procedures, limits, and discipline and agree on consistency between caregivers.

In-Home Child Care Some parents employ a caregiver or nanny to care for their children in their own home. Brazelton (1992) stated that this care may be optimal in the first year. In child care given in the home, the child remains in familiar surroundings, separations are less abrupt, and the routine can be easily maintained. This option works well for children who are sensitive to new environments, have difficulty adjusting to change or novelty, or have problems with separation. The caregiver or nanny must have experience with children and understand the child's temperament in order to create a good fit. One disadvantage of this care is that an inhibited child who experiences this for some time may be isolated from new experiences and have few opportunities to become acclimated to new people and situations.

Family Child Care Some caregivers offer family child care in their homes to small groups of infants and/or children. The quality of this kind of child care depends on the number of children, the home environment, and the caregiver's experience and ability to relate to each child. Family child care can offer a small, safe, nurturing environment for slow-to-warm-up children who have difficulty with large groups. The small size can also benefit the active toddler who is beginning to learn about socialization and the slow-adapting child who dislikes intrusions. The small family child care that has a daily routine and structured activities also benefits easily frustrated children or those who need consistency. Family child care can provide a transition for sensitive or withdrawing children from at-home care to child care in a larger, more formal setting.

As with any kind of care, family child care may vary and may not be ideal for children of every temperament. Lower quality family child care has little structure and too much free play. Problems can arise in family child care with active children if they have too much free play time or too much television time (which is bad for children of any temperament type) without appropriate ways to expend energy. Also, a child who is the oldest among much younger children may get bored easily and may release energy in inappropriate rough-and-tumble play. Highly regular children who need routine, slow-adapters who dislike intrusions or unexpected changes, or children whose lack of persistence makes them easily frustrated by obstacles or delays are especially vulnerable in low-quality child care. High-quality child care, then, is nurturing and structured and has planned activities that fit with children of many temperaments.

Child Care Center   Child care centers or preschools account for approximately 39% of child care in the United States (U.S. Bureau of the Census, 1997). High-quality centers are accredited, have a small child-to-adult ratio (3:1 for infants, 4:1 for toddlers, 6:1–8:1 for 3-year-olds), and hire trained teachers who interact well with the children (Berk, 2002).

Child care centers can vary greatly in organization and philosophy. Some are highly structured and teacher-directed, whereas others are child-directed and primarily provide free play. These centers vary in class size, how the classes are divided (e.g., by developmental level or strictly by age), and whether different age groups are separated or together. These factors influence the fit between the child care setting and children's temperaments.

Child care workers, like parents, seem to evaluate and interact with children on the basis of temperament (Carey & McDevitt, 1995; Zigler & Hall, 1994). Teachers reported that the children they rated as initially withdrawing adjusted more slowly to child care than did high-approach children (Ratekin, 1994). Children rated as difficult by parents and teachers exhibited aggressive behavior in the child care setting (Billman & McDevitt, 1980).

Center caregivers and family caregivers rated children's temperament differently, with the center caregivers perceiving the children they served as more difficult, less compliant, and less likeable than the family care providers rated the children in their care (Griffin & Thornburg 1985). This indicates that care providers such as centers who care for larger numbers of children face more demands than do family child care providers and, thus, are less tolerant of different temperament types. Child care providers working with large numbers of children encounter more variation in temperament and consequently must handle many different temperamental challenges. Knowing how temperamentally distinct children react to similar situations would help child care providers working in centers and other settings with large groups of children respond appropriately to the children's differences.

Before- and After-School Care   Many children attend before- and after-school child care programs in centers. These programs vary greatly in quality and structure, an important consideration, especially for temperamentally challenging children. Children who attend both before- and after-school care must manage extra transitions. The transitions are easier when the before- and after-school care is at the school the children attend rather than in a location where the children must be bussed to and from school. This is a concern for children who are sensitive to changes or who have difficulty with transitions.

Before-School Care   Children often arrive at before-school care drowsy and irritable, having gotten up, dressed, and out of the house quickly. Parents may have had to wake their child in order to get him to child care on time. The child may not have wanted to eat or may have eaten something quickly in the car. For a slow-adapting child, this means he is tired and has already had to deal with a number of transitions by the time he arrives at child care. The child will encounter more changes and intrusions if many children attend the before-school program. If these encounters are negative, they can set the tone for the day.

Some parents find it helpful to wake their child earlier so the morning transitions do not occur as quickly. Others find before-school care that offers breakfast. This can be a good transitional activity each day. The sensitive child will do best with facilities that provide quiet activities to ease the transition into the day. Active, approaching children will have few problems and plunge into the before-school care with abandon, but such programs may present problems for the sensitive or slow-adapting children.

After-School Care   Children often arrive from school over-stimulated, full of unspent energy, frustrated, or depleted of adaptability. Good-quality after-school care addresses these temperament issues. Sensitive children need to reduce sensory overload, so a quiet retreat where they can read or relax will help them decrease stimulation that has built up over the day. Active, flexible children often do well with free play to expend pent-up energy, but children also low on adaptability need structure and routine to prevent unexpected changes or intrusions. The routine that worked for active, slow-adapting Brent began with an after-school snack. This alleviated the hunger that diminished his adaptability and helped with his transition to after-school care. Brent engaged in some active play after his snack to release energy, and then he settled down to homework time. This prevented his energy from escalating further and provided structure. If he had time, he could then play with friends until his parents arrived.

As with all types of child care, a child's temperament determines the best kind of before- and after-school care for a particular child.

REACTIONS TO CHILD CARE BASED ON TEMPERAMENT

Depending on temperament type and combination of types, children will have various reactions to different kinds of child care.

SENSITIVE CHILDREN

Stimulation such as noise, activity, number of children, and environmental distractions affect sensitive children. Even too much artwork on the walls can overstimulate a sensitive child. Bright, loud, exciting, low-structure child care centers can overwhelm these children. Sensitive children tend to withdraw and hide–to be loners or try to stay away from the excitement and group activity. Centers may be able to help such children with their socialization, but only if they can pair them up with another friend to help them navigate the very busy social situations. Sensitive children do best in small centers with low stimulation.

Sensitive children need child care situations that

- Have small numbers of children
- Have quiet and calm caregivers
- Do not overwhelm the senses with color, light, or noise
- Are in a familiar, sheltered setting such as the home of the child or a relative

ACTIVE CHILDREN

Active children need a child care facility in which they can balance activities that expend their energy with quiet activities. Too much activity can "rev" these children up, and too much quiet time can cause energy to emerge in negative ways. These children can function well in large, busy centers, but the larger the group of children, the more possibility they have for intensifying their energy, which can lead to physical aggression and out-of-control behavior. Because these children have the tendency to escalate, too much free play can also present a problem, then. In a large setting, these children benefit from structure and clear limits. Active children also excel in a medium-size group with opportunities for active play interspersed with quiet activities that help the child calm down. Active children often gravitate to older children, so centers that have play periods with slightly older children can help with socialization skills.

Active children need child care that

- Is medium size–not too large
- Allows the child to expend energy but not become too "revved up"
- Has enough room to express energy and play structures that support gross muscle skills
- Has hands-on activities
- Has structure and a daily routine that intersperses active play with quiet activities
- Has child care staff who appreciate energy and can channel it appropriately

INTENSE CHILDREN

Too large a group increases the possibility of intense reactions. Providers must notice which situations trigger intensity and how the situations relate to various temperament traits and then work to prevent the triggers, help the child calm down, or vent reactions positively.

Intense children need child care

- Where staff notice when intensity begins to escalate
- Where staff can help label the triggers and emotions
- Where staff remain calm when responding to intense reactions
- That does not have too large a group of children
- With staff who are willing to help the child learn self-regulation and can provide redirection

IRREGULAR CHILDREN

Children with irregular bodily functions have difficulty fitting into highly structured child care centers with rigid snack, meal, toileting, and nap times. Centers that have staggered snacks and nap times work well. Some centers have snacks available over a period of time and the child can choose when to eat. Rest time can replace nap time for children who cannot sleep at nap time. Smaller facilities have an easier time offering these accommodations than large facilities attending to many children.

Irregular children need child care that

- Has ample free play time
- Has staggered nap, snack, and meal times

SLOW-ADAPTING CHILDREN

Slow-adapting children do best in a smaller child care center that has structure and a daily routine. Large groups and too much free play present the child with too many intrusions, transitions, and unexpected changes.

Slow-adapting children need child care that

- Has small groups of children
- Has a daily structure and routine

- Prepares children for transitions and changes
- Does not have extremely lengthy periods of free play
- Has staff who give warnings and use rituals to signal changes

PERSISTENT CHILDREN

Persistent children do well in child care that allows them to focus on an activity until they complete it. For this reason they can easily occupy themselves during long periods of free play. However, clear limits are necessary because these children can be stubborn. Child care providers must be willing to help the child put closure on an activity before moving on to the next.

Persistent children need child care that

- Has ample free play time so they can focus on an activity or project
- Gives warnings before it is time to stop an activity
- Helps the child put closure on an activity before moving on to another
- Has clear limits

LOW-PERSISTENCE CHILDREN

Low-persistence children have more possibilities for frustration in large centers with long free play periods than do children who are not easily frustrated. Small centers that focus on different short-term activities work well. Having different stations for children to visit allows them to change activities when frustration mounts. Child care providers can work on increasing children's frustration tolerance by helping them to break up difficult projects in order to complete a task.

Low-persistence children need child care that

- Has fewer children to help prevent excess frustration
- Has different short-term activities
- Provides choices in activities so they can go to another when frustration mounts
- Has staff who help redirect the child when he or she becomes frustrated
- Has staff who help the child break up frustrating tasks

HIGHLY DISTRACTIBLE CHILDREN

Highly distractible children do best in centers that limit distractions such as excessive art displays, toys, and noise. These children have problems with too many activities to choose from. Structured activities with limited choices help them stay focused, and teachers can easily redirect them when they become upset or involved in an off-limits activity.

Highly distractible children need child care

- Without excessive toys and noise
- With structured activities that help them stay focused
- With staff who help redirect them when they become distracted

• •

Sherri's child care center asked her parents to find new child care for their 3-year-old because of her biting, aggression, and noncompliance. A temperament assessment described her as persistent, active, and intense. The child care center she attended had 25 children in her class and was structured with a long circle time at the beginning and end of each day. Between circle times, children could play at various stations around the room. If they did not participate in the structured stations, they could choose free play. Sherri had difficulty sitting at circle time and would not follow the teachers' instructions. During free play she often became so involved in an activity that she would not stop and would attack anyone who tried to make her move on. She developed a reputation as a bully, and other parents complained about her aggression.

Sherri's parents found a smaller school with shorter circle times and less free play. Scheduled activities had a limited time frame, making it easy for Sherri to complete an activity before moving on to the next. Her aggression subsided, and Sherri began to make friends.

• •

• •

Casey, 8 years old; Stephanie, 7 years old; and Christophe, 10 years old, attended the after-school program at their elementary school with 35 other children. These three children stood out because of their extremely different temperaments. Casey, active, distractible, approaching, and intense, roared in after school like a hurricane. His activity level could escalate easily into play that turned rough. He touched everything, spoke loudly, disrupted others, and often got into mischief. Some children avoided him, some followed him, and others became out of control as a result of his energy.

Stephanie, on the other hand, entered the room quietly, often without being noticed. She covered her ears when Casey spoke. Sometimes she could not get out of his way quickly enough and was almost bowled over. His sudden intrusions brought her to tears. Her temperament of high sensitivity, slow adaptability, withdrawal, and low distractibility seemed the antithesis of Casey's. She did not readily mix with the other children and had only one friend with whom she played.

Christophe, intense, slow-adapting, persistent, and irritable, usually walked in with a loud complaint and a scowl. He yelled at anyone who got into his space and made a scene whenever things did not go his way. When he felt particularly irritable he would focus on what bothered him and not listen to any other viewpoint. He had one or two friends, but his bossiness sometimes alienated them.

The after-school providers had difficulty containing Casey's energy, helping Stephanie handle the assaults on her sensitivity, and keeping Christophe from exploding. The program had little structure and children were allowed to play outside, do their homework, do art activities, or play games. These three children caused enough difficulty for the program that the providers called in the school psychologist to observe the interactions. His knowledge of temperament allowed him to make recommendations for each child. He spoke to each child, and with the provider they devised an individualized plan to help each child get along better.

Casey needed to expend the energy that had accumulated over the school day. He usually was "starving to death" when he arrived, so they decided a snack would refuel him and cause him to slow down a bit. He loved to shoot baskets, so after his snack he could play one game of hoops with his friends. This would release his energy but not escalate him too much. After that he would do 15 minutes of homework, followed by a less-active game. He would do more homework if necessary, and then, if there was time, he could play another outdoor game until his parents came. The plan established strict rules concerning escalating energy and physicality.

Stephanie needed quiet, so she helped the child care provider create a space in the corner of the room away from all of the activity. Here she could retreat in a comfortable chair with a book and reduce the stimulation that had built up during the day. Other children had to stay out of that corner when Stephanie needed it. Later she could do homework or play a game with her friend, but she always had the option to return to her quiet space if she needed to retreat again.

Christophe had difficulty making the transition from school, and then disliked the unexpected changes and intrusions involved in free play. Together he and the psychologist devised a routine. He would have a snack when he arrived and then do his homework. The snack provided a transitional routine from school and also took care of any hunger that might further deplete his adaptability. Doing his homework next prevented intrusions and added a transitional bridge. After homework, Christophe could choose a free-play activity, but he needed to monitor his intensity during that time. The care provider also agreed to monitor Christophe and help him redirect before his intensity escalated significantly. If an intrusion or change made him angry, he would work on redirecting himself. His persistence made this difficult so he and the psychologist decided on three alternative activities that he liked. Eventually, with practice, he could monitor and redirect himself when necessary.

It took some time for Casey, Stephanie, and Christophe to create a good fit within the after-care program. Depending on what kind of day they had previously had at school, some afternoons were better than others. But eventually all three students were able to function appropriately within the confines of the program.

* *

SUMMARY

Parents must consider the goodness of fit between their children and the child care environment. In addition to quality of care, qualified staff, safety, and developmentally appropriate activities, a knowledge of temperament can guide parents in choosing the best child care. Children who have temperaments that include such traits as high activity, high sensitivity, high intensity, slow-adaptability, low regularity, or low persistence may have problems in certain child care settings. Parents must consider the size of the facility; the amount of structure, routine, or rules; noise level; and sensory stimulation when choosing child care. What may seem an ideal setting to the parent may not fit with the child's temperament. A quiet, sedate child care environment will not make an active child less energetic. Staff must know how to recognize escalation and situations that trigger outbursts with an intense child. The school that has long, involved projects is perfect for the persistent child, but will only cause frustration for the child who is low in persistence. An after-school-care program that offers lengthy French or Spanish lessons may seem a lovely idea to parents, but can induce frustration, obstinacy, or agitation in the child who is active, slow-adapting, or easily frustrated.

Once parents have chosen the child care situation that best fits their child's temperament, they can help the child care provider understand the child's temperament. When behavioral problems arise within the child care setting, child care providers can use that information to devise a behavior plan for the child. A temperament perspective helps providers work effectively with the issues.

CHAPTER 9

Temperament in Educational Settings

● ●

I asked an experienced, successful elementary school teacher, "How do you cope with the differences in children?"

"The first 2 weeks of class I spend just observing them to see how they react and to get to know them," she replied. "And then I do what is necessary. For example, I give the active kids jobs that allow them to get up and move around. They take messages to the office, collect papers, and erase the board."

"Don't the other kids ask why a certain kid gets to move around more?" I asked.

"If they do, I just tell them because he 'needs' to move," she replied. This teacher was one of the favorites in the school. She recognized individual differences and found ways to meet the needs of each child in her classroom.

● ●

As children grow older, they spend more time in school away from the family. The school experience affects social and emotional development and, with the exception of the family, plays one of the most significant roles in childhood. Success or failure in school has far-reaching consequences for the child's development and future. Teachers are crucial to a child's adjustment, achievement, and self-concept. Almost everyone can remember a favorite teacher who made learning exciting and students feel valued. Teachers who elicit such feelings from children are the ones who acknowledge the children's temperament and teach accordingly (Keogh, 2003).

Teachers observe the full range of children's temperaments. Effective teachers recognize differences between children and adjust teaching so that all children in the class benefit. They note that children differ in areas such as their energy levels, their ability to focus, their persistence, their reactions to novelty, and their sensitivities. Effective teachers provide energy outlets for their active students, limit distractions for those who have difficulty focusing, and break up tasks for those who have limited persistence. These teachers are in touch with their students' reactions, sensitivities, and strengths and weaknesses, and they organize their classroom and teaching style so that individual differences are acknowledged. Such teachers create a good fit with their students. They can address students' differences without disrupting classroom functions and the pace of activities while creating appropriate interactions and interventions as needed.

But not all teachers understand children's behavioral styles. Some have narrow ideas about how all children should behave, pay attention, sit still, and be flexible. Teachers who do not understand how temperament affects a child's behavior may misinterpret certain behaviors as disobedience, which could result in classroom difficulties and negative interactions for both teacher and student. Teachers can work more effectively with all children by taking into account children's behavioral styles and which learning techniques fit best with each child, thereby promoting academic success and improving teacher–child relationships. Temperament re-frames how teachers view child behavior and provides a positive structure for behavior management and classroom organization. "Temperament lends itself to the development of innovative, individualized interventions with children that can be used [by]…teachers…and other professionals" (McClowery, 1998, p. 551).

TEMPERAMENT TRAITS AND LEARNING

Aaron always finishes anything he starts, but it is difficult getting him to stop and move on to the next subject. Jennifer works on things in spurts. She is happiest when working on one project and then another, moving between each until both are completed. Vineeta puts her whole body into a project and does best when she can actually manipulate the learning environment rather than sit still and learn. Ken stands back silently and observes what is going on. His teacher sometimes wonders if he understands the assignments because of his initial reluctance to get involved. Usually, however, after a period of observation, he tackles the project completely and competently.

Distractibility, persistence, and activity level are related to attention and how children approach a learning task (Martin, 1989). The four students just mentioned have different temperaments that reflect how they approach learning. Aaron has high persistence and low distractibility, whereas Jennifer exhibits lower persistence and is more distractible. Vineeta's high activity accounts for how she learns best, and Ken is withdrawing and takes time to become familiar with a new task.

Research shows that temperament is related to academic achievement. Certain temperament profiles are more conducive to learning than others. The temperament traits of persistence, adaptability, distractibility, and approach/withdrawal related significantly to academic achievement (Guerin, Gottfried, Oliver, & Thomas, 2003). Children who are less active, more persistent, and less distractible do better in reading and math than their more active, less attentive counterparts (Martin, 1989; Martin, Olejnik, & Gaddis, 1994). Children whom teachers rated as high in persistence, low in distractibility, and low in activity level scored higher on reading readiness tests (Schoen & Nagle, 1994). This does not mean that active, less attentive children cannot succeed at reading and math but that they may need different ways to approach these learning tasks.

A child's temperament contributes to how she learns as well as how she experiences the school environment. Keogh (1986, 2003) differentiated school demands into two categories: 1) academic performance and achievement and 2) socially appropriate and interpersonal behavior. She concluded that significant associations exist between children's temperaments and academic achievement and that students' temperaments affect their classroom behavior, teachers' views of students' abilities to learn, and teachers' attitudes toward their pupils.

LEARNING AND TEMPERAMENT TRAITS

Children differ in their school experiences according to temperament.

High-Sensitivity Children   Highly sensitive children are exquisitely aware of everything around them in school. They react to their environment, both physically and emotionally. For such children, noisy, busy classrooms provide much extraneous stimulation and interfere with performance and focus. Classrooms with walls filled with colorful art projects and diagrams can also overstimulate the highly sensitive student. Noise level, temperature, lighting, and physical comfort affect their school experience. A slight illness or injury during school can influence their concentration. They also respond emotionally to their peers and teachers. These children easily react with hurt feelings to disapproval, criticism, and punishment. A sharp word from a classmate or a reprimand from the teacher can cause the sensitive child to wilt and withdraw. They also respond more to others' moods and emotions.

Low-Sensitivity Children   Children with low sensitivity are not bothered by much in their environments, and they may not be aware of how their behavior affects others. They do not notice that their voices are too loud in class or that they are too close to their neighbor. This can affect peer interactions. They also have difficulty noticing small errors in their class work or picking up nuances in the teacher's explanations. On the other hand, criticism seems to roll off them more easily, and physical comfort rarely is a problem.

Active, Approaching Children   Active, approaching children are enthusiastic learners who find sitting still very difficult. They tend to learn with their entire bodies. Their activity level causes them to move about and explore, and their natural curiosity attracts them to novelty. These children are hands-on learners, the first to volunteer for the science experiment, the last to sit down. They also have a hard time keeping their hands to themselves in class and on the playground. They put all their energy into a task, but when forced to stay still for long periods of time, they may release their pent-up energy in inappropriate ways. When involved in exciting, busy activities they tend to become even more energetic.

Slow-Adapting Children   Slow-adapting children are routine oriented. Because they like to know what to expect, they do well in a classroom that provides routine and structure. An interruption in the daily routine, a substitute teacher, or a field trip can provoke negative reactions from these students. Changing from one task to the next too quickly can cause resistance if the student is not ready to move on. Control issues also occur in nonstructured activities when the child attempts to control the situation if he does not know what to expect. This is often seen during free play periods such as recess and can lead to confrontations with teachers or peers. Slow-adapting children take longer to adjust to any change in the classroom, whether it is a new routine, a different seat arrangement, or a different math concept.

Withdrawing Children   Withdrawing children may be shy in the classroom. They dislike the unfamiliar and take a while to get used to the new class and teacher each year. They resist new skills, unfamiliar activities, and "hands on" tasks, preferring to stand back and watch. They appear to be outsiders looking in, but they are learning through observing rather than doing. These children do not like to be the center of attention. Asking questions, speaking up in class, being put on the spot, or making a presentation provoke anxiety, and these children will resist quietly or try but fail, which makes them more anxious next time.

Low-Persistence Children   Children who are low in persistence have difficulty staying on task if the task is too difficult or if they are bored. They become overwhelmed and then frustrated and move quickly to another activity to reduce their discomfort. These children may engage in attention-seeking behavior to divert the teacher from a difficult task. Many class clowns are low in persistence. Low persistence may be mislabeled as an attention problem, especially if the child is also high in activity level or distractibility.

Distractible Children   Distractible children become sidetracked easily by anything around them. A bird flying past the window, the noise of rustling papers, another student's behavior—all these can interrupt a task or thought. These children notice everything, so busy, noisy environments make it difficult for them to stay focused. They set no priorities in what to attend to; everything is worth their interest. Because they are distractible, they find long lists of instructions difficult to follow. Like the child who is low in persistence, the distractible child may also be labeled as having an attention problem, and his behavior may be misinterpreted as an attention-deficit disorder. Attention-deficit disorders are addressed in more detail later in this chapter and in Chapter 12.

Highly Persistent, Low-Distractible Children   Children with high persistence and low distractibility have excellent focus and attention spans. In fact, they can become so focused on something that they tune out everything around them. When they begin a project they want to see it through to completion. Their motto is "never give up." Problems rarely arise around having this child finish a task, but stopping one activity before it is completed and moving on to the next may be difficult for her. Persistent children often exhibit perfectionist behavior in an attempt to do a good job. They focus so completely on the task that they overextend themselves. Such a child writes a five-page book report when the assignment is to write two pages. Sometimes labeled "stubborn," persistent children also have difficulty letting go of feelings.

All of these traits do not stand alone, but rather, combine in any number of ways to produce behavior. For example, the active, approaching child who is low in persistence will eagerly undertake a new project but will quickly abandon it if he finds it too difficult. The child who is withdrawing, persistent, and distractible will initially refuse to participate in a new project, gradually become involved, and then immerse herself in it. However, if something distracts her, she will attend to that but then return to continue the project.

Intensity is one trait that colors the child's other traits. When a child over-reacts to a situation, it helps to examine which temperament trait or traits and which events triggered the reaction. For example, be-

Table 9.1. Temperament tips for teachers in working with various temperament types*

Trait	High	Low
Sensitivity	Realize that sensitive children do feel physical and emotional discomfort more than less sensitive children; they are not just overreacting or complaining.	Get these students' attention before giving instructions, and express yourself clearly.
	Help these children when possible, but give them some responsibility for solutions.	Help them recognize and interpret body language, gestures, and subtle nuances of communication through stories, observation, and role playing.
	At a neutral time, help these children problem solve how to work with their sensitivities.	Advise these students to ask when they are unclear about another's communication.
Activity	Schedule seat work after physical activities such as recess so high activity students can expend energy before sitting still, and provide a cool-down transition to prepare students for reduced activity.	Allow low activity students extra time to complete tasks, or let them begin earlier if possible.
	Give students plenty of space between desks so that they can sprawl out or move around without bothering others.	Use untimed tests when possible.
	Allow high activity students to expend energy when needed by standing, stretching, sharpening pencils, and so forth, as long as it does not disturb others.	Do not schedule tasks that must be finished in school for the last period of the day.
	Place high activity students near you to decrease active behavior or have them sit in back of the room to prevent them from distracting others.	Let other teachers know that low activity is not a sign of being a slow learner.
	When possible, use teaching methods that allow hands-on learning.	Allow low activity students to finish work at home when necessary.
	Make sure parents and other teachers understand that these students' high energy does not mean willful disobedience.	
Intensity	Inform high intensity students beforehand about situations that may cause them to overreact.	Observe the subtle ways that low intensity students express their feelings.
	Teach students to think before acting (e.g., count to 10); use words to describe feelings and to turn down the intensity.	Encourage these students to try to express their feelings more openly.
	When a child over-reacts remain calm but firm in responding, and do not take it personally.	Provide ways for low intensity students to practice expressing themselves more actively.
	When the student calms down, discuss the reaction and ways to deal with the issue more appropriately next time.	

(continued)

Table 9.1. *(continued)*

Trait	High	Low
Adaptability	Do not overlook the needs of highly adaptable children.	Prepare slow-adapting students for any classroom change beforehand.
		Give 5-minute warnings before switching activities.
		Allow slow-adapting students time to make a change.
		Use routines and rituals to signal changes.
		Go over the day's activities before beginning.
Approach	Provide hands-on tasks for approaching children.	Do not view students' initial withdrawal from school or a new task as dependency or fear.
		Familiarize withdrawing students with new activities by using anecdotes, examples, and so forth.
		Introduce withdrawing students to new things in familiar settings or allow them to have a friend nearby.
		Allow withdrawing students to watch an activity before becoming involved.
		Introduce new experiences by reminding students of ways they handled new events successfully in the past.
Persistence	Be firm but flexible when dealing with persistent students.	Provide encouragement with difficult tasks.
	Help persistent students realize that there are rules and schedules, and that others have rights.	Provide assistance needed to continue when they become frustrated or take a break before continuing.
	Problem-solve together.	Praise or reward students for perseverance.
	Have persistent students postpone starting projects that they may not complete in the allotted time.	Help students break up difficult tasks into doable parts.
	If a task is started but it appears that it cannot be finished on time, help persistent students determine a stopping point.	
	Give advance warning when students must stop work on a task.	
Distractibility	Seat distractible children near front of the room away from distractions.	Help child put closure on one activity before moving on to the next.
	Use short lists to keep the distractible student on task.	Get the chilld's attention before giving directions.
	Monitor distractbility and help direct child back to the task at hand.	
	Get eye contact when giving directions.	

*Because not all temperament traits are problematic in school, not all are listed here.
From Grossman, H. (1990). *Trouble-free teaching: Solutions to behavior problems in the classroom*

coming overstimulated produces a big reaction in a sensitive child, experiencing an unexpected intrusion is a trigger for a slow adapter, and becoming frustrated causes an intense response in a low persistence child. The traits that are more challenging in combination (e.g., high intensity, high activity, slow adaptability, low persistence, high sensitivity) affect how positively teachers and peers view the child. Knowing the child's combination of temperament traits helps parents and teachers know how a particular child approaches learning. The child's temperament also provides clues for what will impede or enhance his or her learning experience. Table 9.1 includes several temperament tips for teachers to help foster success in the classroom.

HOW TEMPERAMENT AFFECTS TEACHERS' ATTITUDES

Students' characteristics influence teachers' attitudes and expectations. Research demonstrates that temperament affects teachers' attitudes toward their students and that students with easier temperaments are often viewed more positively (Keogh, 2003). A study of kindergarten teachers found that teachers overestimated the intelligence of children who were approaching and adaptable and underestimated the intelligence of those who were slow-to-warm-up (Gordon & Thomas, 1967). Such judgments run the danger of becoming self-fulfilling prophecies. Stipek (1998) found that teachers have different interactions with and expectations of high- and low-achieving students. She noted that teachers must be aware of their expectations of students and proposed that they re-examine their beliefs about why students behave as they do because these beliefs influence teaching decisions. Keogh suggested, "This may be helpful when teachers are faced with children with very different temperaments, as temperamental differences are likely contributors to teachers' expectations for children's achievement and behavior" (2003, p. 81).

Another study examined teachers' ratings of temperament and IQ scores and found that children who were rated as more adaptable, approaching, and persistent scored higher on standardized IQ tests (Martin & Holbrook, 1985). Martin (1989) suggested that this could be the result of teachers' bias toward seeing bright children as more adaptable, approaching, and persistent: a classic example of the halo effect (positive characteristics tend to encourage positive ratings). Or it could be that adaptable, approaching, persistent children have a better "fit" with the educational system and score higher because they are better test takers than less-persistent, non-adaptable children.

Martin, Nagel, and Paget (1983; cited in Martin, 1989, p. 42) examined how temperament related to teachers' feelings about students in their classrooms. They asked first-grade teachers four questions:

1. Name three children in your class you would like to have in class again for the sheer joy of it.

2. Name three children you would be least prepared to discuss at a parent–teacher conference.

3. Name three children you would spend more time with if you could.

4. If you could reduce your class by three children, which three would it be?

The questions were said to measure attachment, indifference, concern, and rejection, respectively. Children nominated for the attachment, indifference, and rejection groups were significantly different in temperament from the children not nominated for these groups. According to teacher ratings of temperament, children in the attachment group (question 1) were more adaptable, more approaching, and more persistent than their peers. The indifference group (question 2) had temperaments that were less active, less approaching, and less intense; and the rejection group (question 4) were more active and distractible than their classmates. The concern group (question 3) had no differences in temperament from the other children.

Children who have short attention spans and are distractible tend to receive more criticism and negative attention from teachers (Martin, 1989; Martin, Nagel, & Paget, 1983), and teachers tend to give more instructions, orders, and restrictions to children who are more active and less persistent (Keogh, Pullis, & Cadwell, 1982). These children often are involved in conflict and generate feelings of frustration, anger, and incompetence on the part of adults (Pullis, 1989). Teachers tend to find students who are cooperative, cautious, and responsible preferable to those who are disruptive, independent, and assertive (Wenzel, 1996, as cited in Keogh, 2003). Teacher reports of students who were working hard and behaving appropriately in the classroom correlated with the temperament traits of persistence and predictability, followed by adaptability, mood, distractibility, and intensity (Gurien, Gottfried, Oliver, & Thomas, 2003).

Teachers' perceptions of what causes a child's difficult behavior can also contribute to negative feelings (Keogh, 1986). Teachers often assume that children are being intentionally defiant and that they do not have enough discipline at home. Often, this perception leads a teacher to use more punitive and forcible methods to address the student's difficult behavior. Punishment can cause inhibition and avoidance in the student, leading to school failure, which can result in the student becoming frustrated and defensive (Rothbart & Jones, 1998). This serves only to create more difficult behavior, more conflict in the classroom, and more negative feelings.

As Keogh stated, "Sensitivity to individual differences in children's temperament is an important attribute for an educator to have, and thinking about children's behavior as temperament-related can change the ways teachers interpret behaviors" (2003, p. 90). Later in this chapter, strategies are suggested for working with different temperaments and difficult classroom behavior.

THE "IDEAL" STUDENT

For many teachers, the "ideal" student typically is considered to be one who has a long attention span; sits still when necessary; is adaptable, approaching, and positive in mood; and is low in reactivity (Lerner, Lerner & Zabski, 1985; Keogh, 1989, 1994, 2003). This student learns easily, does not disrupt the classroom environment, and gets along well socially. Teachers interact more with students who have positive temperament profiles, but they also expect higher academic achievement from these students (Lerner, Lerner, & Zabski, 1985). This may also account for the higher IQ scores mentioned previously. Teachers viewed children with more negative temperaments as needing more supervision and direction than those with positive temperaments (Keogh, 2003).

But not all students fit this "ideal." Some are very active and have difficulty sitting still or have short attention spans and are easily distracted. Some are strong-willed and inflexible. Others overreact to extraneous stimulation. Sarason advised educators to "teach children, not subject matter" (1993, p. 124). To do this, teachers must understand students' temperaments as well as they understand their cognitive abilities.

OVERCOMING ATTITUDES TO UNDERSTAND TEMPERAMENTS

When children feel accepted regardless of individual differences, they are more able to meet educational challenges. When teachers understand children's temperaments, they can help their students learn to work with their individual differences and benefit more from the school experience. Teachers can learn to identify students' temperaments by

- Observing their activity level and need to move around during different activities
- Noticing how well they stick with a given task
- Identifying students whose attention is easily diverted
- Observing how students handle transitions from one activity to the next or unexpected changes
- Noting the level of intensity with which students respond and what triggers high levels of intensity
- Being aware of the students who shy away from new people and situations and those who are drawn to any novelty

A teacher can begin to work with children's individual differences by carefully observing each child's typical reactions and responses to daily situations. This will help the teacher identify students' temperaments.

GOODNESS OF FIT BETWEEN TEACHER AND STUDENT

Goodness of fit between a teacher's temperament and expectations and a child's temperament is essential to success in the classroom. Teachers reported that understanding temperament gave them a more sensitive framework for viewing children (Keogh, 1982). When they identify bothersome behavior as temperament-based rather than intentional, it helps them to manage their own negative feelings more effectively, modify their responses to work with the child's temperament, and use supportive techniques that take advantage of a student's strengths (Pullis, 1989). They can better understand a child's behavior, anticipate problematic situations, and shift their focus from believing the child's behavior is purposeful to active problem solving. Accommodations can be made in the classroom and in teaching techniques. For example, a teacher can give an active child appropriate ways to release energy and a low-persistence child assignments in parts rather than one large task. He or she can understand that the student who does not stop reading when it is time to take out his math book may not be intentionally disobedient—he might be slow-adapting and not able to make the transition from reading to math very quickly, or he might be high in persistence and want to finish the chapter before moving on. He may be low in distractibility and so engrossed in the story that he does not hear the request. Or he may be a combination of all three. Knowing this, the method used to have him switch to math can be appropriately adapted. The teacher can give a 5-minute warning before switching subjects. She can suggest a good stopping point so he can move on, and to make sure he heard the request, she might put her hand on his shoulder as she announces that it is time to change. "Recognizing that many classroom behaviors are temperament based, rather than motivationally based, may 'take the edge off' what otherwise might be a disruptive relationship between teacher and child" (Keogh, 2003, p. 90).

Teachers can also benefit by knowing their own temperaments and how their traits affect their students. Some teachers enjoy energetic, intense children because they see them as feisty, interesting, and enthusiastic, whereas other teachers who have difficulty teaching these children prefer quiet, introspective children. The teacher's temperament and teaching style contribute to creating a good fit in the classroom. For example, an active teacher who does well with active students may have a hard time understanding why less active students work so slowly. The intense teacher may find himself provoked by intense students and may lose his temper quickly, whereas the same teacher may overwhelm the sensitive student. The highly adaptable teacher may become angry at the apparent disobedience of the slow-adapters, who cannot appreciate the spontaneity of sudden change. When teachers do not take their own temperaments into account with their students' styles of behavior, they can easily step out of bounds.

Consider the approaching, adaptable teacher with the sensitive, withdrawing child.

Pam, a preschool teacher, encouraged hands-on projects. She loved different tactile experiences, and nothing was considered too messy. One day the children were planting seedlings in the garden. Pam showed them how to plant the seedling by hand. Most of the children had great fun digging in the dirt, but Amy stood back and watched. Pam encouraged her to join in, but Amy was careful not to touch the dirt as she dug. Pam told Amy to use her hands to put the plant in the dirt. She resisted, saying she did not like the way dirt felt, but Pam insisted it was fun and she should try it. When she sprinkled some soil on Amy's hand, Amy howled in protest and ran into the school.

When Mom came to pick Amy up, Pam said, "I'm worried about Amy. She never likes projects like finger painting, gluing, or gardening. She seems overly concerned about cleanliness and often stands back and watches, not joining in. I think she may need play therapy for this problem."

If she had recognized the difference between her own approaching, adaptable (and somewhat persistent) temperament and Amy's sensitive and withdrawing temperament, she might have handled the gardening project differently. She could have provided gardening gloves or given Amy more time to warm up to the new project. In this way, Amy's sensitivities would have been respected and Pam could still involve her in "hands-on" projects.

How teachers respond to their students' temperaments was examined in a study of the interaction between teacher sensitivity and bold children (i.e., high approach, active) or wary children (i.e., withdrawing, inhibited) in the kindergarten classroom (Rimm-Kaufman, Early, & Salujah, 2001). Bold children spent more time off task and made more requests of teachers in the classroom. They were less self-reliant and less socially competent than children who were not bold. Teachers were rated as responsive, intrusive, or detached in how they responded to the children. Bold children with responsive teachers experienced less off-task behavior and became more self-reliant than the bold children whose teachers were either intrusive or detached. The responsive teachers recognized the temperaments of the bold children and were able to moderate their behavior in the classroom.

A teacher who understands students' temperaments has greater tolerance for students' behavior. A teacher who knows his own temperament realizes how much he can tolerate in the classroom. "It's a real balancing act," one teacher said. "Once I know a student's temperament, I can determine what is typical behavior for that child. I know where his strengths are and how much to push him in weaker areas. I also know how tolerant of his behavior I can be, taking into account my own temperament and those of the other students in the class. I find I push myself a bit further than before to accommodate differences." Figure 9.1 includes an informal questionnaire to help teachers gauge where their temperament types fall on a continuum so that they can gain insights into their own temperaments.

ADAPTING THE CLASSROOM ENVIRONMENT FOR DIFFERENT TEMPERAMENT TYPES

Each child experiences a classroom in a different way, and the classroom should reflect this. How desks are arranged, who sits with whom, the amount of art adorning the walls, lighting, and noise levels are just some of the factors that affect a child's experience as influenced by temperament.

For example, teachers often like to change desk, study group, or room arrangements throughout the year. But keeping the changes at a minimum, perhaps corresponding to seasons or holidays, is much easier on slow-adapting and withdrawing children than monthly changes. If monthly changes take place, preparing the children for such changes a few days prior makes for a more comfortable adjustment. Some teachers find that seasonal changes work well. They provide a natural transition for classroom changes, do not occur too often, and can involve the students in preparations for the change.

When planning seating arrangements, teachers can consider children's temperaments. For example, seating a low-persistence child with

Teacher Temperament Survey

Sensitivity: Sensitivity describes how an individual reacts to sensory stimulation. How sensitive are you to textures, tastes, noises, odors? Are you overwhelmed easily? Do your feelings get hurt easily?

1	2	3	4	5
Low				High

Activity: Are you energetic, active, and always on the go, or are you more sedate, moving at a slower pace?

1	2	3	4	5
Low				High

Intensity: How intense are your reactions to the world? Do you tend to be loud, very expressive, and dramatic? Or are you more calm, subdued, and quiet?

1	2	3	4	5
Low				High

Regularity: How predictable are you on a day-to-day basis with eating, sleeping, and other daily patterns? Are you generally more predictable or unpredictable in your daily behavior?

1	2	3	4	5
Predictable				Unpredictable

Approach/withdrawal: Do you hesitate initially with new situations, people, or things? Or do you dive right in, appreciating and seeking out novelty?

1	2	3	4	5
Approach				Withdraw

Adaptability: How well do you adapt to transitions and unexpected changes? How flexible are you? Can you shift gears quickly, or do you need time to adjust? Do you do best with routines or prefer spontaneity?

1	2	3	4	5
Fast				Slow

Persistence: How well do you persist with a task? Do you tend to stay with a task until completed or do you move on to something else if you become frustrated with it?

1	2	3	4	5
High				Low

Distractibility: Are you easily distracted by the surrounding environment, or do you become so engrossed in an activity that you don't hear or see anything around you?

1	2	3	4	5
High				Low

Mood: Is your natural tendency to be happy and positive or more serious and negative? Is the cup half empty or half full for you?

1	2	3	4	5
Positive				Negative

Figure 9.1. A quick, informal survey that can be used to assess a teacher's temperament.

a more persistent child encourages the less persistent child to try a bit longer. Seating two distractible children together can cause problems. How the teacher decorates the room can affect children differently. Walls filled with too much art and decoration can cause diversions for the distractible child and be overwhelming for the sensitive child. Having a quiet corner can provide a retreat for the sensitive, withdrawing child.

STRATEGIES FOR SPECIFIC TEMPERAMENTS

Here are some classroom environments that create a good fit with certain temperament types.

High-Sensitivity Children   Sensitive children need a place to go when they are feeling overstimulated. A corner of the room designated as the quiet area can provide a soothing oasis from the classroom noise and activity. In preschools, a "fort" large enough for one or two children to crawl into, equipped with soft pillows and other comfort objects can provide a quiet hideaway. Elementary classrooms can have a quiet corner with a soft chair or some pillows. Short breaks from the din of classroom activity allow the child to return to his work refreshed and able to continue with renewed vigor.

Sensitive children also react to the room's temperature, odors, lighting, and other physical sensations. These children may feel cold or heat more than less sensitive children. Keeping a sweater at school for cold days will help this child stay comfortable. Discussing what the class notices in the room is a way to make each other aware of individual differences and also can be useful in creating a comfortable atmosphere. The sensitive child will notice a slight change in temperature or that "the room smells funny." A teacher could bring up this subject at the weekly class meeting, and the class could discuss simple changes to make the room comfortable for everyone. Once the changes are made, the subject is closed until the next meeting.

High-Activity Children   Active children have plenty of energy, so classrooms must have space for children to move around freely and to work either standing up or sitting down. Activities can be structured to avoid a lengthy quiet time. Seatwork interspersed with

Sensitive children need

- A quiet retreat within the classroom
- To keep warm and cool clothes at school to manage hot and cold days
- To have their sensitivities acknowledged and addressed

• • • • • • • • • • • • • • • •

Active children need

- Space to move around
- Work interspersed with movement
- To be able to work at different levels (e.g., sitting, standing)
- To be allowed to express energy as long as it does not disrupt the class

• • • • • • • • • • • • • • • •

movement helps the active child who cannot sit still for long periods. The active child may also have difficulties working in his seat, so the teacher can permit work at different levels, including standing at a writing counter or sitting on the floor with a lap desk. One teacher provided large exercise balls to sit on. In another classroom, the teacher allowed children to sit at their desks in whatever way was comfortable, safe, and not disruptive to the class. Some children sat, some kneeled, some stood, some sat on chairs that had been placed upside-down or sideways, and all completed their work more easily when given this choice.

Distractible Children Most teachers who work with distractible children know that seating is crucial to limiting distractions, especially if the child is seated close to the teacher with fewer distractions between them. Distractible children can use cubicles when doing individual work to keep on track. If they are distracted by noise, workstations can be equipped with headphones that provide soothing, nonintrusive music or white noise. Earplugs that mute but do not block noise are useful. And quiet work periods can be scheduled into each day.

Distractible children often forget to take home assignments and materials for homework. A Post-it pad can be used to place reminders on the desktop. At the end of the day, the child removes the Post-it as each reminder is attended to and each task completed. Often, these children miss verbal instructions given in class. One teacher solved the problem this way. "When I give the class instructions I walk over to Jean's desk and put my hand on her shoulder or even on her desk.

This helps her to focus on what I am saying, and there are fewer mistakes or questions later." Writing the instructions on the board as well as giving them verbally is an even better way to assure that the distractible child gets them.

Slow-Adapting Children   Slow-adapting children benefit from a daily schedule. A class calendar can be posted in the front of the classroom and reviewed at the beginning of each day. The teacher can write each day's agenda on the board. Individual, monthly, or weekly calendars also help children know what to expect and can be reviewed at home to help children manage changes at school. Library day, a field trip, or a guest speaker should be discussed beforehand.

Intrusions can be an issue for slow-adapters. They need their space and should be seated away from children who have difficulty keeping their hands to themselves. Teachers can help these students express "I need my space" when necessary during group projects or recess when intrusions are more likely to occur.

Distractible children need
* Seating with few distractions between them and the teacher
* Cubicles for individual work if there are too many distractions
* Ways to block out extraneous noise
* Quiet work periods
* Organizational reminders
* Cues from the teacher when giving instructions

• • • • • • • • • • • • • • •

Slow-adapters need
* Daily routine
* A class calendar or daily agenda
* Reminders before special events (library day, field trips, assemblies)
* Warnings before changes
* Space from intrusions and the ability to express that need

• • • • • • • • • • • • • • •

Slow adapters need to know ahead of time when an activity will change. Teachers can give the class a 5-minute warning before a change. One teacher rings miniature chimes prior to a change or to signal an important announcement. Children who are very slow-adapting may need even more advance warning. Another teacher plays a short song on the tape recorder to signal a change. When the song ends, it is time to move on.

ADJUSTING LEARNING TASKS FOR DIFFERENT TEMPERAMENTS

Children approach learning according to their temperaments. Lessons that require students to manipulate items are more likely to hold the active child's attention than lessons that involve only lecture. When learning about geometric shapes, for example, children can search the room for examples of the shapes. The child who resists hands-on activities can take the role of the observer, pointing out the shapes and writing down or labeling the data that the active child collects.

STRATEGIES FOR ADJUSTING LEARNING FOR SPECIFIC TEMPERAMENTS

The following are some specific strategies for children with various temperament traits.

Slow-Adapting Children   Slow-adapting children have difficulty making transitions. The slow-adapting child may benefit from 5-minute warnings and simple routines paired with transitions. "In 5 minutes we will start our math. When you are finished with your project, walk to the chart and put a sticker by your name and return to your table." Such rituals help the slow adapter make transitions more easily. The slow-adapting child may resist learning a math concept in a different way because it is a change from what he is used to. A child who resists change, whether a change of routine or a different way of learning, takes longer to adjust and benefits from a more gradual approach. The teacher can help ease the adjustment by explaining new concepts and then practicing them with the child before starting. Once slow-adapters get used to a different concept they readily accept it. It just takes time and their initial rejection should not be perceived as an indication of defiance.

Withdrawing Children   Withdrawing students usually are no trouble for the teacher, but they are at risk for not asking for help when they need it. Engaging in new tasks is difficult for the withdrawing child. When the teacher pairs a withdrawing child with another who is slightly more explorative, and gives the withdrawing child certain tasks she knows he can handle, this helps him to go beyond his limits. Similarly, the teacher can help him warm up to a new venture by gradually increasing the expectations of what he must do.

Slow-to-warm-up children may resist learning new concepts because they resist all new tasks. Teachers can ease this problem by relating the new subject to a similar one that the student has mastered. The familiar assignment serves as a stepping stone to the new material. Breaking up the new learning task is another useful technique. The student becomes familiar with one part of the assignment at a time, which prevents apprehension about the new task as a whole. Teachers can also remind the slow-to-warm-up child of past tasks that were difficult for her at first but then mastered. This assures her that she can do it.

Persistent Children The persistent child wants to finish what he has started. He has trouble stopping a task before completing it. When giving persistent children a long task, the teacher can mention how much time they have to work on it and discuss a reasonable stopping point. This helps them believe that they have achieved completion. Persistent children also can be stubborn. If they decide on an answer to a question or the way a problem should be solved, they have a difficult time letting go of their opinion. Confronting them with another way only increases their resistance. Teachers can present them with other possibilities or help them check their answer rather than declaring that it is wrong.

Low-Persistence Children The low persistence child best approaches learning in small pieces rather than as a whole. She is often overwhelmed by a project, especially one that is difficult. Seeing an entire page of spelling words that need sentences can appear too daunting to even begin. Breaking up the task helps. Teach the child to break the task up visually, using another piece of paper to cover all but the first few words. Writing sentences for two spelling words seems much more doable than writing sentences for all of them. The child can then uncover more words as she completes the previous ones. Setting small goals, rather than large ones, helps the child complete the task. Taking small breaks during tasks when possible also keeps frustration down.

Distractible Children   The distractible child has difficulty focusing on the assignment at hand. After the teacher has addressed extraneous distractions as discussed in the last section, the child can use cues to keep himself on track. Often the distractible child's mind will wander, and she may begin to daydream instead of focusing on the task at hand. A short list of instructions or reminders next to the assignment can help the child to re-focus on each part of the task. She can check off each part as she completes it. Post-its also can be placed on the desk to remind the child which tasks to complete.

Impulsive Children   Helping the child who is a combination of high approach, activity, and sometimes intensity (i.e., impulsive) learn to manage impulses can aid the child, the teacher, and others in the classroom who might otherwise follow his lead. The impulsive child needs to learn to slow down and look before leaping. First, identify the places and events that he is likely to rush into. Discuss the expected behavior before those activities, then help him to use self-directed speech at these times. He may need to remind himself to "stop, look, and listen" or "take it slow." Having the child devise the self-talk empowers him and increases his use of the technique. Before any activity or event, a reminder from the teacher to "remember your words" helps set the habit. During the event the teacher can again remind the child or redirect him.

USING TEACHING METHODS
TO CREATE GOODNESS OF FIT

Each teacher brings a distinctive teaching philosophy in how time, physical space, and discipline are structured. Some prefer classrooms where the learning is teacher-led and pupils spend most of their time at their desks completing assignments. Others favor child-centered classrooms where students are more self-directed, taking an active part in the learning and decision making, and working in small cooperative groups on tasks they choose themselves. Project-based learning is a method of teaching whereby students use real-life projects to apply all of their academic skills.

Many prefer combinations of teacher-led, child-centered, and project-based learning. Each style will benefit some temperaments and be difficult for others, so teachers need to consider this once they know the temperamental make-up of the class.

Teacher-led classrooms fit best with students who need quiet and order, but if the class is too rigid, this can cause problems with persistent or slow-adapting children. Child-centered classrooms allow children to move around more and give them more control. This works well for children who need to move and for children who like to feel in control; however, clear limits and directives in how the classroom is managed must be set. With too few limits, child-centered classrooms can become chaotic, with slow adapters trying to control everything, active children expressing too much energy, and sensitive or distractible children bothered by the noise and high level of stimulation.

Project-based learning is a method of teaching that provides ways for children of all temperaments to work together successfully. Students apply their academic skills in solving real-life problems. For example, one fourth-grade classroom took on a project to save the California freshwater shrimp, an endangered species (Rogers, 1996). They researched the subject, decided what had to be done, formed committees, and carried out the work. In doing so, all necessary academic subjects were integrated in the project. Community outreach incorporated language arts in public speaking and letter writing. Fund-raisers incorporated math skills, art design, and bookkeeping. Creek restoration included biology, geography, ecology, and land management. Project-based learning allows children to develop a love for learning, a feeling of responsibility, and a sense of community. It respects children, their capabilities, and their individuality. It allows for a "good fit" by addressing the strengths of children with different temperaments and provides a safe environment that challenges children to go just a bit further than they might have. (See Helm & Katz, 2001; Katz & Chard, 2000; or Rogers, 1996, for a more complete description of project-based learning.)

ADDRESSING SPECIFIC
BEHAVIOR PROBLEMS IN THE CLASSROOM

Certain behaviors are problematic in the classroom: aggression, non-compliance, shyness, daydreaming, lack of attention, and class clown antics. Problems for the teachers often become problems for parents, too. Temperament contributes to each of these issues.

AGGRESSION AND ANGER
Parents of aggressive children fear that these children will be labeled and set up for failure. Teachers are concerned about having a peaceful class in which children feel safe.

. . . .

Desmond is aggressive if things do not go his way and has been kicked out of preschool for biting and hitting. His mother hesitates to try another school because she fears he might not make it and that his self-esteem will be affected. She worries about what will happen when he starts kindergarten.

. . . .

Ellen reacts to frustration or criticism with anger. Often she will lash out at whoever or whatever causes her anger. Recently, when she could not understand a math problem, she threw her pencil, hitting another student in the eye. Her teacher does not tolerate such behavior in her third-grade classroom.

. . . .

Aggression is very common in children who are active and intense. The combination of high energy and intensity can result in physical reactions such as tantrums, biting, kicking, and hitting. Unstructured environments during free play or recess cause activity and intensity to escalate. But other traits such as high sensitivity, slow-adaptability, or low frustration tolerance are the triggers for aggressive behavior.

Knowing which traits trigger the aggression help teachers know how to prevent it.

- Too much noise, stimulation, or commotion can trigger an outburst in a sensitive child who has reached her threshold.

- A child with low persistence will react when frustrated by another student, a difficult activity, or a limit.

- Active children become aggressive when not allowed to release their energy appropriately.

- Children who are active or intense may become aggressive if they become overexcited during free play.

- An unexpected change or intrusion or a transition that occurs too quickly often triggers aggression in a child who is slow-adapting.

For Desmond who is slow-adapting, the type of school may be a factor. If the school is unstructured, mostly free play with a large class size, students must contend with many unexpected changes and intrusions, which can trigger aggression. A smaller, structured classroom with more routine and clear, consistent rules can prevent the triggers that result from slow adaptability. Aggression often occurs during free play or recess because the time is unstructured and the child does not know what to expect. The child then tries to control the situation, which results in peer disagreements and potential aggression.

Teachers can prevent aggression with these children by

- Providing structure during free play by giving the child a task to do during the play period, for example, setting up or putting away play equipment

- Being firm but not rigid when dealing with behavior

- Being willing to give choices rather than commands

- Discussing expected behavior before free play or situations that trigger aggression

- Monitoring the number of changes, transitions, and intrusions the child has had throughout the day

When frustration causes aggression, as in Ellen's case, a teacher can

- Give new, difficult tasks in parts and explain each part thoroughly

- Help her recognize what causes frustration on the playground
- Help her learn more appropriate ways to express her intensity to control aggression

Intrusions, transitions, and changes are cumulative and if there have been more than usual during the day, aggression will be triggered more quickly.

The cooperative school model is another environment that may not be a good fit with children of certain temperaments. This school has a head teacher, assistant teacher, and different parents who work each day as teachers' aides. These parents often vary in terms of discipline and caregiving styles, even though the school strives for uniform rules. These changes are difficult for children who need consistency, familiarity, and few changes and may elicit aggressive responses when too many changes or transitions occur. For the child who is slow-adapting and must attend a cooperative school, teachers can

- Stress the importance that all parent helpers enforce the same school rules in the same way
- Make certain the child knows which parent aid will work each day and announce any changes beforehand
- Follow the same school routine each day

SHYNESS OR INHIBITION

"My son has cried every morning for the past 3 weeks when I leave him at kindergarten," one parent complained. "He won't join in the activities and wants to stay with the teacher. Otherwise he plays by himself. He doesn't talk much to the teacher or the other children. The teacher suggested that maybe he is insecure and not ready for school."

"Jessica is a loner. She is very bright and completes her schoolwork with no problem but is shy and stays by herself during recess," her teacher observed. "If someone approaches her to play she joins in, but she doesn't readily seek out playmates. She has difficulty speaking out in class and becomes very anxious about oral presentations."

Children who are slow-to-warm-up or inhibited are often mislabeled "anxious" or "insecure" and may be referred to a psychologist for treatment (Aron, 2002; Carey & McDevitt, 1995). They prefer to stand back and observe rather than become involved in an activity, and it takes them longer to become comfortable in a new situation. If they are also slow-adapting, they have difficulty making the transition to school and moving from one activity to the next, especially if the activity is new. Their usual reaction is to withdraw, sometimes cry and stay near the teacher, or just play quietly alone. Separation from parents, and later from teachers, is difficult because of their preference for the familiar.

Parents can prepare the slow-to-warm-up child for any new school by talking about it, visiting the school, and meeting the teacher before beginning. In preschool the parent can help the child adjust by staying briefly for the first few days of school and then gradually decrease the transition time. Establishing a consistent way of saying goodbye will help the child know exactly when the parent is leaving.

In elementary school, parents and teachers can help the child create a routine when arriving at school, going into the classroom, and getting ready for the school day. Once in the classroom the teacher can help the child become involved in an activity and then slowly retreat, encouraging the child to become more comfortable with new activities and new children. Pairing the child with another student helps dilute the novelty of the situation. If the other student is more outgoing, it encourages similar behavior in the slow-to-warm-up child. Parents often report that the child labeled shy at school is quite talkative and outgoing at home. The behavior at school exists because the child is not as familiar with the school environment, the teacher, or the other students. As the child becomes familiar with the school, the routine, the children, and the teacher, the evidence of shyness gradually dissipates. The adjustment period can vary from a few days to a few weeks or months.

One parent dealt with her son's separation difficulty in a creative way. "Separating from me was difficult when my son went to school the first time. I gave him a Polaroid picture of me to put in his pocket. Whenever he got lonely, I told him he could look at it and know that I was with him. It took about a week to get used to separating from me, but he still has the photo in his cubby."

Often a child will revert to the shy behavior after an illness, holiday, or a summer break and again need time to readjust. Each new situation evokes the same reaction and parents often notice a pattern.

Leah cried every day for the first 2 weeks of each new school year from preschool until third grade. After third grade she knew the school and the teachers well enough that she did not cry. When she started middle school, this pattern of anxiety repeated itself. She was worried about high school but had enough friends starting ninth grade that the new experience was diluted. When she started college in another state, she made many tearful calls to her family, who reminded her that once she got past the first 2 weeks she would be fine. She was. The move from the dorm to her first apartment elicited the same reaction, as did the move to another city for her first job after college. It helped her to be reminded of the "2-week syndrome" in order to feel comfortable settling into a new situation. Once teachers and children recognize these patterns, the ensuing behaviors can be managed more effectively.

NONCOMPLIANCE

Children who are noncompliant defy adults' requests by ignoring them, doing the opposite of what is requested, or blatantly refusing to obey. When a child refuses to comply, adults may assume that he is stubborn, spoiled, or—in extreme cases—suffering from oppositional defiant disorder. In many cases temperament causes the child's noncompliance.

Jeremy was labeled "noncompliant" because he did not follow instructions in his third-grade class. A temperament assessment revealed that he was slow-adapting and low in persistence. During math class, math stations were set up with a different activity at each table. The children had a specific amount of time to work on each task as they moved from table to table with their group. When it was time to move to the next task, the teacher would ring a bell. Jeremy started with his group at the first table, settled into the project, and began to work. When the bell rang he continued working but slowly got up and moved to the next station after being reminded to join his group, which was already there. He started slowly and was finally working when the bell rang again. Gradually he got up and went to a shelf where he began looking at some toys. The teacher directed him to the next task. When he got there most of the children had finished and the bell rang again. This time he wandered away from the next station, showing no interest in the task, and then left the room. The teacher had to bring him back. This series of events, she said, was a good example of his "noncompliance."

Jeremy's combination of slow adaptability and low persistence explained this behavior. He was not prepared for any of the transitions except the initial one. The bell signaling the change happened too soon for him and he slowed the transition by wandering away. He demonstrated that he had had enough of these transitions when he finally left the room after the bell was rung. Low persistence also played a part in this behavior. When the tasks were difficult, Jeremy was less likely to persist at them. Avoiding the stations assured his not having to do the tasks and prevented frustration.

Jeremy's teacher, parents, and temperament counselor decided to warn him before the bell rang so the transition would not seem so sudden. At the beginning of math class, the teacher described all parts of the tasks in detail. Such techniques increased his adaptability by preparing him for transitions and helped his low persistence by breaking up the frustrating tasks.

• •

Teachers often interpret slow adaptability as noncompliance. If a transition occurs too quickly, the child makes an attempt to slow it down. One way to slow down a transition is to ignore the request. The teacher perceives this as disobedience and it can result in power struggles. These children comply very well when rules and routines are consistent, however, and when teachers prepare them for transitions and provide adequate time to adjust to changes.

High persistence and low distractibility are also perceived as disobedience. Children who insist on completing the entire task before moving on or those who are so engrossed in an activity or thought that they do not hear the next direction are judged as defiant. Suggesting natural stopping points before a task is begun and making eye contact when giving directions generates cooperation.

DAYDREAMING

High distractibility, average to low activity level, and low persistence can contribute to daydreaming. Almost anything can cause the distractible child's mind to wander. When children who are low in persistence are presented with a task that is too difficult or boring, they are more likely to be distracted than those engaged in an interesting task. Because these children are not highly active, their distractibility is more likely to manifest in this form rather than in excessive movement. Seating the child away from major distractions and breaking up tasks to make them less overwhelming also helps the daydreamer. Another technique involves helping the child learn to become attuned to her tendency to daydream so that she can learn to refocus.

David, a second grader, tended to daydream often and this affected his grades as well as his relationship with the teacher. He was referred to his pediatrician for an attention disorder and put on stimulant medication. When this did not solve the problem, the pediatrician discontinued the medication and suggested a consultation with a psychologist. Because David had not experienced any difficulties the previous year, the psychologist suspected a goodness of fit problem. A temperament assessment revealed that David was low in persistence and high in distractibility. The psychologist worked with David to help him learn to notice when his mind started to wander. Together they devised a refocusing technique: When David realized he was not focused, he would hold his pencil at eye level, focus on the point, and follow it with his eyes to the paper in front of him. This brought him back on task. After using this technique for a week, David could refocus by merely thinking of his pencil moving down to the paper, and his ability to stay on task greatly increased.

ATTENTION PROBLEMS

Paying attention in the classroom becomes increasingly important as children grow older. Parents and teachers are now focusing on it at younger and younger ages, however. Children as young as 3 have been referred to pediatricians for attention deficit problems.

• •

Zadie, 3 years old, was referred to the psychologist for an inability to sit still and focus at circle time and for being disruptive in class. In Zadie's school, students were expected to be obedient and quiet, to sit still, and to attend silently during story time. If Zadie was not interested in the story, she would leave it and do something else. When she had to sit for a long time, she often disrupted the others. The teachers were disturbed by this behavior and advised her mother to take Zadie to a psychologist for her lack of attention.

A temperament assessment revealed that Zadie was active, intense, approaching, low in persistence, and moderate in adaptability. None of these scores was extreme, however. Zadie's behavior was that of a normal, approaching, active 3-year-old child. Working with her temperament could help her gain some self-control during certain activities, but if the school's expectations were unrealistic for an active 3-year-old, it might be a poor fit for her. The consequence for Zadie's behavior was to sit in a time-out chair, which only increased the problem. She needed ways to expend energy and incentives for controlling her behavior. Because of her low persistence, the psychologist advised her parents and teacher to focus only on one activity in which Zadie had to sit still. The teacher would specify the behavior she expected and give Zadie a stamp or sticker when she was successful. If the school combined this with appropriate ways for Zadie to release energy, more success was sure to follow. If, on the other hand, this did not fit with the school's philosophy, perhaps this school was not right for Zadie.

• •

In elementary school most teachers seat the low-attention students near them where there are fewer distractions and the teacher can help keep them on track. Low-approach students, however, might not like being so close to the teacher, preferring some physical distance. Another tactic is cooperative learning, in which the teacher places the student with a more persistent student who will keep the child on task but not take over the task. Often the low-attention student is merely overwhelmed by the difficult task. In this case, the teacher can show the child how to break up the assignment and do one part at a time.

Children who have difficulty staying on task can use timers to help them focus when working on homework. The child sets the timer and works on the assignment for the designated time, and then takes a short break and returns to work. This method cannot be used in class because it would disrupt the other students, so one teacher suggested a watch that would vibrate or flash when the time was up. Another teacher suggested an hourglass timer. At the signal, the child can take a short "mental break" (e.g., sharpen or change pencils, shift sitting positions) and set the timer again. As the child becomes used to this method, she can increase the work time. Eventually, children do away with the timer altogether, as the habit becomes well established.

CLOWNING

The class clown always has a wisecrack or funny face to make the other students laugh. But usually this is a ploy to distract others from the fact that he does not know the answer or is frustrated by the activity. Class clowns are often low in persistence, active, and approaching. Clowning derails the activity or buys them time to come up with an answer. Tactics mentioned as helpful for low-persistence children are useful for class clowns, as well as the use of positive reinforcement for behavior that does not involve clowning. But clowning can also be indicative of high persistence as illustrated by Blake.

• •

Blake's fourth-grade teacher advised that he be evaluated by a child therapist. Blake had experienced no classroom problems when school started, but as the year wore on, he became more and more disruptive. A good student and sociable, Blake had the ability to clown around until the class was in an uproar and the teacher had no control. Going to the principal's office became a daily event. Blake's parents consulted a temperament counselor who found that Blake was adaptable, high in persistence, approaching, and active. Temperament techniques produced some changes. But when a substitute teacher filled in one week while the regular teacher attended a conference, she made an astonishing discovery. She noticed that Blake was always the first to finish his work and then began to disrupt the others. After this observation the teacher began giving him additional work, which he readily completed. As long as he was occupied, he was not disruptive, but his combination of high activity and approach propelled him into his role as class clown when there was nothing else to engage his attention.

• •

EFFECTIVE HOME–SCHOOL COMMUNICATION

When working with behavior problems, parents and teachers must openly communicate. Events at school and at home can affect behavior, especially for children with more challenging temperaments. Teachers should be made aware of any issues at home, just as parents should know of any changes at school that could affect the child's behavior. Parents can alert the teacher to any events or changes at home by telephoning or sending notes. Some teachers have sign-in logs or places in the children's daily homework agenda book, in which parents can note relevant information. Likewise, teachers can alert parents of changes in school events by issuing a weekly or monthly calendar.

Children who are slow-adapting or withdrawing will be affected by anything that varies from the normal school routine. Even changes that happen regularly but occasionally such as assemblies, library day, holiday parties, or new seat assignments can have an impact. Listing events on the school calendar and discussing them in advance helps prepare children for them.

Changes that occur at home, such as visitation with a divorced parent, can affect school behavior the next day because it changes the child's usual routine. A parent who leaves on a business trip, a house-guest, or a new sibling also can make a difference in school behavior. Even a long plane or car trip can affect a child's behavior the next day at school. When teachers know of these changes, they can go more slowly with the child. The teacher might devise a special routine to ease the school transition when these outside changes occur. Giving the child choices within the routine or some other means of control after such changes can help.

WORKING ON PROBLEMS AT HOME AND SCHOOL

When a child experiences or causes a problem at school, parents can also work with the child at home. Parents and teachers can devise plans together to address the problem in both environments (see Table 9.2). For example, parents can work on aggression at home by moni-toring the television and movies that are viewed, modeling peaceful in-teractions, and reminding the child to use words. Rules for certain be-haviors and warnings for changes and transitions can be the same at school and at home.

By keeping communication open between school and home, many problems can be prepared for or prevented. Those that cannot be prevented can be handled much more easily once parents and teachers understand the cause.

Using Consequences and Rewards   Teachers often use con-sequences and rewards to change negative behavior. The child's tem-perament determines what is most effective. Consequences are neces-sary, but if they have no effect, consider an incentive. Slow-adapting children often respond better to incentives than punishment because they feel that they have more control in gaining a reward. The child's persistence level determines the schedule of rewards. Children with low persistence need small, immediate rewards. They have a difficult time sustaining behavior over the course of an entire day, let alone an entire week. Choose a specific behavior and divide the day into parts: for example, before and after recess in the morning and in the after-noon, or focus on specific activities during the day when the behavior occurs most often (during math, reading, and history). The child then

Table 9.2.   Temperament factors that affect behavior at home and at school

Temperament trait	Factors at home that can affect school behavior	Factors at school that can affect home behavior
High sensitivity	Illness or injuries that occurred at home	Illness or injuries
		Being too hot or cold
	Overstimulating activities the day or night before	Loud or chaotic activities
High activity	Rainy days—too much indoor time	Rainy days—too much indoor time
	Long car or plane trips	Having to sit still for long periods
		Waiting in line
Intensity	Tantrum or argument at home before school	Triggers from other traits (e.g., transitions, frustration)
Slow adaptability	Visitation weekend with divorced parent	Substitute teacher
	Illness (parent or child)	Changing room or classes (e.g., music, physical education)
	Moving (e.g., house, room)	Changing activities quickly
	New sibling	Rearranging the room
	Visitors staying in home	Field trips
	Parent gone on business trip	Changing the daily routine
	Coming home from a vacation or trip	Illness
	Any big change	Being reprimanded or disciplined
Approach	No major effects	Tasks involving observation
		Having to wait too long to take a turn
Withdrawal	Being ill at home for an extended period	Having to do "hands-on" tasks
	Moving	New teacher
	New child care provider	Returning to school after illness or vacation
		Field trips
		New activity or learning task
High persistence	Power struggle at home before school	Having to stop a task and move on
	Being "locked in" to an idea or power struggle	Being "locked in" to an idea or power struggle
Low persistence	Frustrating experience before school	Difficult task that seems overwhelming
		Boring, tedious tasks
Low distractibility	Upsetting experience before school that child locks into	Upsetting experience at school that child locks into
	Not wanting to stop an activity before school	
High distractibility	Chaotic situations or environments that interfere with child's ability to maintain homework routines	Lots of activity in the room
		Being with a noisy group
		Too many instructions at once

has several possibilities to succeed. A child with high persistence has an easier time of sustaining the behavior over a longer time—an entire day or a week.

Parents can also reinforce rewards at home. The teacher might give the child a star each time he succeeds, and the parent can then reinforce the child at home for the number of stars received. Again, the more home and school work together, the faster negative behavior is resolved.

Kinds of incentives vary according to what motivates the child. Motivation is either intrinsic (an internal desire to do something for its own sake) or extrinsic (an external reward or punishment). A sticker may motivate one child, whereas being allowed to collect the papers is an incentive for another. Both are considered extrinsic motivators. An individual goal such as breaking one's own broad jump record is an example of intrinsic motivation. But most often both intrinsic and extrinsic motivators are at work. When the student learns better study habits, he feels proud (intrinsic motivation), but this also results in higher grades (extrinsic motivation). Teachers and parents may begin with extrinsic incentives in order to establish a behavior, and then gradually phase them out as the intrinsic motivation takes its place.

HELPING CHILDREN LEARN SELF-MANAGEMENT

By elementary school, children can develop more self-control by understanding their own temperaments and their reactions to certain situations. Whereas at younger ages the adult watches for cues of rising intensity and then manages the behavior, in elementary school the child can learn to recognize intensity as it increases and do something to redirect it. Chapter 6 discusses ways children can learn about their own temperaments and learn to self-manage.

• •

Suzanne was a very slow-adapting, intense child, but she controlled her behavior on the playground at school, even though she could be very bossy with her friends. When asked how she could control her intense feelings at school, she replied, "When I start to get mad, my ears get hot. When I feel this way I go to the swings. After I swing for a while, I'm not mad anymore." Children who are in touch with their temperaments have more self-control.

• •

Teachers who validate children's feelings by acknowledging their temperaments from an early age help them to begin self-management. Prompts such as, "I know it's hard for you to make a change but I will give you a 5-minute warning before we line up," or "You don't like Jared to get too close to you during recess, but let's figure out what you can do instead of pushing him," teach children about their own reactions, work on problem-solving skills, and provide tools for managing the behavior. Teachers can use the method described in Chapter 6 to help children understand their own and others' temperaments to solve classroom problems. When a problem exists between peers, they can discuss the temperaments of those involved and figure out how that contributes to the problem. Then they can use a temperament perspective to find solutions that address each person's differences. This enables students to appreciate each other's differences while teaching them problem-solving skills.

To foster children's self-management skills, teachers can

- Help children become aware of their temperaments by validating their traits ("I know it's hard for you to switch subjects")

- Suggest a way to work with the trait ("I will give you a 5-minute warning when it's time to change")

- Focus on one area in which the child has difficulty with self-management ("We will work on switching from reading to math")

- Share control by having the child help devise ways to self-manage the problem area ("What do you think might help make it easier to switch?")

- Use small incentives to encourage successful self-management ("Each time you switch from reading to math with no problem, you'll get a sticker")

ATTENTION DISORDER OR TEMPERAMENT?

Ruff and Rothbart (1996) describe the temperament traits that are related to attention as extraversion (including impulsivity, activity, and positive intensity), fear (behavioral inhibition), and effortful control (the ability to control impulses). When these temperament dimensions are viewed in terms of attention deficits, they describe a child who is extremely outgoing and novelty seeking (high in extraversion and low on behavioral inhibition) and who has difficulty controlling his behavior (low effortful control). The ability to control impulses and sustain attention increases as the child develops, so school-age children who are active, inattentive, and impulsive may be considered immature. Some children do take longer to acquire these controls than do others. A temperament approach, however, suggests that these traits rather than developmental immaturity explain the child's behavior.

Those who do not understand the role that temperament traits play in attention might assume that children who are low in attention have attention-deficit/hyperactivity disorder (ADHD). As children reach elementary school age, teachers expect them to be able to sit and attend. But children vary greatly in activity level and attention span. The temperament traits of high activity, low persistence, high distractibility, and low adaptability can account for differences in attention. Confusion may occur because some of the symptoms of ADHD are similar to temperament characteristics.

The difference between temperament characteristics and ADHD can be found in the degree to which a child expresses behaviors. Children who have ADHD exhibit behaviors that are excessive and that go beyond traits of children with difficult temperaments (Keogh, 2003). Carey and McDevitt (1995) pointed out that it is often difficult to determine what is considered "excessive" behavior. ADHD behavior not only exceeds temperament-based behavior, but also it is recognized early, persists over time, disrupts daily activities, and is consistent (Keogh, 2003). The behaviors continue whether the child is in the classroom, with friends, at lunch, or on the playground, and they do not change greatly when the situation or instructional task is modified. On the other hand, temperament-based behaviors are evident in particular situations and respond to modifications in the environment and the organization of the setting.

The past two decades have witnessed an enormous increase in ADHD diagnoses (Carey, 2003). Hancock (1996) identified it as America's "number 1 psychiatric disorder" and reported that the number of children taking medication for the disorder has increased 2.5 times since 1990 in the United States. ADHD is diagnosed in 3%–9% of boys and somewhat less in girls, depending on the criteria used (Hudziak, Heath, & Madden, 1998).

Carey (1999) reported that only 1%–2% of the population can be readily identified as having clinical problems caused by disorganized high activity and extremely short attention spans. According to Carey (1988, 1999), ADHD is not a coherent syndrome and there is no standardization in assessing attentional or hyperactivity problems. He believes that no clear evidence that ADHD is related to brain malfunction exists, and that questionnaires that assess it are subjective and impressionistic. He asserts that ADHD symptoms are not clearly distinguished from normal temperament variations and that children diagnosed with the disorder may be more active and less attentive than average. He contends that the ADHD etiology neglects the effects of the child's surroundings and environmental interactions, an important consideration in behavior (Carey, 2003).

Attentional symptoms can be improved or worsened depending on the fit between the environment and the child's temperament (Biederman et al., 1995; Tizard & Hodges, 1978). The highly active child with low persistence and high distractibility can benefit from different teaching approaches or managing the environment. When teachers have realistic expectations for active, distractible children with low persistence by allowing energy outlets, reducing extraneous distractions, and dividing school work into parts, active children can sit still and focus quite well. Stella Chess told this story about her mother, a former third-grade teacher:

> When Burt began to be restless, my mother suddenly found errands that she needed done and asked Burt to help. Paper needed to be passed out, which required that Burt go to each desk; classroom books needed to be rearranged; the blackboard needed erasing. When Burt again began to appear distracted, my mother used her "ace." She sent a very important message to another teacher whose room was located at the far end of the corridor. The note she sent said, "I just needed to get Burt's muscles in motion. Please send me a sealed note back and

thank him for doing such an important job." This device helped Burt stay focused until the lunch break. (as cited in Keogh, 2003, p. xi)

Our educational system often does not adequately address the needs of active children. Perhaps the number of ADHD referrals received by pediatricians could be reduced if those needs were considered. When a child has characteristics of inattention, parents and teachers could request a temperament assessment as a first step before testing for ADHD. A temperament behavioral plan can address the issues at school, and if the behaviors respond to temperament management techniques, the child needs no further tests. If the techniques have no effect, parents should consider further testing by a qualified professional. Chapter 12 discusses how to determine if an attention problem is more than temperament.

SUMMARY

Temperament is an integral part of learning and success in the classroom. Administrators, teachers, and paraeducators can benefit from temperament information. When teachers recognize their students' individual differences in temperament, as well as their own, they can create a learning environment that capitalizes on their students' strengths and challenges them to move beyond their weaknesses. Knowledge of temperament can help teachers and administrators develop better educational programs, prevent negative behavior, and cope with classroom behavior problems more effectively. When temperament-related problems arise that teachers cannot handle on their own, they can call a temperament counselor to observe the difficult behavior and recommend temperament strategies. Temperament counselors can also help parents and teachers work together. After parents and teachers each complete a temperament assessment, the temperament counselor can help them understand temperament's role in the behavior issue and suggest strategies to use at school and at home.

Parents also play an important part in understanding how their child reacts in the school environment. Parents who take an active role in their child's learning and who communicate openly with the school regarding any events at home that might influence school behavior help their child to have a more successful school experience.

When educators and parents work together to utilize temperament concepts at schools and at home, students learn more readily, have better self-esteem, and acquire self-management skills. If behavior problems occur, teachers can identify and manage them more effectively.

CHAPTER 10

Temperament in Health Care Settings

Four-year-old Lisa reacted strongly when she saw her pediatrician. At each visit she would cling to her father and resist the doctor's examination. As her anxiety increased so did her intensity, and most procedures required the nurse and her mother to hold her down. Lisa's nurse dreaded her visits, considering her behavior that of a "spoiled child" who had an overly permissive parent.

Wesley, age 8, often complained of persistent stomach pains, but the doctor found no physical explanation for his symptoms. Although the problem seemed to occur randomly, closer analysis indicated that the pains preceded situations such as beginning a new class, going on a field trip, or attending a birthday party. Wesley's doctor noted that these events triggered anticipation and joy in most children, so he believed that the stomach problems reflected an emotional disturbance. He referred Wesley to a psychologist for further evaluation and treatment.

Terrance's mother brought him in for his 2-year well-child visit. She claimed he had no problems and was happy and active. But when the doctor examined his ears, she saw a raging ear infection with an eardrum near rupture. She suspected Terrance's mother of neglect for not noticing such a blatant condition. She warned Terrance's mother that neglected ear infections could lead to ear damage and hearing loss and found it hard to believe that Terrance had not alerted his mother to his infection.

• •

The ways in which children react to illness and medical procedures depend not only on their developmental levels, their familiarity with the situation, and the understanding and support of others, but also on their particular temperaments. Temperament also contributes to the occurrence of certain physical disorders and, in some cases, prognosis. Health care providers who do not utilize temperament information may make harsh judgments and incorrect diagnoses, and they may use inappropriate treatments (Carey, 1997).

In Lisa's example, had the nurse known that Lisa's temperament included high sensitivity, withdrawal, and high intensity, she may have approached the situation differently. "I notice that I judge children less now that I've learned about temperament. Rather than 'Oh, here's a little brat,' I think, 'Here's a child who's slow-to-warm-up and really having a hard time with this new, frightening situation," states Rona Renner, R.N. (Kaiser Permanente, 1995).

If Wesley's doctor had made a temperament assessment, he would have known that Wesley's problem involved slow-to-warm-up behavior rather than an emotional problem. He could have advised Wesley's mother to help him gradually adjust to these new situations in order to minimize any somatic effects. Likewise, Terrance's doctor would not have suspected neglect if she knew that Terrance's low sensitivity and low intensity caused the boy to react to pain less than other children would. Instead, she could have discussed with Terrance's mother how to identify possible subtle cues that might indicate early signs of illness and thereby prevent possible ear damage.

When health care providers recognize temperament differences, they understand why, for example, some children have sleeping or feeding difficulties, while others do not, and they can better advise parents about these issues. They also know which children may be at risk for developing behavior problems because of temperament risk factors. A temperament risk factor is any temperament trait or combination of traits that increases the risk of developing behavior problems or pathology when interacting with other factors (Strelau, 1989). People who have four or more risk factors acting together are 20% more likely to develop a behavior disorder (Rutter, 1979). When health care providers consider the number of temperament risk factors a child possesses, they can help prevent the development of behavior problems and provide appropriate intervention.

QUALITY OF CARE

Health care providers notice individual differences in infants' behavior from birth, and these differences affect how caregivers respond. Temperament affects how health care providers decide when a child needs medical intervention, the kind of medical care needed, and also certain physical conditions. How physicians and nurses interpret an infant's individual differences corresponds to how well they understand temperament, and this can influence the quality of care the child receives in the nursery.

Newborn nursery nurses reported that infants 20–40 hours old showed differences in alertness, activity level, and fussiness, which affected the care they received (Breitmayer & Ricciuti, 1988). Alert infants received the most nurturing and social contact and active infants received the least, although caregivers expressed more concern about active infants' health. Hospital or medical caregivers who interpret high activity level as physical discomfort or health problems may mistakenly refer these infants for more unnecessary medical procedures than less active babies. Nurses also tend to soothe fussy infants more than they do active or alert infants. Fussiness, in addition to indicating health issues, can also relate to an infant's negative mood or high sensitivity, and nurses can soothe these babies more effectively when they know the cause of the fussiness. For example, sensitive infants need lower levels of stimulation to reduce fussiness. If the soothing methods stimulate these infants further, irritability will increase. Whereas an active infant might respond to walking and bouncing, the sensitive infant might need soft stroking or a gentle voice. Knowing how different babies react because of temperament would help care-givers select the most effective soothing technique for each baby and prevent misinterpretation of infant cues.

TEMPERAMENT EFFECTS ON PHYSICAL CONDITIONS

Carey and McDevitt (1995) described three areas of physical condi-tions that temperament affects: organic conditions such as accidents, child abuse and neglect, and tooth decay; feeding and growth problems such as failure to thrive (FTT) and obesity; and physiological func-tions such as elimination, sleep, and pain. Children's temperament also plays a role in maternal postpartum depression; the behavior of pre-term and low birth weight (LBW) infants; and chronic illness and devel-opmental delays in children. These conditions are described in roughly chronological order.

FAILURE TO THRIVE

Nonorganic FTT is a growth disorder in which infants do not grow at the expected rate even though they are offered food and do not have a serious illness. Although a lack of stimulation and an inade-quate parent–child relationship can cause the disorder, the interaction between a mother's sensitivity and an infant's temperament can also be a contributing factor. Compared with infants who had no feeding difficulties, those with feeding problems were higher in negative emo-tionality and had less sensitive mothers (Hegekull, Bohlin, & Rydell, 1997). Infants rated as irregular had more problems at age 2, when their mothers were not sensitive to their signals. Other studies have found infants with FTT to be more fussy and demanding and less per-sistent than typically developing children (Wolke, Skuse, & Mathisen, 1990). Carey and McDevitt (1995) urged caution when interpreting the temperaments of these infants, however, because it may be that under-nourishment results in negative mood rather than negative mood re-sulting in undernourishment. In all cases, analyzing temperament and the goodness of fit with parents and the environment provides valu-able information when deciding how to cope with the problem.

LOW BIRTH WEIGHT

Preterm infants are those born 3 weeks or more before a full-term 38-week pregnancy. Low-birth-weight (LBW) infants weigh less than 2,500 grams (approximately 5 1/2 half pounds). Both types of infants have the possibility of physical, psychological, and developmental issues. Whereas some of these infants develop severe problems, others show no disabilities. Both environmental and biological factors play a role in outcome.

Preterm and LBW infants are sleepy and unresponsive, and when awake they often fuss or cry. Their appearance can cause parents to be less responsive and sensitive to them compared with the way they react to full-term babies. Parents hold, touch, and talk to these babies less and risk overstimulating them or behaving intrusively when trying to elicit a response (Baratt, Roach, & Leavitt, 1996). Preterm infants are less distractible, less sensitive, more intense, and less adaptable for their first 3 years (Hertzig, 1983), and mothers rated them as more difficult than full-term infants (Gennaro, Tulman, & Fawcett, 1990; Langkamp, Kim, & Pascoe, 1998). Although these infants are more likely to have a difficult temperament, these traits often diminish over time. In a study of LBW infants, 32% had difficult temperaments at 6 months, but at 12 months only 12% remained difficult, the average in a typical population (Medhoff-Cooper, 1986).

Successful programs to optimize preterm and LBW infants' development utilize family support, parent education, and interventions to enhance the children's developmental skills. Teaching parents about temperament as part of the intervention program helps them understand that certain infants typically exhibit difficult behavior. Parents can then learn to recognize subtle behavioral cues and to use appropriate methods to optimally stimulate or soothe their infant, enhancing the parent–child relationship. The Early Infant Temperament Questionnaire (Medhoff-Cooper, Carey, & McDevitt, 1993) assesses temperament as early as age 1 month in preterm and LBW infants. (See Appendix A for information on obtaining questionnaires.)

Familiarity with the concept of temperament increases the clinicians' understanding of medical problems and can help them suggest further treatment options. Knowing how infant characteristics and environmental stressors interact provides opportunities for more comprehensive intervention programs for children and parents.

Postpartum Depression

Temperament affects children's health *and* mothers' health, specifically in terms of maternal depression. A health care professional providing services to a difficult, fussy, or irritable infant should take note of the mother's mental state. Studies have found significant relationships between postpartum depression and infant temperament, suggesting that maternal perception of infant difficulty contributes to a mother's depression, particularly during the second postpartum month (Beck, 1996; Mayberry & Alfonso, 1993). A mother often expects to have a positive, "easy" infant, but having an infant she perceives to be "difficult" often makes parenthood extremely trying and unsatisfying. This may cause the mother to respond less to her baby, which increases the baby's irritability. The cycle, in combination with few social supports, could lead to child neglect or even abuse. Health care providers can help put social supports in place for mothers of "difficult" infants.

Tooth Decay

Parents will try anything to soothe a fussy baby, including giving extra bottles of milk or juice. This practice can lead to *dental caries* (i.e., tooth decay) (Carey & McDevitt, 1995), especially when a parent puts a child to bed with a bottle of milk or juice, which causes the liquid to pool in the child's mouth overnight. Health care practitioners should caution parents of irritable infants against bottle soothing. Because certain temperament traits contribute to irritability, the infant's temperament will also determine the most acceptable ways to soothe. See Chapter 4 for suggestions for soothing infants of different temperaments.

Accidents

Certain children have more accidents than others, and their parents may label them as "accident prone." Research on temperament effects and accident occurrence found that "difficult" temperaments correlated with lacerations (Carey, 1972) and to hospitalizations for various injuries in a child's first 5 years (Nyman, 1987). Children hospitalized because of accidents were significantly more persistent, more negative in mood, more active, and higher in intensity than children who were not hospitalized. In another study, boys tended to sustain more injuries than did girls and had temperaments with negative mood, withdrawal, low persistence, and slow adaptability (Irwin, Cataldo, Matheny, & Peterson, 1992).

• •

Winston, age 7, visited the emergency room five times last year. The nurses came to know him by name. The first visit involved a laceration. He fell and cut his head on the edge of the counter when he ran into the house from outside. The following visits involved a broken leg from jumping off a tree, a cut finger from climbing a fence, a large "goose egg" on his head from falling off of his bike when rounding a corner too fast, and a dislocated thumb from diving to catch a baseball.

• •

Carey (Carey & McDevitt, 1995) stated that the temperament traits that cause conflict or put the child out of touch with his or her setting increase the possibility of accidents. For example, highly active, intense children tend to get into more conflicts than do children of other temperaments because they react physically. Similarly, high negative persistence or slow adaptability increases the likelihood of stubborn behavior and "fight, not flight" reactions. Consider Bruce and Abe: When persistent, slow-adapting Bruce would not let active, intense Abe on top of the climbing structure, Abe pushed Bruce off, causing him to sprain his ankle. Inattentive children, who have traits of high or low distractibility or low persistence, tend to notice less around them or shift their attention constantly: They trip on the rock they did not see or run into the street after the ball without looking for cars. These qualities, combined with an overwhelmed or low activity caregiver, make injuries a real possibility.

A study at Kaiser Permanente Medical Center (Hansen, Rosen, Cameron, Rice, & Kristal, 1991) examined the relationship of temperament to accidents and identified three groups of children who had many accidents. The first group, composed of active, intense, approaching children, had more motion-related accidents such as falling, bumps, and cuts because of their tendency to "go for it." The second group of children—average in activity, lower in adaptability, and less persistent—had more self-inflicted accidents such as getting into dangerous places, ingesting hazardous materials, and pulling objects down on themselves. The third group, whose members tended to be persistent, adaptable, distractible, positive in mood, and less active, had accidents involving "other-inflicted" harm such as being hurt by a sibling or knocked down by a dog. Similarly, another study (Irwin, et al., 1992) found that withdrawn, slow-adapting, less attentive children were prone to unintentional injuries. Table 10.1 includes these three main types of accidents and the temperament types associated with them.

Schwebel and Plumert (1999) found that children who overestimate their abilities not only have more accidents but also have temperament traits of high activity and approach and low inhibitory control. These children are likely to seek out novelty and to rush impulsively into risky situations. Because of their high approach, they are attracted to new places. Their high activity level and low impulse control causes them to rush into potentially dangerous places. For example, 8-year-old Tisa, playing with friends in the woods, came across a rabbit on the other side of a stream and decided to try to catch it. She

Table 10.1.   Relationship of temperament type to kinds of accidents

	Motion-related accidents	Self-inflicted accidents	Other-inflicted accidents
Temperament	Active Approaching Intense	Average activity Slow-adapting Low persistence	Persistent Adaptable Distractible Average activity Positive mood
Average age at occurrence	15 months	9.6 months	15 months
Age range at which most cases (95%) occurred	12–18 months	7–12 months	10–21 months
Examples	Broken arm: Fell off a slide Cut head: Tripped when running	Burned: Pulled hot coffee off table and onto self Abrasions: Got arm caught in fence	Eye injury: Hit by branch when following brother Dog bite: Tried to pet strange dog

Source: Hansen, R.L., Rosen, D.L., Cameron, J.R., Rice, D., and Kristal, J. (1991).

did not think twice before trying to leap across and landed in the stream on a sharp rock. Her arm required three stitches. Active, approaching, uninhibited Winston would often overestimate his ability to jump from a tree, make the corner on his bike, climb a fence, or catch a baseball—behaviors that led to frequent accidents.

Health care providers can advise parents of children like Tisa to actively monitor their children's behavior and to teach safety rules early in order to prevent emergency room visits. Parents must teach precaution and insist on the consistent practice of safety rules both at home and in new situations to keep children like Winston and Tisa from injury.

CHILD ABUSE AND NEGLECT

Although many issues play a part in child abuse and neglect, studies have identified temperament as a significant factor in predicting maltreatment (Bagley & Mallick, 2000; Famularo, Fenton, & Kinscherff, 1993; George & Main, 1979; Harrington, Black, Star, & Dubowitz, 1998). "Difficult" children place additional stress on already overwhelmed parents or those who have abusive tendencies. Difficult temperament is also a risk factor when combined with other problems parents face, such as few social supports, poor psychological adjustment, and little preparation for parenting (Dukewich, Borkowski, & Whitman, 1996; Engfer, 1992). When parents do not have the personal or social supports to cope with an extremely challenging child, temperament may serve as the trigger for abuse. The therapeutic efforts by clinicians should include helping at-risk parents to understand their child's temperament, particularly those traits that are a challenge to manage or that particularly distress parents. A child's temperament cannot be altered, but parents can learn to understand why a behavior occurs, to anticipate or avoid situations that may trigger that behavior, and to work on changing their reactions to the child.

Another study found that neglected children had more difficult temperaments than a control group (Brayden, Altmeier, Tucker, Dietrich, & Vietze, 1992). Although difficult temperament can trigger neglect, Carey and McDevitt (1995) pointed out that other temperaments might also play a role in neglect. "Easy" children often require little attention and may get overlooked by preoccupied parents. A shy or sensitive child may consistently reject new situations or opportunities set up by the parent until the parent gives up trying new things, consequently neglecting the child's development.

OBESITY

Some evidence indicates that temperament can serve as a contributing factor to obesity. When Carey (1985b) compared typical-weight and overweight 6- to 12-month-old infants, he found that the "difficult" infants gained significantly more weight than the "easy" infants. He speculated that mothers fed fussy infants more in an attempt to soothe them. In a study of obesity in middle childhood, Carey and colleagues found that 8- to 12-year-old obese children were less predictable and less persistent than same-age children who were not obese (Carey, Hegvik, & McDevitt, 1989). Perhaps unpredictable children do not have regular eating patterns, which could contribute to obesity, and the frustrations that low-persistence children face could prompt them to eat to ease frustration. Low activity could be another contributing trait because children who are less active may burn fewer calories than do highly active children. The environmental fit with these temperament traits can determine the outcome of childhood obesity.

ENCOPRESIS

Pediatricians and nurses often treat children with encopresis, the retaining of feces that causes soiling from leakage. Physicians usually attribute this to constipation caused by the child's diet or to emotional conflicts, but temperament may also play a part. Carey and McDevitt (1995) suggested that low adaptability contributes to toileting resistance because it can lead to stubbornness. Temperament counselors from Kaiser Permanente have observed that children rated as slow-adapting, persistent, withdrawing, and intense tend to develop encopresis more often than do adaptable children (Cameron, personal communication December, 12, 2002). Slow-adapting and persistent children may resist parental control by retaining stools. Withdrawing children hold on due to the newness of using the toilet, and intense children protest loudly. Sensitive children who have had pain from a hard bowel movement may retain their stools in order to avoid pain. Chapter 5 describes problems related to this condition in more detail.

CHRONIC ILLNESS

Children with chronic conditions often must make major adjustments for their illnesses. How easily a child makes an adjustment depends on his or her temperament more than on the nature or severity of the illness (Carey & McDevitt, 1995). For example, children with acute lymphoblastic leukemia undergo painful lumbar punctures (LP). Those with higher sensitivity undergo greater anxiety and pain before and during the procedure than less sensitive children. In one study, sensitive children who met with a therapist who helped them manage the procedure by re-evaluating their last LP and enhancing their beliefs about their ability to cope showed less LP distress than sensitive children who had not received the intervention (Chen, Craske, Katz, Schwartz, & Zeltzer, 2000). Measuring physical sensitivity in children could help increase the effectiveness of identifying children who would benefit most from psychological interventions.

Children diagnosed with insulin-dependent diabetes must alter their diet and learn to manage daily injections or to use a pump for this purpose. These new routines affect family and social dynamics. Poor adjustment can lead to treatment resistance and behavior problems (Weissberg-Benchell & Glasgow, 1997). Children who have diabetes and who are less active and more adaptable have fewer behavior problems than inflexible children, whereas persistent children with low distractibility have fewer social problems while making this adjustment. Those who were most flexible achieved better metabolic control than did children with challenging temperaments. Active children who scored low in sensitivity and high in regularity and distractibility had good metabolic control (Rovet & Ehrlich, 1988). Compliance with medical regimens was more common in children who had a long attention span and were very predictable and positive in mood (Garrison, Biggs, & Williams, 1990). Slow-adapting children have difficulty with diet and injections because they involve change, intrusion, and the loss of control. When they are also sensitive, these children must cope with the pain of injections.

Health providers can use temperament strategies to help ease adjustments to illnesses. They can teach parents to establish routines for meals and insulin injections so the child knows what to expect. They can share control by letting the child choose where to have the injection (e.g., bedroom or bathroom, arm or leg) and what acceptable foods will be included when planning menus. Sensitive or distractible children can use techniques such as positive imagery or a pleasant distraction such as a game or music during injections. Children who are not distractible can focus on a favorite book or video. Giving a child control in other areas such as clothes and hairstyle choice helps her to adjust to other choices over which she has no control.

Parental involvement and consistency is vital in establishing healthy habits and providing support. Knowing a child's intensity level helps parents understand how large a reaction they can expect while the child makes these adjustments. Parents' temperaments can also affect children's health; one study found that mothers rated as inflexible, rigid, and negative in mood tended to have children with poor metabolic control, the inability to maintain sufficient blood insulin levels through food and insulin intake (Garrison, Biggs, & Williams, 1990). In order to establish good metabolic control, parents must be flexible, consistent, and maintain a positive attitude.

DEVELOPMENTAL DELAYS OR DISABILITIES

The impact of a developmental delay or disability is determined not only by the severity of the problem but also by environmental effects and child characteristics. A temperament assessment will not explain how a delay or disability will affect a child but it will predict the child's reactions. Children with developmental delays are more likely to have a behavior disorder than their typically developing peers, and a difficult temperament increases the probability of developing problems (Goldberg & Marcovitch, 1989). For example, when an infant has highly intense reactions and is difficult to soothe, this can be problematic for parents because such traits can relate to externalizing behavior. Extremely low intensity of reaction also can cause problems, especially in social interactions. A temperamentally challenging child with delays or disabilities causes additional stress for parents (Thomas & Chess, 1977). Therefore, identifying the temperaments of these children helps health care providers develop services for families.

Much of the literature on developmental delay focuses on the temperaments of children diagnosed with Down syndrome (see Goldberg & Marcovitch, 1989; Nygaard, Smith, & Torgersen, 2002; Ratekin, 1996). These children demonstrate a wide range of temperamental variation but, in general, they vary more greatly from a typical comparison group in terms of the dimensions of approach/withdrawal and persistence. The temperaments of children with Down syndrome were assessed as higher in approach, more distractible, more positive in mood, and lower in persistence than children without developmental delays (Ratekin, 1996). They also experienced less attentional focusing and lower inhibitory control (Nygaard, Smith, & Torgersen, 2002). Although children with Down syndrome are rated as less persistent, with time their temperaments tend to shift toward the "easy" direction in that they become more approaching, more positive in mood, and more predictable as they get older. They usually do not become more sullen or stubborn when they reach adolescence (Gunn & Cuskelly, 1991).

Goldberg and Marcovitch (1989) cautioned that, because the measures commonly used to assess temperament were developed with a population of typically developing children, results can have different meanings depending on population (e.g., Carey & McDevitt, 1978; Fullard, McDevitt, & Carey, 1984). For example, understanding the behavior of a child with a disability who has very low intensity may be problematic for the child's parents because the child's emotional cues are difficult to read. Parents of babies with Down syndrome often express frustration with their children's subdued expressions, for example, whereas the population of typically developing, low-intensity children are considered "easy."

Chess and Thomas (1986) pointed out other disabilities that temperament could affect. For example, deaf children need extra supervision due to their inability to perceive auditory cues. An impulsive, active, approaching deaf child faces greater danger because he cannot hear an oncoming car if he dashes into the street after a ball. Children with motor disabilities will have an easier time controlling muscular movements if their activity level is low rather than high.

Children with congenital or acquired limb deficiencies must adapt both psychologically and socially. Factors such as family support, family harmony, and temperament help predict how well children with limb deficiencies are able to adapt to their conditions (Varni, Rubenfeld, Talbot, & Setoguchi, 1989). Children with high emotionality have both internalizing and externalizing behavior problems and less social competence than those with less emotionality. These children would most likely react to their limb deficiencies by loudly acting out or by demonstrating withdrawing, anxious behavior.

TEMPERAMENT STRATEGIES FOR CHILDREN WITH DISABILITIES

To use temperament strategies with a child with a disability or developmental delay, a health provider must examine the extent of the problem, assess the amount of parental stress involved, determine the child's temperament, and decide whether the interactions between the environment and child match. The health care provider can then determine the best techniques, depending on the amount of parental stress and the child's temperamental difficulties. For example, the child who is high in intensity and easily frustrated may react to frustration in the environment with aggression or tantrums. Parents can watch for signs of frustration and intervene with redirection or by having the child take a break before frustration mounts to a tantrum. When aggression or a tantrum does occur, parents can learn to remain calm and firm in addressing the behaviors. Temperament techniques used with children with developmental delay or disability are similar to those used with typically developing children. Parents of a child who has developmental delays, however, must learn to identify their child's behavioral cues that may differ from other children. Research has shown that children with disabilities who have difficult temperaments benefit from more frequent professional monitoring and additional support or preventive intervention (McDevitt, 1988).

EFFECT OF TEMPERAMENT ON CHILDREN'S RESPONSE TO MEDICAL PROCEDURES

Medical procedures such as blood tests, immunizations, and hospitalizations are challenging for most children, but those with temperament traits such as high sensitivity, withdrawal, slow adaptability, or high intensity have particularly strong reactions.

TEMPERAMENT-BASED REACTIONS TO PAIN

Children handle pain in various ways, and individual differences in temperament play a role in coping style and in pain response. Highly sensitive Kelly faints at the slightest bruise, whereas low-sensitivity Matt does not notice that he has cut himself. High-intensity Chrissie shrieks loudly and at length after falling. Distractible, intense Charlie wails at a scraped knee, but his cries quickly subside as his attention turns elsewhere.

Parents' responses to their children's pain reflect family structure and parental boundaries and reinforce family patterns (Segal-Andrews, Altschuler, & Harkness, 1995). Parents who express distress and anxiety intensely whenever their child experiences pain teach the child to react similarly. Children soon learn that they can get extra attention when ill or in pain. Knowing that a child has intense reactions helps his parents modulate their responses to the child's illness or pain.

In a study of school-age children's reactions to pain from venipuncture (i.e., taking blood from the arm), those with higher sensitivity had increased heart rates and higher pain reactions (Bournaki, 1997). Distractible children had lower reactions. Activity, mood, approach, adaptability, intensity, and sensitivity correlated with children's pain responses in another study (Lee & White-Traut, 1996). Sensitive, intense children had increased responses to pain, and those with the difficult traits of high activity and intensity, low adaptability, withdrawal, and negative mood reacted more negatively than did children without those traits.

A child's intensity determines the volume and drama of the reaction. The active child might physically resist a procedure and then react aggressively to the pain. When active, intense Abby gets an injection, she angrily shouts and then kicks the nurse or whomever is near. The new procedure intrigues adaptable, approaching Omar, whereas it frightens sensitive, withdrawing Chang. Slow-adapting Else resists the loss of control and reacts strongly to the intrusion of the procedure. Adaptable, active Ginger reacts to the pain but gets over it quickly. Negative Leslie whines and complains before, during, and after the procedure. Distractible, low-persistence Norah winces until she notices the bright poster on the wall.

In addition to affecting a child's reactions to pain, temperament can also influence the development of a physical problem. Abdominal pain is one example. Numerous health factors can contribute to recurrent abdominal pain, but one study found that more children (age 68 months, or 6½ years) with this ailment had temperaments rated as intense and negative than did children with other temperament types (Huttunen & Nyman, 1982). Other researchers found that difficult children who had trouble adapting to new routines at the beginning of the school year were more likely to report abdominal pain (Davison, Faull, & Nicol, 1986). Carey explained that in a slow-to-warm-up child, the stress of adjusting to a new situation might mobilize the sympathetic nervous system and cause some physical disturbance (Carey & McDevitt, 1995). Withdrawing or sensitive children with low intensity may respond to fearful, new situations by internalizing their anxiety in stomach pain or other somatic complaints. Kowal and Pritchard (1990) found that sensitive or shy children complained of recurrent headaches more often than did children in a control group. As one pediatrician explained,

> When a child comes in with recurrent belly aches or headaches and I can find no organic cause or major familial conflict or change, I look for a temperament cause. Not only can I explain the symptoms, but also I can offer the parent some concrete advice.

Having a temperament profile in the child's medical chart helps the provider diagnose the problem, predict reactions, and offer advice for treatment.

RESPONSES TO HOSPITALIZATION

One study found that the temperament traits of predictability, approach, adaptability, and mood predicted how children responded to hospitalization for tonsillectomy (Carson, Council, & Gravely, 1991). Children higher in predictability, approach, and adaptability responded better to the experience than did children with the opposite temperaments. McClowery (1990) found that the variables of mood and approach/withdrawal predicted response to hospitalization for school-age children. Children rated as negative in mood and withdrawing had a more difficult time with their hospitalization than approaching, positive children.

Temperament also influences the amount of pain medication that children receive following a surgical procedure. Intense children received more medication following genitourinary surgery than children rated as low in intensity (Ruddy-Wallace, 1989). The adage "the squeaky wheel gets the grease" seems appropriate because the louder the complaint, the more medication is administered, so easy or low-intensity children run the risk of being overlooked. They may experience as much pain as intense children, but they do not express their needs as vocally and therefore may not receive the medication they need.

TEMPERAMENT IN DIAGNOSIS, TREATMENT, AND PREVENTION: CAREY'S MODEL

William Carey, M.D., one of the first pediatricians to recognize the importance of using temperament in a pediatric practice, suggests four steps for health care practitioners to use temperament in diagnosis, treatment and prevention (Carey & McDevitt, 1995):

1. *Recognize temperament vulnerability.* Normal temperament variations affect a child's vulnerability to stressors or unpleasant environments. The magnitude of the child's complaints and the occurrence of symptoms may reflect the child's intensity or sensitivity to current environmental issues. Practitioners can evaluate the extent to which a given child's temperament has made him vulnerable to this illness.

2. *Consider temperament's influence on a child's response to symptoms.* When physical findings do not correspond to subjective reports, or if the child typically complains too much or not at all, the health care professional can consider the role temperament plays. A minimally red eardrum in a screaming child could indicate the beginning of a major infection, a cry for attention, or a highly sensitive and intense child. Treatment plans can then address the child's real needs rather than just the intensity of the complaints.

3. *Remember temperament's role in adjusting to chronic illness or disability.* Primary health care providers and parents who acknowledge and accommodate the child's temperament can expect fewer behavior problems and easier management. Practitioners can help parents develop ways to manage the illness that suit their particular child's temperament. For example, as mentioned previously, children who are adaptable have an easier time coping with a new

diagnosis of insulin-dependent diabetes than do children who are slow-adapting. Parents can help children who are slow-adapting manage the dietary changes and medication by such methods as sharing control and establishing routines around administering medication.

4. *Modify the environment to control the stressors.* The clinician can identify environmental factors that fit poorly with the child and can attempt to change them. This includes helping the parents adjust their expectations of the child's behavior to the child's temperament. Health care practitioners understand that children respond differently to stressful medical procedures, so they can provide support to fit the child's temperament. Being hospitalized is stressful for most children, but the child who is intense may react by kicking the nurse, the child with slow-adaptability may refuse to cooperate, the withdrawing child may become anxious or depressed, and the child who has low intensity may not express any displeasure. Although difficult and shy children have obvious needs, easy children might be overlooked because their positive mood and mild expressions of pain may conceal true emotions. Knowing how the child will react helps health care providers and parents adjust the environment to create a good fit. A nurse can learn to go slowly with the child who is intense and help provide positive ways to express her intensity. The child who is slow-adapting can visit the hospital before being admitted, and doctors and nurses can prepare the child for any procedure beforehand. The child with low intensity should be adequately prepared for the hospitalization even though he appears unconcerned.

Patient treatment begins with a comprehensive health history that includes medical and environmental information, and a temperament profile can be part of this process. An examination determines the physical extent of the child's problem. The child's temperament provides information about the child's reactions to the problem, treatment approaches, and possible contributing environmental factors. When the problem concerns behavioral issues such as discipline, tantrums, or daily issues such as feeding or sleeping, health care providers can use temperament to give concrete advice.

Six-year-old Lily developed a stomachache a few days before her teacher went on maternity leave. Being very sensitive to changes in her environment and withdrawing, she did not openly express her feelings about this event. The pain in her stomach increased until she began to react loudly. Because her reaction was so intense, her parents rushed her to her pediatrician thinking she might have appendicitis. After finding nothing physically wrong, her physician, knowing Lily's temperament, realized that her reaction resulted from the impending departure of her teacher and her high sensitivity to change and fear of the new situation rather than from a serious illness.

TEMPERAMENT PROGRAMS IN MEDICAL FACILITIES

Following Carey's lead in using temperament in a pediatric practice, other clinicians have established temperament programs in medical centers. James Cameron, Ph.D., studied the original data from the New York Longitudinal Study (NYLS) and found relationships between parental attitudes, child temperament, and behavior problems (Cameron, 1977, 1978). In 1986, Dr. Cameron teamed up with David Rosen, M.D., chief of psychiatry at Kaiser Permanente Medical Center, San Rafael, California, and began a large-scale 3-year study of temperament guidance for parents (Cameron, Hansen, & Rosen, 1989). All parents of 4-month-old infants in the study received a temperament questionnaire. The 35% of parents who completed the questionnaire were divided into four groups: a control group and three experimental groups. The control group completed the questionnaire and received no feedback, but the temperament profile was placed in their child's medical chart. Experimental Group 1 (E-1) received written information by mail regarding their infant's temperament profile and anticipatory guidance about issues likely to occur in children with that temperament. Experimental Group 2 (E-2) received personal feedback from a temperament counselor, and Experimental Group 3 (E-3) received a profile and written information and met with a temperament counselor to discuss their infant's temperament. The temperament counselors were child development specialists and pediatric nurses within the department who had been specially trained. This research followed a preventive model to help parents understand their infant's individuality at an early age and use that information to manage issues such as feeding, sleeping, and separations. The information also helped parents anticipate behaviors that were likely to occur and to plan for those situations.

The research reconfirmed Chess and Thomas's findings that children's temperament affects the incidence of behavioral problems and that fewer problems develop when parents understand their child's temperament (Cameron et al., 1989; Cameron, Rice, Hansen, & Rosen, 2000). Parents in all experimental groups who received temperament information felt more confident as parents and understood their children better than did those who received no information. Parents in group E-2, who received personal guidance from a temperament counselor, reported significantly fewer problems in managing behavior issues than those in the other groups. Parents who received written information (E-1) found it particularly helpful in managing issues with their slow-adapting infants. In all three experimental groups, parents with temperamentally difficult children managed their children's behavior better and used fewer pediatric services than did parents of difficult children in the control group (Cameron, Rice, & Rosen, 1994; Rosen, Cameron & Rice, 1996).

After this initial research, the preventive program expanded to include toddlers and preschoolers. This program intended to prevent temperament-related behavioral issues from becoming behavior problems. The program had a trial run first in the psychiatry department that then was established in pediatrics. Parents preferred to have the temperament program in pediatrics so it could be part of their regular pediatric care. Having it in the psychiatric department seemed to pathologize temperament.

Many parents who received a questionnaire found it so helpful that they requested the services for a sibling. Pediatricians began to refer patients to the temperament counselors and several Kaiser facilities set up meetings to educate their physicians and nurses about temperament. The program expanded to include children up to 12 years old with referrals from physicians, nurses, and parents who had heard of the program. Facilities incorporated temperament-based parenting classes and temperament counseling services, and different medical centers developed variations of the program according to the populations they served and their budgets.

More than 25,000 children, ages 4 months–12 years, have participated in the Kaiser temperament program, which provides anticipatory guidance to prevent behavior problems and counsels parents whose children have behavioral issues. Because the individualized advice is based on the child's temperament, the outcome is highly positive. Follow-up data of all participating Northern California Kaiser pediatric departments noted the following:

> Two-thirds of the pediatricians rated the temperament information as helpful to parents and rated the temperament program as having a positive impact on their practice. More than half of these pediatricians said that the temperament program enabled them to handle behavioral questions from parents more easily and quickly (Rosen, Cameron, & Rice, 1996, p. 141).

Clinicians who are not interested in handling behavioral issues during office visits stated that they like having a temperament-trained professional in the department to whom they can refer parents. The program has expanded to other medical facilities throughout California, the Northwest, the Southwest, Canada, and the Midwest (e.g., Anderson, 1994; Ostergren, 1997; Smith, 1994).

In Sioux Falls, South Dakota, the Temperament Project at Avera McKenna Hospital and South Dakota Children's at Sioux Valley Hospital developed a similar program, which offers temperament screening to parents of all 9-month-old children born at either hospital. A corresponding program sponsored by the local United Way provides families with free temperament screening and an opportunity to receive follow-up services to help them better understand their infants. The program also provides training, in-service workshops, and screenings for babies in the community. Free classes tailored to meet the needs of specific groups are available to parents, teachers, child care providers, and local businesses.

Nursing Programs

The Kaiser Permanente temperament program trains pediatric nurses as temperament counselors. In addition to providing individual counseling for parents, the nurses use temperament concepts in routine pediatric care. Nurses find it easier to approach a child for an immunization, weight and height check, or ear wash when they know the child's temperament. Nurses also use temperament concepts to "reframe exhibited behavior patterns within a temperament perspective" (McClowery, 1992, p. 323) and use the concept of goodness of fit to identify high-risk families and determine the success of temperament-based interventions.

Arizona State University School of Nursing offers an interactive, on-line Temperament Assessment and Counseling class. The program is a semester-long class that teaches nursing students about temperament theory, temperament assessment, and temperament concepts that can be used when working with children. To the best of my knowledge, this is the first on-line temperament counseling class that has been developed. As the importance of temperament becomes increasingly evident in diagnosis and treatment, more university medical classes will incorporate these concepts.

Pediatrics Practices

In an informal evaluation survey conducted by the author, a group of pediatricians described how they used temperament concepts in their practices. They found temperament concepts useful when working with pediatric patients and their parents or caregivers in five areas: customizing advice, understanding siblings, strengthening parenting skills, approaching an examination, and working with specific behavioral and medical issues. The following sections include some of their comments taken from the survey.

Customizing Advice for Parents   Pediatricians often talk to parents about behavioral issues such as limit setting; tantrums; and sleep, feeding, and toileting. Many use the concepts of temperament to customize their advice in these areas. Many parents ask their pediatricians about parenting strategies they use and how their children respond. One pediatrician noted, "Temperament is often important in understanding a child's response to a parenting strategy."

• •

Leigh's parents were frustrated with her tantrums. Even though the parents responded consistently and did not give in to the tantrums, the tantrums still occurred. Leigh's parents described the tantrums as random and occurring over seemingly inconsequential issues. Their pediatrician checked Leigh's temperament profile, which showed high intensity, high sensitivity, and low adaptability. She determined that quick transitions, unexpected changes, and overstimulation could trigger Leigh's intensity and advised her parents to make more time for transitions, to prepare Leigh for changes, and to minimize stimulating experiences. Leigh's parents reported that the tantrums decreased dramatically.

• •

Understanding Sibling Differences   Another pediatrician found that temperament concepts helped parents understand differences between siblings. Parents who have one easy child and one challenging child often feel they have done something wrong with the more challenging child. When the parents can compare the differences in temperament profiles, the behaviors become clearer and so do the solutions. Parents realize that children from the same family may react differently in similar situations. They learn to customize their responses to their children according to each child's unique temperament.

Educating and Empowering Parents   Other pediatricians described temperament as "a wonderful source of knowledge and empowerment for patients' parents—an excellent resource to help parents be better parents. It puts behavior issues and problems into a framework for discussion and explanation." Health care providers use temperament to reframe behavior issues and help parents understand that certain behaviors are "normal" for a particular temperament. This helps parents learn appropriate management strategies while reducing parental blame and guilt.

Conducting an Examination   The pediatricians described in the evaluations how they use the information during an examination. "If I know the child is sensitive to change, I talk to her in the mom's lap for a while before I approach for the exam." Another said the child's temperament determines how quickly she can perform parts of an examination. "Some kids react strongly to being touched or are okay until you try to look in their ears, so I do that last." Knowing the child's temperament is essential in improving compliance. "If I am going to do something that is associated with pain or unfamiliar to the child, I try to tailor my interaction to what I know or suspect of his or her temperament." Having the temperament profile in the chart aids the doctor in approaching the patient and in discussing behavior problems with parents.

Working with Specific Behavioral and Medical Issues   Understanding temperament also helps pediatricians deal with particular issues. "I have found that temperament counseling has been particularly helpful in older children's resistant non-toileting. It provides clues as to the resistance." If the child is sensitive it may be due to a painful experience, but if a child is low in sensitivity he may not be noticing his body's cues. If the child uses toileting as a means of maintaining control, control issues often relate to slow adaptability or high persistence. Each trait determines the best approach.

One pediatrician surveyed explained,

> In our well-child exams we cannot but help touch upon issues that fall within this [temperament] realm, whether eating issues, toileting, sleep concerns and so forth. It is likewise common for a parent to throw in a 'by the way' question regarding a specific behavior issue while in for an ill visit. Temperament can play a role with straightforward medical issues as well. I frequently use it for questions on maintaining discipline with children with serious medical problems. The previous dynamic between parent and child is disrupted and the parent is uncertain as to whether it is appropriate to go back to old routines and requirements with a child who appears to be trying to manipulate using illness as an excuse.

Pediatricians find that having a temperament counselor available in the office enhances their time-limited visits. The service allows parents more time with a professional to work on behavioral issues. One doctor concluded,

> Raising a child is so difficult, the fragmentation of the nuclear family, loss of extended families, and two parents working make parents seek help more often in issues pertaining to the interactions with their children. Despite our age-appropriate handouts and our own experience, our skills or time is limited and I find temperament counseling to be invaluable to help my parents. It is a very distinct "value added" service that I can offer to [my patients] and they are universally appreciative.

SUMMARY

Health care providers and pediatrics offices increasingly incorporate temperament concepts into their practices. Understanding a child's temperament increases the quality of care provided to families by helping nurses, doctors, and other health care providers understand the child's behavior and respond in the best way to create a good fit with the child. It aids in diagnosis of physical and mental conditions and is essential in preventive medicine. For example, temperament helps physicians know which children may be at risk for accidents, child abuse, obesity, and more. They can also help mothers of "difficult" infants who may be at risk for post-partum depression. When a child develops a chronic illness a temperament profile helps the practitioner know how the child will react to procedures and how to best proceed.

Medical facilities that have temperament programs provide a valuable service for families. Parents involved in these temperament programs have fewer problems with their children, and learn how to best handle situations if they occur. Temperament programs with temperament counselors allow physicians to refer behavioral issues to the counselors so that they can concentrate primarily on medical problems. Whether physicians, nurses, or temperament counselors utilize temperament concepts with parents or children, families benefit as well as the pediatric departments providing these services.

CHAPTER II

Temperament in Mental Health Settings

A child therapist who was unfamiliar with temperament concepts observed 3½-year old Joseph at preschool because of concerns about his inability to follow rules and his aggressive behavior toward peers. She watched him for 1 hour during free-choice time and outside play. Joseph refused his teacher's request to let another child play on the computer, and the teacher had to physically remove him. Next, he went to the art table, where the children were stringing cereal necklaces. The teacher explained the craft to Joseph and asked if he wanted to participate, but he refused. Instead, he began to eat handfuls of the cereal. The teacher removed the bowl and Joseph became angry, made a face, crossed his arms, and left the table. Still, he stayed nearby and watched. He came back a few minutes later, said he would like to do the craft, and spent 15 minutes stringing cereal and talking about school. He was calm and articulate as he talked about the rules at school and how you could get in trouble.

Next he went outside and pushed a friend around the yard in a car and crashed into a group of children. When the bell rang to go inside, Joseph ran to the front of the line and then into school, although the teacher called him to come back and line up. Circle time was next: Joseph rolled on the floor, argued with and pushed another boy, and would not sit down until the teacher made him sit next to her.

The therapist described Joseph as a bright boy with no cognitive delays who had a few friends. She observed that he was self-directed and understood the rules but did not always follow them. She concluded that he was extremely noncompliant, sought negative attention, was impulsive, and thought of himself as a "bad boy." She recommended an evaluation by a neurodevelopmental or behavioral pediatrician to rule out attention-deficit/hyperactivity disorder (ADHD) or oppositional defiant disorder (ODD), direct and immediate family support for Joseph, counseling for the entire family, play therapy for Joseph, a shortened school day because of behavioral issues, and one-to-one time each day with Joseph to give him positive attention and approval.

Joseph's parents, upset by this report, called their pediatrician, who arranged an evaluation by a temperament counselor. The results of the assessment revealed that Joseph was low in sensitivity, average in distractibility, very active, moderate in intensity, slow-adapting to intrusions and changes, very approaching, easily frustrated, and high in negative persistence. Using a temperament perspective, the counselor explained Joseph's behavior in ways that differed from those of the therapist. For example, when the teacher asked Joseph to leave the computer, this was a change for which he was not prepared and an intrusion when she physically removed him. This created frustration and a rise in intensity. When his intensity escalated, his adaptability decreased, which resulted in his refusal to do the craft. When he ate the cereal he exhibited negative persistence and also an attempt to control the situation after his loss of control when taken from the computer. He eventually did join in on his own terms and participated without incident for 15 minutes. Outdoors he demonstrated active, approaching, and impulsive behavior when he pushed the car into the children. Aggressive or physical behavior often increases in free play among active, approaching, intense children who are also slow-adapting to intrusions. If the transition to going inside was made too quickly, this could account for his lack of compliance about lining up and going in. Difficulty at circle time is common for active children who have been playing vigorously outside and are then expected to stop and sit quietly.

Joseph's mother reported that he had not experienced behavioral difficulties at his previous school and was considered an "active boy" there. She had changed schools because she believed he would have more friends entering kindergarten from this school. The other school was very small, but his class in his new school had 45 children. Joseph's mother did not report any major changes at home apart from the new school, and issues with Joseph's 8- and 11-year-old siblings were typical. The parents' relationship was good, and there were no unusual environmental circumstances.

• •

From a temperament perspective, such a large class was a poor fit for Joseph. His aggression and refusal to follow rules were typical behaviors for a child with his temperament. In these circumstances, a temperament counselor might recommend that before considering family therapy or play therapy, the family try using temperament strategies. The evaluations for ODD and ADHD might have been premature based on the limited observation and the young age of the child.

A counselor might also recommend that Joseph's parents look into a smaller school setting. If this was not possible, perhaps Joseph's present school could make some minor modifications such as structuring the free play period to limit the number of intrusions. One way to do that would be to give Joseph a "helper" task to break up the length of the free play. Teachers could prepare him for changes in a consistent way when moving between activities. If they saw his activity level escalate, redirecting him to calmer activities could prevent physical or aggressive behavior. His parents could review the daily routine and school rules each day before school, which would prepare him for what to expect. Incentives would help him to control his behavior during free play periods. Being low in frustration tolerance, Joseph would do best with several incentives spread throughout the day rather than one reward at the end of the day.

• •

Based on the temperament counselor's recommendations, Joseph's mother decided to take him out of school until she found a smaller school setting. In the meantime, she worked with him at home on his low adaptability and frustration tolerance and his expression of intensity.

• •

Psychotherapists increasingly use temperament concepts in their practices. Still, many do not recognize the significance of temperament in the children they see. Although many psychotherapists do recognize the contribution of "nature" to children's behavior, most do not understand how a child's temperament interacts with the environment to create behavior problems. As child therapists learn more about the contribution of "nature" to behavior, temperament is one way of making sense of that biological influence.

Temperament dimensions by themselves may not constitute an explanation for psychopathology in childhood or adulthood. Their real significance lies in how these characteristics interact with a number of environmental factors (Garrison & Earls, 1987). The duration, nature, and intensity of the stress, the emotional support available to the family, and the child's temperament all play parts in the manifestation of behavioral symptoms (Wertlieb, Weigel, & Feldstein, 1989). Even when a factor such as parental dysfunction is the cause of a problem, children respond differently and the pattern between dysfunction and pathology is not consistent (Chess & Thomas, 1989). For example, one child may respond to harsh, authoritarian treatment with opposition and defiance, whereas another child may become anxious and withdrawn. Research that examined the relationship between temperament and stressful experiences found that the temperament traits of high activity level, low adaptability, withdrawal, high intensity, negative mood, low persistence, and low rhythmicity were related to the development of behavior problems when stress was present (Wertlieb, Weigel, Springer, & Feldstein, 1987). In other words, temperament plays a significant role in how children cope with stress and, as a result, whether they develop behavior problems.

Psychotherapists or physicians unfamiliar with temperament run the risk of either under- or overestimating the magnitude of a problem and then providing the incorrect treatment (Carey & McDevitt, 1995). Knowledge about temperament allows therapists to discern how a particular child is likely to respond to a particular traumatic experience and helps determine which treatment options will work best with each client.

Child therapists are eager to learn concepts that help them better understand their clients. Temperament concepts will help them differentiate typical temperament-related problems from pathological behavior and will help them determine the best treatment options that fit with each individual child. They can use these concepts when working with parents, children, adolescents, and other adults.

This chapter describes how a group of therapists who actively apply temperament concepts in their practices use a temperament perspective when working with children and their families. Psychotherapists provided the case examples.

CHILDREN IN THERAPY

Psychotherapists usually see children younger than the age of 12 for problems relating to school (e.g., rules, attention, peer interaction, academic achievement, homework), to home and the family (e.g., compliance, sibling rivalry, death, divorce, illness), or to delayed developmental milestones at expected times (e.g., late toilet training, poor self-regulation) (Rice, 2001). As Griffin (1993) pointed out, very few of the behaviors that therapists see are pathological; rather, they are related to day-to-day living and reflect the condition of the family system and temporary adjustment problems. Therapy is an attempt to modify significant environmental elements, beliefs, psychic structures, and interaction patterns. Once the problem is determined, interventions include play therapy for the child, family therapy, work with the teachers, parent guidance, and/or a referral for a medical evaluation.

Many therapists learn to interpret behavior as a product of the child's environment and view behavior problems or dysfunction as evidence of unhealthy caregiving, traumatic events, or a combination of factors (Chess & Thomas, 1989). Even though information is available to therapists regarding the importance of temperament in child behavior (e.g., Carey & McDevitt, 1995; Chess & Thomas, 1986; Rowe, 1994), many child therapists do not see temperament as a major factor in behavior problems. Because many child therapists recognize the role biological differences play in behavior, temperament is a natural extension to explain how individual differences can affect the ways children behave. They can begin by seeing how children react differently in similar situations, how the child's nature and the caregiver's responses to the child interact to create behavior, and how a mismatch between the caregiver or the environment and the child's innate temperament can cause behavior problems. Utilizing temperament information when assessing a behavior problem can aid therapists in understanding the whole child; it provides one more piece of the puzzle. Psychotherapists and mental health professionals who do not understand individual differences may interpret behavior as pathological when it is instead indicative of a response based on an extreme temperament trait. As a result, these professionals may misdiagnose, prescribe unneeded medication for, or inappropriately label a child. Even therapists who are aware of temperament may not understand how to apply the concepts in their psychotherapy practice. Learning to understand, assess, and implement temperament concepts can help child therapists gain a better understanding of their clients and provide effective tools for working with problem behavior.

TEMPERAMENT AND BEHAVIOR PROBLEMS

Most children who see therapists have behavior problems, and research confirms the relationship between temperament and behavior problems (Barron & Earls, 1984; Garrison & Earls, 1987; Webster-Stratton & Eyberg, 1982). On the one hand, temperament traits may predispose children to develop later problems; on the other hand, a behavior problem may occur regardless of a child's temperament. Nevertheless, temperament can determine the severity, direction, or the extent of the problem (Lemery, Essex, & Smider, 2002; Rothbart, Posner, & Hershey, 1995). Behavior symptoms may also represent the extremes of temperament. The New York Longitudinal Study (NYLS; Thomas, Chess, & Birch, 1968, discussed in more detail in Chapter 1) found that "difficult" children developed a proportionately higher number of behavior problems. These children's slow adaptability and irregular, intense, negative reactions to new situations and demands made positive peer relations, socialization, and school situations arduous when compared with "easy" children. Thomas and colleagues (1968) found five combinations of temperament traits associated with behavior problems:

1. A combination of irregularity, slow adaptability, withdrawal, negative mood, and high intensity

2. A combination of withdrawal, low intensity, and slow adaptability

3. Markedly high or low intensity

4. Excessive persistence

5. Excessive distractibility

Earls (1981) found that low distractibility, high intensity, and low adaptability were associated with the number of behavior problems in 3-year-old children. Barron and Earls (1984) later labeled this temperament constellation as temperamental inflexibility. They found that this inflexibility combined with poor parent–child interaction and family stress contributed to a child's behavioral problems in preschool. Other researchers confirmed the connection between parenting and temperament, and found that in 4-year-old children, insecure attachment and uninhibited temperament predicted aggressive behavior and externalizing behavior problems (Burgess, Marshall, Rubin, & Fox, 2003). Children who exhibited high emotionality and under-controlled behavior at age 2 initiated aggressive conflicts that predicted externalizing behavior problems at age 4. The externalizing problems were greatest for toddlers who experienced high maternal negativity (Rubin, Burgess, Dwyer, & Hastings, 2003). Murray and Kochanska (2002) found that *effortful control*, the temperamentally based ability to inhibit a primary reaction and initiate a secondary response, was related to adaptive functioning. Mothers reported higher quantities of behavior problems with children who had low levels of effortful control.

Kolvin, Nicol, Garside, Day, and Tweedle (1982) found a correlation between the traits of high intensity, high activity, and assertiveness with antisocial, aggressive behavior in elementary school-age boys. Researchers found that difficult temperament in infancy predicted later aggression. Children and adolescents from that group who were also novelty seekers (uninhibited) were more likely to be diagnosed with conduct disorders than other clinical categories (e.g., anxiety disorders, depressive disorders) (Schmeck & Poustka, 2001). Terestman (1980) found that children identified as both high in negative mood and intensity were more likely to already have had a behavior disorder or to develop one before age 9. In general, children who exhibit extreme temperament characteristics are more likely to be regarded as disordered during the early school years (Garrison & Earls, 1987). Child therapists can use temperament information to help determine how characteristics contribute to a child's problem behavior and influence the extent of the problem and how parenting and environment interact with temperament.

The majority of children seen by therapists have high maintenance temperaments: highly active, intense, slow adapting, easily frustrated, and/or highly sensitive (Rice, 2001). Parents who have no problem rearing their other children often seek help when they are unable to successfully manage the behavior of temperamentally challenging children. When identifying the source of a maladaptive behavior, temperament must be considered in addition to other possibilities. A functional behavioral evaluation differentiates between temperament-based reactions, maladaptive coping mechanisms used to deal with temperament reactions, responses to inappropriate contingencies, difficulties managing imposed challenges, and deliberate manipulation (Teglasi, 1998). For example, a child who is withdrawing may be reacting to novelty, trying to avoid a difficult or boring situation, responding to excessive stimulation, or experiencing anxiety. Not only does the therapist run the risk of misdiagnosis but also he or she is significantly less effective in treating the child unless he or she can distinguish between causes and is able to clarify temperamental influences.

Counseling parents about their child's temperament can improve the treatment outcome. Professionals can attain a temperament assessment and explain the child's temperament to the parents. From this explanation they can guide the parents in what strategies to use and determine which treatment options are best for the child. Mettatal

(1996) found that children ages 5–11 whose parents received temperament information and guidance experienced long-lasting cognitive and behavioral changes much like those that occur during traditional psychotherapy. Another study (Teerikangas, Aronen, Martin, & Huttunen, 1998) found that "difficult" temperament in infancy predicted psychiatric symptoms in adolescence, but that a home-based family counseling intervention during infancy protected these temperamentally at-risk infants from developing symptoms in adolescence. The early management of temperament-related issues can prevent the development of later behavior problems (Cameron, 1978).

Those therapists who routinely use temperament concepts incorporate them into their practices in a number of ways depending on the client, the presenting problem, and the goals of therapy. One therapist stated, "Temperament is incorporated into all aspects of my practice. [It] is so thoroughly integrated into my thinking about my work that I use it continuously. It is an integral part of how I view clients in an overall assessment." Another commented, "While not all behavioral issues are temperament-based, I'm willing to bet that more temperament-based behaviors get called something other than temperament than the other way around."

A therapist who is working with a child and who has a collateral relationship with the parents often does a formal temperament assessment to gain as complete an understanding of the child as possible. He or she then shares information with the parents concerning the child's salient temperament traits and offers guidance about environmental changes that will facilitate goodness of fit. The therapists notes areas where the parents may have difficulty making the necessary changes and, in subsequent sessions, follows up and supports those changes while paying close attention to resistances or defenses that may come up.

• •

Jamal and Denise were concerned about their 7-year-old son Martin's noncompliance and volatile, unpredictable behavior. They went to see a child therapist and requested that she see Martin for play therapy. When the therapist took a history, Jamal and Denise expressed worry that because Denise had suffered postpartum depression, this accounted for his behavior. They described how Martin had struggled at the beginning of first and second grade and how he became easily frustrated in school. Jamal described a recent incident that occurred when he and Martin had walked to school as they often did. This usually was a fun time for them to connect and be together. On this particular morning, Jamal decided to cross the street in a different place than their routine. Martin refused to cross and had a tantrum, which worried Jamal. As the therapist listened, she thought this sounded like the behavior of a slow-adapting child. She offered some suggestions about working with adaptability such as preparing Martin for changes and transitions and providing structure and routine. She also recommended a temperament assessment.

The assessment confirmed the therapist's hunch about Martin's slow adaptability. It also confirmed that he was withdrawing, intense, and low in frustration tolerance. The temperament assessment and ensuing discussion greatly relieved the parents. They had noticed a change in Martin's behavior following the therapist's initial suggestions, and the therapist determined Martin did not need play therapy.

A year later, Jamal returned to discuss some new behaviors. After discussing how these behaviors related to Martin's temperament, Jamal stated that he finally understood that Martin behaved as he did not because he was bad but because of his temperament. Jamal left armed with new strategies and feeling relieved.

•   •

HOW TEMPERAMENT CONCEPTS ARE USED IN VARIOUS TYPES OF THERAPY

Often, a child does not fit neatly into a psychiatric diagnostic category but comes to the clinic with a problem needing intervention. Telling the parents the child is "normal" invalidates their impressions that something is wrong and offers them little hope for making changes; yet providing an unnecessary psychopathological diagnosis could be harmful or unethical. Knowing temperament characteristics helps a therapist distinguish a temperament problem from pathology. A history of similar patterns of behavior over time suggests that certain problems are temperament-based. The therapist can then help the parent understand that theirs is a typical child with a unique—although perhaps extreme—temperament. Once parents understand their child's natural tendencies, they can begin to empathize with the child, to let go of their guilt and the idea that the child is "bad" or "out to get them," and to begin to work with the behaviors. Besides learning how to handle current problems, they can begin to anticipate where new issues might arise, preventing problems from escalating.

Becoming familiar with their clients' temperaments helps the therapist get to know them more quickly at the onset of therapy and understand how the clients are likely to react to certain approaches or treatments. Perhaps a child is likely to react in intense ways. Another child may be slow-to-warm-up to therapy or resist changes that might be suggested. The therapist can predict if a child may stick with a change or become easily frustrated by it. Knowing a child's temperament allows therapists to consider their own temperament and understand their relationship with the child. For example, an exuberant therapist who realizes that the child is sensitive and withdrawing knows to go slowly and to tone down his or her usual style of interaction. The therapist who understands the child's temperament from the start is better able to create a good fit with the child and to honor his or her individual differences.

• •

Four-year-old Naomi was brought to therapy because of her refusal to speak with teachers, relatives, other adults, and most children. Her parents were worried about her socialization and the possible labeling of her as a "problem child." She was also silent and unresponsive during therapy sessions. She would not interact at all, and the therapist's usual methods for enticing a child to play did not work. The therapist decided a temperament assessment would give her more information.

The temperament assessment revealed that Naomi was extremely slow-adapting, low in intensity, withdrawing, and sensitive to novelty. This information allowed the therapist to approach her from a temperament perspective. She asked Naomi's parents to bring a favorite toy from home to serve as a bridge between home and her office. The therapist asked to see the toy and Naomi shyly handed it to her, watched as she played with it, and gradually joined in, slowly warming up to the situation; however, Naomi still did not speak. Naomi's therapist devised rituals and routines to begin and end the session, initiated play that was familiar to the child and involved minimal interaction, and broke up the entire therapeutic experience into small, nonthreatening components. She provided Naomi with repeated opportunities to adapt to new experiences. She kept the office quiet and subdued, used low lighting, and eliminated some of the toys that might be overstimulating for Naomi. She deliberately used a very soft voice when speaking. Naomi was encouraged to express herself through nonverbal means, especially at the beginning of therapy, using art, a doll house, or a sand tray. The therapist believed that by making these modifications, the therapeutic process moved along more smoothly and quickly than if she had not known the child's temperament. Naomi eventually began to talk with the therapist, and through play therapy they were able to work on ways to make communication with new people less threatening.

• •

ASSESSING TEMPERAMENT

Therapists have different ways of assessing temperament. They may use observation, a questionnaire, or an informal interview depending on their style, the child's needs, the presenting problem, and the therapy goals. Some therapists prefer to discuss the temperament-related issues as they come up in therapy. Others only use temperament questionnaires, and still others combine assessment methods. For a detailed discussion of assessments see Chapter 3.

Interview or Discussion   Structured interviews or more informal discussions can be used to determine a child's temperament. When a therapist meets with parents for a detailed developmental history prior to meeting with the child, they can ask questions about what the child was like as an infant, toddler, and preschooler. Asking specific questions during the intake interview gives the therapist an initial indication of the child's temperament as well as the parents' temperaments. Therapists might ask questions such as the following:

- Does your child prefer active or quiet play?
- How does your child react to changes and transitions?
- Is your child sensitive to tastes, textures, or odors?
- Can your child stick with a difficult activity until he or she completes it?
- In what way is your child similar to or different from you?

The therapist can then give the parents feedback on how temperament relates both to their conflicts and their successes.

Some therapists use a combination of assessment questions and discussion in initial interviews with parents. From this, the therapist can use examples of the child's behavior and typical reactions to illustrate the child's temperament. For example, a parent might say that the child will stick with an activity, leave it when he hears the telephone ring, but then return to it. This would initiate a discussion about how distractibility differs from persistence: The child is easily distracted but persistent with the activity. Once parents are familiar with temperament concepts, they can use them as part of an ongoing dialogue.

For many parents, temperament's impact on behavior is better understood when they are working directly with feelings and issues in therapy. When temperament comes up unexpectedly, such as when a parent describes a child's noncompliance that is clearly related to an inability to transition quickly (slow adaptability), temperament concepts can be introduced and then followed up with a few informal questions.

Questionnaires   Clinicians often use questionnaires or checklists to obtain information in therapy with children and adults. Psychiatric evaluations or psychological testing may include a temperament assessment. A temperament assessment can provide an opportunity to discuss behavior with the parent or help in the diagnostic process. A temperament profile from a standardized questionnaire gives parents a concrete way to understand their child's behavior. It legitimizes their concerns and helps them see current behavior and problems that may be due to poorness of fit. The process of filling out the questionnaire is helpful in itself. It makes parents think specifically about their child's behavior in new ways. One therapist reported,

> I use [questionnaires] mostly with children when a behavioral issue is presented. I also find the profiles helpful in building therapeutic relationships with parents. I like the nonblaming quality of temperament interventions and the information that can be shared about the positive qualities of a challenging temperament. I also find that parents like to have something concrete to work on, and temperament counseling provides suggestions for specific tasks.

Another therapist skips using a temperament questionnaire when parents are already overwhelmed, when there are time constraints, or when the added expense of an assessment is an issue.

Many therapists like to have both parents complete a temperament questionnaire on their child. Because parents vary in how they perceive the child's behavior, the contrast of two questionnaires provides a basis for discussion: Mom's expectations for behavior may not match Dad's, and the child might behave differently with each parent. A therapist can plot both parents' results by hand on one profile sheet. This makes it easy for parents to see the similarities and differences in how they perceive their child, and it establishes a foundation for working together on the issues.

Therapists are likely to use temperament questionnaires when a discrepancy is reported between behavior at home and in another environment, such as school. The questionnaire may also be helpful for gaining insight into younger children who are presenting unusual challenges. At times, parents' expectations are unrealistic for their child's temperament, or parents cannot understand where the child's reactions come from. The temperament profile is a concrete way to help them appreciate their child's unique characteristics. "[The] use of temperament questionnaires for adults, children and siblings offers a wealth of information that can be relevant to family evaluation and treatment" (Garrison & Earls, 1987, p. 68).

WORKING WITH FAMILIES EXPERIENCING DIVORCE

Hetherington (1989) found that children with easier temperaments are better able to cope with their parents' marital transitions. The stress associated with divorce and remarriage is likely to exacerbate children's already existing behavioral issues (Hetherington, Bridges, & Insabella, 1998). Those with more difficult temperaments elicit more negative responses from parents and then have a harder time handling parental negativity. They also have a more difficult time eliciting support from those around them.

Therapists who work with divorce or co-parenting issues find temperament assessments useful when children are having difficulty adjusting after a divorce or remarriage. Temperament concepts are also helpful when transitions between homes are problematic, when behavior is different at one parent's home from another, or when parents are working together to create consistent discipline and routines between homes. For example, knowing a child's level of adaptability helps the therapist to work with the parents to develop routines for making visitation transitions easier or to provide recommendations for custody arrangements. Focusing on the child's temperament may also decrease the blame between parents and helps them to begin parenting from a more neutral point.

• •

Fred, 6 years old, lives with his mother, Connie, during the week and with his father, Chuck, one night a week and every other weekend. Fred's parents sought counseling because their son had trouble with the transitions. He would talk back and not comply with his mother's requests for a few days after returning from visiting his father. He would throw a tantrum when things did not go his way. A temperament assessment indicated that some of Fred's need for control was due to his temperament, but the counselor cautioned that the large amount of parental conflict that he had experienced could also account for his controlling behavior.

When both parents completed temperament questionnaires about Fred, their ratings showed similarities and differences. Chuck and Connie agreed that Fred was irregular in rhythmicity, moderately low in distractibility, and mild in sensitivity. Chuck and Connie rated Fred very differently from one another in some areas, however. On the one hand, Connie saw him as low in activity level, high in intensity, slow-adapting, negative in mood, and moderately low in persistence. According to Connie he preferred staying at home to going out to play. He did not like his routines disrupted and would protest loudly, often dissolving into a tantrum. He became easily frustrated when playing and often seemed irritable. Chuck, on the other hand, saw Fred as average in activity level, average in approach/ withdrawal, fast-adapting, positive in mood, low in intensity, and average in persistence. Fred liked going places with his father, always seemed happy, and did not need a routine during his visits.

The therapist used this information to discuss how Fred was reacting to the divorce. Their discussion on co-parenting therapy centered on why they viewed him so differently in the key areas of adaptability, approach/ withdrawal, and mood. Perhaps Fred acted differently when he was with each of them because his relationship with each of them was different. He could have been testing his mother more and his father less when visiting alone; the presence of other children or his half-sisters at home could have influenced his behavior. Also, his parents might have only seen segments of Fred's behavior. Connie may have seen the part of Fred's behavior that showed separation difficulties during transitions from one house to the other, and Chuck may have only seen him as he settled in quickly at his house. At home with his mother he "let it all out," experiencing a delayed reaction to the transition of going between homes. Another possibility is that Fred, like many children, was able to maintain a level of self-control and adaptability in certain situations. Fred's behavior may have been more contained at Chuck's home than at Connie's because he spent less continuous time there. He may have been better able to control his behavior there, but expressed more after returning to his mother. Increasing the length of time at his father's house might have made it difficult for him to maintain this coping strategy.

That Fred's parents viewed him so differently could have become problematic if the range of difference was too wide. Fred needed more integration in his parents' perceptions of who he was in order to form a coherent self-view. Without the temperament assessment, Fred's therapy might have helped him cope with parental conflict and his behavior differences between households. But the temperament assessment provided a set of strategies for making transitions more routine and consistent, and these transitions eventually became easier for Fred.

Unfortunately, the parental conflict Fred was experiencing still remained a factor. The therapist worked with the family to reduce parental and family conflict and to help Fred's parents see his temperament in a more integrated way. Fred was very angry because of the divorce, and the therapist worked with his anger in play therapy. She helped his mother and father work with his temperament by setting up routines for the transitions between homes. His mother learned how to watch for intensity triggers and redirect him before the intensity escalated and how to work with his low frustration tolerance to lessen the frequency of tantrums.

• •

USING TEMPERAMENT CONCEPTS TO ADDRESS SCHOOL PROBLEMS

Therapists see many children for school-related problems. The beginning of the chapter described the recommendations of a therapist who was consulted about a school-related problem and did not consider temperament. Behavior problems in school may reflect difficulties at home, with peers, lack of fit with teachers, or combinations of issues. Chapter 8 discusses typical problems that occur at school and in the classroom. When a teacher cannot manage a problem, a therapist may be called in. Having information about temperament can help the therapist determine if the problem is one of "fit," home environment, or a possible behavior disorder. Following is an account of a therapist who used temperament concepts successfully. With this preschool child, understanding temperament was crucial to the positive outcome.

A therapist was called to observe 4-year-old Sean and make recommendations because of his destructive tendencies. His teachers found it difficult to work with him and the usual discipline of time-outs did not work. The therapist first observed Sean in his preschool classroom at the beginning of the school year. He was so destructive that he often had to be sent home. He acted like a small but ferocious cyclone; he could turn a classroom upside down in seconds. He would climb under tables or get into boxes or corners and wreck anything in his way. At first glance, he appeared oppositional and defiant.

The therapist requested a team meeting including both Sean's family and the school staff. The therapist had the teachers and the parents complete a temperament questionnaire. The results showed that Sean was highly sensitive and easily overstimulated. He was also high in intensity. At the meeting, the therapist distributed a chapter from Greenspan's (1995) The Challenging Child on the highly sensitive child. It described how sensitive children can melt down over seemingly minor things, how they can be bossy and demanding, and how they each convey their sensitivities in their own special way. The response was unanimous that the description fit Sean perfectly. Looking at his behaviors in a new light, everyone understood that when overwhelmed with stimuli he needed a "safe place." When he did not have a safe place, his intensity took over and he became destructive. In the classroom he would make a safe place himself out of a table and a large cardboard box. His family was able to create this at home in the form of a tent. As the staff learned the amount and frequency of stimulation Sean could tolerate, they helped him begin to learn to regulate himself. They provided a quiet fort in a corner of the room. The adults became more in tune with his temperament needs. At first, when he showed signs of overstimulation (when his activity and intensity began to escalate), the teachers would steer him toward his quiet place. Once he became used to that, they would suggest that he needed some quiet time, and eventually he would go to his space himself when he needed to.

● ●

USING TEMPERAMENT CONCEPTS WITH ADOPTED CHILDREN

Adoptive parents seeking child therapy have additional reasons to be confused by their child's behavior. Not sharing the same biological make-up as their child, they do not know how much of their child's behavior is due to environment, parenting, attachment issues, or genetics. When parents are not certain of the prenatal history or the birth parents' history, they may fear that the child was prenatally exposed to some teratogen or has a genetic predisposition to mental illness. Working with temperament concepts as part of therapy can allay certain fears that a child is "abnormal" in some way.

● ●

Myra, a 6-year-old girl, had been adopted from an orphanage in Guatemala at 6 months old. She was a fussy, highly sensitive baby who became a strong-willed, intense child prone to outbursts. Her mother, Linda, brought her to therapy because of constant power struggles, prolonged tantrums, and difficulty making friends. Linda had a very hard time understanding her daughter's behavior. She worried that there had been neglect in the orphanage resulting in a psychological disorder and that this accounted for Myra's difficulties. Linda was a quiet, gentle woman, the exact opposite of her daughter. She had great difficulty understanding and responding to Myra's behavior.

A temperament assessment helped distinguish Myra's natural tendencies from her early environmental experiences. Not knowing exactly what had transpired in the first 6 months of Myra's life, the therapist decided to work with what she did know to help alleviate current problems. Myra was highly sensitive, intense, withdrawing, slow-adapting, and low in persistence, and most of the difficult behaviors that she exhibited could be explained by her temperament. From this, the therapist was able to determine what triggered her outbursts. Transitions, unexpected changes, or becoming overstimulated or frustrated could cause Myra to have a tantrum. Together, Linda and the therapist worked on preventing the triggers and helping Myra calm down when an outburst did occur. The temperament assessment also explained some of Myra's problems with peers. High sensitivity, withdrawal, and slow adaptability made it difficult for her to maintain friendships. Before play dates, Linda learned to discuss the play and planned activities so Myra knew what to expect. She invited children who were more flexible than Myra in order to prevent power struggles. She kept the play dates short at first and required breaks during active play to reduce Myra's stimulation and help maintain her adaptability. Because Myra's temperament was so different from her mother's, Linda needed frequent reminders of Myra's needs based on her temperament assessment. She was able to use a temperament perspective in dealing with daily challenges, which eliminated many of the power struggles and outbursts.

Therapists not versed in temperament concepts might assume that Myra suffered from an attachment disorder and that this alone explained her behavior. For a therapist who uses temperament concepts, the first step is to create a good fit between Myra and her mother. After that is accomplished, if there are still difficulties, the possibility of an attachment disorder could be investigated.

Using Temperament Concepts with Other Treatment

When a child has a serious psychological problem and needs treatment beyond temperament guidance, a temperament model of behavior is still useful. The interaction of environmental influences with a child's disorder can exacerbate or minimize clinical outcomes and the underlying temperament influences the child's response. Understanding the child's temperament aids the therapist and parents in deciding the best approach and the appropriate expectations for that child. A serious loss or trauma, a learning disability, or any other psychological issue is best served when temperament is taken into account and is responded to in a way that is most helpful to that particular child (Chess & Thomas, 1986). For example, a child with a speech disorder who is low in persistence, active, intense, and approaching needs a speech-language therapist who can set boundaries, find appropriate ways for the child to expend energy, and break up sessions to reduce frustration. Therapists who modify their styles according to a child's temperament increase the effectiveness of their treatment.

● ●

A 5-year-old girl, Ella, was referred to a therapist because she cried frequently and had angry outbursts and her parents were concerned this would affect her adjustment to kindergarten. Ella's history revealed she had numerous, inconsistent caregivers since infancy, resulting in many disruptions in her attachments. Her mother had been disabled due to back problems when the child was 2, and Ella's father was emotionally distant. A temperament assessment indicated that Ella was very slow-adapting and high in intensity. The therapist worked with the parents by teaching them to prepare Ella for changes and to be more consistent with routines. They learned to notice Ella's rising intensity and to use calming techniques such as redirection, breathing deeply, coloring, or playing with play-dough, while also teaching Ella ways to release intensity appropriately. At the same time, Ella worked in her play therapy on issues of attachment and security. The temperament assessment gave Ella's parents concrete strategies that they could use to provide more consistency and security, and the therapist worked directly with Ella to improve her attachment relationships.

● ●

WORKING WITH ADOLESCENTS

Therapists are most likely to use temperament concepts when working with young children, but some find it successful with adolescents as well. Parents expect their teenagers to take more responsibility for their lives and adolescents want more independence from their parents. Mothers reported more parenting satisfaction and better communication with adolescents who are positive in mood, flexible, higher in task orientation, and approaching, whereas fathers found it easier to set limits, communicate and become involved with teens who had positive moods (Guerin, Gottfried, Oliver, & Thomas, 2003). Fathers promoted autonomy easily with flexible teens and mothers found discipline, communication, and independence easier to promote when their adolescents were positive in mood, flexible, approaching, and task oriented than when they had difficult temperaments (Guerin et al., 2003).

Adolescents are eager for self-awareness, and teaching them about their own temperaments provides them with valuable information concerning their typical reactions and response patterns. This enables them to overcome some obstacles and effectively plan for the future. Motivation becomes a powerful ally to temperament during adolescence and may help overcome temperamental weaknesses (Chess & Thomas, 1986). For example, the withdrawing student who loves to write joins the school newspaper, and his love of writing helps him overcome the anxiety he feels when interviewing new people. The distractible student who wants to succeed in the test learns to place strategic reminders around the house to help him prepare. When adolescents achieve temperament self-awareness they can take more personal responsibility for their behavior and decide on an appropriate course of action (Carey & McDevitt, 1995).

• •

Mary, a senior in high school, was an intelligent girl who was dealing with a variety of issues in therapy including her inability to finish tasks, make commitments, and find direction in her life. Her future was a main concern, and her goals included going to college and having a professional career. Mary kept putting off her college applications, and some deadlines had passed with no action. Her therapist worked with these issues psychodynamically, but progress was slow. In addition to their therapeutic work, the therapist decided to have Mary complete a temperament questionnaire.

Mary completed the temperament assessment enthusiastically, hoping for some answers to her problems. The results indicated that she was active, approaching, slow-adapting, and low in persistence. When her therapist described how these characteristics contributed to her behavior and assured her that they were "normal" for her, Mary seemed greatly relieved. She liked that her results showed that she easily approached others and what that might mean for her meeting new people at college. Mary wondered if her activity level might explain her difficulty falling asleep at night. Her therapist helped her to see the importance of having a relaxed, quiet time each night before bed. She understood that being low in persistence contributed to her difficulty sticking with boring or difficult activities and that this also suggested that she might be a competent "multitasker." They discussed how she could divide boring tasks into parts and work on other duties when frustration mounted.

Understanding her slow adaptability had the greatest impact on Mary's behavior. The fact that slow-adapters have difficulty with changes and transitions helped her understand the challenge of completing her college applications and of moving away from her family. These tasks were still overwhelming for her, but the idea that this was normal for her temperament helped her move forward. The result was that she immediately completed the college forms and was accepted at the three colleges to which she applied.

Mary was also intrigued that each temperament scale could be explained in both beneficial and challenging terms. She said, "This is who I am. It's not all bad. There may be things I have trouble with but I'm okay."

• •

Temperament can be the great normalizer, helping people to understand how their traits affect their behavior and how this information can aid them in creating the best fit between the environment and their responses.

During adolescence, self-development becomes more complex and better organized. Adolescents' quest for identity affects cognitive, emotional, and social aspects of development. As they struggle to become independent and make sense of their world, they spend less time with family and more time with peers, which helps them develop self-concept and self-esteem. Knowing their temperaments helps adolescents understand themselves and gives them tools to make positive changes. Therapists working with adolescents can help them

- Improve self-awareness by having them complete a temperament assessment
- Understand how temperament affects their reactions, choices, and behavior
- See the strengths and weaknesses of each temperament trait
- Plan strategies to overcome temperamental weaknesses
- Know that their behavior is "normal" for their temperament

WORKING WITH ADULTS

Adult therapy generally deals with the client's own behavior or interactions. A therapist who can give clients an understanding of their own temperament can help them see how they affect others. When adults in therapy have children, understanding how their own temperaments affect behavior can help them realize the impact their own temperaments have on their children. This in turn affects their approaches to parenting and family dynamics. One therapist commented, "I love the 'aha' moments and relieved laughter when they see their behavior in this new light. It reduces their defensiveness and self-deprecation and normalizes the behavior."

In their psychotherapy work with adults, Burks and Rubenstein (1979) found that particular temperament constellations appeared repeatedly. Although they used these clusters with adult clients, therapists could also apply them to other ages. These groupings provided a conceptual tool for identifying individuals' styles. They were:

- The Withdrawer (withdrawal, slow adaptability, low mood, and average to low intensity), who tends to hold back from any new situation, is cautious, worried, but also thoughtful and reliable.
- The Persister (high persistence, slow adaptability, and sometimes low distractibility), who finds it difficult to tolerate interruption or input from others and is a perfectionist.

- The Intenser (high intensity, high sensitivity, average to high persistence), who expresses himself with great force and tends to overreact.

- The Approacher (high approach, high sensitivity, adaptable), who is always quick to become involved.

- The Adapter (fast adaptability, high activity level, high distractibility, positive mood), who is pleasing company, goes along with others, and rarely asserts her own position.

- The Doer (high activity, high intensity, and variable mood), who is an achiever and a problem solver and always has a plan of action.

Burks and Rubenstein found that individuals understood and responded quickly to the use of temperament in therapy. The structure of their approach was didactic explanation, self-identification, group feedback, further self-examination and response, and explanation of communicative interactions. In all cases they were able to make temperament concepts understood and the clients were able to identify their temperaments.

Therapists often use a less formal structure to impart temperament concepts to their clients by discussing the concepts during therapy. One therapist suggested having individuals think about their own parents' temperaments and how that influenced their relationships. This facilitates insight into their own parenting issues and problems they have had with their children. Looking back on these problems and the relationship to both parent and child temperament, individuals can understand current behavior patterns and use that information to resolve existing problems. This therapist used temperament concepts with adults who were troubled by their relationships with their adult children:

> On one such occasion I loaned [the book] *Raising your Spirited Child* (Kurcinka, 1991) to a mother who had been in and out of treatment for many years with her now adult daughter. I also discussed some principles from *Goodness of Fit* (Chess & Thomas, 1999). It made a dramatic difference in her life and her relationship with her daughter. She grieved the fact that she had not discovered this information earlier.

• •

Jamie had seen her therapist in weekly sessions for 2 years to help resolve a highly conflicted relationship with her mother, whom she viewed as highly narcissistic and unavailable. Six months into the therapy, Jamie became pregnant, which intensified her struggle with her mother. She had her baby and several months passed, but at 4 months of age, her baby still woke every 2 hours at night and napped irregularly. Jamie wrestled with her feelings of exhaustion, inadequacy as a mother, and negative feelings toward the baby. Her therapist referred her and her husband to a temperament counselor to help with the sleeping problems and the baby's behavior while continuing to work with Jamie about her feelings about the baby, her feelings as a mother, and her feelings about her own mother. Even though the therapist was very familiar with temperament consultation, she chose to refer Jamie to temperament counseling based on the unique psychodynamic relationship she had built with her client. The therapist believed it would be counter-therapeutic to include her husband in one of their therapy sessions to focus attention on the baby's temperament rather than on Jamie's feelings. Following the temperament consultation, the therapist wove the temperament counselor's recommendations into therapy, as Jamie worked on her feelings about the baby crying, her worry about not being a good mother, and her anger at her own mother and her husband.

• •

Referring clients to a temperament counselor provides therapists with a way to not disrupt the fragile client–therapist relationship. Therapists can also work with temperament counselors by bringing them into a session with the client who has difficulty with a child. The client completes a temperament assessment and the temperament counselor presents the results to the therapist and the parent. As they discuss strategies to work with the child, the therapist can provide added insights as to which techniques will work best with the family.

Therapists working with adult clients can

• Help them identify their own temperaments
• Have them think about their parents' temperaments and how that affected their own development and interactions

- Help them see how their parents' temperaments affected their own parenting style
- Have them identify their children's temperaments and the effects on their parent–child interactions
- Identify the role each family member's temperament plays in family dynamics
- Refer them to a temperament counselor so the therapeutic relationship is not disturbed
- Have a temperament counselor meet with the client and the therapist to present temperament information and suggest strategies.

WORKING WITH COUPLES

Parents often comment about their own temperaments when going over their child's profile. A parent might realize, "That's just like me" or "That's just like her dad." Goodness of fit is an important concept between child and adult and it is also important between parents or partners.

The temperament traits most useful in addressing couples issues are approach/withdrawal, adaptability, sensitivity, and intensity. For example, couples who are opposites in terms of approach/withdrawal may have issues involving social situations.

• •

High-approach Bill loves going to parties and having people over for dinner, but his wife Ivy dislikes social events because they involve new situations and people. Sometimes Bill will invite a new co-worker over for dinner and forget to tell Ivy, which results in a fight. Bill is resentful and cannot understand why this is a problem. He feels Ivy is holding him back from having any fun.

Their son Andy is like his mother. On the weekends Bill loves to plan spontaneous outings with his friends and their sons. Andy does not like doing new things with unfamiliar people and either protests these outings or goes but refuses to participate. Bill cannot understand why Andy cannot be "one of the guys." When their couple's counselor pointed out how Ivy's responses were similar to Andy's, they began to examine solutions that considered temperament. Bill learned to plan ahead and to talk over a plan or outing with Ivy or Andy first, making the experience much more pleasant for everyone.

• •

Imagine the fury in the disagreements of couples when both are intense or the possibilities when one is very sensitive and the other is not. Picture the reaction of a slow-adapting man when he walks into a surprise party given by his highly adaptable partner, with 40 of their "closest" friends as guests. Imagine the impact on a family with children whose temperaments may not fit with one or both parents. Learning about temperament helps couples be curious rather than furious about their temperamental differences. It helps them understand their impact on each other as well as their children, it removes blame without abdicating responsibility, and it allows partners to recognize and address the underlying needs.

SUMMARY

Professionals use temperament concepts for various therapeutic settings and reasons: with child behavior problems, divorced families, adopted children, couples counseling, adult and adolescent therapy, and as an adjunct to other treatment. Chess and Thomas (1984) were quick to point out that temperament guidance is not a magic formula for all problems. In some cases temperament plays a major role as it interacts with the environment, whereas in other cases it plays a minor role. For example, if there is evidence of psychopathology or brain damage, temperament usually plays a minor part in understanding the problem. A trained therapist can sift out the parts played by temperament, motivation, distorted sensory function or perception, or delayed cognition or development. In addition, all these factors interact with the environment.

Temperament provides a neutral basis from which to assess a problem and can help therapists understand and explain a client's behaviors. All individuals have temperaments, and their temperaments determine how they respond to certain situations and stresses. Cameron (1977) used the analogy that temperament is the "fault line" and the family or other environmental stress is the "strain." Both fault line and strain must be present to produce an "earthquake" behavioral disorder. As one family therapist stated, "I always have an ear open for temperament and bring it up whenever it seems relevant. When you know what to listen for, you hear temperament a lot since everyone has one."

CHAPTER 12

Beyond Temperament

When to Seek Outside Help

• •

Ashton's mother came to the temperament counselor because she had had problems disciplining Ashton at home and his teacher had reported that he was having problems with aggression at preschool. He was not affected by redirection, encouragement, or punishment. He had difficulty with bedtime and dinnertime transitions. He seemed unresponsive to social cues; would not greet people or respond to greetings; and had an intense fascination with lights, light switches, and vacuum cleaners. His temperament profile revealed average sensitivity, above-average activity, slow adaptability, withdrawal, persistence, and low distractibility.

His profile explained some of the troubling behaviors. Discipline problems could result from slow adaptability or high negative persistence depending on how his parents asked him to comply. Aggression could result from a combination of his high activity level causing him to react physically, high persistence resulting in stubbornness, and slow adaptability making him want control. His initial withdrawal from new people could explain his apparent unresponsiveness to social cues. Slow adaptability could account for his fascination with lights because turning on and off lights gave him a sense of control, whereas low distractibility could contribute to his intense focus on vacuum cleaners.

Ashton's parents decided to work on bedtime issues first, so the counselor helped them set a bedtime routine using a visual chart. At their next appointment they reported that the chart had worked and bedtime was going well. But Ashton still had problems at preschool with aggression and his parents wondered if the problems were related to the school's large number of students and loose structure. After discussing his activity level, adaptability, and tendency to become overstimulated, they decided to move Ashton to a small preschool program with only 15 students. Ashton adjusted to the new school, but he still lacked social skills. At times he attacked children for no apparent reason, had no empathy when he hurt them, and made little eye contact with students or teachers. The teacher could get him to comply by letting him examine the school's vacuum cleaner. He made some progress and his parents continued to use temperament strategies. But his fascination with lights continued. His parents took him to a neighbor's outdoor barbecue and had to leave early when Ashton discovered the landscape lighting and attempted to dismantle it. At a restaurant he somehow found the main light switch and turned off all of the restaurant lights. The manager asked them to leave.

When Ashton was kindergarten age, his parents decided on a small private school. At the admission interview, his lack of social skills, difficulty sitting still, fascination with the light switch, and constant inquiry about the school's choice of vacuum caused the headmaster to cut the interview short. When the parents described to the temperament counselor what had transpired at school, at the restaurant, and with the neighbors, he recommended further testing because these behaviors seemed to be increasing. Although temperament techniques had helped to an extent, Ashton had challenges that extended beyond his temperament.

• •

WHEN AN ISSUE IS MORE THAN TEMPERAMENT

There is a saying, "If all you have is a hammer, everything looks like a nail." If all a clinician knows is temperament, everything appears to be temperament-related. Clinicians must know when a problem goes beyond temperament and when to refer the child to the appropriate specialist.

Many problems do relate to a child's temperament. A temperament profile can explain some behaviors, and some problems may be resolved with temperament techniques. But at times it becomes necessary to look at other causes, particularly because of the frequency and duration of the problem, its interference with family and social life, and the lack of improvement using temperament techniques. In behavioral issues in which family dysfunction or serious pathology does not appear initially, clinicians can approach a problem by examining temperament as a first line of defense. Clinicians can always perform further evaluations if necessary, but it is harder to retract a serious clinical diagnosis than to arrive at it after simpler explanations have been insufficient.

Conditions that May
First Appear to Be Temperament Based

Many behavioral concerns or conditions have qualities similar to temperament traits. What makes them different is that they endure regardless of temperament strategies, they occur much more frequently, and they are more intense than the "normal" extremes of temperament. Parents or teachers often say they "have a feeling" about a certain behavior, that it does not seem "normal" in comparison to other behaviors. Those feelings must be respected, especially when they arise after giving temperament techniques a sufficient trial. A physician or therapist can then do further testing or make a referral to the appropriate professional. A temperament counselor who works *only* with parent guidance should always refer the client to a professional when any doubt appears.

The following behavioral disorders at first may appear to be temperament issues but later may be diagnosed (they are not always diagnosed) as a serious concern: obsessive-compulsive disorder (OCD), bipolar disorder, Asperger's syndrome, attention-deficit disorder (ADD) and attention-deficit/hyperactivity disorder (ADHD), anxiety disorders, oppositional defiant disorder (ODD), conduct disorders, sensory integrative dysfunction, and childhood depression. This is not intended to be a complete listing; careful observation and diagnosis must be made by a professional or professionals in the field in order to determine the nature of the disability or condition, if any. Also keep in mind that children may have more than one challenge or disability.

Obsessive-Compulsive Disorder

• •

Todd had a difficult time going to bed at night. He needed his superman pajamas, his red pillow placed to the left of his blue pillow, his Pokemon figure on the night table facing him, and four of his stuffed animals lined up at the side of his bed in order. He had to turn off the light himself three times. When he did not follow his routine, he could not fall asleep. This behavior worried his mother. She explained to Todd's pediatrician that he had always been particular about his toys, but in the month since they had moved to a new house and he had started a new school this behavior had increased. His pediatrician performed a temperament assessment, which revealed high sensitivity to change, slow adaptability, withdrawal, and low distractibility. His doctor suspected that Todd might be trying to maintain some control over his new environment. As Todd became more comfortable with his new surroundings, the behaviors decreased until he only lined up his animals beside his bed before going to sleep.

• •

Sophie worried about locking all the windows and doors before bedtime. Even though she watched her parents lock them each night, she often awoke to check again. Her parents consulted a psychologist about this behavior, which had begun after a local kidnapping, and he assured them that many children had had the same reaction. He told Sophie's parents to call him if the behavior continued or worsened, but after the kidnapper's capture the behavior disappeared.

• •

Many children exhibit compulsive or obsessive behaviors at one time or another. Children who need to know what to expect or who feel as if things are out of control often try to control their lives in ritualistic ways. As they grow older or events in their lives become more predictable, the ritualistic behaviors often decrease and become a typical part of their expressions of temperament. For other children, however, age and predictability do not lessen the OCD behaviors. Let's look at another child, Adam.

• •

When he was 3 years old, Adam had started lining his cars up by color, and he would become very upset when someone changed the order. He always ate from his Barney bowl, wore his purple dragon tee-shirt, and walked on tiptoe over the tiles on the kitchen floor. Adam's doctor assured his mother that this behavior typified a preschooler's striving for independence and for individuation. The family's life was stable with no major changes or dysfunction. But at his kindergarten check-up, Adam's mother reported that the rituals had increased. Adam needed to open and close the door three times while counting to 10 each time they entered the house. The rituals for eating breakfast often made him late for school, and he worried about getting dirty, especially in the bathroom. Adam refused to touch his penis, the toilet seat, or door handles, and washed his hands over and over. These behaviors also affected his behavior at school as he resisted touching door handles and frequently wanted to wash his hands. Adam's doctor referred him to a psychiatrist for evaluation, and Adam was diagnosed with OCD.

• •

According to the diagnostic criteria from DSM-IV-TR (American Psychiatric Association, 2000), children who have OCD have recurrent obsessions and/or compulsions that cause severe distress and interfere in their lives. Obsessions are not just excessive worries about real issues or preoccupations, like Sophie's worry about locked doors based on a frightening event. They are recurrent, persistent thoughts, images, and impulses that cause anxiety because of their intrusive, inappropriate nature. Compulsions are repetitious behaviors or rituals that children use to ward off the anxiety they experience. These might include washing hands, counting objects, or flicking light switches. The thoughts and rituals are not reasonable and the child, particularly as he grows older, recognizes them as excessive and inappropriate. When these rituals and thoughts interfere with normal routine and daily functioning and occupy more than one hour a day, the child is considered to have OCD.

Approximately 1 in 200 children have OCD, and boys are more likely to have prepubertal onset and have a family member with OCD (March & Mulle, 1998), although children may develop the disorder with no family history. OCD results from a disregulation of the brain circuits between the frontal cortex and the basal ganglia. The neurotransmitters serotonin and dopamine greatly influence this neurobehavioral disorder.

Extensive testing by a child psychiatrist or psychologist can determine the extent of the disorder and rule out learning disabilities. The child may be treated with cognitive behavioral therapy, medication such as serotonin re-uptake inhibitors, and behavioral interventions at home and school (March & Mulle, 1998). Most children with OCD live happy, productive lives with a combination of medication and cognitive behavioral therapy.

Bipolar Disorder

● ●

Miranda had extraordinary mood swings. She could be sweet one moment, then go into a rage that could last for hours. Her parents had to remove from her room anything that could be a danger during one of her rages—she had already thrown a ball through the window, broken a lamp, and torn her bed sheets into shreds during past rampages. At other times Miranda's enthusiasm amazed everyone. When she decided to build a dollhouse, she brought all of her father's tools into the basement along with all of the scrap wood she could find, and she hammered and nailed for hours, not wanting to stop for dinner or bed. A temperament assessment might attribute such behavior to intensity, activity level, and persistence, but the volatility of her moods indicated a problem other than temperament. Miranda was eventually diagnosed with bipolar disorder.

• •

Adults with bipolar disorder alternate between periods of intense mania and deep depression (Myers, 1996). In children the moods can vary between affection, silliness, rage, and despair. Children cycle rapidly between these states more often than adults who have the disorder. The cycles can occur several times a week or month, or even several times a day (Papolos & Papolos, 1999). Children with bipolar disorder appear inflexible, noncompliant, and irritable and have episodes of explosive rage. These behaviors can resemble the temperament traits of slow adaptability, negative persistence, negative mood, and negative intensity. But the severity and duration of these traits and children's response to temperament techniques determine whether this goes beyond temperament. Children with bipolar disorder have tantrums for hours, punch holes in walls, and threaten or attack family members and pets. The triggers of the rage are not the same as typical temperament triggers such as experiencing a change too quickly or lacking energy outlets. No one symptom identifies bipolar disorder, but hyperactivity, extreme mood shifts, prolonged rage, and a family history of mood disorders all increase the possibility of that diagnosis (Papolos & Papolos, 1999).

Children with bipolar disorder display several unique characteristics starting in infancy. They have erratic sleep patterns, often sleeping no more than 4–6 hours a night, and they take few or no naps. They can have extreme separation anxiety. Other symptoms include night terrors with violent, emotionally charged imagery, rages that occur several times a day and last for hours, frequent mood shifts, oversensitivity to stimulation, racing thoughts, lethargy, and depression (Papolos & Papolos, 1999).

When a clinician suspects that a child has bipolar disorder, he or she should refer the child to a psychiatrist for an evaluation. The psychiatrist may use medication to stabilize the child's moods, in addition to psychotherapy or family therapy. A team effort, with parents, pediatrician, psychiatrist, therapist, and school personnel working together, ensures the best treatment.

Asperger's Syndrome   Children with Asperger's syndrome, a pervasive developmental disorder, have problems in social interactions, exhibit stereotypical behavior, and have restricted interests and activities. Asperger's syndrome is within the autism spectrum. Autism is a disorder characterized by impaired social interactions; delayed or deviant speech and language patterns; repetitive behaviors such as whirling, rocking, or clapping; and a rigidity about maintaining specific routines and extreme distress when routines are disrupted (Maxmen & Ward, 1995; Palombo, 2001).

Children with Asperger's syndrome function at a much higher level than most children with autism. They often have good language abilities, although their voices tend to be flat, stilted, or repetitive, and conversation often revolves around themselves (Ozonoff, Dawson, & McPartland, 2002). Cognitively, these children can be anywhere in the IQ score range, although many are above average in verbal ability and below average in performance abilities (Edelson, 1995). Parents often describe them as eccentric because of their intense interests in topics such as specific aspects of history or certain mechanical devices.

These children may have clumsy and awkward motor skills, difficulty interacting with peers, trouble reading facial expressions and gestures, and difficulty making eye contact. They prefer playing alone and engaging in activities such as counting passing cars or taking apart the lawn mower. They may seem unaware of social cues or the effect that their behavior has on others.

At first glance, temperament may seem to explain these behaviors. Low sensitivity and withdrawal can account for negative social interactions. High persistence and low distractibility explains the individual's becoming overly focused on a subject or activity. Slow adaptability can account for becoming fixated on routine or order. But when temperament guidance produces little improvement, these children may need a further evaluation.

Ashton, described at the beginning of the chapter, was eventually diagnosed with Asperger's syndrome. At first, his symptoms seemed to reflect his temperament, but they could not all be accounted for by temperament. He was enrolled in a small school with teachers who worked well with him. He was able to keep up academically and began a social skills program with a therapist who specialized in pervasive developmental disorders. Although he still had an eccentric fascination with mechanical devices, he could get along at school and made a few friends.

Asperger's syndrome has no known cure, but interventions can help children learn social skills to get along better in society. Many adults with Asperger's syndrome can lead normal lives and hold jobs.

Attention-Deficit/Hyperactivity Disorder and Attention-Deficit Disorder   Many children have attention problems. Inability to stay on task is particularly significant when a child reaches school age and may relate to the child's temperament; however, clinicians who do not know about temperament may attribute the cause to a disorder. Teachers and professionals may suspect that the child has ADHD when children have difficulty paying attention, behave impulsively, and are very active. Children who have attention problems without the impulsivity or elevated activity level may be labeled as having ADD.

• •

Tracey got by in school. She was never in trouble but she did not excel and often "spaced out." She had difficulty completing her schoolwork and struggled through elementary school. Middle school teachers had higher expectations, and school became harder for Tracey. Her teachers said she did not apply herself, and she became increasingly depressed. Her mother talked to a psychologist about her depressed behavior and problems in school. When he heard about the situation he said, "I think Tracey may have a learning disability or an attention deficit; we should test her." After completing a thorough assessment, the psychologist determined that Tracey had ADD. They decided to give Tracey a trial run of medication.

Tracey started her medication on the weekend. She came home after her first day at school on the medication with a big smile. "I can't believe it," she said. "This is the first day I've ever been able to really concentrate on anything!" Tracey went on to excel in school, graduate from college, and attend graduate school. For her, the diagnosis and medication offered what she needed to succeed.

• •

Daniel was in constant motion. His school's long "circle time" and extensive seatwork caused him difficulty. His teacher expected all students to sit still and work quietly. After 1 month of unsuccessfully admonishing Daniel to stop moving and sit still, his teacher suggested that his parents have him evaluated for ADHD. Daniel's pediatrician assured his worried parents that his activity level did not suggest an ADHD diagnosis. Instead, he recommended that they find a school where Daniel did not have to sit quietly for long periods of time. They found a new school with a good balance between movement and seatwork and Daniel excelled.

• •

Matt had more energy than anyone else in the first grade. His eyes darted around the room as he noticed every sight and sound. He leaped from his seat for no apparent reason and he blurted out answers to questions without raising his hand. He lost his assignments or would not finish them because he would start another project instead. His teacher worked with him, making sure he had plenty of time to exercise during recess, seating him directly in front of her to cut down on distractions, and using an incentive program to help him control his behavior and finish his work. After 3 months, nothing had changed. At a conference with his parents, they decided on an ADHD evaluation. Matt's assessment indicated ADHD, but his parents were reluctant to use medication, and so the school scheduled an individualized education program (IEP) meeting to determine the best course of action.

• •

Both ADHD and ADD can appear as typical extremes of temperament. Children with high activity, low persistence, and high distractibility can have attention problems and have a hard time sitting still, bouncing from one thing to the next. Children with low persistence and high distractibility without high activity may also have attention problems but they sit still and tend to daydream. These behaviors become more than temperament problems when a child can never stay on track and never sits still and when they affect both home life and academic life.

According to the *Diagnostic and Statistical Manual of Mental Disorders* (4th ed., text revision) (DSM-IV-TR; American Psychiatric Association, 2000), children must have six or more symptoms of inattention and/or hyperactivity as described for a positive diagnosis. Inattention symptoms include making careless mistakes, not listening, not following through, having difficulty organizing tasks, and being distractible, among others. Hyperactivity criteria include leaving one's seat, fidgeting, excessive talking, blurting out answers, and not taking turns. Many of these symptoms describe temperament-related behaviors that can cause confusion in diagnosis. Because some children may have temperament traits similar to those used to diagnose ADHD, this does not mean that these children have ADHD. "Compared with temperament-related behaviors, the behavior of children with ADHD is excessive in degree and goes beyond the characteristics of children with difficult temperaments. The problem, of course, is to determine what defines *excessive*" (Keogh, 2003, p. 118). The DSM-IV-TR does not define "excessive," and Carey (1999) pointed out that the DSM-IV-TR criteria can be easily misinterpreted. For example, raters might vary greatly in their definition of "talks excessively." He suggests examining the "fit" between a child and the classroom and teacher before assuming the child has ADHD or ADD.

Keogh (2003) noted that true ADHD behavior is extreme, ongoing, consistent, and apparent in a variety of settings such as school, playground, or home, and the behaviors do not change when the tasks or situations vary. In contrast, temperament-related behaviors are often obvious in certain situations or with particular activities, and they respond to changes in the environment. For this reason, clinicians must recognize the differences between ADD/ADHD and temperament to prevent over-diagnosis or misdiagnosis.

Anxiety Disorders   All children experience anxiety at one time or another; the trigger could be the first day of school, going to the doctor for a booster shot, or staying away from home overnight for the first time. Young children may fear the dark or monsters, but these fears usually do not last long. When fears become overwhelming and prevent the child from participating in daily activities such as going to school, separating from parents, and making friends, the child may have an anxiety disorder.

• •

Melanie's parents described their 10-year-old daughter as shy. She resisted new places and people and liked having her parents nearby. Over the years they had successfully used temperament techniques to help Melanie adjust to new situations and overcome childhood fears. She usually adapted to changes after a time, but this year, when the new school year started, she did not want to go. Over the summer there had been a small fire in the cafeteria of her school and Melanie feared the school could burn down with her inside. Her parents explained how the fire had begun and that the firefighters had quickly contained it with no damage, but that did not help. They visited the school and saw where the fire damage had been repaired. They also talked to the principal who assured Melanie of the school's safety. But after her first day at school she came home in a panic. The usual techniques for assuaging her fear did not work. She refused to go to school and began to worry about fires at home. She had problems going to sleep and felt constantly on edge as her worry increased. Melanie's parents took her to a psychologist who diagnosed childhood anxiety disorder.

• •

Davis, age 6, wanted to play only at home. He cried at birthday parties and would not go on play dates. His parents tried forcing him into new situations but this caused him such increased distress that they eventually shielded him from new situations. His parents worried about his reticent behavior and consulted their pediatrician, who assessed his temperament as sensitive and withdrawing. They began to use temperament strategies to help Davis accept new situations. It took 2 months before they saw any change. Each time Davis experienced additional stress, he became fearful again. But for every one step backward he took two steps forward and continued with his slow, gradual progress.

• •

The temperament traits of high sensitivity and withdrawal can seem like anxiety. Children with that temperament tend to be more fearful than outgoing children, and inhibited children may be at risk for developing anxiety disorders. Inhibited children have more internalizing behaviors such as anxiety, worry, and phobias than uninhibited children (Aron, 2002; Kagan, Snidman, Arcus, & Reznick, 1994). One study asked people diagnosed with panic, social phobia, and depression whether they were shy or fearful as children. All three groups reported more signs of childhood inhibitions than did adults who did not have these symptoms (Kagan et al., 1994).

Working with a child's sensitivity or withdrawal at an early age can help prevent the development of anxiety disorders later on. If temperament techniques do not solve the problem, however, a psychologist or psychiatrist can evaluate both psychological and physiological symptoms. Psychological symptoms include apprehension, worry, and tension without a known reason or specific cause; hypervigilance; irritability; or insomnia. Physiological symptoms can include tremors, jitters, twitches, sweating, racing heart, dizziness, and hot and cold spells (Maxmen & Ward, 1995). According to the DSM-IV-TR (American Psychiatric Association, 2000), the symptoms of generalized anxiety disorder (including overanxious disorder of childhood) include restlessness, edginess, fatigue, difficulty concentrating, irritability, muscle tension, and sleep disturbance. These symptoms cause clinical distress and impair daily functioning. Play therapy, cognitive behavioral therapy, and family therapy can help the child overcome anxiety. Medication may also be prescribed in moderate to severe cases of anxiety disorder (Maxmen & Ward, 1995).

Oppositional Defiant Disorder

• •

Miles refused to do anything his parents asked. He had temper tantrums, behaved aggressively, and argued constantly. At 7 years old, he terrified his parents and they worried that he would become unmanageable as a teenager. At school, although these characteristics emerged at times, he behaved much better. Miles's parents sought the help of a psychologist who noted that he could have oppositional defiant disorder (ODD). In order for the psychologist to make that diagnosis, Miles had to exhibit four or more symptoms from the DSM-IV-TR criteria for ODD, and these symptoms had to have lasted at least 6 months and caused social or academic impairment. Miles had four of the symptoms and they had occurred since pre-school, but he had friends and behaved reasonably well at school with few outbursts. The psychologist decided to examine Miles's temperament and concluded that the boy's intensity, negative persist-ence, and slow adaptability accounted for his behavior. He began to teach Miles's parents how to work with those traits and they slowly began to see his behavior improve.

• •

ODD usually begins by age 8. More boys have this disorder than girls before the onset of puberty, but the gender ratio evens out after puberty (Maxmen & Ward, 1995). Children with ODD often have low frustration tolerance, mood fluctuations, and temper outbursts. Mazi-ade and his colleagues (1990) found that children who have difficult temperaments and poor fit in their family environment often devel-oped ODD. These findings indicate that learning strategies to manage difficult temperament traits early in a child's life and to create a good fit between adults and child can help prevent the development of this disorder.

A child presenting with ODD symptoms should first be evalu-ated for coexisting disorders such as ADHD, learning disabilities, and depression or bipolar disorder (Maxmen & Ward, 1995). Treatment often includes parent training programs, child pyschotherapy to help with anger management, cognitive behavioral therapy, family pyschotherapy to improve communication, and social skills programs.

Conduct Disorder   The DSM-IV-TR lists conduct disorder (CD) under the umbrella term of ADHD, not otherwise specified. It is one of the most commonly diagnosed conditions in outpatient and inpatient mental health facilities for children. The DSM-IV-TR categorizes conduct disorder behaviors into four main groupings: 1) aggressive conduct that causes or threatens physical harm to other people or animals, 2) non-aggressive conduct that causes property loss or damage, 3) deceitfulness or theft, and 4) serious violations of rules. In terms of temperament, poor frustration tolerance, irritability and temper outbursts, and recklessness often characterize someone with CD. These traits do not mean that a person has this condition, however; as in other disorders, individuals with CD exhibit several of these behaviors and traits, consistently.

Sensory Integrative Dysfunction

• •

Toby would sit on his father's lap and rock back and forth as hard as he could, banging into his father's chest. Toby refused to eat many foods because of their texture, preferring crunchy foods such as crackers or chips. At age 4½ years he had not learned to use the toilet regularly, having accidents and sometimes not having bowel movements for days. He chased the family cat and pulled her tail, and the natural consequence of getting scratched had no effect on his behavior. His fine motor skills seemed delayed and he resisted holding a pencil. His parents had difficulty disciplining him and he often refused to go to bed. They came to see a temperament counselor for discipline, bedtime, and toilet learning issues.

Toby's temperament assessment revealed that he was low in activity level, very slow-adapting, withdrawing, intense, low in frustration tolerance, and average in sensitivity. His parents found that setting up bedtime routines and working with his adaptability around discipline issues helped. But the temperament techniques that usually work with the toileting and food issues had no effect. He also continued to torment the cat. Although temperament counseling addressed some of the issues, clearly he had problems not related to temperament.

Toby's parents decided to continue with the temperament counseling for daily parenting issues, but they sought further help for the other issues. They discovered a book called The Out-of-Sync Child by Carol Kranowitz (1998), which seemed to describe Toby's different behavior and found an occupational therapist who identified his condition as sensory integrative dysfunction.

• •

Children who have sensory integrative dysfunction cannot analyze, organize, or integrate sensory messages, and this affects their ability to respond to sensory information. The child may have difficulty reading verbal or nonverbal cues or organizing incoming sensory information. Kranowitz (1998) explained that children with this disorder can be oversensitive, undersensitive, or oversensitive to some sensations and undersensitive to others.

Oversensitive children react strongly to touch, movement, sounds, sights, and smells. For example, they may refuse to wear shoes or labels on clothing because these things "feel funny," react so strongly to certain smells that they vomit, and become motion-sick on elevators. Undersensitive children seek out physical sensation and may seem oblivious to sensory input. They may bump into things, spin around and around, or not notice the odor of their baby brother's dirty diaper. Other children may have oversensitivity to some sensations and not notice others. They may detest the sound of the vacuum cleaner, and not notice facial expressions, be clumsy, and hate getting dirty.

Sensory integrative dysfunction may look like a combination of temperament-related issues at first. As just mentioned, the child may appear very sensitive or not at all sensitive. A child with motor difficulties may seem like he tends toward an extreme in activity level, and a child who holds back from situations may look like he tends toward withdrawal or slow adaptability. Sensory integrative dysfunction is distinguished by the duration, frequency, and degree of the issues and by the lack of response to modifications in environment. Kranowitz (1998) explained that the determining factors of sensory integrative dysfunction are the child's unusual reactions to touch and body position and to moving or being moved.

Treatment involves occupational therapy to help the child better integrate sensory stimulation. Occupational therapists (OTs) may use activities such as obstacle courses to help motor planning, special brushes that can be used on children's arms and legs with different textures to reduce tactile sensitivity or defensiveness, balls and beanbags to improve visual-spatial coordination, and magnets to increase fine motor skills. The therapist also devises activities that the child can do at home such as taking a shower, bouncing on a therapy ball, pushing or pulling heavy loads, or rocking or swinging. With treatment these children can begin to integrate sensory stimulation and become competent at home and school.

Childhood Depression

Megan, a feisty infant, grew into a challenging child. Her mother, a high-powered executive, had difficulty disciplining her and at school Megan gave her teachers a hard time. When each infringement occurred in school, Megan's mother assumed the school was a poor fit with her daughter and moved her to another. With all of these moves, Megan had difficulty sustaining friendships and became more agitated with each change. Megan's self-esteem plummeted. Eventually, her mother sought the help of a therapist, but when results did not come soon enough she asked another therapist to take over. Again, with each change, Megan got the message that the problem was with her. She became more agitated and caused more problems at school. A therapist eventually determined that Megan suffered from depression.

Children manifest their depression in different ways than adults do. They may cause trouble at home or school, and because they do not always seem sad, parents can misinterpret the behavior. Other symptoms may include bursts of exhilaration followed by lethargy, daydreaming or lack of concentration, and frequent crying. Depressed children may isolate themselves socially or have difficulty with relationships. They may be extremely sensitive to rejection or failure, have increased anger or irritability, exhibit poor concentration, and complain of illness.

On the surface, temperament may seem to explain these behaviors. Exhilaration can reflect activity level or intensity. Sensitive, intense, withdrawing children often cry and react deeply to rejection or failure. Anger and irritability can indicate intensity, negative persistence, activity, and slow adaptability. But the clinician must determine if the symptoms represent a change from usual behavior or if they have been mounting over time. Diagnosis is easier when the symptoms are a change from usual behavior. A child who used to play with friends now spends time alone. Fun events now bring little joy and the child reacts with anger or irritability. The child may talk about dying or suicide. These behaviors and reactions clearly do not reflect the child's usual temperament. But when the behavior seems the expression of a difficult temperament, the diagnosis is not as simple and it takes an experienced clinician to know the difference. A family history of depression increases the likelihood of the child having it. When behavior does not respond to the usual temperament strategies or if the depression lasts, a psychotherapist should evaluate the child. Early diagnosis and treatment of depression are essential. Treatment often includes family and individual therapy and antidepressant medication. Once treated, children can lead happy, productive lives.

DISORDERS THAT RESEMBLE OR CO-EXIST WITH OTHERS

When clinicians feel that temperament alone does not account for the child's behavior, they may have difficulty determining the exact cause. Many disorders mirror others or co-exist. For example, clinicians may misdiagnose the child with sensory integrative dysfunction as having ADHD or ADD. The fidgeting and distractibility caused by too much stimulation can mirror ADHD. A medication may help a child with

ADHD but have no affect on the child with sensory integrative dysfunction. A child may have sensory integrative dysfunction as well as ADHD or learning disabilities. A thorough, extensive evaluation will determine the difference.

Similarly, depression in children can look like ADHD but also may resemble bipolar disorder or an anxiety disorder. A child with depression may have a learning disability or attention disorder that contributes to the depression. Difficult cases may have numerous aspects to the problem and it may take visits with several professionals to tease out what role temperament plays and what disorders affect the child.

COPING WITH SEPARATION OR LOSS

Issues other than psychiatric disorders can at first appear to be caused by temperament. A child who experiences separation or loss may react the way a sensitive, slow-adapting, intense child would, although this does not represent her innate temperament. Children, regardless of temperament, respond to loss or the risk of loss with anxiety and anger (Bowlby, 1988). Likewise, a new sibling, a divorce, an ill parent, or a death prompts behavior that may appear to be temperament-based but does not result from temperament. But temperament can predict the typical response a given child might have to an event such as a divorce or a new sibling. Children with easier temperaments will adjust to the changes more quickly, whereas children with more difficult temperaments will take longer to adjust and have loud, dramatic reactions.

Children who undergo many changes and who do not have a stable environment eventually react badly to their chaotic existence even if their innate temperament does not lead them to respond negatively.

• •

Hannah had become increasingly clingy and noncompliant at home and at school. Her mother claimed that no major environmental changes had occurred. A temperament assessment revealed low persistence, sensitivity to changes, and withdrawal. In talking to her mother the clinician found out that her uncle had recently died in a violent crime. Her mother thought this had not affected Hannah because she had not known her uncle well and the mother had made a point of not talking openly about it. But Hannah sensed the effect the death had on her parents and reacted to it.

• •

Jo's mother had abused drugs and alcohol. As a toddler, Jo had never known where her mother would take her or at what hour. She could not count on waking up in the same house, let alone the same bed, each morning. Meals had been erratic. Now sober for 9 months, Jo's mother had a job and an apartment. Jo attended child care each day but at home she was demanding and had frequent tantrums. Her mother explained that she had been an easy baby and had become increasingly difficult as her mother's addiction progressed. The problem behavior remained despite the improved circumstances.

• •

Extremely chaotic conditions can make even adaptable children react as a slow-adapter would in order to maintain control over their environment. Once the chaos subsides, children need time to realize that they now have a stable environment and that their parents now respond with consistency. Only then can they began to relinquish control. Until that happens, parents must respond with greater consistency to establish the stability these children crave.

SUMMARY AND RECOMMENDATIONS

Many conditions and disorders may underlie a child's behaviors, or a child might just be exhibiting a normal range of temperament but be leaning toward a temperament extreme at a particular time. To determine whether a child has an identifiable disability, clinicians often take a detailed history of a child. They learn family histories and patterns, environmental changes, and the duration of the problem. This alone may determine if the problem relates to temperament. If the clinician remains uncertain, he or she can begin with a temperament assessment to provide parents with explanations for behavior and techniques for working with the child. Sometimes the parents want only a temperament evaluation because they prefer not to pathologize the problem or they deny that there is a problem. In these situations, beginning with a temperament assessment can still help. It will provide the parents with some information and open the door to further evaluations if necessary. When temperament may not account for all of the issues, a professional should further evaluate the child. If the clinician makes additional diagnoses, he or she can still use temperament information in conjunction with other treatments.

CHAPTER 13

Temperament Stability and Future Directions

Kellen changed from an easy baby to a challenging child when he turned 3. He became irritable, shy, and active—the exact opposite of his infant and toddler behavior. In middle childhood, his temperament seemed easier again, and through high school it varied, sometimes becoming quite challenging.

Morgan entered the world screaming and always expressed her emotions loudly. She smiled and approached strangers and her activity level kept her moving. Easily distracted, with many interests, she bounced from one activity to the next. In elementary and high school and into college she loudly expressed her emotions, loved social events, and always had several projects going at once.

STABILITY OF TEMPERAMENT

Some children's behavior styles remain the same from birth and others change throughout their lives. Because of this variability, researchers have questioned the stability of temperament and what accounts for change. Most researchers agree that temperament can change over time. Development, neurological organization, and the environment contribute to its stability or change (Bates, 1989). Temperament appears to follow a developmental course. Some temperament-related patterns, such as those concerning fear and attention, develop over time and are not present in early infancy (Rothbart, 1989c). Characteristics present in infancy expand as the child matures. For example, distress expressed in early infancy evolves into the emotions of anger and fear later on (Fox, 1991). The infant who reacts to stimulation with distress at 4 months often develops into the child who is fearful or inhibited in early and middle childhood (Kagan, Snidman, & Arcus, 1998). Before 4 months of age, orienting or attention is more reflexive, but after that time infants can disengage and change focus from one event to another (Rothbart, Derryberry, & Hershey, 2000). Infants rated as fearful showed lower impulsivity, low activity level, positive anticipation, and aggression later in childhood than did infants who were not fearful (Rothbart et al., 2000).

As motor, cognitive, and socioemotional skills develop, behavior also changes. Infants from 6 to 12 months old are more intense and active than in their first 6 months, and they become more regular in eating, sleeping, and elimination and notice more changes in their surroundings (Hagekull & Bohlin, 1981). Infants who at 4 months exhibit motor activity combined with positive mood become approaching, positive, outgoing toddlers (Calkins, Fox, & Marshall, 1996). Quiet, "easy" infants can develop into active and negative toddlers as their motor ability improves and their drive for independence increases. During the second half-year, infants become less sensitive to environmental stimulation and their lower persistence, decreased attentiveness, and increasing negative mood make their behavior less manageable. Overall, temperament becomes more stable after a child reaches the age of 3 (Carey & McDevitt, 1995; McDevitt, 1986).

Most temperament changes occur during a child's preschool years as compared with his middle childhood. Guerin and Gottfried (1994) confirmed Thomas and Chess's (1986) findings that by age 5 years, a child's adaptability, biologic regularity, and positive mood increased while intensity decreased. In addition, they found that persistence and sensitivity increased and activity level decreased. In middle childhood children's activity and intensity levels decreased, and they showed less sensitivity and greater approachability than during preschool age. Distractibility remained stable during all time intervals, and persistence and sensitivity showed stability from ages 8 to 12. Developmentally, children tend to experience a shift toward less activity and intensity beginning in preschool and continuing through middle childhood.

• •

Miriam was alert and engaging in early infancy. By 9 months of age she walked, and, with her increased mobility, she got into everything. In her toddler years she became more active and distractible and less persistent. Miriam bounced from one activity to another, becoming frustrated and protesting loudly when her mother interrupted her pursuits. By preschool, although still active, she could maintain attention and sit still during storytime and participate in art projects involving small motor skills. In early childhood Miriam became quieter and focused in her class. She channeled her high activity level into ballet class three times each week. Although her intense reactions surfaced at home, she could control them at school and ballet class. This continued into middle school and high school, where she continued to show increased persistence and inhibitory control.

• •

Temperament often appears to change in different stages of development when, in fact, different behaviors may express the same temperament traits. For example, in infancy parents can easily soothe a distractible baby by redirecting his attention. As a preschooler this distractible child moves quickly from one new activity to the next, and in elementary school the child daydreams instead of focusing on his schoolwork. All of these behaviors are different manifestations of distractibility at different periods of development.

Outside influences also can affect neurological development, which plays a role in temperament variability. For example, chronic over- or understimulation can change children's levels of sensitivity (Strelau, 1983), and when children get adequate sleep, they become less irritable and demanding (Weissbluth, 1999). Environmental influences, particularly parents' response to children, can influence temperament. For example, anxious kindergarten boys whose mothers protected them became less anxious by fifth grade (Bowen, Vitaro, Kerr, & Pelletier, 1995). The goodness of fit between the environment and temperament strongly affects the stability of temperament (Chess & Thomas, 1999).

STABILITY IN CHILDREN WITH EXTREME AND/OR DIFFICULT TEMPERAMENTS

Stability is greatest in children with extreme temperaments. In general, one half to one third of children have moderate changes in temperament, but very few make extreme changes such as from difficult to easy temperament (Prior, Sanson, & Oberklaid, 1989). Extremely inhibited preschoolers remained shy at age 7 or 8 years and outgoing 2- and 3-year-olds stayed sociable in later years (Kagan, Reznick, & Gibbons, 1989). Undercontrolled, impulsive children at age 3 became danger-seeking, impulsive, and emotionally negative in young adulthood, whereas inhibited children became overcontrolled, nonassertive, and restrained in young adulthood (Caspi & Silva, 1995).

Parents who perceived their infants as fussy, difficult, and demanding continued to see them as difficult throughout childhood. Difficult 18-month-old behavior was associated with high activity, low adaptability, and negative mood throughout childhood (Guerin & Gottfried, 1994). Difficult infants exhibited withdrawing behavior at preschool age and low persistence and increased intensity in the elementary school years. "Difficultness consistently related to negative mood, high activity, and low adaptability from two to twelve years" (Guerin & Gottfried, 1994, p. 419). Bates and Bayles (1984) also found strong connections between early difficult behavior and later difficult behavior and with slow adaptability and resistance to control. Thus, behaviors of young children who have difficult temperaments tend to remain the same when they grow up.

STABILITY OF SPECIFIC TEMPERAMENT TRAITS

Research has found that certain temperament traits have more stability than others. Findings from the New York Longitudinal Study (NYLS) showed stability in activity level in children from ages 1 to 5 years (Thomas & Chess, 1986), and the Fullerton Longitudinal Study (Guerin & Gottfried, 1994) found activity level stability from age 2 to

12 years. During the preschool period (3–5 years), children's temperaments became more predictable (biologically rhythmic), positive in mood, persistent, sensitive, and less intense. Boys were found to be more active than girls at age 3 and less adaptable at age 5. In middle childhood (8–12 years) children's activity, intensity, and sensitivity levels decreased and approach increased.

TEMPERAMENT PREDICTABILITY

Rothbart et al. (2000) found that inhibitory control increases with age. They also looked at stability of temperament traits from children at ages 3 months, $6\frac{1}{2}$ months, 10 months, and $13\frac{1}{2}$ months to 7 years. In a small sample they found that infants who were distressed at 3 months of age became fearful at 7 years old, and those who were fearful at 10 and $13\frac{1}{2}$ months became shy at 7 years old. Infants who expressed distress when confronted with limitations showed anger, frustration, and aggression at 7 years. A readily approaching child of 3 months later showed impulsivity and positive anticipation. They also found that the intensity and duration of frustration increased over time while the intensity of fear decreased with development. Irritability and frustration in infancy predicted anger, frustration, aggression, activity, and risk taking at age 7. Smiling and laughter in infancy predicted impulsivity and less inhibitory control (Rothbart et al., 2000).

CONSISTENCY AND CHANGE

When Chess and Thomas (1996) re-examined their NYLS data, they concluded that temperament was not immutable. They found in their sample several instances of temperament change from infancy to adulthood. For example, one child rated as "difficult" in infancy and early childhood became "easy" in middle childhood and adolescence and then "difficult" again in college. Other children's temperaments remained relatively stable over time. When analyzing the data, they identified six factors that accounted for temperamental change: social cognitive capacity, self-awareness of temperament, motivation, support networks, self-esteem, and fortuitous events. Any one or a combination of these factors can explain the change:

1. *Social cognitive capacity* refers to the individual's social competence, the understanding of acceptable and expected social behavior. Children who have good social cognitive capacity respond appropriately in social situations, even if it seems contradictory to their

temperament. For example, shy children who prefer not to talk to new people but learn to greet them may appear approaching instead of initially withdrawing. Their temperament has not changed, but their understanding of socially acceptable behavior has superseded their temperamental hesitancy.

2. *Self-awareness* regarding temperament accounts for changes that the child can control. Children who understand their temperamental reactions can learn to handle situations in ways that work best for them. Slow-adapting children who know that they do not like unexpected events can use a calendar to keep track of extracurricular activities, school assignments, and upcoming commitments. By doing this, they can eliminate their own unwanted reactions to something unexpected. Having control over schedules helps these children plan ahead and seem more adaptable than they actually are.

3. *Motivation* can override temperament reactions. The intense child who wants to be elected class president may realize that intense negative reactions drive people away. Her motivation to win the election helps her contain those reactions or express them outside of the public forum.

4. *Support networks* provide children with positive feedback and help them lower stress and handle negative reactions. Children with particularly challenging temperaments need adults and peers around them who understand their temperaments and can create a good fit with the children's environments. People in these support networks monitor children's behavior, teach them to maintain control, offer ways to release intensity appropriately, help them plan how to handle difficult situations, and provide positive role models. Children need such support systems less as they learn to use these tactics themselves.

5. Children with *high self-esteem* can overcome negative situations more easily than those with poor self-esteem. The withdrawing child who becomes nervous and forgets the poem he must recite realizes that his temperament makes this a difficult task. But he does not take this to heart because he can remember other times when he has succeeded. He feels confident that next time he will plan better and do well. Children with low self-esteem feel inade-

quate, perhaps because of a poor fit with their environment. They expect to fail and each failure reinforces the view that their temperament creates problems rather than opportunities.

6. *Fortuitous events* can also change temperament. A slow-adapting homeless child whose parents find housing and employment appears to be adaptable in the stable environment. This fortunate turn of events has created a change in his behavioral style. Negative events can also precipitate changes in a child's environment. The active, adaptable, positive child who breaks her leg and arm from a fall must be immobile for several weeks and becomes demanding, intense, and easily frustrated. The extent of the injury determines the length of her recovery and if her positive active temperament will return. Many life events present changes that can affect temperament either temporarily or permanently.

To most professionals working with children, temperament stability is less important than a specific child's presenting problem and current temperament profile. A sudden, extreme change in temperament can provide clues as to the problem's cause, but small changes over time are not considered pathological. The predictive value of temperament makes early interventions worthwhile in circumventing later problems, however. For example, by knowing that uninhibited children often become impulsive, risk-taking, negatively intense adolescents, professionals can intervene in early childhood to moderate those traits. The interaction between a child's temperament and the environment and the difficulties it causes are more important to the treatment than temperament stability over time. Knowing about the stability and predictability of temperament over time and its developmental course helps in establishing temperament programs.

INNOVATIVE TEMPERAMENT PROGRAMS FOR DIFFERENT SETTINGS

Today, temperament programs are used in a number of clinical settings. William Carey, M.D., demonstrated the significance of using temperament in pediatric practices (Carey, 1970, 1982, 1985, 1994); namely, in educational discussions with parents, to clarify understanding of a child's temperament, and to provide interventions when dissonance exists in the temperament–environment interaction. Cameron and colleagues initiated temperament programs in health maintenance organizations to provide temperament guidance on a large scale, which increased parental understanding and management of child behavioral issues (Cameron, Hansen, & Rosen, 1989; Cameron, Rice, Hansen, & Rosen, 1994). A temperament program in Wisconsin, based on Cameron and colleague's model, examined the best way to convey temperament information to parents. Parents who received individualized temperament information when their child was 4 months old that sensitized them to the importance of temperament, and then again when their child was 3 years old, gave higher ratings for the preschool advice they received than did parents who received generic preschool advice. Parents who had temperamentally "difficult" children found the program more useful than did parents of easy children (Ostergren, 2003).

Other clinicians have developed their own temperament programs. For example, Stanley Turecki, M.D., a child psychiatrist, wrote *The Difficult Child* (Turecki, 1985; Turecki & Tonner, 2000), one of the first books for parents of temperamentally difficult children. He established The Difficult Child Center in New York to help parents and children with temperament-related behavioral problems, providing them with techniques to minimize family stress (Turecki, 1989).

In La Grande, Oregon, The Temperament Program was established in 1988 to offer guidance to parents, stepparents, grandparents, foster parents, and those who work with children, using its comprehensive psychoeducational parenting program (Smith, 1994). It trains parents as temperament specialists to provide temperament education and interventions. Parents reported that the program helped them in their parenting skills, and they affirmed that concepts they had learned resulted in an improvement in their children's behavior.

Mary Sheedy Kurcinka, a teacher and parent educator, put a positive spin on the notion of difficult behavior when she wrote *Raising Your Spirited Child* (1991, 1998a); *The Raising Your Spirited Child Workbook* (1998); and *Kids, Parents and Power Struggles* (2001). She established Spirited Child Workshops for Minnesota's Early Childhood Family Education Programs and continues to educate parents, professionals, and organizations across the country about temperament. Other temperament programs, such as the Sioux Falls, South Dakota, hospital program, are described in Chapter 10.

Temperament programs such as these show how temperament information and evaluations are effective tools that aid professionals in their work with child behavior. These programs have a significant impact on parent–child relationships and on school behavior, and they reduce the development of behavior problems by helping parents and professionals understand behavior and manage behavioral issues more effectively than those who do not have temperament knowledge. Whether used in medical or therapeutic settings, with parents or in schools, temperament concepts increase awareness and treatment effectiveness.

FUTURE DIRECTIONS FOR TEMPERAMENT PROGRAMS

Clinical programs need empirical research to prove their efficacy. Many temperament programs mentioned in previous chapters provide information about temperament and behavioral issues. Some have outcome measures that show their impact. Other programs need research and outcome studies so that professionals can fine-tune temperament strategies and develop new programs. There are many possibilities for new temperament programs in specific settings or with particular populations.

ON-SITE COUNSELING

In some existing programs, a temperament counselor works with another professional. For example, temperament counselors in pediatric departments work alongside physicians and nurses to handle behavioral issues or to provide advice on approaching a medical problem according to temperament.

In a similar vein, temperament counselors in schools could work with teachers, resource specialists, special educators, and school psychologists to resolve school-based temperament issues. Counselors could observe in classrooms, develop individualized education programs, and improve goodness of fit between teacher and child.

Temperament specialists also could work in therapy practices, providing assessments and temperament consultation for child psychotherapists, co-parenting specialists, family therapists, and marriage counselors. Other professionals such as pediatric dentists, occupational therapists, and physical therapists could also use temperament consultations concerning challenging patients.

PROGRAMS FOR AT-RISK POPULATIONS

Temperament programs could serve many at-risk populations. Temperament-based counseling could be used in high schools, domestic violence programs, and drug rehabilitation programs, and infant/toddler temperament programs could be part of teen pregnancy centers. They could be part of child abuse prevention programs and reunification programs for parents who have had their children taken away by Child Protective Services. Temperament information can be integrated into therapeutic preschools that work with traumatized children to help clinicians understand the different reactions children have and to help them devise interventions that fit best with each child. It can be used with families of children who have disabilities or chronic illness.

Temperament programs are valuable for families going through divorce to help parents understand their children's responses to divorce, to aid in co-parenting strategies, and to help in determining healthy custody arrangements. Preventive programs help people understand and work with their children's temperament to cope with daily stress, create positive relationships, and promote healthy communication.

Programs for School-Age Mothers   Horizon's School-Aged Mothers, a high school program in Pleasanton, California, works with pregnant adolescents or teenagers who have infants or toddlers. As part of the parenting program, the school incorporates temperament concepts to help the girls understand their infants' behavior and learn the best way to work with them. The temperament approach works well because it gives the girls a common, neutral language to describe their babies' behavior. Rather than using terms such as "brat" or "mama's boy," they can say "low in frustration tolerance" or "sensitive" to understand and describe the behaviors.

First, the teenage mothers learn about differences in temperament, both theirs and their baby's. Then they complete a temperament questionnaire with a therapist who discusses the questions with them. Once they have the results, they discuss how the babies' temperaments differ and what kind of environment and care will best create a good fit. The school's child care provider meets with the parents and therapist to discuss the children's temperament and the child care experience. The school also uses temperament concepts in their parenting classes and the parents read *Temperament Tools* (Neville & Johnson, 1998) as a text.

Many of these teenage mothers live with their parents. A class for the infants' parents and grandparents would provide them with a common, nonjudgmental understanding of the babies and create a strong support system for the teen mothers.

Child Abuse Prevention Programs   Early intervention programs, rehabilitation programs, and child welfare services can teach temperament concepts to parents identified as at risk for child abuse. Ideally, pregnant couples would receive temperament information during prenatal classes. But some at-risk parents may not get prenatal care. In these cases, temperament information can be included in the infant care information that parents receive in the hospital. If the parent needs more support, an in-home intervention program could include temperament techniques to give the parents the support they need.

Domestic Violence Programs   Programs related to domestic violence often involve classes and counseling for the women who have taken their children and left abusive relationships. Women who have "difficult" children have added stresses to deal with. Temperament counseling can teach these women the most effective parenting strategies to help alleviate stress and to provide the additional support they need. These classes are particularly useful as the women make the transition from the shelter to other independent living arrangements. A temperament program also would help fathers in anger management domestic-violence programs.

Drug or Alcohol Treatment and Reunification Programs   Drug addicted or alcoholic parents may have their babies placed in foster care or treatment programs at birth. Sometimes, parents live on the premises of the treatment program and can interact with their children daily. Some programs teach life skills and provide support to help parents succeed once they complete the program and are sober. As a program reunites the child with the parent, it provides parenting classes and supervision as parents spend increasingly more time with their children. Teaching parents temperament concepts can help the reunification proceed smoothly and lessen parenting stress.

Therapeutic Child Care or Preschool Programs   Children who attend therapeutic preschools because of physical or sexual abuse or neglect must work through their traumatic experiences. Temperament information can give therapists insight into a child's reactions, treatment strategies, and individualized behavioral management approaches to help with internalizing or externalizing behavior problems.

Family and Community Service Agencies   Family and community service agencies provide many support services for individuals, families, and children and often serve populations who cannot afford private mental health services. Information about temperament can be part of an agency's individual psychotherapy, parenting classes, and support groups. These agencies can also train therapy interns to incorporate temperament concepts into their work with children, adults, and couples.

SCHOOL AND CLASSROOM APPLICATIONS

Children who exhibit behavior problems in the classroom can benefit from educators and others holding a temperament perspective, as stated in Chapter 9. A temperament evaluation can help parents and teachers work together to determine causes of behavior and appropriate behavior plans. When classroom problems are caused by more than temperament, a temperament assessment can still provide additional valuable information that can be used in addition to other interventions. A temperament perspective also can be used in special education classes and classes for children with disabilities. Children in these classes have a range of temperaments, and teachers can benefit from understanding what role temperament plays in their classroom behavior.

Children's Socialization Groups   Children who have challenging or inhibited temperaments often have problems getting along in group settings or interacting appropriately with peers. These children may miss social cues or react to them inappropriately. Other children may reject a "difficult" child because of his aggressive, intrusive, moody, or loud behavior or because he exhibits shy or sensitive behavior.

Temperament-based social groups can teach these challenging children appropriate behavior in order to improve their peer status. Social groups would improve children's socialization skills by teaching them about their temperaments and those of others and by providing strategies to cope with their temperaments. The literature provides no references to any programs working with groups of children to improve socialization using a temperament perspective; however, McClowry's INSIGHTS program, which provides interventions to change the interpersonal dynamics between children, their peers, and caregivers in order to improve goodness of fit, reduce behavior problems, decrease parental distress, and increase children's self-perceptions (mentioned in Chapter 7), is comparable to such a program.

Socialization groups could teach temperament concepts through structured activities and interactive games. Group leaders could turn difficult situations into learning experiences. Weekly sessions could focus on different themes determined by problem behaviors identified by parents or teachers. Children would learn appropriate outlets and calming activities for their energy, intensity, and aggression. Socially inhibited children would learn assertiveness techniques and ways to help them feel comfortable in novel situations.

Parents could meet with the group leader prior to the first session. In one model, a second parent meeting could be scheduled part way through the series to discuss progress. De-briefing meetings after the series could include suggestions for continuing socialization work at home. Another variation would have parents attend temperament-related parenting classes while their children attend the socialization group. Each week these parents would have an assignment of activities to use at home to reinforce the lessons. Outcome studies regarding the efficacy of these groups would be necessary to determine if there is a decrease in the number of target behaviors and an increase in socially acceptable behaviors, and whether the child was using techniques that indicated an understanding of his temperament.

TEMPERAMENT APPLICATIONS
WITH ADOLESCENTS AND ADULTS

Until recently, most clinical temperament work has been with infants, preschoolers, and school-age children as old as age 12. Clinicians who work with adolescents and adults can use temperament concepts, but there are few questionnaires to assess temperament for these age groups (see Appendix A for a list of commonly used questionnaires). As temperament questionnaires continue to be developed for adolescents and adults, clinicians will increasingly use temperament concepts in these populations. Chapter 11 presents examples of how psychotherapists have used temperament in their work with adolescents and adults.

Adolescents

Temperament questionnaires make it easier to assess adolescents' temperaments. The questionnaires that adolescents complete themselves increase their self-awareness. Discussions with a temperament specialist can highlight temperament's relationship to behavioral responses, learning issues, and peer problems. Clinicians can use adolescent temperament assessments in therapy or with at-risk teens. School counselors and academic advisors can use them to help the teen make the best fit in a class, with the curriculum, or in college placements.

Adult and Couples Therapy

Temperament awareness helps adults understand their own responses and anticipate their reactions to people and situations. Adults can use temperament concepts to change their own behavior and to understand the fit between them and their partners, co-workers, children, or jobs.

Temperament information is a useful tool in couples' therapy. Couples with different temperaments may not understand how their relationship problems relate to their temperament differences. When they understand their own and each another's behavioral style, they can realize that reactions may not be purposeful or meant to hurt. They can begin to create a better fit between their expectations of their partner and the partner's temperament.

SUMMARY

Possibilities for applications of temperament concepts are limitless. Beginning with the work of Chess and Thomas, the construct of temperament has helped explain differences in child behavior and the development of behavior problems. The concept of goodness of fit provides a framework for understanding how friction between children and their environments can develop and which strategies work best to eliminate that friction. This increases the potential for prevention and intervention.

Children express their temperaments differently as they develop. The behavioral issues that present difficulties vary with infancy, early childhood, middle childhood, and adolescence. When adults understand a child's temperament early, these behavioral issues need not develop into problems, and if they do, temperament can provide a key to resolving those problems. As children get older they can learn about their own and others' temperament and individuality. Increasing this awareness increases the acceptance of individual differences.

To create more awareness of individual differences and a better fit for our children, parent education can include temperament information. Medical, educational, and child care systems can incorporate temperament concepts. Mental health providers can consider temperament when making a diagnosis and deciding on a treatment. Expanding temperament programs to include at risk populations can help improve the development of intervention programs for children with learning and physical disabilities, children who have experienced trauma, those going through divorce, pregnant teenagers, or children or adolescents who cannot get along with peers. Adult at-risk populations also can benefit from incorporating temperament into programs that work with domestic violence, drug or alcohol treatment, or child abusers. Temperament concepts can be used to provide anticipatory guidance to prevent problems from developing and in child abuse and neglect prevention. As new temperament programs are developed, applications would need to be evaluated empirically to assess their efficacy.

Temperament research in different cultures allows us to understand how temperament applies to different cultures within our society. Different cultures value different temperament traits, and what one culture views as a challenging trait, another sees as an asset. Because of these differences, culturally appropriate assessment tools must be developed and counselors must be trained to work within the contexts of different ethnic groups.

We are on the verge of an exciting era for temperament counseling. We can apply temperament concepts in many settings and with many populations: when working in schools, medical centers, and child care facilities; with parents; and with mental health practitioners. The temperament counselor possesses unique knowledge that can benefit parents and professionals and enhance any program that works with children. As the importance of temperament becomes better understood and accepted, temperament counseling will emerge as a new mental health profession, an adjunct to the broad range of social services.

References

Aboud, F., & Skerry, S. (1983). Self and ethnic concepts in relation to ethnic constancy. *Canadian Journal of Behavioral Science, 15,* 3–34.

Ainsworth, M.D.S., Bell, S.M., & Stayton, D.J. (1971). Individual differences in Strange Situation Behaviour in 1–year-olds. In H.R. Schaffer (Ed.), *The origins of human social relations.* London: Academic.

Ainsworth, M.D.S., Blehar, M.C., Waters, E., & Wall, S. (1978). *Patterns of attachment: A psychological study of the Strange Situation.* Mahwah, NJ: Lawrence Erlbaum Associates.

American Psychiatric Association. (2000). *Diagnostic and statistical manual of mental disorders* (4th ed., Text rev.). Washington, DC: Author.

Anderson, C. (1994, Spring). Temperament differences and the child in family child care. *Individuals (Publication of the Temperament Project, Vancouver, BC), 6,* 7–8.

Anderson, C.J. (1994). Parent support groups. In W.B. Carey & S.C. McDevitt (Eds.), *Prevention and early intervention: Individual differences as risk factors for the mental health of children* (pp. 226–234) New York: Brunner/Mazel.

Anderson-Goetz, D., & Worobey, J. (1984). The young child's temperament: Implications for child care. *Childhood Education, 61,* 134–140.

Arcus, D. (2001). Inhibited and uninhibited children: Biology in the social context. In T.D. Wachs & G.A. Kohnstamm (Eds.), *Temperament in context* (pp. 43–60). Mahwah, NJ: Lawrence Erlbaum Associates.

Arcus, D., & Gardner, S. (1993, March). *When biology is not destiny.* Paper presented at the biennial meeting of the Society for Research in Child Development, New Orleans, LA.

Arcus, D., Gardner, S., & Anderson, C. (1992, May). Infant reactivity, maternal style, and the development of inhibited and uninhibited behavioral profiles. In *Temperament and environment.* Symposium conducted at the biennial meeting of the International Society for Infant Studies, Miami, FL.

Arcus, D., & Kagan, J. (1995, March). *Temperamental contributions to social behavior.* Paper presented at the biennial meeting of the Society for Research in Child Development, Indianapolis.

Arend, R., Gove, F., & Sroufe, L.A. (1979). Continuity of individual adaptation from infancy to kindergarten: A predictive study of ego-resiliency and curiosity in preschoolers. *Child Development, 50,* 950–959.

Aron, E.N. (2002). *The highly sensitive child: Helping our children thrive when the world overwhelms them.* New York: Broadway Books.

Atkinson, E., Vetere, A., & Grayson, K. (1995). Sleep disruption in young children: The influence of temperament on the sleep patterns of pre-school children. *Child Care, Health and Development, 21,* 233–246.

Bagley, C., & Mallick, K. (2000). Predictions of sexual, emotional, and physical maltreatment and mental health outcomes in a longitudinal cohort of 290 adolescent women. *Child Maltreatment: Journal of the American Professional Society on the Abuse of Children, 5,* 218–226.

Bagnato, S.J., Neisworth, J.T., Salvia, J.J., & Hunt, F.M. (1999). *Temperament and Atypical Behavior Scale (TABS): Early indicators of developmental dysfunction.* Baltimore: Paul H. Brookes Publishing Co.

Bandura, A. (1977). *Social learning theory.* Englewood Cliffs, NJ: Prentice-Hall.

Baratt, M.S., Roach, M.A., & Leavitt, L.A.(1996). The impact of low-risk prematurity on maternal behavior and toddler outcomes. *International Journal of Behavioral Development, 19,* 581–602.

Barber, B.K., Olson, J.E., & Shagle, S.C. (1994). Associations between parental psychological and behavioral control and youth internalized and externalized behaviors. *Child Development, 65,* 1120–1136.

Barker, R., & Wright, H.F. (1951). *One boy's day.* New York: HarperCollins.

Barron, A.P., & Earls, F. (1984). The relation of temperament and social factors to behavior problems in three-year-old children. *The Journal of Child Psychology and Psychiatry, 25,* 23–33.

Bates, J.E. (1980). The concept of difficult temperament. *Merrill-Palmer Quarterly, 26,* 299–319.

Bates, J.E. (1989). Concepts and measures of temperament. In G.A. Kohnstamm, J.E. Bates, & M.K. Rothbart (Eds.), *Temperament in childhood* (pp. 2–26). New York: John Wiley & Sons.

Bates, J.E., & Bayles, K. (1984). Objective and subjective components in mothers' perceptions of their children from age 6 months to 3 years. *Merrill-Palmer Quarterly, 30,* 111–130.

Bates, J.E., Freeland, C.B., & Lounsbury, M.L. (1979). Measurement of infant difficultness. *Child Development, 50,* 794–803.

Bates, J., Marvinney, D., Keyy, T., Dodge, K., Bennet, T., & Pettit, G. (1994). Childcare history and kindergarten adjustment. *Developmental Psychology, 30,* 690–700.

Bates, J.E., Pettit, G.S., Dodge, K.A., & Ridge, B. (1998). Interaction of temperamental resistance to control and restrictive parenting in the development of externalizing behavior. *Developmental Psychology, 34,* 982–995.

Bates, J.E., Viken, R.J., Alexander, D.B., Beyers, J., & Stockton, L. (2002). Sleep and adjustment in preschool children: Sleep diary reports by mothers relate to behavior reports by teachers. *Child Development, 73,* 62–74.

Baumrind, D. (1966). Effects of authoritative parental control on child behavior. *Child Development, 37,* 887–907.

Baumrind, D. (1971). Current patterns of parental authority. *Developmental Psychology Monographs, 4*(1).

Baumrind, D. (1997). Necessary distinctions. *Psychological Inquiry, 8,* 176–182.

Baumrind, D., & Black, A.E. (1967). Socialization practices associated with dimension of competence in preschool boys and girls. *Child Development, 38,* 291–327.

Bayley, N. (1969). *Bayley Scales of Infant Development.* New York: The Psychological Corporation.

Beck, C.T. (1996). A meta-analysis of the relationship between postpartum depression and infant temperament. *Nursing Research, 54,* 225–230.

Belsky, J. (1984). The determinants of parenting: A process model. *Child Development, 55,* 83–96.

Belsky, J. (1990). Developmental risks associated with infant day care: Attachment insecurity, noncompliance and aggression? In S. Cherazi (Ed.), *Psychosocial issues in day care* (pp. 37–68). Washington DC: American Psychiatric Press.

Belsky, J., Rha, J., & Park, S. (2000). Exploring reciprocal parent and child effects in the case of child inhibition in U.S. and Korean sample. *International Journal of Behavioral Development, 24,* 338–347.

Belsky, J., & Rovine, M. (1987). Temperament and attachment security in the Strange Situation: An Empirical Rapprochement. *Child Development, 58,* 787–795.

Belsky, J., Rovine. M., & Taylor, D.G. (1984). The Pennsylvania Infant and Family Development Project 3: The origins of individual differences in mother-infant attachment: Maternal and infant contributions. *Child Development, 55,* 178–728.

Berk, L.E. (2002). *Infants, children, and adolescents* (4th ed.). Boston: Allyn & Bacon.

Biederman, J., Milberger, S., Faraone, S.V., Keily, K., Guite, J., Mick, E., Ablon, S., Warburton, R., Reed, E., & Davis, S.G. (1995). Impact of adversity on functioning and comorbidity in children with attention-deficit hyperactivity disorder. *Journal of the American Academy of Child and Adolescent Psychiatry, 34,* 1495–1503.

Billman, J., & McDevitt, S.C. (1980). Convergence of parent and observation ratings of temperament with observations of peer interaction in nursery school. *Child Development, 51,* 395–400.

Birch, L.L., Zimmerman, S., & Hind, H. (1980). The influence of social-affective context on preschool children's food preferences. *Child Development, 51,* 856–851.

Birns, B. (1965). Individual differences in human neonates' responses to stimulation. *Child Development, 36,* 249–256.

Block, J.H., & Block, J. (1980). The role of ego control and ego-resiliency in the organization of behavior. In W.A. Collins (Ed.), *Minnesota symposium on child psychology, Vol. 13* (pp. 39–101). Mahwah, NJ: Lawrence Erlbaum Associates.

Bournaki, M.C. (1997). Correlates of pain-related responses to venipunctures in school-aged children. *Nursing Research, 46,* 147–154.

Bowen, F., Vitaro, F., Kerr, M., & Pelletier, D. (1995). Childhood internalizing problems: Prediction from kindergarten, effect of maternal overprotectiveness, and sex differences. *Development and Psychopathology, 7,* 481–498.

Bowlby, J. (1969). *Attachment and loss. Vol.1. Attachment.* New York: Basic Books.

Bowlby, J. (1973). *Attachment and loss. Vol.2. Separation.* New York: Basic Books.

Bowlby, J. (1982). *Attachment and loss. Vol.1. Attachment* (2nd rev. ed.) New York: Basic Books.

Bowlby, J. (1988a). *Attachment and loss. Vol.3. Loss, sadness, and depression.* New York: Basic Books.

Bowlby, J. (1988b). *A secure base: Parent-child attachment and healthy human development.* New York: Basic Books.

Braungart-Reiker, J., Garwood, M.M., & Stifter, C.A. (1997). Compliance and noncompliance: The roles of maternal control and child temperament. *Journal of Applied Developmental Psychology, 18,* 411–428.

Brayden, R.M., Altmeier, W.A., Tucker, D.D., Dietrich, M.S. & Vietze, P. (1992). Antecedents of child neglect in the first two years of life. *Journal of Pediatrics, 120,* 426–429.

Brazelton, T.B. (1973). *Neonatal Behavioral Assessment Scale.* London: Spastics International Medical Publications.

Brazelton, T.B. (1984). *Neonatal Behavioral Assessment Scale* (2nd ed.). London: Spastics International Medical Publications.

Brazelton, T.B. (1992). *Touchpoints: Your child's emotional and behavioral development* (pp. 443–450). New York: Addison-Wesley.

Brazelton, T.B., Nugent, J.K., & Lester, B.M. (1987). Neonatal Behavioral Assessment Scale. In J.D. Osofsky (Ed.), *Handbook of infant development* (pp. 780–817). New York: John Wiley & Sons.

Bredekamp, S., & Copple, C. (Eds.) (1997). *Developmentally appropriate practice in early childhood programs* (Rev. ed.). Washington, DC: National Association for the Education of Young Children.

Breitmayer, B.J., & Ricciuti, H.N. (1988). The effect of neonatal temperament on caregiver behavior in the newborn nursery. *Infant Mental Health Journal, 9,* 158–172.

Burgess, K.B., Marshall, P.J., Rubin, K.H., & Fox, N.A. (2003). Infant attachment and temperament as predictors of subsequent externalizing problems and cardiac physiology. *Journal of Child Psychology & Psychiatry & Allied Disciplines, 44,* 819–831.

Burks, J., & Rubenstein, M. (1979). *Temperament styles in adult interaction: Applications in psychotherapy.* New York: Brunner/Mazel.

Buss, A.H., & Plomin, R. (1975). *A temperament theory of personality development.* New York: Wiley-Interscience.

Buss, A.H., & Plomin, R. (1984). *Temperament: Early developing personality traits.* Mahwah, NJ: Lawrence Erlbaum Associates.

Buss, D.M., Block, J.H., & Block, J. (1980). Preschool activity level: Personality correlates and developmental implications. *Child Development, 51,* 401–408.

Calkins, S.D., & Fox, N.A. (1992). The relations among infant temperament, security of attachment, and behavioral inhibition at twenty-four months. *Child Development, 63,* 1456–1472.

Calkins, S.D., Fox, N.A., & Marshall, T.R. (1996). Behavioral and physiological antecedents of inhibition in infancy. *Child Development, 67,* 523–540.

Cameron, J.R. (1977). Parental treatment, children's temperament, and the risk of childhood behavior problems: 1. Relationships between parental characteristics and changes in children's temperament over time. *American Journal of Orthopsychiatry, 47,* 568–576.

Cameron, J.R. (1978). Parental treatment, children's temperament, and the risk of childhood behavior problems: 2. Initial temperament, parental attitudes, and the incidence and form of behavioral problems. *American Journal of Orthopsychiatry, 48,* 140–147.

Cameron, J.R. (1992, September). *Temperament counseling II: Training for counseling and coordinators.* Paper presented at Kaiser Permanente, San Rafael, CA.

Cameron, J.R. (1994, October). *Goodness of fit.* Unpublished diagram presented at The Children's Temperament Conference, Berkeley, CA.

Cameron, J. (2003). Common temperament scale combinations. In *Introduction to Temperament Assessment.* Retrieved November 12, 2003, from http://asu.edu/xed/temperament/noncredit.html

Cameron, J., Hansen, R., & Rosen, D. (1989). Preventing behavior problems in infancy through temperament assessment and parental support programs. In W.B. Carey & S.C. McDevitt (Eds.), *Clinical and educational application of temperament research.* Berwyn, PA: Swets & Zeitlinger.

Cameron, J.R., Neville, H., & Renner, R. (2002, October). Pilot project results from an internet discussion group for parents of temperamentally problematic young children. Paper presented at the 14th Occasional Temperament Conference, Newport Beach, CA.

Cameron, J., & Rice, D. (1999). *Cameron-Rice Temperament Questionnaires.* Retrieved June 9, 2004, from http://www.preventiveoz.org

Cameron, J., Rice, D., Hansen, R., & Rosen, D. (1994). Developing temperament guidance programs within pediatric practice. In W.B. Carey & S.C. McDevitt (Eds.), *Prevention and early intervention: Individual differences as risk factors for the mental health of children.* New York: Brunner/Mazel.

Cameron, J.R., Rice, D., Hansen, R., & Rosen, D. (2000). *How infant temperament works: A causal model analysis of the interrelationships between infant temperament scales.* Unpublished manuscript.

Cameron, J.R., Rice, D., & Rosen, D.L. (1994, October). *Evaluating the clinical and cost effectiveness of the Kaiser temperament program.* Paper presented at the 10th Occasional Temperament Conference, Berkeley, CA.

Campbell, S. (1979). Mother-infant interaction as a function of maternal ratings of temperament. *Child Psychiatry and Human Development, 10,* 67–76.

Capaldi, D.M., & Rothbart, M.K. (1992). Development and validation of an early adolescent temperament measure. *Journal of Early Adolescence, 12,* 153–173.

Carey, W.B. (1970). A simplified method for measuring infant temperament. *Journal of Pediatrics, 77,* 188–194.

Carey, W.B. (1972). Clinical applications of infant temperament measurements. *Journal of Pediatrics, 81,* 823–828.

Carey, W.B. (1974). Night waking and temperament in infancy. *Journal of Pediatrics, 84,* 756–758.

Carey, W.B. (1982). Clinical use of temperament data in pediatrics. In R. Porter & G.M. Collins (Eds.), *Temperament differences in infants and young children* (pp. 191–205). London: Pitman.

Carey, W.B. (1982). Validity of parental assessments of development and behavior. *American Journal of the Diseases of Children, 136,* 97–99.

Carey, W.B. (1985a). Clinical use of temperament data in pediatrics. *Journal of Developmental and Behavioral Pediatrics, 6,* 128–131, 137–142.

Carey, W.B. (1985b). Temperament and increased weight gain in infants. *Journal of Developmental and Behavioral Pediatrics, 6,* 128–131.

Carey, W.B. (1988). A suggested solution to the confusion in attention deficit diagnoses. *Clinical Pediatrics, 27,* 348–349.

Carey, W.B. (1992). Pediatric assessment of behavioral adjustment and behavioral style. In M.D. Levine, W.B. Carey, & A.C. Crocker (Eds.), *Developmental–behavioral Pediatrics* (2nd ed., pp. 609–616). Philadelphia: W.B. Saunders.

Carey, W.B. (1994). Specific use of temperament data in pediatric behavioral interventions. In W.B. Carey & S.C. McDevitt (Eds.), *Prevention and early intervention: Individual differences as risk factors for the mental health of children* (pp. 215–225). New York: Brunner/Mazel.

Carey, W.B. (1997). *Temperament and the pediatrician: Pediatric development and behavior.* Retrieved from Developmental-Behavioral Pediatrics Online Community, http://www.dbpeds.org/section/fall97/temperament.html

Carey, W.B. (1999). Problems in diagnosing attention and activity. *Pediatrics, 103,* 664–667.

Carey, W.B. (2003, Autumn). The great debate, ADHD: An epidemic? *AAP Section on Developmental and Behavioral Pediatrics Newsletter.*

Carey, W.B., Hegvik, R.L., & McDevitt, S.C. (1989). Temperamental factors associated with rapid weight gain and obesity in middle childhood. *Journal of Developmental and Behavioral Pediatrics, 9,* 194–198.

Carey, W.B., & McDevitt, S.C. (1978). Revision of the Infant Temperament Questionnaire. *Pediatrics, 61,* 735–739.

Carey W.B., & McDevitt, S.C. (1995). *Coping with children's temperament: A guide for professionals.* New York: Basic Books.

Carson, D.K., Council, J.R., & Gravely, J.E. (1991). Temperament and family characteristics as predictors of children's reactions to hospitalization. *Journal of Developmental and Behavioral Pediatrics, 12,* 141–147.

Caspi, A. (1998). Personality development across the life course. In W. Damon (Ed.-in-Chief) and N. Eisenberg (Vol. Ed.), *Handbook of child psychology: Vol. 3. Social, emotional and personality development* (5th ed., pp. 311–388). New York: John Wiley & Sons.

Caspi, A., Henry, B., McGee, R.O., Moffit, T.E., & Silva, P. (1995). Temperamental origins of child and adolescent behavior problems: From age three to fifteen. *Child Development, 66,* 55–68.

Caspi, A., & Silva, P.A. (1995). Temperamental qualities at age three predict personality traits in young adulthood: Longitudinal evidence from a birth cohort. *Child Development, 66,* 486–498.

Chen, E., Craske, M.G., Katz, E.R., Schwartz, E., & Zeltzer, L.K. (2000). Pain sensitive temperament: Does it predict procedural distress and response to psychological treatment among children with cancer? *Journal of Pediatric Psychology, 25,* 269–278.

Chess, S., & Thomas, A. (1959). Characteristics of the individual child's behavioral response to the environment. *American Journal of Orthopsychiatry, 24,* 791–802.

Chess, S., & Thomas, A. (1984). *Origins and evolution of behavior disorders from infancy to early adult life.* New York: Brunner/Mazel.

Chess, S., & Thomas, A. (1986). *Temperament in clinical practice.* New York: Guilford Press.

Chess, S., & Thomas, A. (1987). *Know your child: An authoritative guide for today's parents.* New York: Basic Books.

Chess, S., & Thomas, A. (1989). The practical application of temperament to psychiatry. In W.B. Carey & S. McDevitt (Eds.), *Clinical and educational applications of temperament research* (pp. 23–35). Berwyn, PA: Swets North America.

Chess, S., & Thomas, A. (1992). Dynamics of individual behavioral development. In M.D. Levine, W.B. Carey, & A.C. Crocker (Eds.), *Developmental-behavioral pediatrics* (2nd ed., pp. 84–92). Philadelphia: W.B. Saunders.

Chess, S., & Thomas, A. (1996). *Temperament theory and practice.* New York: Brunner/Mazel.

Chess, S., & Thomas, A. (1999). *Goodness of fit: Clinical applications from infancy through adult life.* New York: Brunner/Mazel.

Childcare Video Magazine. (1990). *Flexible, fearful, and feisty: The different temperaments of infants and toddlers.* California State Department of Education, Sacramento.

Colder, C.R., Lochman, J.E., & Wells, K.C. (1997). The moderating effects of children's fear and activity level on relations between parenting practices and childhood symptomatology. *Journal of Abnormal Child Psychology, 25,* 251–263.

Coletta, N. (1979). Support systems after divorce: Incidence and impact. *Journal of Marriage and the Family, 41,* 837–846.

Cost, Quality, & Child Outcomes Study Team. (1995). *Cost, quality, and child outcomes in child care centers, public report.* Denver: Economics Department, University of Colorado at Denver.

Crockenberg, S. (1981). Infant irritability, mother responsiveness, and social support influences on the security of infant-mother attachment. *Child Development, 52,* 857–865.

Crockenberg, S.B. (2003). Rescuing baby from the bathwater: How gender and temperament (may) influence how child care affects child development. *Child Development, 74,* 1034–1038.

Crockenberg, S.B., & Smith, P. (2002). Antecedents of mother-infant interaction and infant irritability in the first 3 months of life. *Infant Behavior and Development, 25,* 2–15.

Crowell, J., Keener, M., Ginsberg, N., & Anders, T. (1987). Sleep habits in toddlers 18–36 months old. *Journal of the American Academy of Child and Adolescent Psychiatry, 26,* 510–515.

Dantrock, J.W. (2000). *Children* (6th ed.). Boston: McGraw Hill.

Davison, I.S., Faull, C., & Nicol, A.R. (1986). Research note: Temperament and behaviour in six-year-olds with recurrent abdominal pain: A follow-up. *Journal of Child Psychology and Psychiatry, 27,* 539–544.

Denham, S.A., Renwick, S.M., & Holt, R.W. (1991). Working and playing together: Prediction of preschool social-emotional competence from mother-child interaction. *Child Development, 62,* 242–249.

Dixon, W.E., Jr., & Shore, C. (1997). Temperamental predictors of linguistic style during multiword acquisition. *Infant Behavior and Development, 20,* 99–103.

Dixon, W.E., Jr., & Smith, P.H. (2000). Links between early temperament and language acquisition. *Merrill-Palmer Quarterly, 46,* 417–440.

Dodge, K. (1985). Facets of social interaction and the assessment of social competence in children. In B.H. Schneider, R.K. Rubin, & J.E. Ledinghom (Eds.), *Assessment and Intervention.* New York: Springer-Verlag.

Dukewich, T.L., Borkowski, J.G., & Whitman, T.L. (1996). Adolescent mothers and child abuse potential: An evaluation of risk factors. *Child Abuse and Neglect, 20,* 1031–1047.

Earls, F. (1981). Temperament characteristics and behavior problems in three-year-old children. *Journal of Nervous and Mental Disorders, 169,* 367–373.

Edelson, S.M. (1995). *Asperger's syndrome.* Center for the Study of Autism, Salem, Oregon [Online]. Retrieved July 19, 2004, from http//www.autism.org/asperger.html

Eisenberg, N., Fabes, R.A., Bernzweig, J., Karbon, M., Poulin, R., & Hanish, L. (1993). The relation of emotionality and regulation to preschoolers' social skills and sociometric status. *Child Development, 64,* 1418–1438.

Emery, R. (1982). Interparental conflict and the children of discord and divorce. *Psychological Bulletin, 92,* 310–330.

Engfer, A. (1992). Difficult temperament and child abuse: Notes on the validity of the child-effects model. *Analise Psicologica, 1*(10), 51–61.

Erickson, M., Sroufe, L.A., & Egeland, B. (1985). The relationship between the quality of attachment and behavior problems in preschool in a high-risk sample. In I. Bretherton & E. Waters (Eds.), Growing points of attachment theory and research. *Monographs of the Society for Research in Child Development, 209,*(50), 147–166.

Escalona, S.K. (1968). *The roots of individuality: Normal patterns of development in infancy.* Chicago: Aldine.

Eysenck, H.J. (1947). *Dimensions of personality.* London: Routledge & Kegan Paul.

Famularo, R., Fenton, T., & Kinscherff, R. (1993). Medical and developmental histories of maltreated children. *Clinical Pediatrics, 31,* 536–541.

Far West Laboratory. (1993). *Module I: Social-emotional growth and socialization.* Sacramento: California State Department of Education.

Feldman, R., Greenbaum, C.W., & Yirmiya, N. (1999). Mother-infant affect synchrony as an antecedent of the emergence of self-control. *Developmental Psychology, 35,* 223–231.

Field, T. (1991). Quality infant day-care and grade school behavior and performance. *Child Development, 62,* 863–870.

Fox, N.A. (1991). If it's not left, it's right: Electroencephalograph asymmetry and the development of emotion. *American Psychologist, 46,* 863–872.

Franyo, G.A., & Hyson, M.C. (1999). Temperament training for early childhood caregivers: A study of the effectiveness of training. *Child & Youth Care Forum, 28,* 329–347.

Freud, S. (1940). *An outline of psychoanalysis.* London: Hogarth Press.

Freud, S. (1950). *Collected papers.* London: Hogarth Press.

Fullard, W., McDevitt, S.C., & Carey, W.B., (1984). Assessing temperament in one- to three-year-old children. *Journal of Pediatric Psychology, 9,* 205–216.

Galambos, N., & Lerner, J.V. (1987). Child characteristics and the employment of mothers with young children: A longitudinal study. *Annual Progress in Child Psychiatry and Child Development,* 177–193.

Garrison, W.T., Biggs, D., & Williams, K. (1990). Temperament characteristics and clinical outcomes in young children with diabetes mellitus. *Journal of Child Psychology and Psychiatry, 31,* 1079–1088.

Garrison, W.T., & Earls, F.J. (1987). *Temperament and child psychopathology.* Newbury Park, CA: Sage Publications.

Gennaro, S., Tulman, L., & Fawcett, J. (1990). Temperament in preterm and full term infants at three and six months of age. *Merrill-Palmer Quarterly, 36,* 201–215.

George, C., & Main, M. (1979). Social interactions of young abused children: Approach, avoidance and aggression. *Child Development, 50,* 306–318.

Gesell, A. (1928). *Infancy and human growth.* New York: Macmillan.

Gesell, A., & Ames, L.B. (1937). Early evidences of individuality in the human infant. *Scientific Monthly, New York, 45,* pp. 217–225.

Ghosh, C. (1995, March). *Authoritarian versus authoritative parental behaviors and children's active participation during an interactive play task.* Paper presented at the biennial meeting of the Society for Research in Child Development, Indianapolis, IN.

Goldberg, S., & Marcovitch, S. (1989). Temperament in developmentally disabled children. In G.A. Kohnstamm, J.E. Bates, & M.K. Rothbart (Eds.), *Temperament in childhood* (pp.387–403). New York: John Wiley & Sons.

Goldsmith, H.H. (1996). Studying temperament via construction of the Toddler Behavior Assessment Questionnaire. *Child Development, 67,* 218–235.

Goldsmith, H.H., Buss, A.H., Plomin, R., Rothbart, M.K., Thomas, A., Chess, S., Hinde, R.A., McCall, R.B. (1987). Roundtable: What is temperament? Four approaches. *Child Development, 58,* 505–529.

Goldsmith, H.H., & Campos, J.J. (1982). Toward a theory of infant temperament. In R.N. Emde & R.J. Harmon (Eds.), *The development of attachment and affiliative systems* (pp. 161–193). New York: Plenum.

Goldsmith, H.H., & Rothbart, M.K. (1992). *The Laboratory Assessment Battery: Locomotor Version.* Eugene: University of Oregon, Personality Development Laboratory.

Goodman, K., Zukin, B., Tyler, B., & Shick, L. (1995). *Temperament talk: A guide to understanding your child.* LaGrande, OR: Center for Human Development.

Gordon, E.M., & Thomas, A. (1967). Children's behavioral style and the teacher's appraisal of their intelligence. *Journal of School Psychology, 5,* 292–300.

Greenspan, S.I. (1995). *The challenging child.* Cambridge, Massachusetts: Perseus Books.

Griffin, S., & Thornburg, K.R. (1985). Perceptions of infant/toddler temperament in three child care settings. *Early Childhood Development and Care, 18,* 151–160.

Griffin, W.A. (1993). *Family therapy: Fundamentals of theory and practice.* New York: Brunner/Mazel.

Gross, C.B. (1995). Temperament in toddlerhood. *Journal of Pediatric Nursing, 10,* 146–151.

Grossman, H. (1990). *Trouble-free teaching: Solutions to behavior problems in the classroom.* Mountain View, CA: Mayfield.

Guerin, D.W., & Gottfried, A.W. (1994). Developmental stability and change in parent reports of temperament: A ten-year longitudinal investigation from infancy through pre-adolescence. *Merrill-Palmer Quarterly, 40,* 334–355.

Guerin, D.W., Gottfried, A.W., Oliver, P.H., & Thomas, C.W. (2003). *Temperament infancy through adolescence.* New York: Kluwer Academic/Plenum Publishers.

Gunn, P., & Cuskelly, M. (1991). Down syndrome temperament: The stereotype at middle childhood and adolescence. *International Journal of Disability, Development & Education, 38,* 59–70.

Hagekull, B., & Bohlin, G. (1981). Individual stability in dimensions of infant behavior. *Infant Behavior and Development, 4,* 97–108.

Hancock, L. (1996, March 18). Mother's little helper. *Newsweek,* 51–56.

Hansen, R.L., Rosen, D., Cameron, J.R., Rice, D., & Kristal, J. (1991, September). *Predicting accident risk from infant temperament.* Paper presented at the meetings of the Society for Behavioral Pediatrics, Baltimore.

Hanson, M.J., & Lynch, E.W. (2004). *Understanding families: Approaches to diversity, disability, and risk.* Baltimore: Paul H. Brookes Publishing Co.

Harrington, D., Black, M.M., Star, R.H., Jr., & Dubowitz, H. (1998). Child neglect: Relation to child temperament and family context. *American Journal of Orthopsychiatry, 68,* 108–116.

Harris, M.P. (1998). The relationship of parenting style to early childhood temperament (Doctoral dissertation, Wright Institute, US). *Dissertation Abstracts International, 59* (5–B), 2454.

Harter, S. (1986). Processes underlying the construction, maintenance, and enhancement of the self-concept in children. In J. Suis & A. Greenwald (Eds.), *Psychological perspectives on the self* (Vol. 3., pp. 137–181). Mahwah, NJ: Lawrence Erlbaum Associates.

Harter, S. (1999). *The construction of the self: A developmental perspective.* New York: Guilford Press.

Head Start Bureau Press, (2003). *2003 Head Start fact sheet.* Retrieved from www.acf .hhs.gov/programs/hsb/research/2003.htm

Hegekull, B., Bohlin, G., & Rydell, A.M. (1997). Maternal sensitivity, infant temperament, and the development of early feeding problems. *Infant Mental Health Journal, 18,* 92–106.

Hegvik, R. (1989). Application of temperament theory to an individualized educational environment. In W.B. Carey & S.C. McDevitt (Eds.). *Clinical and educational applications of temperament research.* Berwyn, PA: Swets North America.

Hegvik, R.L., McDevitt, S.C., & Carey, W.B. (1982). Middle Childhood Temperament Questionnaire. *Developmental and Behavioral Pediatrics, 3,* 197–200.

Helm, J., & Katz, L.C. (2001). *Young investigators: The project approach in the early years.* New York: Teachers College Press.

Hertzig, M.E. (1983). Temperament and neurological status. In M. Rutter (Ed.), *Developmental neuropsychiatry* (pp. 164–180). New York: Guilford Press.

Hetherington, E.M. (1989). Coping with family transitions: Winners, losers, and survivors. *Child Development, 60,* 1–14.

Hetherington, E.M., Bridges, M., & Insabella, G.M. (1998, February). What matters? What does not? Five perspectives on the association between marital transitions and children's adjustment. *American Psychologist, 53,* 167–184.

Howes, C., & Olenick, M. (1986). Family and child care influences on toddler's compliance. *Child Development, 57,* 202–216.

Howes, C., Phillips, D., & Whitebook, M. (1992). Thresholds of quality: Implications for the social development of children in center-based child care. *Child Development, 63,* 449–460.

Hudziak, J.J., Heath, A.C., Madden, P.A.F., Reich, W., Bucholz, K.K., Slutske, W., et al. [etc.] (1998). Latent class and factor analysis of DSM-IV ADHD: A twin study of female adolescents. *Journal of the American Academy of Child and Adolescent Psychiatry, 37,* 848–857.

Huttunen, M., & Nyman, K. (1982). On the continuity, change, and clinical value value of value of infant temperament in a prospective epidemiological study. In R. Porter & G.M. Collins (Eds.), *Temperamental differences in infants and young children* (pp. 240–251). London: Pitman.

Irwin, C.E., Cataldo, M.F., Matheny, A.P., Jr., & Peterson, L. (1992). Health consequences of behavior: Injury as a model. *Pediatrics, 90,* 798–807.

Johnson, C.M. (1991). Infant and toddler sleep: A telephone survey in one community. *Journal of Developmental and Behavioral Pediatrics, 12,* 108–114.

Kagan, J. (1982). *Psychological research on the human infant: An evaluative study.* New York: W.T. Grant Foundation.

Kagan, J. (1984). *The nature of the child.* New York: Basic Books.

Kagan, J. (1994). Inhibited and uninhibited temperaments. In W.B. Carey & S.C.

McDevitt (Eds.), *Prevention and early intervention: Individual differences as risk factors for the mental health of children*. New York: Brunner/Mazel.

Kagan, J. (1998). Biology and the child. In W. Damon (Series Ed.) & N. Eisenberg (Vol. Ed.), *Handbook of child development: Vol. 3. Social, emotional, and personality development* (pp. 178–235). New York: John Wiley & Sons.

Kagan, J., Reznick, S., & Gibbons, J. (1989). Inhibited and uninhibited types of children. *Child Development, 60,* 838–845.

Kagan, J., Reznick, S., & Snidman, N. (1987). The physiology and psychology of behavioral inhibition in young children. *Child Development, 58,* 1459–1473.

Kagan, J., & Snidman, N. (1991a). Infant predictors of inhibited and uninhibited behavioral profiles. *Psychological Science, 2,* 40–44.

Kagan, J., & Snidman, N. (1991b). Temperamental factors in human development. *American Psychologist, 46,* 856–862.

Kagan, J., Snidman, N., & Arcus, D. (1998). Childhood derivatives of infant reactivity. *Child Development, 69,* 1483–1493.

Kagan, J., Snidman, N., Arcus, D., & Reznick, J.S. (1994). *Galen's prophecy: Temperament in human nature*. New York: Basic Books.

Kaiser Permanente. (1995). *Using temperament concepts to prevent behavior problems* [Motion picture]. (Available from The Kaiser Permanente Temperament Program, Audio Visual Department, 1950 Franklin, Oakland, CA)

Kaler, S.R., & Kopp, C.B. (1990). Compliance and comprehension in very young toddlers. *Child Development, 61,* 1997–2003.

Kaplan, J.A. (1991). *Differences between mother's and father's parenting style: Their effect on preschooler's behavior in the family*. Poster presented at the biennial meeting of the Society for Research in Child Development, Seattle, WA.

Karraker, K.H, Lake, M.A., & Parry, T.B (1991). Poster presented at the biennial meeting of the Society for Research in Child Development, Seattle, WA.

Katz, L.G., & Chard, S.C. (2000). *Engaging children's minds: The project approach* (2nd ed). Norwood, NJ: Ablex Publishing.

Kaye, K. (1982). *The mental and social life of babies*. Chicago: University of Chicago Press.

Keener, M.A., Zeanah, C.H., & Anders, T.F. (1988). Infant temperament, sleep organization, and nighttime parental interventions. In S. Chess & M.E. Hertzig, (Eds.), *Annual Progress in Child Psychiatry & Child Development,* 257–274.

Kelmanson, I. (1999). Parent–infant bed sharing and behavioural features in 2–4 month old infants. *Early Childhood Development and Care, 149,* 1–9.

Keogh, B.K. (1982). Children's temperament and teachers' decisions. In R. Porter & G.M. Collins (Eds.), *Temperamental differences in infants and young children* (pp. 269–279). London: Pitman.

Keogh, B.K. (1986). Temperament and schooling: Meaning of "goodness of fit"? In J.V. Lerner & R.M. Lerner (Eds.), *Temperament and social interactions in infants and children* (pp. 89–108). San Francisco: Jossey-Bass.

Keogh, B.K. (1989). Applying temperament research to school. In G.A Kohnstamm, J.E. Bates, & M.K. Rothbart (Eds.), *Temperament in childhood* (pp. 437–450). New York: John Wiley & Sons.

Keogh, B.K. (1994). Temperament and teachers' views of teachability. In W.B. Carey & S.C. McDevitt (Eds.), *Prevention and early intervention: Individual differences as risk factors for the mental health of children*. New York: Brunner/Mazel.

Keogh, B.K. (2003). *Temperament in the classroom: Understanding individual differences*. Baltimore: Paul H. Brookes Publishing Co.

Keogh, B.K., Pullis, M., & Cadwell, J. (1982). Teacher Temperament Questionnaire–Short Form. *Journal of Educational Measurement, 29,* 323–329.

Klein, H. (1980). Early childhood group care: Predicting adjustment from individual temperament. *The Journal of Genetic Psychology, 134,* 155–159.

Kochanska, G. (1995). Children's temperament, mothers' discipline, and security of attachment: Multiple pathways to emerging internalization. *Child Development, 66,* 597–615.

Kochanska, G. (1997a). Mutually responsive orientation between mothers and their young children: Implications for early socialization. *Child Development, 68,* 94–112.

Kochanska, G. (1997b). Multiple pathways to conscience for children with different temperaments: from toddlerhood to age 5. *Developmental Psychology, 33*(2), 228–240.

Kochanska, G., Murray, K., & Coy, K. (1997). Inhibitory control as a contributor to conscience in childhood: From toddler to early school age. *Child Development, 68,* 263–277.

Kolvin, I., Nicol, A.R., Garside, R.F., Day, K.A., & Tweedle, E.G. (1982). Temperamental patterns in aggressive boys. In R. Porter & G.M. Collins (Eds.), *Temperamental differences in infants and young children* (pp. 252–268). London: Pitman.

Kowal, A., & Pritchard, D. (1990). Psychological characteristics of children who suffer from headache: A research note. *Journal of Child Psychology and Psychiatry, 30,* 637–649.

Krakow, J.B., & Johnson, K.L. (1981, April). *The emergence and consolidation of self-control processes from 18 to 30 months of age.* Paper presented at the biennial meeting of the Society for Research in Child Development, Boston.

Krakow, J.B., Kopp, C.B., & Vaughn, B.E. (1981, April). *Sustained attention during the second year: Age trends, individual differences, and implications for development.* Paper presented at the biennial meeting of the Society for Research in Child Development, Boston.

Kranowitz, C.S. (1998). *The out-of-sync child: Recognizing and coping with sensory integration dysfunction.* New York: The Berkeley Publishing Group.

Kristal, J., Neville, H., & Renner, R. (1994). *The instructor's manual for temperament based parenting classes.* Oakland, CA: Kaiser Permanente Regional Health Education.

Kurcinka, M.S. (1991). *Raising your spirited child: A guide for parents whose child is more intense, sensitive, perceptive, persistent, energetic* New York: HarperCollins.

Kurcinka, M.S. (1998a). *Raising your spirited child: A guide for parents whose child is more sensitive, perceptive, persistent* (rev. ed.). New York: HarperCollins.

Kurcinka, M.S. (1998b). *The raising your spirited child workbook.* New York: Harper-Collins.

Kurcinka, M.S. (2001). *Kids, parents and power struggles.* New York: Quill.

Kurdek, L.A., & Fine, M.A. (1994). Family acceptance and family control as predictors of adjustment in young adolescents: Linear, curvilinear, or interactive effects? *Child Development, 65,* 1137–1146.

LaFreniere, P., & Sroufe, L.A. (1985). Profiles of peer competence in the preschool: Interrelations between measures, influence of social ecology, and relation to attachment history. *Developmental Psychology, 21,* 56–69.

Lamb, M.E., Chase-Lansdale, L., & Owen, M.T. (1979). The changing American family and its implications for infant social development: The sample case of maternal employment. In M. Lewis & A. Rosenblum (Eds.), *The child and its family* (pp. 267–291). New York: Plenum.

Landy, S. (2002). *Pathways to competence: Encouraging healthy social and emotional development in young children.* Baltimore: Paul H. Brookes Publishing Co.

Langkamp, D.L., Kim, Y., & Pascoe, J.M. (1998). Temperament and preterm infants at 4 months of age. Maternal ratings and perceptions. *Journal of Developmental and Behavioral Pediatrics, 19,* 391–396.

Lee, L.W., & White-Traut, R.C. (1996). The role of temperament in pediatric pain response. *Issues in Comprehensive Pediatric Nursing, 19,* 49–63.

Lemery, K.S., Essex, M.J., & Smider, N.A. (2002). Revealing the relationship between temperament and behavior problem symptoms by eliminating measurement confounding: Expert ratings and factor analyses. *Child Development, 73,* 867–882.

Lemery, K.S., Goldsmith, H.H., Klinnert, M.D., & Mrazek, D.A. (1999). Developmental models of infant and childhood temperament. *Developmental Psychology, 35,* 189–204.

Lerner, J.V., Lerner, R.M., & Zabski, S. (1985). Temperament and elementary school children's actual and rated academic performance: A test of a 'goodness of fit' model. *Journal of Child Psychology and Psychiatry, 26,* 125–136.

Locke, J. (1892). Some thoughts concerning education. In R.H. Quick, *Locke on Education* (pp. 1–236). Cambridge, England: Cambridge University Press. (Original work published 1690)

Londerville, S., & Main, M. (1981). Security of attachment, compliance, and maternal training methods in the second year of life. *Developmental Psychology, 17,* 289–299.

Lorenz, K. (1971). *Studies in animal and human behavior* (Vol. 2). Cambridge, MA: Harvard University Press.

Maccoby, E.E. (1984). Socialization and developmental change. *Child Development, 55,* 317–328.

Maccoby, E.E. (1992). The role of parents in the socialization of children: An historical overview. *Developmental Psychology, 28,* 1006–1017.

Maccoby, E.E., & Martin, J.A. (1983). Socialization in the context of the family: Parent-child interaction. In P.H. Mussen (Ed.), *Handbook of child psychology* (4th ed., Vol. 4). New York: John Wiley & Sons.

Main, M., & Solomon, J. (1990). Procedures for identifying infants as disorganized/ disoriented during the Ainsworth Strange Situation. In M. Greenberg, D. Cicchetti, & M. Cummings (Eds.), *Attachment in the preschool years: Theory, research and intervention* (pp. 121–160). Chicago: University of Chicago Press.

Mangelsdorf, S.C., Schoppe, S.J., & Burr, H. (2000). The meaning of parental reports: A contextual approach to the study of temperament and behavior problems in childhood. In V.J. Molfese & D.L. Molfese (Eds.), *Temperament and personality across the life span* (pp. 121–140). Mahwah, NJ: Lawrence Erlbaum Associates.

March, J.S., & Mulle, K., (1998). *OCD in children and adolescents: A cognitive behavioral treatment manual.* New York: Guilford Press.

Martin, R.P. (1988a). Child temperament and educational outcomes. In A.D. Pellegrini (Ed.), *Psychological bases for early education.* London: John Wiley & Sons.

Martin, R.P. (1988b). *The Temperament Assessment Battery for Children.* Brandon, VT: Clinical Psychology Publishing Co.

Martin, R.P. (1989). Temperament and education: Implications for underachievement and learning disabilities. In W.B. Carey & S.C. McDevitt (Eds.), *Clinical and educational applications of temperament research* (pp. 37–51). Amsterdam: Swets Zeitlinger.

Martin, R.P., Halverson, C.H., & Duke, H. (1996, October). *A typal analysis of preschool children based on temperamental characteristics.* Poster presented at the Occasional Temperament Conference, Eugene, Oregon.

Martin, R.P., & Holbrook, J. (1985). Relationship of temperament characteristics to the academic achievement of first grade children. *Journal of Psychoeducational Assessment, 3,* 131–140.

Martin, R.P., Nagel, R., & Paget, K. (1983). Relationships between temperament and classroom behavior, teacher attitudes, and academic achievement. *Journal of Psychoeducational Assessment, 1,* 377–386.

Martin, R.P., Olejnik, S., & Gaddis, L. (1994). Is temperament an important contributor to schooling outcomes in elementary school? Modeling effects of temperament and scholastic ability on academic achievement. In W.B. Carey & S.C. McDevitt (Eds.), *Prevention and early intervention. Individual risk factors for the mental health of children*. New York: Brunner/Mazel.

Matheny, A.P., Jr. (1989). Temperament and cognition: Relations between temperament and mental test scores. In G.A. Kohnstamm, J.E. Bates, & M.K. Rothbart (Eds.), *Temperament in childhood* (pp. 185–205). New York: John Wiley & Sons.

Matheny, A.P., Jr. (2000). Standardized play assessment of infant and toddler temperament. In K. Gitlion-Weiner, A. Sandgrund, & C. Schaefer (Eds.), *Play diagnosis and assessment* (2nd ed.). New York: John Wiley & Sons.

Matheny, A.P., Jr., Reise, M.L., & Wilson, R.S. (1985). Rudiments of infant temperament: Newborn to nine months. *Developmental Psychology, 21,* 486–494.

Matheny, A.P., Jr., Wilson, R.S., & Thoben, A.S. (1987). Home and mother: Relations with infant temperament. *Developmental Psychology, 23,* 323–331.

Maxmen, J.S., & Ward, N.G. (1995). *Essential psychopathology and its treatment*. New York: W.W. Norton & Company.

Mayberry, L.J., & Alfonso, D.D. (1993). Infant temperament and postpartum depression: A review. *Health Care for Women International, 14,* 201–211.

Maziade, M., Caron, C., Cote, R., Merette, C., Bernier, H., Laplante, B., et al. (1990). Psychiatric status of adolescents who had extreme temperaments at age 7. *American Journal of Psychiatry, 147,* 1531–1536.

McCartney, K., Scarr, S., Rocheleau, A., Phillips, D., Eisenberg, M., Keefe, N., et al. (1997). Social development in the context of typical center-based child care. *Merrill-Palmer Quarterly, 43,* 426–450.

McClowry, S.G. (1990). The relationship of temperament to pre- and post hospitalization behavioral responses of school-aged children. *Nursing Research, 39,* 30–35.

McClowry, S.G. (1992). Temperament theory and research. *IMAGE: Journal of Nursing Scholarship, 24,* 319–325.

McClowry, S.G. (1995a). The development of the School-Age Temperament Inventory. *Merrill-Palmer Quarterly, 41,* 271–285.

McClowry, S. (1995b). The influence of temperament on development during middle childhood. *Journal of Pediatric Nursing, 10,* 160–165.

McClowry, S.G. (1998). The science and art of using temperament as the basis for intervention. *School Psychology Review, 27,* 551–563.

McClowry, S. (2002). Transforming temperament profile statistics into puppets and other visual media. *Journal of Pediatric Nursing, 17,* 11–17.

McClowry, S.G. (2003). *Your child's unique temperament: Insights and strategies for responsive parenting*. Champaign, IL: Research Press.

McClowry, S., & Galehouse, P. (2002). Planning a temperament-based parenting program for inner city families. *Journal of Child and Adolescent Psychiatric Nursing, 15,* 97–105.

McClowry, S.G., Snow, D.L., & Tamis-LeMonda, C.S. (in press). *An evaluation of the effects of INSIGHTS on the behavior of inner city primary school children*. Paper submitted for publication.

McDevitt, S.C. (1986). Continuity and discontinuity of temperament in infancy and early childhood: A psychometric perspective. In R. Plomin & J. Dunn (Eds.), *The study of temperament: Changes, continuities and challenges* (pp. 27–38). Mahwah, NJ: Lawrence Erlbaum Associates.

McDevitt, S.C. (1988). Assessment of temperament in developmentally disabled children infants and preschoolers. In T. Wachs & R. Sheehan (Eds.), *Assessment of young developmentally disabled children*. New York: Plenum.

McDevitt, S.C., & Carey, W.B. (1975–1995). The Behavioral Style Questionnaire for

3- to 7-year-old children. *The Carey Temperament Scales*. Behavioral Development Initiatives: B-DI.com.

McDevitt, S.C., & Carey, W.B. (1978). The measurement of temperament in 3- to 7-year-old children. *Journal of Child Psychology and Psychiatry, 19,* 245–253.

McGurk, H., Caplan, M., Hennessy, E., & Moss, P. (1993) Controversy, theory, and social context in contemporary day care research. *Journal of Child Psychology and Psychiatry, 34,* 3–23.

Medhoff-Cooper, B. (1986). Temperament in very-low-birth-rate infants. *Nursing Research, 35,* 139–143.

Medhoff-Cooper, B. (1994). Specific prevention and intervention strategies used to accommodate individual needs of newborn infants. In W.B. Carey & S.C. McDevitt (Eds.), *Prevention and early intervention: Individual differences as risk factors for the mental health of children.* New York: Brunner/Mazel.

Medhoff-Cooper, B., Carey, W.B., & McDevitt, S.C. (1993). The Early Infancy Temperament Questionnaire. *Journal of Developmental and Behavioral Pediatrics, 14,* 230–235.

Melvin, N. (1995). Children's temperament: Intervention for parents. *Journal of Pediatric Nursing, 10,* 152–159.

Mettatal, G. (1996). Non-clinical interventions for families with temperamentally difficult children. *Early Child Development and Care, 121,* 119–133.

Milliones, J., (1978). Relationship between perceived child temperament and maternal behaviors. *Child Development, 49,* 1255–1257.

Minde, K., Faucon, A., & Faulkener, S. (1994). Sleep problems in toddlers: Effect of treatment on their daytime behavior. *Journal of the American Academy of Child and Adolescent Psychiatry, 33,* 1114–1121.

Mirsky, E., Dodge, K., & Schiller, M. (1999). *Parental socialization and child compliance, temperament and self-control.* Paper presented at the biennial meeting of the Society for Research in Child Development, Albuquerque, NM.

Mischel, W. (1983). Delay of gratification as process and as person variable in development. In D. Magnusson & V.L. Allen (Eds.), *Human development: An interactional perspective* (pp. 149–165). New York: Academic Press.

Morris, A.S., Silk, J.S., Steinberg, L., Sessa, F.M., Arenevoli, S., & Essex, M.J. (2002). Temperamental vulnerability and negative parenting as interacting of child adjustment. *Journal of Marriage and Family, 64,* 461–471.

Murray, K.T., & Kochanska, G. (2002). Effortful control: Factor structure and relation to externalizing and internalizing behaviors. *Journal of Abnormal Child Psychology, 30,* 503–514.

Myers, D.G. (1996). *Exploring psychology* (3rd ed.). New York: Worth Publishers.

Nelson, N.N. (1987). Child temperament, gender and teacher-child interactions: An observational study. *Early Child Development and Care, 29,* 343–365.

Neville, H., & Johnson, D.C. (1998). *Temperament tools: Working with your child's inborn traits.* Seattle, WA: Parenting Press.

NICHD Early Child Care Research Network. (1998). Early child care and self-control, compliance, and problem behavior at twenty-four and thirty-six months. *Child Development, 69,* 1145–1170.

Northam, E., Prior, M., Sanson, A., & Oberklaid, F. (1987). Toddler temperament as perceived by mothers versus care givers. *Merrill-Palmer Quarterly, 33,* 213–229.

Nygaard, E., Smith, L., & Torgersen, A.M. (2002). Temperament in children with Down syndrome and in prematurely born children. *Scandanavian Journal of Psychology, 43,* 61–71.

Nyman, G. (1987) Infant temperament childhood accidents and hospitalization. *Clinical Pediatrics, 26,* 398–404.

Oberklaid, F., Sanson, A., Pedlow, R., & Prior, M. (1993). Predicting preschool behavior problems from temperament and other variables in infancy. *Pediatrics, 91,* 113–120.

O'Dell, S.L., O'Quinn, J., Alford, B., O'Briant, A.L., Bradlyn, A.S., & Giebenhain, J.E. (1982). Predicting the acquisitions of parenting skills via four training models. *Behavior Therapy, 13,* 194–208.

Ostergren, C.S. (1997). Differential utility of temperament-based guidance materials for parents of infants. *Family Relations, 46,* 63–71.

Ostergren, C.S. (2003). *Evaluation of a temperament-based parenting program: Factors affecting program usefulness, ease of understanding, preferred amounts of materials and parental attitudes.* Unpublished doctoral dissertation, University of Wisconsin–Madison.

Ozonoff, S., Dawson, G., & McPartland, J. (2002). *A parent's guide to Asperger syndrome and high functioning autism.* New York: Guilford Press.

Palombo, J. (2001). *Learning disorders and disorders of the self in children and adolescents.* New York: W.W. Norton & Co.

Papolos, D.F., & Papolos, J. (1999). *The bipolar child.* New York: Broadway Books.

Phelan, T.W. (1995). *1–2–3 magic: Effective discipline for children ages 2–12.* Glen Ellyn, IL: Child Management, Inc.

Phillips, D., Scarr, S., & McCartney, D. (1987). Dimensions and effects of child care quality. In D. Phillips (Ed.), *Quality in child care* (pp. 57–80). Washington, DC: National Association for the Education of Young Children.

Piaget, J., & Inhelder, B. (1969). *The psychology of the child.* New York: Basic Books.

Prior, M. (1992). Childhood temperament. *Journal of Child Psychology and Psychiatry, 33,* 249–279.

Prior, M.R., Sanson, A.V., & Oberklaid, F., (1989). The Australian temperament project. In G.A. Kohnstamm, J.E. Bates, & M.K. Rothbart (Eds.), *Temperament in childhood* (pp. 537–554). New York: John Wiley & Sons.

Pullis, M. (1989). Goodness of fit in classroom relationships. In W.B. Carey & S.C. McDevitt (Eds.), *Clinical and educational applications of temperament research* (pp. 117–120). Berwyn, PA: Swets North America.

Ratekin, C. (1994, October). *Temperament and its role in adjustment in child care.* Paper presented at the Tenth Occasional Temperament Conference, Berkeley, CA.

Ratekin, C. (1996). Temperament in children with Down syndrome. *Developmental Disabilities Bulletin, 24,* 18–32.

Rice, D. (2001). *Temperament and psychotherapy with children.* Unpublished manuscript.

Rimm-Kaufman, S., Early, D., & Saluja, G. (2001). *Bold children in the classroom: The moderating role of the teacher.* Paper presented at the biennial meeting of the Society for Research in Child Development, Minneapolis, MN.

Rogers, L. (1996). *The California Freshwater Shrimp Project: An example of environmental project based learning.* Berkeley, CA: Heyday Books.

Rosen, D.L., Cameron, J., & Rice, D. (1996). The temperament program: A children's preventive mental health program. *HMO Practice, 10,* 140–142.

Rothbart, M.K. (1981). Measurement of temperament in infancy. *Child Development, 52,* 569–578.

Rothbart, M.K. (1986). Longitudinal observation on infant temperament. *Developmental Psychology, 22,* 356–365.

Rothbart, M.K. (1988). Temperament and the development of inhibited approach. *Child Development, 59,* 1241–1250.

Rothbart, M.K. (1989a). Biological processes in temperament. In G.A. Kohnstamm, J.E. Bates, & M.K. Rothbart (Eds.), *Temperament in childhood* (pp. 77–110). Chichester, UK: Wiley.

Rothbart, M.K. (1989b). Temperament in childhood: A framework. In G.A. Kohnstamm, J.E. Bates, & M.K. Rothbart (Eds.), *Temperament in childhood*. Chichester, UK: Wiley.

Rothbart, M.K. (1989c). Temperament and development. In G.A. Kohnstamm, J.E. Bates, & M.K. Rothbart (Eds.), *Temperament in childhood*. Chichester, UK: Wiley.

Rothbart, M.K., Ahadi, S.A., & Evans, D.E. (2000). Temperament and personality: Origins and outcomes. *Journal of Personality and Social Psychology, 78,* 122–135.

Rothbart, M.K., Ahadi, S.A., & Hershey, K.L. (1994). Temperament and social behavior in childhood. *Merrill-Palmer Quarterly, 40,* 21–39.

Rothbart, M.K., Ahadi, S. A., Hershey, K., & Fisher, P. (2001). Investigations of temperament at three to seven years: The Children's Behavior Questionnaire. *Child Development, 72*(5), 1394–1408.

Rothbart, M.K., & Bates, J.E. (1998). Temperament. In W. Damon (Series Ed.) & N. Eisenberg (Vol. Ed.), *Handbook of Child Development: Volume 3: Social, emotional, and personality development* (pp. 105–176). New York: John Wiley & Sons.

Rothbart, M.K., & Derryberry, D. (1981). Development of individual differences in temperament. In M.E Lamb & A.L. Brown (Eds.), *Advances in developmental psychology* (Vol. I, pp. 37–86). Mahwah, NJ: Lawrence Erlbaum Associates.

Rothbart, M.K., Derryberry, D., & Hershey, K. (2000). Stability of temperament in childhood: Laboratory infant assessment to parent report at seven years. In V.J. Molfese & D.L. Molfese (Eds.), *Temperament and personality development across the life span* (pp. 85–120). Mahwah, NJ: Lawrence Erlbaum Associates.

Rothbart, M.K., & Goldsmith, H.H. (1985). Three approaches to the study of infant temperament. *Developmental Review, 5,* 237–260.

Rothbart, M.K., & Jones, L.B. (1998). Temperament, self-regulation, and education. *School Psychology Review, 27,* 479–491.

Rothbart, M.K., Posner, M.I., & Hershey, K.L. (1995). Temperament, attention, and developmental psychopathology. In D. Cicchetti & D.J. Cohen (Eds.), *Manual of developmental psychopathology* (Vol. 1, pp. 315–340). New York: John Wiley & Sons.

Rovet, J., & Ehrlich, R. (1988). Effect of temperament on metabolic control in children with diabetes mellitus. *Diabetes Care, 11,* 77–82.

Rowe, D.C. (1994). *The limits of family influence: Genes, experience, and behavior.* New York: Guilford Press.

Rubin, K.H., Bukowski, W., & Parker, J.G. (1998). Peer interactions, relationships, and groups. In W. Damon (Series Ed.) & N. Eisenberg (Vol. Ed.), *Handbook of child psychology: Vol. 3. Social, emotional and personality development* (5th ed., pp. 619–700). New York: John Wiley & Sons.

Rubin, K.H., Burgess, K.B., Dwyer, K.M., & Hastings, P.D. (2003). Predicting preschoolers' externalizing behaviors from toddler temperament, conflict, and maternal negativity. *Developmental Psychology, 39,* 164–176.

Rubin, K.H., Burgess, K.B., & Hastings, P.D. (2002). Stability and social-behavioral consequences of toddlers' inhibited temperament and parenting behaviors. *Child Development, 73,* 483–495.

Rubin, K.H., Hastings, P.D., Stewart, S.L., Henderson, H.A., & Chen, X. (1997). The consistency and concomitants of inhibition: Some of the children all of the time. *Child Development, 68,* 467–483.

Rubin, K.H., Stewart, S.L., & Coplan, R.J. (1995). Social withdrawal in childhood: Conceptual and empirical perceptions. In T.H. Ollendick & R.J. Prinz (Eds.), *Advances in clinical child psychology* (Vol. 17, pp. 157–196). New York: Plenum.

Ruddy-Wallace, M. (1989). Temperament: A variable in children's pain management. *Pediatric Nursing, 15,* 118–121.

Ruff, H.A., & Rothbart, M.K. (1996). *Attention in early development: Themes and variations.* New York: Oxford University Press.

Rutter, M. (1979). Protective factors in children's response to stress and disadvantage. In M.W. Kent & J.E. Rolf (Eds.) *Primary prevention of psychopathology* (Vol. 3, pp. 49–74) Hanover, NH: University Press of New England.

Rutter, M. (1982). Temperament: Concepts, issues, and problems. In R. Porter & C.G. Collins (Eds.), *Temperamental differences in infants and young children* (pp. 1–19). Ciba Foundation Symposium No. 89. London: Pitman.

Rutter, M., & Garmezy, N. (1983). Developmental psychopathology. In P.H. Mussen (Series Ed.) & E.M. Hetherington (Vol. Ed.), *Handbook of child psychology: Vol. 4. Socialization, personality, and social development* (4th ed., pp. 775–911.). New York: John Wiley & Sons.

Sadeh, A., Lavie, P., & Scher, A. (1994). Sleep and temperament: Maternal perceptions of temperament of sleep disturbed toddlers. *Early Education and Development, 5,* 311–322.

Sanson, A., Smart, D., Prior, M. & Oberklaid, F. (1993). Precursors of hyperactivity and aggressions. *Journal of the American Academy of Child and Adolescent Psychiatry, 32,* 1207–1216.

Sarason, S.B. (1993). *The case for change: rethinking the preparation of educators.* San Francisco: Jossey Bass.

Scarr, S. (1998, February). American child care today. *American Psychologist,* 95–108.

Scarr, S. & McCartney, K. (1983). How people make their own environments: A theory of genotype (environment interactions. *Child Development, 54,* 424–435.

Schaefer, C.E., (1990). Night waking and temperament in early childhood. *Psychological Reports, 67,* 192–194.

Schmeck, K., & Poustka, F. (2001). Temperament and disruptive behavior disorders. *Psychopathology, 34,* 159–163.

Schoen, M.J., & Nagle, R.J. (1994). Prediction of school readiness from kindergarten temperament scores. *Journal of School Psychology, 32,* 135–147.

Schwebel, D.C., & Plumert, J.M. (1999). Longitudinal and concurrent relations among temperament, ability estimation, and injury proneness. *Child Development, 70,* 700–712.

Segal-Andrews, A.M., Altschuler, S.M., & Harkness, S.E. (1995). Chronic abdominal pain: Treating the meaning of pain. *Family Systems Medicine, 13,* 233–243.

Seifer, R., Sameroff, A.J., Barrett, L.C., & Krafchuk, E. (1994). Infant temperament measured by multiple observations and mother report. *Child Development, 65,* 1478–1490.

Seifer, R., & Schiller, M. (1995). The role of parenting sensitivity, infant temperament, and dyadic interaction in attachment theory and assessment. In E. Waters, B.E. Vaughn, G. Posada, & K. Kondo-Ikemura (Eds.), New growing points of attachment: Theory and research. *Monographs of the Society for Research in Child Development, 244, 60,* 146–174.

Sheeber, L.B., & Johnson, J.H. (1994). Evaluation of a temperament-focused, parent-training program. *Journal of Clinical Psychology, 23*(3), 249–259.

Sher, A., Epstein, R., Sadeh, A., Tirosh, E., & Lavie, P. (1992). Toddlers sleep and temperament: Reporting bias or valid link? A research note. *Journal of Child Psychology and Psychiatry, 33,* 1249–1254.

Shirley, M.M. (1931). *The first two years: A study of twenty-five babies: Vol. 1. Postural and locomotor development.* Minneapolis: University of Minnesota Press.

Skinner, B.F. (1938). *The behavior of organisms.* Englewood Cliffs, NJ: Prentice-Hall.

Skinner, B.F. (1974). *About behaviorism.* New York: Vintage Books.

Slomkowski, C.I., Nelson, K., Dunn, J., & Plomin, R. (1992). Temperament and language: Relations from toddlerhood to middle childhood. *Developmental Psychology, 28,* 1090–1095.

Smith, B. (1994). The temperament program: Community-based prevention of behavior disorders in children. In W.B. Carey & S.C. McDevitt (Eds.), *Prevention and early intervention; Individual differences as risk factors for the mental health of children.* New York: Brunner/Mazel.

Sroufe, L.A. (1985). Attachment classification from the perspective of infant-caregiver relationships and infant temperament. *Child Development, 56,* 1–14.

Steinberg, L., Dornbusch, S.M., & Brown, B.B. (1992). Ethnic differences in adolescent achievement: An ecological perspective. *American Psychologist, 47,* 723–729.

Steinberg, L., Lamborn, S.D., Darling, N., Mounts, N.S., & Dornbusch, S.M. (1994). Overtime changes in adjustment and competence among adolescents from authoritative, authoritarian, indulgent, and neglectful families. *Child Development, 65,* 754–770.

Stevenson-Hinde, J., & Simpson, A.E. (1982). Temperament and relationships. In R. Porter & G.M. Collins (Eds.), *Temperamental differences in infants and young children* (pp. 51–61). Ciba Foundation Symposium 89. London: Pitman.

Stipek, D. (1998). Communicating expectations. In D. Stipek (Ed.), *Motivation to learn: From theory to practice* (pp. 203–220). Boston, MA: Allyn & Bacon.

Strauss, M.E., & Rourke, D.L. (1978). A multivariate analysis of the neonatal behavioral assessment scale in several samples. In A.J. Sameroff (Ed.), Organization and stability of newborn behavior: A commentary on the Brazelton Neonatal Behavioral Assessment Scale. *Monographs of the Society for Research in Child Development, 43*(Serial No. 177) Nos. 5–6, 81–91.

Strelau, J. (1983). *Temperament, personality, activity.* San Diego: Academic Press.

Strelau, J. (1989). Temperament risk factors in children and adolescents as studied in Eastern Europe. In W.B. Carey & S.C McDevitt (Eds.), *Clinical and education applications of temperament research* (pp. 65–77). Berwyn, PA: Swets North America.

Strelau, J. (2001). The role of temperament as a moderator of stress. In T.D. Wachs & G.A. Kohnstamm (Eds.), *Temperament in context* (pp. 153–172). Mahwah, NJ: Lawrence Erlbaum Associates.

Sullivan, S.A., & Birch, L.L. (1990). Pass the sugar, pass the salt: Experience dictates preference. *Developmental Psychology, 26,* 546–551.

Susman-Stillman, A., Kalkoske, M., Egeland, B. & Waldman, I. (1996). Infant temperament and maternal sensitivity as predictors of attachment security. *Infant Behavior and Development, 19,* 33–47.

Teerikangas, O.M., Aronen, E.T., Martin, R.P., & Huttunen, M. (1998). Effects of infant temperament and early intervention on the psychiatric symptoms of adolescents. *Journal of the American Academy of Child and Adolescent Psychiatry, 37,* 1070–1076.

Teglasi, H. (1998). Temperament constructs and measures. *School Psychology Review, 27,* 564–585.

Temple, K.M. (1991, April). *Toddlers' shyness as related to parental attitudes and behavior: A function of child and parent gender.* Poster presented at the biennial meeting of the Society for Research in Child Development. Seattle, WA.

Tennes, K., Downey, K., & Vernadakis, A. (1977). Cortisol excretion levels and daytime sleep in one-year old infants. *Clinical and Endocrinology Metabolism, 44,* 175–179.

Terestman, N. (1980). Mood quality and intensity in nursery school children as predictors of behavior disorders. *American Journal of Orthopsychiatry, 50,* 125–138.

Thomas, A., & Chess, S. (1977). *Temperament and development.* New York: Brunner/Mazel.

Thomas, A., & Chess, S. (1980). *Dynamics of psychological development.* New York: Brunner/Mazel.

Thomas, A., & Chess, S. (1986). The New York Longitudinal Study: From infancy to early adulthood. In R. Plomin & J. Dunn (Eds.), *The study of temperament: Changes, continuities and challenges.* Mahwah, NJ: Lawrence Erlbaum Associates.

Thomas, A., Chess, S., & Birch, H. (1968). *Temperament and behavior disorders in children.* New York: New York University Press.

Thomas, A., Chess, S., Birch, H., Hertzig, M.E., & Korn, S. (1963). *Behavioral individuality in early childhood.* New York: New York University Press.

Thompson, R.A., Connell, J.P., & Bridges, L.J. (1988). Temperament, emotion, and social interactive behavior in the Strange Situation: A component process analysis of attachment system functioning. *Child Development, 59,* 102–110.

Tizard, B., & Hodges, J. (1978). The effect of early institutional rearing on the development of 8-year old children. *Journal of Child Psychology and Psychiatry 19,* 99–118.

Turecki, S. (1985). *The difficult child.* New York: Bantam.

Turecki, S. (1989). The difficult child center. In W.B. Carey & S.C. McDevitt (Eds.), *Clinical and educational applications of temperament research* (pp. 141–154) Berwyn, PA: Swets North America.

Turecki, S., & Tonner, L. (2000). *The difficult child* (Rev. ed.). New York: Bantam.

U.S. Bureau of the Census. (1997). *Who's minding our preschoolers?* (Current population Reports, P70–62). Washington, DC: U.S. Government Printing Office.

U.S. Bureau of the Census. (2000). *Statistical abstract of the United States* (120th ed). Washington, DC: U.S. Government Printing Office.

U.S. House of Representatives, Committee on Ways and Means. (1996). Section 10: Child Care. In *Green Book.* Washington, DC: U.S. Government Printing Office.

van Bakel, H.J.A., & Riksen-Walraven, J.M. (2002). Parenting and development of one-year-olds: Links with parental, contextual, and child characteristics. *Child Development, 73*(2), 256–273.

Vandell, D.L., & Corasaniti, M.A. (1988). The relation between third-graders after school care and social, academic, and emotional functioning. *Child Development, 59,* 868–875.

Vandell, D.L., & Corasaniti, M.A. (1990). Child care and the family: Complex contributors to child development. *New directions for Child Development, 49,* 23–37.

Varni, J.W., Rubenfeld, L.A., Talbot, D., & Setoguchi, Y. (1989). Family functioning, temperament, and psychologic adaptation in children with congenital or acquired limb deficiencies. *Pediatrics, 84,* 323–330.

Vaughn, B.E., Lefever, G.B., Seifer, R., & Barglow, P. (1989). Attachment behavior, attachment security, and temperament during infancy. *Child Development, 60,* 728–737.

Volling, B., & Feagans, L. (1995). Infant day care and children's social competence. *Infant Behavior and Development, 18,* 177–188.

Walker, S., Berthelsen, D., & Irving, K. (2001). Temperament and peer acceptance in early childhood: Sex and social status differences. *Child Study Journal, 31,* 177–192.

Weber, R.A., Levitt, M.J., & Clark, M.C. (1986). Individual variation in attachment security and Strange Situation Behavior: The role of maternal and infant temperament, *Child Development, 57,* 55–65.

Webster-Stratton, C., & Eyberg, S. (1982). Child temperament: Relationship with child behavior problems and parent-child interactions. *Journal of Clinical Child Psychology, 11,* 123–129.

Webster-Stratton, C., Hollingsworth, T., & Kolpacoff, M. (1989). The long-term effectiveness and clinical significance of three cost-effective training programs for families with conduct-problem children. *Journal of Consulting and Clinical Psychology, 57,* 550–553.

Weikart, D.P. (1998). Changing early childhood development through educational intervention. *Preventive Medicine, 27,* 233–237.

Weissberg-Benchell, J., & Glasgow, A. (1997). The role of temperament in children with insulin-dependent diabetes mellitus. *Journal of Pediatric Psychology, 22,* 795–809.

Weissbluth, M. (1982). Sleep duration and infant temperament. *Journal of Pediatrics, 99,* 817–819.

Weissbluth, M. (1987). *Healthy sleep habits, happy child.* New York: Ballantine.

Weissbluth, M. (1989a). Sleep loss, stress and temperamental difficultness: Psychobiological processes and practical considerations. In G.A. Kohnstamm, J.E. Bates, & M.K. Rothbart (Eds.), *Temperament in childhood.* New York: John Wiley & Sons.

Weissbluth, M. (1989b). Sleep-temperament interactions. In W.B. Carey & S.C. McDevitt (Eds.), *Clinical and educational applications of temperament research.* Berwyn, PA: Swets North America.

Weissbluth, M. (1999). *Healthy sleep habits, happy child.* New York: Ballantine Books.

Wertlieb, D., Weigel, C., & Feldstein, M. (1989). Stressful experiences, temperament and social support: Impact on children's behavior symptoms. *Journal of Applied Developmental Psychology, 10,* 487–503.

Wertlieb, D., Weigel, C., Springer, T., & Feldstein, M. (1987). Temperament as a moderator of children's stressful experiences. *American Journal of Orthopsychiatry, 57,* 234–245.

Whitebook, M., Howes, C., & Phillips, D. (1989). *The national child care staffing study: Who cares? Child care teachers and the quality of care in America.* Oakland, CA: The Child Care Employee Project.

Wilson, R.S., & Matheny, A.P., Jr. (1986). Behavior genetics research in infant temperament: The Louisville twin study. In R. Plomin & J. Dunn (Eds.), *The study of temperament: Changes, continuities and challenges* (pp. 81–98). Mahwah, NJ: Lawrence Erlbaum Associates.

Windle, M., & Lerner, R. M. (1986). Reassessing the dimensions of temperamental individuality across the life span: The Revised Dimensions of Temperament Survey (DOTS–R). *Journal of Adolescent Research, 1,* 213–230.

Wolke, D., Skuse, D., & Mathisen, B. (1990). Behavioral style in failure-to-thrive-infants: A preliminary communication. *Journal of Pediatric Psychology, 15,* 237–254.

Young, S., Fox, N., & Zahn-Waxler, C. (1999). The relation between temperament and empathy in two-year-olds. *Developmental Psychology, 35,* 1189–1197.

Zajdeman, H.S., & Minnes, P.M. (1991). Predictors of children's adjustment to child care. *Early Child Development and Care, 74,* 11–28.

Zigler, E., & Hall, N. (1994). Seeing the child in child care: Child care, individual differences, and social policy. In W.B. Carey & S.C. McDevitt (Eds.) *Prevention and early intervention* (pp. 237–245). New York: Brunner/Mazel.

Zigler, E., & Styfco, S.J. (Eds.) (2004). *The Head Start debates.* Baltimore: Paul H. Brookes Publishing Co.

Temperament Questionnaires

INFANT QUESTIONNAIRES

Name/Author(s)	Type/Age	Scale/Dimensions
Cameron-Rice Infant Questionnaire Cameron & Rice (1999)	Parent report Infants	46-item scale: Sensitivity, Movement, Reactivity, Frustration Tolerance, Adaptability, Regularity, and Soothability
Early Infancy Temperament Questionnaire (EITQ) Medhoff-Cooper, Carey, & McDevitt (1993)	Parent report 1- to 4-month-old infants	76-item scale: Thomas and Chess dimensions
Infant Behavior Questionnaire (IBQ) Rothbart (1981)	Parent report 3- to 12-month-old infants	96-item scale: Activity, Distress to Limits, Fear, Duration of Orienting, Smiling and Laughter, Soothability
Infant Characteristics Questionnaire (ICQ) Bates, Freeland, & Lounsbury (1979)	Parent report Difficult infants	32-item scale: Unadaptable, Persistent, Unsociable and Intense Expression of Negative Affect
Revision of the Infant Temperament Questionnaire (RITQ) Carey & McDevitt (1978)	Parent report 4- to 8-month-old infants	95-item scale: Thomas and Chess dimensions

EARLY CHILDHOOD QUESTIONNAIRES

Name/Author(s)	Type/Age	Scale/Dimensions
Behavioral Style Questionnaire (BSQ) McDevitt & Carey (1978)	Parent report 3–7 years old	100-item scale: Chess and Thomas dimensions
Cameron/Rice Preschooler Scale Cameron & Rice (1999)	Parent report 3–5 years old	69-item scale: Sensitivity (3 subscales), Distractibility, Intensity (3 subscales), Adaptability (3 subscales), Approach/Withdrawal (3 subscales), Frustration Tolerance (2 subscales), Regularity (2 subscales), Soothability
Cameron-Rice Toddler Questionnaire Cameron & Rice (1999)	Parent report 1–3 years old	69-item scale: Sensitivity (2 subscales), Movement (2 subscales), Intensity (2 subscales), Distractibility, Frustration Tolerance, Adaptability (3 subscales), Regularity, and Soothability
Child Temperament Questionnaire (CTQ) Thomas & Chess (1977)	Parent report 3–7 years old	72-item scale: Chess and Thomas dimensions
Children's Behavior Questionnaire (CBQ) Rothbart, Ahadi, & Hershey (1994)	Caregiver report 3–7 years old (For research purposes only)	Activity Level, Anger/Frustration, Approach–Anticipation, Attentional Focusing, Discomfort, Falling Reactivity-Soothability, Fear, High Intensity Pleasure, Impulsivity, Inhibitory Control, Low Intensity Pleasure, Perceptual Sensitivity, Sadness, Shyness, Smiling and Laughter
Colorado Childhood Temperament Inventory (CCTI) Rowe & Plomin (1977)	Parent report 1–6 years old	Five items in each of five scales: Sociability, Emotionality, Activity, Attention Span, Soothability
The Temperament Assessment Battery for Children (TABC) Martin (1988b)	Parent, teacher report 3–7 years old	48-item scale: Activity, Adaptability, Approach/Withdrawal, Emotional Intensity, Distractibility, Persistence
Temperament Assessment Battery for Children–Revised (TABC-R) Martin & Bridger (1999)	Parent, teacher report 2–7 years old	37-item scale (parent) & 29-item scale (teacher): Negative Emotionality, Inhibition, Activity Level Task Persistence
Toddler Temperament Scale (TTS) Fullard, McDevitt, & Carey (1984)	Parent report 1–3 years old	97-item scale: Chess and Thomas dimensions

MIDDLE CHILDHOOD AND EARLY ADOLESCENCE QUESTIONNAIRES

Name/Author(s)	Type/Age	Scale/Dimensions
Early Adolescent Temperament Questionnaire (EATQ) Capaldi and Rothbart (1992)	(for research purposes only) 9–16 years old	92-item scale: Sensitivity, Autonomic Reactivity, Motor Activation, Fear, Irritability, Shyness, Sadness, High and Low Intensity, Pleasure, Activity Level, Attentional Control
Middle Childhood Temperament Questionnaire (MCTQ) Hegvik, McDevitt, & Carey (1982)	Parent report 8–12 years old	99-item scale: Chess and Thomas dimensions
School-Age Temperament Inventory (SATI) McClowry (1995)	Parent report 8–11 years old	38-item scale: Approach/Withdrawal, Task Persistence, Negative Reactivity, Energy

MULTIAGE QUESTIONNAIRES

Name/Author(s)	Type/Age	Scale/Dimensions
Adult Temperament Questionnaire (ATQ) Chess & Thomas (1995)	Self-report 18–40 years old	54-item scale: Activity Level, Rhythmicity, Approach or Withdrawal, Adaptability, Threshold of Responsiveness, Intensity, Persistence, Distractibility
Dimensions of Temperament Survey–Revised (DOTS-R) Windle & Lerner (1986)	Parent report, teacher report, parent and child self-report Early childhood to young adulthood	54-item scale: Activity Level, Attention Span or Distractibility, Adaptability or Approach/Withdrawal, Rhymicity, and Reactivity
Emotionality, Activity, and Sociability (EAS) Buss & Plomin (1984)	Parent, teacher, or self-report Child/adolescent	20-item scale: Emotionality, Activity and Sociability, Shyness
Parent and Teacher Temperament Questionnaire (TTQ) Keogh, Pullis, & Cadwell (1982)	Parent report, teacher report Preschool and elementary school	23-item scale: Task Orientation (3 subscales), Personal-Social Flexibility (2 subscales), Reactivity (3 subscales)
Reactivity Rating Scale (RRS) Friedenberg & Strelau (1982)	Adult report Preschool, elementary, and secondary school students	3- to 9-item scale: Reactivity and Activity
Temperament and Atypical Behavior Scale (TABS) Bagnato, Neisworth, Salvia, & Hunt (1999)	Parent report 11–71 months old	15-item scale: Atypical behavior in four categories: Detached, Hypersensitive-Active, Underreactive, and Dysregulated

Temperament Reading List

BOOKS FOR PROFESSIONALS

Bates, J.E., & Wachs, T.D. (1994). *Temperament and individual differences at the interface of biology and behavior.* Washington, DC: APA Press.

Carey, W., & McDevitt, S. (Eds.). (1989). *Clinical and educational applications of temperament research.* Berwyn, PA: Swets North America.

Carey, W., & McDevitt, S. (Eds.). (1994). *Prevention and early intervention: individual differences as risk factors for the mental health of children.* New York: Brunner/Mazel.

Carey, W., & McDevitt, S. (1995). *Coping with children's temperament: A guide for professionals.* New York: Basic Books.

Chess, S., & Thomas, A. (1986). *Temperament in clinical practice.* New York: Guilford.

Chess, S., & Thomas, A. (1996). *Temperament theory and practice.* New York: Brunner/Mazel.

Chess, S., & Thomas, A. (1999). *Goodness of fit.* New York: Bruner/Mazel.

Eliasz, A., & Anglieitner, A. (Eds.) (2001). *Advances in research on temperament.* Lengerich, Berlin, Germany: Pabst Science Publishers.

Garrison, W.T., & Earls, F.J. (1987). *Temperament and child psychopathology.* Beverly Hills: Sage Publications.

Guerin, D.W., Gottfried, A.W., Oliver, P.H., & Thomas, C.W. (2003). *Temperament from infancy through adolescence: The Fullerton Longitudinal Study.* New York: Kluwer Academic/Plenum.

Halverson, C., Martin, R., & Kohnstamm, G. (1994). *The developing structure of temperament and personality from infancy to adulthood.* Mahwah, NJ: Lawrence Erlbaum Associates.

Kagan, J. (1994). *Galen's prophecy: Temperament in human nature.* New York: Basic Books.

Keogh, B.K. (2003). *Temperament in the classroom: Understanding individual differences.* Baltimore: Paul H. Brookes Publishing Co.

Kohnstamm, G.A., Bates, J.E., & Rothbart, M.K. (Eds.). (1989). *Temperament in childhood.* New York: John Wiley & Sons.

Lerner, J.V., & Lerner, R.M. (Eds.) (1986). *Temperament and social interacton in infants and children.* San Franciso: Jossey Bass.

Molfese, V.J., & Molfese, D.L. (Eds.). (2000). *Temperament and personality development across the life span.* Mahwah, NJ: Lawrence Erlbaum Associates.

Strelau, J. (Ed.). (1998). *Temperament: A psychological perspective.* New York: Plenum Press.

Wachs, T., & Kohnstamm, G. (Eds.). (2001). *Temperament in context.* Mahwah, NJ: Lawrence Erlbaum Associates.

BOOKS FOR PARENTS

Aron, E.N. (1996). *The highly sensitive person.* New York: Broadway Press.

Aron, E.N. (2002). *The highly sensitive child: Helping our children thrive when the world overwhelms them.* New York: Broadway Books.

Budd, L. (1991). *Living with the active, alert child.* New York: Prentice Hall.

Carey, W.B. (1997). *Understanding your child's temperament.* New York: Simon & Schuster.

Chess, S., & Thomas, A. (1987). *Know your child: An authoritative guide for today's parents.* New York: Basic Books.

Greene, R.W. (2001). *The explosive child.* New York: HarperCollins.

Greenspan, S. (1995). *The challenging child: Understanding, raising, and enjoying the five "difficult" types of children.* Reading, MA: Addison-Wesley.

Hidson, G. (1997). *Child Magazine's guide to quarreling.* New York: Pocket Books.

Kurcinka, M.S. (1998). *Raising your spirited child: A guide for parents whose child is more intense, sensitive, perceptive, persistent, energetic.* New York: HarperCollins.

Kurcinka, M.S. (1998). *The raising your spirited child workbook.* New York: HarperCollins.

Kurcinka, M.S. (2001). *Kids, parents and power struggles.* New York: Quill.

Neville, H., & Johnson, D.C. (1998). *Temperament tools: Working with your child's inborn traits.* Seattle: Parenting Press.

Shick, L. (1999). *Understanding temperament: Strategies for creating family harmony.* Seattle: Parenting Press.

Turecki, S. (1994). *Normal children have problems, too.* New York: Bantam Books.

Turecki, S., & Tonner, L. (2000). *The difficult child* (Rev. ed.). New York: Bantam.

Weissbluth, M. (1999). *Healthy sleep habits, happy children.* New York: Ballantine Books.

APPENDIX C

Resources

VIDEOTAPES

FOR INFANT AND TODDLER CAREGIVERS

Flexible, Fearful, or Feisty: The Different Temperaments of Infants and Toddlers

Available from
California State Department of Education
Post Office Box 944272
Sacramento, CA 95814
916-310-0800

Kaiser Permanente Health Maintenance Organization Temperament videos

FOR HEALTH CARE PROVIDERS

Using Temperament Concepts to Prevent Behavior Problems
Understanding the High-Intensity, Slow-Adapting Child
Understanding the High-Activity, Slow-Adapting Child with Low Rhythmicity
Understanding the Withdrawing Child with High Sensitivity and Intensity

FOR PARENTS

Knowing Your Child
Understanding Your High-Intensity, Slow-Adapting Child
Understanding Your High-Activity, Slow-Adapting Child with Low Rhythmicity
Understanding Your Sensitive and Withdrawing Child

Available from
Child Development Media
5632 Van Nuys Boulevard, Suite 286
Van Nuys, CA 91401
818-994-0933

WEB SITES

Behavioral Development Initiatives: http://www.b-di.com, or
http://www.temperament.com
Temperament resources, including books, workshops, Carey Temperament Scale questionnaires, CTS scoring software, and more

Highly Sensitive Persons: http://www.hsperson.com
Resources, books, newsletter, workshops, and classes for individuals
with high sensitivity

INSIGHTS:
http://www.nyu.edu/education/nursing/insights/currentstudies.html
Information on the INSIGHTS program, research studies, books, workshops, on-line temperament questionnaire for school-age children

Mary Kurcinka: http://www.parentchildhelp.com
Temperament resources for parents and professionals, books, workshops for parents and professionals

**A Parenting Resource: Parenting Your Unique Child (University
of Wisconsin Extension):**
http://www.uwex.edu/ces/flp/parenting/unique.html
A resource on child temperaments for parents

Preventive Ounce: http://www.preventiveoz.org
On-line temperament questionnaires, temperament information and
advice

The Temperament Perspective: http://www.kidtemp.com
Information about temperament, resources for parents and professionals, books, workshops and classes for professionals and parents,
temperament counseling training.

Temperament Talk: http://www.chdinc.org
A unique training curriculum for parents and professionals, trainings
and workshops for parents and professionals

Temperament Tools: http://www.temperamenttools.com
Temperament information, resources, books, workshops for parents
and professionals

PROGRAMS

Baker Pediatric Consulting Services
Temperament counseling and assessment for private pediatric offices.
Contact: E-mail: embaker@sonic.net

INSIGHTS
INSIGHTS provides interventions for disadvantaged minority children, their parents, and their teachers through a parenting program, an intervention for teachers, and a universal drama therapy program for the targeted children and their classmates.
Contact: E-mail: sm6@nyu.edu
212-998-9039
http://www.nyu.edu/education/nursing/insights/currentstudies.html

The Kaiser Permanente Temperament Program
Kaiser Permanente offers individual temperament counseling services and temperament-based parenting classes at selected medical facilities in Northern California, Oregon, and Washington.

Contact local Kaiser pediatric or health education departments to learn which services are available in your area.

Practical Parenting!
A temperament-based parent education service in West Chester, Pennsylvania. Classes are offered on helping parents learn strategies for children who are challenging to raise.
Contact: 866-228-9235 ext. 3754; E-mail: RobHegvik@aol.com

The Temperament Program
A temperament-based community prevention program located in La Grande, Oregon. This program offers individual and small group temperament counseling utilizing Temperament Talk, the program curriculum; and experiential presentations and workshops for parents, professionals, schools, and workplace.

Contact:
541-962-8835; E-mail: bzukin@chdinc.org
http://www.chdinc.org/temperament

The Temperament Project at Avera McKenna Hospital and South Dakota Children's at Sioux Valley Hospital
Offers temperament screening to parents of all 9-month old children born at either hospital. A corresponding program provides families with free temperament screening and an opportunity to receive follow-up services to help them better understand their infants. The program also provides trainings, in-service workshops, and screenings for babies in the community.

Contact:
CHILD Services
Sioux Valley Hospital and Health System
115 West 41st Street
Sioux Falls, SD 57105

PROFESSIONAL TRAINING PROGRAMS AND UNIVERSITY CLASSES

Arizona State University

Introduction to Temperament Assessment (recommended prior to credit course)
This noncredit continuing education course is provided on-line by the Continuing and Extended Education Program at Arizona State University's College of Nursing. The course teaches about the concept of temperament, using an online assessment of a child's temperament, interpreting a temperament profile, how temperament "works" to create behavioral problems, understanding common temperament trait combinations, and forecasting what temperament issues are likely to occur for a particular child. It also provides advice on what works best for a particular temperament-related issue.

HCR 598: Principles of Temperament Counseling

This on-line, 15-week, 3-credit course reviews current theory and research on the contribution of children's temperament to the origins of sleep, separation, shyness, temper tantrums, discipline problems, and other childhood issues. Child care professionals will learn about assessment of the temperament of infants, toddlers, preschoolers, and older children; how the child's temperament, parenting styles and other environmental factors combine to create specific behavioral issues and problems; and how to select the appropriate approach to manage these temperament-related issues. (Note: Students must be admitted to ASU's graduate college and pay associated fees to enroll in course.) To register for either one of these courses, call 480-965-9200 or visit http://www.asu.edu/xed/nursing

Dominican University of California
Temperament and Child Behavior

This course, offered as a 1-unit class or as a 3-unit psychology elective, examines inborn traits and how temperament affects behavior and development throughout childhood. Interactions between temperament and the environment are explored in terms of "goodness of fit" in creating positive relationships. Students learn the history of temperament, various theories, cultural differences in temperament, assessments, and clinical applications. To register, call 415-457-4440; E-mail: enroll@dominican.edu

Index

Page references followed by *f* indicate figures; those followed by *t* indicate tables.